Access™ 2007

The L Line,™
The Express Line to Learning

Access™ 2007

The L Line,™
The Express Line to Learning

Kenneth Hess

Wiley Publishing, Inc.

Access™ 2007: The L Line™ The Express Line to Learning

Published by
Wiley Publishing, Inc.
111 River Street
Hoboken, NJ 07030-5774
www.wiley.com

For general information on our other products and services, please contact our Customer Care Department within the U.S. at 800-762-2974, outside the U.S. at 317-572-3993, or fax 317-572-4002.

For technical support, please visit www.wiley.com/techsupport.

Wiley also publishes its books in a variety of electronic formats. Some content that appears in print may not be available in electronic books.

Library of Congress Control Number: 2006939475

ISBN: 978-0-470-10790-4

Manufactured in the United States of America

10 9 8 7 6 5 4 3 2 1

WILEY

About the Author

Kenneth Hess is an avid database enthusiast and administrator. He has worked with many different types of database software over the past 20 years. Ken currently focuses his database interests and research on MySQL and SQLite. He has worked with every version of Windows since 3.0, most versions of Linux, most MacOS versions since 7.x, and almost every flavor of commercial Unix although Linux remains as his passion and favorite above all the others.

Ken maintains his technical edge through his day job, his research with Linux, PHP, MySQL, SQLite, and other open source applications. He maintains his sanity through involvement with his family, fiction writing, art, and watching a few select TV shows.

Ken may be contacted through his website at www.kenhess.com.

Publisher's Acknowledgments

Acquisitions, Editorial, and Media Development

Project Editor
Pat O'Brien

Acquisitions Editor
Greg Croy

Copy Editor
Barry Childs-Helton, Laura Miller

Technical Editor
Vince McCune

Editorial Manager
Kevin Kirschner

Media Development Specialists
Angela Denny, Kate Jenkins,
Steven Kudirka, Kit Malone

Media Development Coordinator
Laura Atkinson

Media Project Supervisor
Laura Moss

Media Development Manager
Laura VanWinkle

Editorial Assistant
Amanda Foxworth

Sr. Editorial Assistant
Cherie Case

Special Help
Joe Stockman

Composition Services

Project Coordinator
Erin Smith

Layout and Graphics
Denny Hager, Barbara Moore,
Heather Ryan, Ronald Terry

Proofreaders
Laura Albert, Debbye Butler,
Charles Spencer, Brian H. Walls

Indexer
Broccoli Information Management

Anniversary Logo Design
Richard Pacifico

Publishing and Editorial for Technology Dummies

Richard Swadley, *Vice President and Executive Group Publisher*

Andy Cummings, *Vice President and Publisher*

Mary Bednarek, *Executive Acquisitions Director*

Mary C. Corder, *Editorial Director*

Publishing for Consumer Dummies

Diane Graves Steele, *Vice President and Publisher*

Joyce Pepple, *Acquisitions Director*

Composition Services

Gerry Fahey, *Vice President of Production Services*

Debbie Stailey, *Director of Composition Services*

Author's Acknowledgments

I wish to thank my wife, Melissa, who encourages me to write in spite of the amount of time it takes. Also thanks to the good people at Microsoft who have the skill and vision to create programs like Access.

Dedication

I dedicate this book to my family who encourages me to pursue my dreams: Melissa, Connor, Walker, and Maria.

Contents at a Glance

Contents

Preface

From the Publisher

Welcome to *Access 2007: The L Line, The Express Line to Learning*. This book belongs to a tutorial series from Wiley Publishing created for independent learners, students, and teachers alike. Whether you are learning (or teaching) in a classroom setting, or gaining skills for fun, this book is for you.

Like all titles in *The L Line, The Express Line to Learning* series, this book's design reflects the concept of learning as a journey — a trip on a subway system — with navigational tools and real-world stops along the way. The destination, of course, is mastery of the key applications and core competencies of Access 2007.

From the Author

Access 2007: The L-Line is described as "The Express Line to Learning." The concept of this series is to introduce computer applications to you as if you were on a long subway trip. I really like this concept and was very excited when the book was assigned to me. The idea of a subway trip appeals to me (though I have never ridden one) because learning a new application is a journey of sorts. The chapters build upon each other somewhat, and generally you should follow them in order. The chapters do not necessarily introduce more advanced concepts as you progress through the book, so don't be intimidated by higher chapter numbers. Where needed, I have split the chapters into multiple levels. In those instances, Level I is introductory material, and Level II is more advanced. I have made an effort to make any advanced material optional but recommended.

Can Anyone Use Access?

Knowing Access certainly seems to be a skillset that is in demand in a lot of companies. There are also many jobs available that require knowledge of Access in addition to other skills. Additional skills, like knowing Access, will make you more marketable and employable.

The following jobs require knowledge of Access:

- Database Administrator
- Access Developer
- Access Consultant
- Administrative Assistant
- Marketing Coordinator
- Data Entry Clerk
- Project Manager
- Systems Analyst
- Inventory Control Manager
- Database Developer
- Receptionist

How Do You Get Started in Access 2007?

This book assumes no prior knowledge of databases or Microsoft Access. This book is for anyone who wants to begin or expand their skills with databases and Access. It is a great first book for someone wanting to learn a lot about Access in a short amount of time and with a bit of a different approach. You do not have to be a technology expert, nor do I assume that you are a computer novice. Microsoft Access is not a tool for someone who is new to computers. The assumption is that you have worked with a computer long enough to be familiar with the Windows Operating System and applications like Microsoft Word or Microsoft Excel.

What's in the Book?

Each chapter begins with the "Stations Along the Way," which outlines at a glance the topics to be covered in the chapter. This element is followed by "Enter the Station" which is a list of study questions, a pretest designed to get you thinking about each chapter's content up front (and to help you study). The Express Line element directs you ahead if you're already up to speed on a particular chapter's subject.

At the end of each chapter are a couple of important elements:

- **Street Jargon.** This glossary lists all the important terms introduced in the chapter.

- **Practice Exam.** Your last stop before exiting a chapter is the Practice Exam, which will test you on the concepts you learn in each chapter. All answers can be found in Appendix B.

Icons Used in the Book

There are several handy icons you'll find along the way:

Information Kiosk

These icons point out or additional explanations of concepts discussed in the regular text.

Transfer

These icons refer you to other places in the book for more information on a particular subject.

Watch Your Step

These icons point out potential pitfalls you might encounter as you begin programming — and advise caution when necessary.

Step into the Real World

These sidebars discuss problems or issues you might run into out in the real world — or additional considerations for you to mull over.

Using the Web Site

If you're following the book from front to back, you'll use and modify a few examples while you practice the steps. But if you're skipping around, there are practice files you can download from the Web site so you can use any individual chapter.

For Instructors and Students

Access 2007: The L Line has a rich set of supplemental resources for students and instructors. **Instructors** can find a test bank, PowerPoint presentations with course and book outlines, and instructor's manual and sample syllabi online. Please contact Wiley for access to these resources.

Students and independent learners: resources such as chapter outlines and sample test questions can be found at www.wiley.com.

Your Next Step

Starting any new project comes with excitement and a bit of nervous tension. It is normal to feel as if you may fail. Getting this far means that you want to do something new for your career, to solve a problem, or maybe just for your own edification. Whatever your reason or background, it is now time to take the next step, turn the page, and get started—The L-Line is waiting for you to board.

Designing Databases

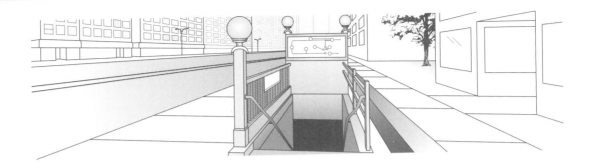

 # Enter the Station

Questions

1. What is a database?

2. What are the parts of a database?

3. What is a relational database?

4. How do you create a database in Microsoft Access?

5. What's the most basic element of database design?

6. How do you delete a database?

7. How can you tell whether a database is well-designed?

Express Line

If you already understand the basics of database structure and design, then skip ahead to Chapter 2.

This chapter guides you through an introduction to databases, the parts of a database, some design principles, a little database theory, and practical examples. In this chapter, you can figure out how to design, name, create, and delete databases.

Discovering Databases

A *database* is an object that stores related data. In some database programs, the database is simply a folder on your hard drive, but in Microsoft Access, it's much more. An Access database is a specialized container that holds such information as data, tables, macros, modules, forms, and reports. Most database systems don't provide such a feature-rich environment. In most other database programs, a database is simply a storage-and-retrieval engine for large amounts of table data, and other programs handle all the remaining features.

Microsoft Access provides a database *client* (the program that shows you your data) and a database server, plus data-entry forms that you create, reports for summarizing and displaying data, and two programming languages.

Information Kiosk

Technically, Microsoft Access isn't a database server. However, multiple clients can connect to it simultaneously, like a server. You can share your database with anyone who has the Microsoft Access program. Several people can work on the same database at the same time.

Information Kiosk

A database program is usually referred to as a Database Management System (DBMS) or as a Relational Database Management System (RDBMS). Though most people use the terms *database* and *DBMS* interchangeably, I use *database* to mean a single container of data; *DBMS* refers to Microsoft Access itself. I don't use *RDBMS* at all because Access is a relational database, so the relational part of the definition is assumed.

You can think of a database (in general terms) as a collection of similar or related data. Typically, when you create a database, you have some idea of the type of data that you plan to store in it — all that data should have something in common. For example, you could put all the data for your company in one database and data about all the books in a library in another database, but you might not want to put all the data of both types into the same database. Trying to keep different types of data in one database may cause your single database to grow to an unmanageable size.

In the following section, I show you the basic database-design principles that let your databases grow and progress normally — and point out how to avoid some common database pitfalls.

Designing a Database

Before you open Access and start putting things in database files, take some time to consider what you want to put in your database — and the ways you want to use that information. The more carefully you've thought out a design for your database *before* you build it, the more useful Access will be to you.

Design principles

The most basic design element of a database is the consistent naming of its components. Simply put, a *naming convention* is a way of categorizing and managing the items in a database by creating and using descriptive labels for those items.

This naming process may sound very simple, but you must decide on a naming convention for your database work and stick to that convention throughout your project. Consistency and clarity are very important attributes of any naming convention.

Information Kiosk

A naming convention is a standard way of naming and referring to items such as databases, tables, forms, reports, and so on. You must decide for yourself on the naming convention for your projects. Although there's no standard naming convention that works for all databases, it's a good idea to keep the names short and descriptive — for example, you might use `Publishers` for a list of book publishers and `Titles` for book titles in a `Books` database.

Although nobody has created ironclad standards for naming database objects, the next section offers a few guidelines for coming up with your own consistent naming convention — and sticking to it. Note that the idea here is to create *scalable* names (able to grow with the project); they'll be easier to migrate to a higher-end database product such as Microsoft SQL Server if you have to scale up to a client/server database at some point.

Practical rules for scalable naming conventions

A naming convention should follow these rules:

- Easy to decipher
- Consistently capitalized

(ONE CARE) Descriptive of the data

(ONE CARE) Relatively short

A naming convention should avoid these pitfalls:

(ONE CARE) Don't use *spaces*.

(ONE CARE) Don't be *cryptic* or use a *foreign language*.

(ONE CARE) Don't use *numbers* unless they're significant in some logical way (such as the date, part of the name of a company, or a musical group).

(ONE CARE) Don't use any characters except *capital letters* (A–Z), *lowercase letters* (a–z), *numbers* (0–9), *underscored spaces* (_), and *hyphens* (-).

For example, if you name a database `Guestbook`, your naming convention has the first letter capitalized and the remainder of the name in lowercase. This type of naming convention is common — but what if you have two or three different guest books, each representing a different company? Well, you could name them `Guestbook1`, `Guestbook2`, and `Guestbook3` — but those numbers don't offer any information about which company is using which guest book. Instead of numbering the guest books, you could put company initials in your naming convention — something like `Guestbook_DBD`, `Guestbook_SMS`, and `Guestbook_KDS`. These descriptive names give you immediate clues about the guest-book data contained in each database.

Remember, if you have fifty guest books and two companies have the abbreviated name of DBD, then you should change your naming convention accordingly. For example, say you're creating databases for both Delta Boat Disassemblers and Data Bank Dynamics. You could expand their guest-book names to `Guestbook_Delta_Boat_Dis` and `Guestbook_Data_Bank_Dyn`.

You want to group similar data into a single unit and keep it separate from other (unrelated) data — and a database is the primary object for grouping data. In the preceding example, you wouldn't put salary information in a `Guestbook` database designated to hold guest data such as names, addresses, e-mail addresses, and comments.

Step into the Real World

You may find the best way to organize your ideas about a database project is to write down your thoughts about organizing data on paper before starting with Access. The following section describes the process you can go through in detail.

Accounting data offers a good example. Suppose you created a database named `Accounting` that contained tables with such names as `Accounts_Rec`, `Accounts_Pay`, `Payroll`, and `Taxes`. Here you're using separate tables for accounts receivable, accounts payable, and so on — but not separate databases. It's a matter of scale: the Accounting department is usually kept separate from other departments within a company, so it gets its own database. The Human Resources department is another good example of a data grouping. A database called `Human_Resources` may have such tables as `Employees`, `Management`, `Executives`, `Salaries`, `Pension`, and `401K` — but all of these belong in the same database because they're all Human Resources concerns.

Information Kiosk

Create databases sparingly. Many companies follow the practice of creating a single database that contains many tables. You can also create databases that break up the data into logical subcategories, such as Accounting, Human Resources, and Manufacturing (for an automaker) or Stamps, Books, and Grades (for a school).

Organize your data

Creating a database can be as simple as saying, "I need a database for all of my recipes," and so you create a database and name it `Recipes`. You can create a database for your postage stamp collection and name that database `Stamps`, but the way to group your data is often far less obvious. That's when the process becomes a little more complicated.

Say you're creating a database for your company, Delta Boat Disassemblers, to use to keep track of employee information. You create a database named `DBD`, and inside the database, you decide to create a list of tables that will store employee data of all kinds, including salaries, insurance, Human Resources information, customer data, sales, and inventory information. This scenario may work just fine, but you should consider many issues before deciding to take this approach, the greatest of which is organization of the data.

Putting the concept to work

The design of your database is absolutely critical to your success.

The following list shows my design progression, which you can use to create a database. These steps are effective and efficient:

1. **Write the name and purpose of the database.**

Watch Your Step

Always keep the purpose of your database in mind. By remembering why you're creating your database, you're less likely to include faulty or unrelated data. For instance, if you create a database to store all your recipes, you probably don't want to add your stamp or music collection to that database. The data within a database should be related in some logical way.

2. **List the major categories of data.**

These categories usually become the tables within the database.

3. **List the elements within the categories.**

These elements can become the columns in each table.

4. **Remove redundancies.**

Watch Your Step

Removing redundancies is the most important step. Chapter 3 covers removing redundancies in detail.

5. **Add and remove categories and elements.**

Add categories for items that appear often in your data (if you haven't already) and clean up by removing any unneeded categories or elements.

6. **Create the database, tables, and columns.**

Creating a Database

Access requires that you either open an existing database or create a new one upon opening the program.

To create a new database when first opening Access, follow these steps:

1. **Start Microsoft Access.**

   When Access is open, your screen should look like Figure 1-1.

2. **Click Blank Database.**

   The right side of the application updates with a default database name of `Database1.accdb`. You can accept this name or use another name.

3. **Click Create to create the database and open it in Microsoft Access.**

Watch Your Step

Don't change the extension of the database (`.accdb`). If you change the extension, Access automatically appends the name with `.accdb`.

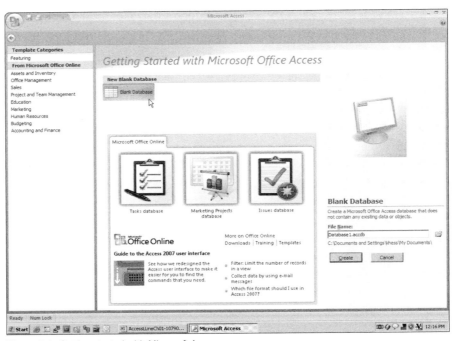

Figure 1-1: Getting started with Microsoft Access.

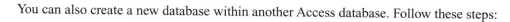

You can also create a new database within another Access database. Follow these steps:

1. **Click the Microsoft Office icon.**

2. **Click New.**

The Getting Started with Microsoft Office Access page opens, as shown in Figure 1-1. The right side of the application updates with a default database name of `Database1.accdb`. You can accept this name or use another name.

3. **Click Create to create the database and open it in Microsoft Access.**

Deleting a Database

You can delete a database in two ways:

- As you would any other file on your computer
- From within Access

To delete a database from within Access, follow these steps:

1. **Click the Microsoft Office icon (in the upper-left corner of the program).**

2. **Click Open.**

Your list of available databases appears in the window.

3. **Right-click the database file you want to delete.**

4. **Select Delete from the menu.**

5. **Confirm the deletion by clicking Yes.**

To delete a database from outside of Access, simply drag the icon to the Recycle Bin or highlight the file name and press Delete.

Watch Your Step

You can't delete a database that's open. When you delete a database (inside or outside of Access), you can recover it only if it's still in your Recycle Bin.

The true purpose of a database is to store and retrieve data quickly. It's a centralized repository of information that's organized in such a way that you can easily access that information. Data doesn't generally get changed within a database, so you need to make sure that the data is of very high quality when you enter it into the database. Data is of *high quality* if it doesn't have redundancies, mistakes, or *anomalies* (faulty data).

database: An object that stores related data.

DBMS: Database Management System refers to a program for managing and storing data. Microsoft Access is a DBMS.

naming convention: A method of using consistent and easily deciphered names for database objects.

object: A database or any part of a database (such as a table).

RDBMS: Relational Database Management System is a DBMS that has the added feature of allowing objects, such as tables, to share data with each other. Microsoft Access is an RDBMS.

relational database: A database whose tables share common data elements with each other, making those tables related.

Last Stop

Practice Exam

1. **Which of the following is the best definition of a database?**

   A) A collection of objects with similar names

   B) A storage facility for data

   C) An object that contains data

   D) An object that stores a collection of related data

2. **You have three notebooks filled with information that you want to put into Access. One notebook contains the names and addresses of your friends and family, another contains information related to your home-based business, and the third contains information about your music collection. When using Access to organize and store this data, you would:**

   A) Create a database named Info and put the data from all three notebooks in it.

   B) Create a database and put only your business information in it because databases are far too important to store personal data.

   C) Create two databases, one named Personal and one named Business, and put your addresses and music in Personal and your business info in Business.

   D) Create three databases, one for each of the three general types of information.

3. **Which of the following would be the best name for a database that holds information for the Destructo Demolition company?**

   A) Destructo

   B) DDemo

   C) DeDeCo

   D) Destructo Demolition Company

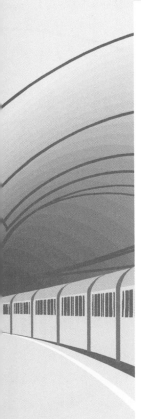

4. **Which of the following steps is the most important when designing a new database?**

A) List the elements within the categories.

B) Remove redundancies.

C) Add and remove categories and elements.

D) Create the database, tables, and columns.

5. **When developing a naming convention for your databases, you should:**

A) Use simple, easily decipherable names.

B) Be creative.

C) Use cryptic names.

D) Use very long and very descriptive names.

6. **True or false: You can create a new database from within Access. If true, explain how.**

_____

_____

_____

7. **If you delete a database accidentally, you may be able to retrieve it if:**

A) No changes have been made to the database since it was deleted.

B) The database is less than 50 megabytes in size.

C) It's still in the Recycle Bin.

D) It has the appropriate security locks.

8. **What's the true purpose of a database?**

A) To organize data

B) To stick with a naming convention

C) To store and retrieve data

D) To locate faulty data

9. True or false: A database should contain data that's related. Explain why or why not.

_____

_____

_____

10. Explain why you shouldn't name three new databases Stuff, Miscellaneous, and New.

_____

_____

_____

Creating and Using Tables — Level I

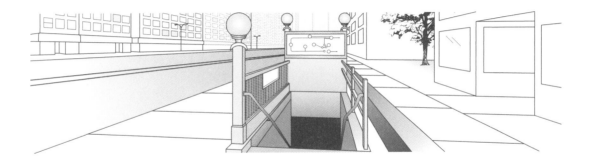

Enter the Station

Questions

1. What are the parts of a table?

2. How is a table different than a spreadsheet?

3. How do you create a table in Microsoft Access?

4. What's the most basic element of table design?

5. How can you change data or column names?

6. How do you delete a table?

7. How can you get your data into a table?

Express Line

If you're already up on creating tables and directly entering data into them, then skip ahead to Chapter 4.

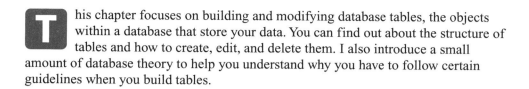

This chapter focuses on building and modifying database tables, the objects within a database that store your data. You can find out about the structure of tables and how to create, edit, and delete them. I also introduce a small amount of database theory to help you understand why you have to follow certain guidelines when you build tables.

Building Tables

The most basic object in a database is the table. A *table* is a named object composed of columns, rows, and cells, very similar to a spreadsheet. And like a spreadsheet, it lets you order (or sort) the data, but the particular order in which you place the data in a table doesn't matter — and neither does the order of the columns. Spreadsheets, on the other hand, usually rely on some ordering of the columns so that the data makes more sense and is easier to read and maintain. Information in a database is usually easier to read and maintain because you typically never look at all the data at once, as you do in a spreadsheet. Databases have a special language called *Structured Query Language (SQL)* that collects specific data into a readable and convenient form. You can find out more about this language in Chapter 13.

Information Kiosk

Tables are composed of columns, rows, and cells.

Transfer

If you want to know more about the database language (SQL), Chapter 13 has the details.

You have several good reasons to use Access rather than a spreadsheet when you store and maintain data. As you add data to a spreadsheet, that data becomes cumbersome to work with when the spreadsheet gets very large. The technical limits of a spreadsheet far exceed the human limits for viewing data comfortably. If you use a spreadsheet with many columns of data, the data becomes

- **Difficult to navigate:** In a spreadsheet with many columns, you often scroll way out to the right and then back to the left to view the data. You can very easily become lost and frustrated when dealing with an amount of data that you can't easily view on a single page.

- **Difficult to view when printed:** You can have a really hard time making sense of a printed version of your spreadsheet unless you print multiple pages and tape them together.

If you have a spreadsheet that's much more than one screen wide, consider putting the data into a database. Figure 2-1 shows data in a spreadsheet, and Figure 2-2 shows the same data in Access.

Figure 2-1: Example data in Excel.

Figure 2-2: Example data in Access.

When you deal with several hundred records and dozens of columns, you'll probably find using a database much easier than using a spreadsheet.

Transfer

Microsoft Access makes the transition from Excel, Microsoft's spreadsheet, to Access very simple with an import wizard. Chapter 3 shows how to use the wizard.

Tables, in general, are the part of the database that you interact with when using data. Databases are typically composed of multiple tables that are related to one another by a common column of data. The data in that column isn't repeated in both tables — instead, one table keeps the real data and the other table simply refers to that data.

Step into the Real World

Spreadsheets are very handy for

- Data that you can basically view in one page (or multiple pages if you use multiple worksheets)
- Small amounts of data

Creating a Table

You can create a new table in Access very simply.

Transfer

If you already know how to create an Access table and manually input data into it, you can skip ahead to the section "Putting Data into a Table," later in this chapter.

Follow these steps:

1. Click the Create tab on the Menu Bar.

The Create tab contains the options for creating new database objects.

2. Use the first icon on the left (Table) to create a blank table.

The blank table created is called Table1 because it's your first table.

After you create Table1, Figure 2-3 shows what your new table should look like. In the right pane, you see a tab named `Table1`. This is the datasheet view. (It looks very much like a spreadsheet.)

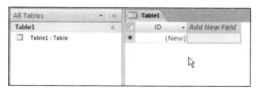

Figure 2-3: Table1, on the right, is your new table.

When you create an Access database, the first column (ID) is set up automatically for you. It's assigned the data type AutoNumber. This is Access's way of keeping each row unique for good database design.

The other x columns are yours to create and fill as you need.

Transfer

Chapter 13 explains data types.

It's a good idea to create all the columns you think you'll need for the table before you enter any data. You might not get them all in the first try, but you'll be able to focus on entering data instead of adding columns.

The following example is very straightforward: an address book. Table 2-1 lists a set of sample columns. To add columns to a table, follow these steps:

1. Double-click Add New Field (the second column heading).

When you start a new table, Access automatically creates the ID column. The Add New Field column is immediately to the right of the ID column.

2. For each column name, type the new field name and then press Enter.

To begin adding the sample columns from Table 2-1, type **First_Name**, and then press Enter.

When you press Enter, the cursor goes directly to the next column name field. A new blank column is added to the right of your newest column, labeled Add New Field, as you can see in Figure 2-4. You don't have to add a new column, but you have the option. This is a new feature introduced with Access 2007 that makes adding new columns to your table very easy.

Figure 2-4: Table1 gives you the option to Add New Field.

3. When you're done adding fields, press Enter without typing a field name in the column heading.

When you press Enter, the cursor goes to the first cell in the first row under the ID column heading.

Table 2-1   Columns for an Address Book Table

Column Name	Data Type
ID	AutoNumber
First_Name	Text
Last_Name	Text
Address	Text
City	Text
State	Text
Zip	Text

Figure 2-5 shows the address book table with named columns.

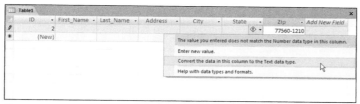

Figure 2-5: This Table1 layout includes all the named columns.

In this example, I use the text data type for all of the columns because a text column lets you enter letters, numbers, dashes, underscores, and the # sign — all without causing problems. Zip codes don't include any letters, but if you enter **77560-1210** into a numeric column, the hyphen isn't allowed. If you create `Zip` as a Numeric column, Access doesn't let you make this mistake — after you enter the numbers (with hyphen), Access asks whether you want to convert the column to text because the value you entered is inappropriate for the Numeric column type. Figure 2-6 shows the message you see when you make this entry.

Figure 2-6: Access prompts you to convert the column type.

Information Kiosk

In the address book example, I use two columns (`First_Name` and `Last_Name`) rather than a single `Name` column. Splitting the full name into two separate columns is good table design. This separation makes operations that use names (such as sorting by last name) easier.

The `Address`, `City`, `State`, and `Zip` columns all adhere to good table design because the data they'll contain are *indivisible,* which means the columns can't be logically split any further.

Information Kiosk

Use the smallest bit of data that can stand on its own for each column.

Step into the Real World

Developing a naming convention is wise when working with databases. Use descriptive names that aren't too long but let you know the types of data that the tables store.

- If your data is relatively simple and cohesive, you can use a naming convention such as States and Addresses.
- If your data is more complex, then you may need to expand the names to be more descriptive, such as `Data_Error_Codes` and `Checked_Files`.

A naming convention makes your database easier to maintain and support later.

Information Kiosk

If you use previous versions of Access, you may prefer to design your tables in Design View. To get to Design View, right-click the Table tab and click Design View (shown in Figure 2-7).

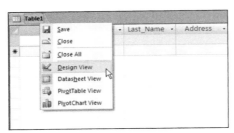

Figure 2-7: You can change your table to Design View.

That's the essence of table creation. You create a new table, add columns, name them, and then add data to the table.

Altering a Table

Changing a table's structure by altering column names, data types, and even the table's name is a very common practice.

Access conveniently gives you a way to edit, modify, and change every aspect of your database and its contents:

- You can change the name of any column without affecting the data within the column.
- Changing a column's data type is risky. You may lose some or all of your data by doing so.

Access warns you of the data loss if the new data type you choose is incompatible with the data in the column. Figure 2-8 shows this warning.

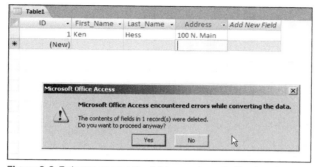

Figure 2-8: Trying to convert the Address column to Number data type gets this warning message.

To change the name of a column, double-click the column name, and type in the new name. For instance, you may want to change the name of the `Address` column to `Home_Address`. Follow these steps:

1. Double-click the `Address` **column name.**

2. Type in Home_Address.

3. Click into any other cell, press Enter, or use an arrow key to accept the change.

Altering a table in Access is very similar to altering information in an Excel spreadsheet. You can alter data in a cell by clicking the cell that you want to alter and typing in the new value.

Deleting a Table

You can create a very complex table and add thousands of records to it, and with a few simple clicks, you can delete the table and all of its contents forever.

Step into the Real World

Rarely does anyone create a database, or a table within a database, that's perfect from the start. A database is a dynamic object. All objects within a database are also dynamic. Objects such as tables and reports within a database are naturally dynamic because you routinely add, delete, and change data. A table may undergo several structural changes over its lifetime. Don't think you must create the perfect database, table, or set of tables. Most of the time that just isn't possible.

Watch Your Step

After you delete a table, you can't recover it. Be sure that you really want to delete it before you actually do.

To delete a table, follow these steps:

1. Close the table that you want to delete (shown in Figure 2-9).

Access doesn't let you delete an open table. If you try, you receive a warning that you can't delete an open table. You're instructed to close the table first, and then delete it.

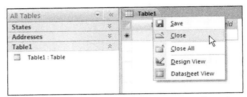

Figure 2-9: Close Table1 by selecting Close from the menu.

2. Right-click the table's name and select Delete from the menu (shown in Figure 2-10).

Access warns you that you're about to delete the table.

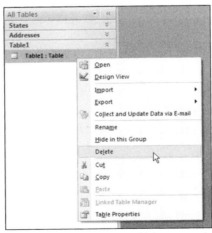

Figure 2-10: Right-click the table's name and select Delete to delete that table.

3. Confirm the table deletion by clicking Yes (shown in Figure 2-11).

The table disappears from view and is deleted from the database.

If you want to cancel the deletion, click No rather than Yes.

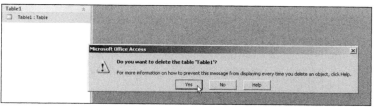

Figure 2-11: Confirm that you want to delete your table by clicking Yes.

Putting Data into a Table

A table isn't useful at all without data in it. Storing data for easy retrieval is a table's main purpose.

Typing the data in manually is the easiest and most direct way to enter a small amount of data into a table. It's time and labor intensive. but it's the classic data entry method to get data into a table.

The quality of your data depends largely on your accuracy as you enter the data. How accurately you input your data directly determines the effectiveness and efficiency of your database.

To begin entering data into a table, you need to create a table to put the data in. I'll reuse the address book example from the section "Creating a Table," earlier in this chapter — check out that section to see how to create a table.

After you create the table, it's time to enter data into the datasheet:

1. **Click into the cell that appears directly under** First_Name.
2. **Enter the first name for this record — or the value described in the column heading.**
3. **Press the Enter key, Tab key, or right arrow.**

   The data is accepted, and you proceed to the next cell in the row (Last_Name).
4. **Repeat Steps 2 and 3 to keep adding your data in the cells.**

   After you fill in the last cell and press Enter, Tab, or the right arrow, the cursor automatically appears in the ID column of the next row.
5. **Repeat Steps 2 through 4 with new information for each row until you've entered all your data.**

   You can add as many rows as you want for practice.

Figure 2-12 shows the address book table with two records (rows of data) in it.

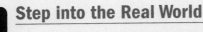

Step into the Real World

Many jobs posted in newspapers and on the Internet require data-entry skills, which require fast typing skills and attention to detail. Now you know why — everyone's looking for someone to fill their tables with data.

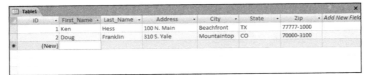

Figure 2-12: I've added two entries to my address-book table.

In Chapter 3, you can discover other methods of getting data into a table that are more advanced but far less labor intensive.

cell: A single item of data at the intersection of a column and a row in a table. A cell is more commonly used in spreadsheet discussions.

column: A collection of data in a database table related by a single data type. Also referred to as a *field*.

data type: A description of the data within a column. The type of data can be such formats as Number, Text, or Memo.

field: A collection of data in a database table related by a single data type. This information appears in a database table *column*.

record: A single entry of data defined by the columns or fields in a table. This information appears in a database table *row*.

relationship: A relationship between tables exists where a column of data in one table is identical to a column of data in another table. One column holds the actual data, and the other column contains a reference to the actual data.

row: A single record of data in a table.

table: A collection of data arranged in *columns (fields)* and *rows (records)*.

Last Stop

Practice Exam

1. Which of the following would be the best table name for storing information about a postage-stamp collection?

A) Stamp Collection Table

B) Stamp_Collection

C) Stamps

D) Postage_Stamps_From_Around_the_World

2. You've accidentally deleted a table from your database. Describe the steps you'll take to recover it.

_____

_____

_____

3. About how many columns should you limit a table to?

A) 5

B) 10

C) 15

D) 20

4. What are the characteristics of a good naming convention?

A) Simple, descriptive, and short

B) Simple, vague, and short

C) Complex, vague, and lengthy

D) Complex, descriptive, and lengthy

5. True or false: The order in which you create the columns in a table is very important. Explain why or why not.

_____

_____

_____

6. Database tables are very similar to spreadsheets because they're both:

A) Great at storing huge amounts of data

B) Equally capable in handling predictive scenarios

C) Designed for historical data analysis

D) Made up of columns and rows

7. Describe the process of adding a new column to a table.

_____

_____

_____

8. Which of the following is true of database tables?

A) They never need revision or changes.

B) Tables require very long names to be effective.

C) Tables are dynamic entities.

D) Tables aren't different from spreadsheets.

9. True or false: You can delete only very small tables by using the method shown in this chapter. Explain why or why not.

_____

_____

_____

10. Write down the column names and data types that you would use to create the table for the following scenario. Imagine you are asked to develop a table to store information about company employees, using the following information as a guide: Name, address, phone number, salary, city, state, Zip code, number of dependents, and marital status.

_____

_____

3

Creating and Using Tables — Level II

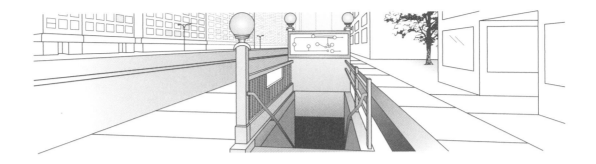

Enter the Station

Questions

1. How do you enter data into Access?

2. What's an external data source?

3. How do you import data into Access?

4. How do you link to external data from Access?

5. Can Access share its data with other programs?

6. How do you export data from Access?

Express Line

If you already have experience using external data in Access, then skip ahead to Chapter 4.

This chapter focuses on how to enter data into Access by importing directly from another program or by linking to an external source for the data. You can find out various ways to acquire information and make the necessary changes so that Access can use the data. This chapter also talks about exporting data from Access to demonstrate how to share your data with others.

Gathering Data

It's easy to put data into a new table in Access. After you create the table and columns (which you can read about in Chapter 1), you can type in the information directly, just as you would for a word-processing document or a spreadsheet (as shown in Chapter 2). This is the easiest (but most time-consuming) method of getting data into a table. If data is already in an electronic format, you can use faster and more efficient ways of getting it into your database.

You can acquire data for your database from many sources, such as spreadsheets, other database systems (including other Access database files), word-processing documents, plain text files, Web pages, and e-mail programs.

Information Kiosk

After you understand the concept of getting data from external sources, you can gather data from a variety of electronic sources, even if Access doesn't have a special feature to import that source.

External Data Sources

Using external data sources is so common and important that a large portion of Access is now dedicated to it. On the menu bar, you see a tab named External Data. When you click the External Data tab, you see separate sections for Import, Export, Collect Data, and SharePoint Lists.

Import

You can import data into Access in several ways. The External Data tab shows you the following list:

- Access
- Excel
- SharePoint List

- Text File
- XML File
- ODBC (Open Database Connectivity) Database
- HTML File
- Outlook Folder
- dBase File
- Paradox File
- Lotus 1-2-3 File

Paradox, dBase, and Lotus 1-2-3 are other database programs that have files you can directly convert into Access format.

Export

The ability to export your Access data to other programs gives you the opportunity to share your data in a variety of formats. You can export to the following formats:

- Excel
- SharePoint List
- PDF (Portable Document Format) or XPS (XML Paper Specification)

  PDF is the current industry standard for creating files that can be used on any operating system. XPS is Microsoft's new open-document format that's integrated into Windows Vista. (To view XPS documents on Windows XP and Windows Server 2003, you must use the XPS Document Viewer.)

- RTF (Rich Text Format)

  A wide variety of word-processing programs can use RTF, including Microsoft Word, WordPad, and OpenOffice.

- Text File
- Access
- XML File
- ODBC Database
- HTML File
- dBase File
- Paradox File

- Lotus 1-2-3 File
- Microsoft Word Mail Merge

Collect Data

With the new feature of Access 2007, Collect Data, you can gather table data using e-mail. If you choose Create E-mail from the Collect Data area of the menu, you're presented with a wizard that lets you send data to a list of recipients. The e-mail recipients can view the data, update it, and send it back so that you can update your original data. The Manage Replies option lets you update your e-mail responses. This feature can be very handy for updating personal information or conducting surveys.

SharePoint Lists

If you have access to a SharePoint Portal Server, the SharePoint Lists feature gives you the ability to export your data directly to SharePoint for immediate consumption. It also lets you synchronize any changes when you make the connection.

The SharePoint Lists feature has the following options:

- Move to SharePoint
- Synchronize
- Take All Offline
- Discard Changes

If you want to try SharePoint for free, go to www.sharepointtrial.com. The site is fully functional, and it's a great introduction to the possibilities that the SharePoint Portal Server offers.

Importing Data

Importing data is a very rapid and common method of getting data into a database. Data may be imported from a variety of sources: Other Access databases, Excel spreadsheets, text files, and so on.

Access

Another Access database gives you a good source of data that you can import into your own database. You can use a database from the current or a previous version of Access.

Before you can use the examples in this chapter, you need two databases with one table each. You can either download the databases Database2 and Database3 from this book's Web site or create the databases yourself by following these steps:

1. **Create a new database and name it** Database2.accdb.
2. **Add three columns named** First_Name, Last_Name, **and** Grade.
3. **Enter the following data into the table:**
   - Bob, Smith, 96
   - John, Doe, 84
   - Jane, Johnson, 99
4. **Create a second database and name it** Database3.accdb.
5. **Add three columns named:** First_Name, Last_Name, **and** Grade.
6. **Enter the following data into the table:**
   - Linda, Jones, 88
   - David, Davis, 67
   - Betty, Sherman, 79

At this point, you should have Database3 still open. To import data from another Access database, follow these steps:

1. **From the External Data tab, click Access.**

   You're asked to select the source and destination of the data. The default location for your databases is shown in the `File name` field.
2. **Click the Browse button to open an Explorer window.**
3. **Select** Database2.accdb **from the list. Click Open.**
4. **Click OK.**

   The Import Objects dialog box appears, displaying `Table1`.
5. **Click** Table1 **and then click OK.**

   The Save Import Steps screen opens.
6. **Click Close.**

If you're following the example, you should now have two tables: Table1 and Table11. Table11 is the data from the other table exactly as you entered it into Database2. There's no way to import into an existing table in Access. The only way to put all the records into the same table is to import the data into a new table, copy or cut the data from the imported data table, and paste it into your original table.

To copy data from one table to another, follow these steps:

1. **Open both tables (double-click each table name).**

2. **Select the imported data table (for example,** Table11**).**

3. **Highlight all the records in the table by clicking the upper-left corner of the datasheet, as shown in Figure 3-1.**

Figure 3-1: Click the upper-left corner of the datasheet to highlight all the records.

4. **Right-click the datasheet.**

5. **Click Cut or Copy.**

If you click Cut, you receive a warning that you're about to delete the records and you can't undo this operation.

6. **Click Yes.**

7. **Select the table (for example,** Table1**).**

8. **Click the cell with the asterisk (*) in it to select the entire row.**

Figure 3-2 shows the row selected.

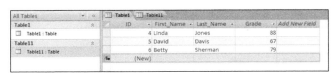

Figure 3-2: Selecting the entire row.

9. **Right-click the row.**

10. **Click Paste.**

You receive a message that you're about to paste three records.

11. **Click Yes to paste the records.**

If you're following the example, you now have all six records in Table1.

Excel

Excel is a very common source of data to import into Access. When an Excel spreadsheet grows to an unmanageable size, the next step is usually an Access database.

Importing an Excel spreadsheet as a new Access table

To create an Excel spreadsheet to import into Access as a new table, you can either download the ready-made spreadsheet from this book's Web site or follow these steps in Excel:

1. Open Excel and type in the data shown in Table 3-1.

Table 3-1   Excel Data

First Name	Last Name	Grade	
Jenna	Schwartz	90	
Al	Colson	67	
Audrey	Payton	85	

2. Save the spreadsheet as Book1.

3. Close Excel.

To import the data from an Excel spreadsheet to Access, follow these steps:

1. Click Excel in the External Data tab.

The *Select source and destination data* screen opens with three options available.

2. Click Browse and select your Excel spreadsheet (for example, the Book1 spreadsheet).

3. Click Open.

4. Select *Import the source data into a new table in the current database* (the first option).

5. Click OK.

The Import Spreadsheet Wizard screen displays the data from the spreadsheet.

6. Click Next.

7. Click First Row Contains Column Headings.

The data in the first row moves up and becomes column headings, leaving the data from the spreadsheet in the list.

8. Click Next.

9. Change First Name and Last Name to First_Name and Last_Name.

This step is very important in the Import Spreadsheet Wizard because it lets you edit field (column) names, data types, indexing, and whether to import specific fields. You can change the column names by clicking the column name and typing the new name in the Field Options area, as shown in Figure 3-3.

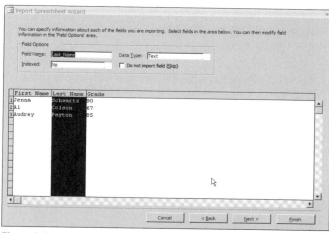

Figure 3-3: You can edit spreadsheet features in the Import Spreadsheet Wizard.

10. **Click Next.**

The screen prompts you to select a primary key (or not) for your new table.

 Information Kiosk

A *primary key* uniquely identifies each record in your table, and allows you to retrieve data more quickly.

11. **Click Next to accept the current settings.**

12. **Change the name of the table from Sheet1 to** Table2.

13. **Click Finish.**

14. **Click Close.**

For this example, Table2 contains the data from Book1. At this point, you can copy and paste the data in the same way I describe in the "Access" section earlier in this chapter.

Importing an Excel spreadsheet into an existing Access table

In this section, you can find out how to import data from an Excel spreadsheet and append that data into an existing table.

Information Kiosk

If your spreadsheet doesn't have the same number of columns and column names as your Access table, then you must edit the spreadsheet; create a new spreadsheet with correctly formatted data; or import the data into a new Access table (which I discuss in the preceding section), then copy and paste it into the correct Access table. When appending data into an existing table, you can't rename columns, omit columns, or alter indexes.

To import and append the data from the `Book1.xls` example spreadsheet into Table1, follow these steps:

1. **Open Book1 in Excel and change First Name to** First_Name **and Last Name to** Last_Name.

2. **Save Book1 and Close Excel.**

3. **Click Excel in the External Data tab.**

   The *Select source and destination data* screen opens with three options available.

4. **Click Browse and select your Excel spreadsheet (Book1).**

5. **Click Open.**

6. **Choose** *Append a copy of the records to the table* **(the second option).**

7. **Select** Table1 **from the drop-down list.**

8. **Click OK.**

   If Table1 is open, you receive a message telling you so. You can save and close Table1 and continue.

   The Import Spreadsheet Wizard opens, displaying your spreadsheet data.

9. **Click Next.**

10. **Select First Row Contains Column Headings.**

11. **Click Next.**

   Make sure that the `Import to table` field has `Table1` in it.

12. **Click Finish.**

   The data from Book1 is now appended to Table1.

If your spreadsheet data is in a format that you don't want to change (or you can't change it), then your best option is to import the data into a new table, which you can read about in the preceding section. By importing into a new table, you have more flexibility and options available.

SharePoint lists

This section uses the public SharePoint server described in the "SharePoint Lists" section earlier in this chapter. I've created a list on the server that's basically an online database or spreadsheet through their editor.

My SharePoint list, named `Gradebook`, contains the entries shown in Table 3-2.

Table 3-2   Gradebook

ID	First_Name	Last_Name	Grade
1	Maria	Trumbull	95
2	Connor	Stevens	59
3	Walker	Tucker	68

To import a SharePoint list into the currently open database, follow these steps:

1. **Click SharePoint List from the External Data tab in Access.**

   The *Select the source and destination data* screen appears, requesting the SharePoint site URL.

2. **Enter your SharePoint URL into the Specify a SharePoint site field.**

   I use `http://kenhess.sharepointsite.com`.

3. **Click Next.**

   A user name and password prompt appear.

4. **Enter your user name and password. Click OK.**

   The *Import data from list* screen appears with all your available lists.

5. **Select the list you want to import. Click OK.**

   My list is called `Gradebook`.

   The SharePoint list is imported into the current database as a new table (mine is called `Gradebook`). Use the instructions described in the "SharePoint Lists" section (earlier in this chapter) to copy and paste this data into Table1.

Text files

Text files are a great source of data for databases. Of all the sources available, I've used text files most often. Many programs have the ability to export their data in plain text as comma-delimited text. *Comma-delimited text* is text in which the individual items (values) in the file are separated by commas.

Information Kiosk

You can use comma-delimited text to share data between dissimilar applications. Files that have their data set up in this way are called *comma-separated values* (CSV), *comma-delimited text files*, or simply *delimited text* (when the comma is assumed). You can also use other common delimiters (separators), including tabs, spaces, and quotes.

To create a comma-delimited text file suitable for importing into Access, follow these steps:

1. **Open Notepad (Start → Run → Notepad → OK) and enter the values exactly as shown in Table 3-3.**

Table 3-3   Text File

First_Name,Last_Name,Grades
Larry,Yoder,66
Bob,Green,78
Lisa,Cash,83

2. **Save the file as** Grades.txt **and close Notepad.**

3. **Click Text File in the External Data tab.**

The *Select source and destination data* screen opens with three options available.

4. **Click Browse and select your text file (`Grades.txt`).**

5. **Select the *Import the source data into a new table in the current database* option (the first option in the list).**

6. **Click OK.**

Your data appears on this page.

7. **Click Next.**

A page opens that lets you specify the delimiter if the wizard couldn't determine it automatically. Your delimiter is recognized as Comma.

8. **Click First Row Contains Field Names.**

9. **Click Next.**

Your file is in the correct format, and you want all the fields.

10. **Click Next.**

11. Click the *Let Access add primary key* radio button. Click Next.

12. Make sure the name of the table is Grades and click Finish.

13. Click Close.

Your data appears in a new table named `Grades`. You can now copy and paste the data from Grades to Table1.

Information Kiosk

If you're importing data into a new table, the wizard helps you make very flexible choices, regardless of the data source. The data you're importing can contain any number of columns and different data types that don't have to match those of an existing table. If you're importing data that's going to be appended to a current table, you must make sure that the external data source (such as a spreadsheet, SharePoint list, or text file) is correctly formatted. It must be designed exactly like your table, with matching column names and the same number of columns.

You should now have a good grasp of importing data into Access. In the following section, you can figure out how to connect to external data sources without importing the data into your database.

Linking to External Data

The ability to link to an external data source makes Access a very powerful database program. This feature lets you connect to external data and use that data without any design or ownership issues on your part. So you can use data from a wide variety of data sources without actually having to edit or maintain the data. If the external data is updated, you and the users of your database get that updated information without any intervention.

External Access databases

This example illustrates how to link to external data. Just follow these steps:

1. Close Database3 (which you opened earlier in this chapter) by opening a new database (Database4).

2. Close Table1 (which you opened earlier in this chapter).

3. Click Access in the External Data tab.

4. Click Browse and select Database3 from the list that appears. Click Open.

5. Select *Link to the data source by creating a linked table.*

6. **Click OK.**

A list of tables from Database3 appears. You can link to any number of tables.

7. **Select Table1 and click OK.**

If you're following this example, Table1 from Database3 is now linked to Table1 in Database4. Open Table1 and look at the data. Because no one has placed any security on Table1 from Database3, you can enter new data into it — changing Table1 in Database3. You can't always edit the original data, however. In many instances, you're given read-only access to a database or other external file, so you can see the data but you can't make permanent changes to it. To make permanent changes to the data, you must first import it into Database4.

External Excel spreadsheets

Linking to an Excel spreadsheet gives you a different method of updating and viewing information in a spreadsheet.

To link to an Excel spreadsheet, follow these steps:

1. **Click Excel in the External Data tab.**

You don't need a copy of Excel to link to an Excel spreadsheet file.

2. **Click Browse and select the spreadsheet (for example, Book1). Click Open.**

3. **Select** *Link to the data source by creating a linked table.*

4. **Click OK.**

5. **Click Next.**

6. **Select First Row Contains Column Headings. Click Next.**

7. **Change the name of Sheet1 to** Table2. **Click Finish.**

If you're following this example, you get a message that the spreadsheet has been linked, and you can now see Table2. To compare the data in both, follow these steps:

1. **Open Table2 to view the data.**

2. **Open Book1 in Excel.**

You receive a message that tells you Book1 is locked for editing, but you can open a read-only copy.

3. **Click Cancel.**

When a linked table is opened in Access, it locks the external file for editing — but you can only edit records that already exist. You can't add new records. You can add new records and columns only either from within Excel or when Access doesn't have a lock on the Excel spreadsheet.

Watch Your Step

When two applications access the same spreadsheet file, it's "first come, first served." The first application to open a file gets an exclusive lock for editing on the file. When the file is open, all other applications that access the file get a read-only copy of the file. This feature protects the file from having its contents simultaneously overwritten, which could lead to file corruption and errors in the data.

SharePoint lists

You can link to a SharePoint list in Access.

To link to a SharePoint list, follow these steps:

1. **Click SharePoint List in the External Data tab.**

2. **Enter your SharePoint URL into the Specify a SharePoint site field.**

I use `http://kenhess.sharepointsite.com`.

3. **Click Next.**

A user name and password prompt appears.

4. **Enter your user name and password. Click OK.**

5. **Select the list that you want to import. Click OK.**

My list is called `Gradebook`.

The SharePoint list is linked as a table in your current database. The table name is the same as the list name — in my example, `Gradebook`. Linking to a SharePoint list is superior, in many ways, to linking to other external data sources. Access can update the SharePoint list through the linked table, and users of the online SharePoint list can also update the list. A refresh shows the updates to either application.

Information Kiosk

In Windows applications, the F5 key on the keyboard *refreshes*, or reloads, your current page or application data.

External text files

The same rules apply for linking to an external text file as importing one, which you can read about in the "Text files" section earlier in this chapter. The file should be plain text (no formatting) with values *delimited* (separated) by such characters as commas, tabs, spaces, or semicolons.

To link an external text file, follow these steps:

1. **Click Text File in the External Data tab.**
2. **Click Browse, select the Grades text file, and click Open.**
3. **Select *Link to the data source by creating a linked table*.**
4. **Click OK.**
5. **Click Next.**
6. **Select First Row Contains Column Headings. Click Next.**

   Here you can perform such changes as changing field names, omitting fields, or creating indexes.

7. **Click Next.**
8. **Accept the name (for example, Grades) for the linked table or change it to another name. Click Finish.**

You receive a message stating that the link has been created. Unlike a linked spreadsheet, you can edit the table created from the external text file in Access by adding new records or changing existing ones.

Linking to external data provides a wide range of possibilities for accessing data from a variety of sources. For read-only data viewing, linking to an external data source gives you the shortest path for expanding your database. In some cases, linking (for example, linking to a spreadsheet) can become cumbersome. Using a SharePoint Portal Server to share data with Access lets users share data stored in a central location.

Exporting Data

Access has the ability to export data to a wide variety of other formats, sharing data between applications. Very often, people ask for a *data dump* (writing all table data to a file) from a database. Understanding how to export data from Access is as important as knowing any other aspect of the program. Users export data from Access more often than they perform any other database operation. Because everyone uses different programs and may need access to information, you must be able to provide data to them quickly and in the correct format.

Excel

For Windows users, Excel is by far the most requested format for exported data. Excel can read several types of files with which you're probably familiar, such as comma-separated values (CSV), text files, HTML files, and Access databases.

Exporting Access data to Excel

To export data from Access to Excel, follow these steps:

1. **Open a database (for example, Database3).**

2. **From the Export Section of the External Data tab, click Excel.**

The name of the Excel file you're exporting data to is the same as the Table you're exporting (for example, Table1), and the file format is Excel 2007 (`.xlsx`). If users have older versions of Excel, choose a different value from the File Format drop-down list — such as Excel 97 - Excel 2003 Workbook (*.xls).

3. **Select Export data with formatting and layout.**

4. **Select Open the destination file after the export is complete.**

This step automatically launches Excel and opens your table (for example, `Table1.xlsx`).

5. **Click OK.**

Give Excel a few seconds to open. An Access dialog box notifies you that the export was successful.

6. **Click Close on the Access window.**

Exporting Access data to delimited files

Exporting data to Excel is one way to ensure that Excel users can share your data. But what if everyone who needs that data isn't using Excel? A more generic way of exporting the data is to export it to a text file by using a delimiter, such as a comma or tab.

To export data from Access to a delimited text file, follow these steps:

1. **From the Export Section of the External Data tab, click Text File.**

The name of the text file you're exporting data to is the same as the table you're exporting (Table1).

2. **Click OK.**

The Export Text Wizard starts and displays your data from Table1.

3. **Click Next.**

A page of the wizard that displays the value delimiter and text delimiter if it can determine them automatically appears. By default, Comma is selected and the Text Qualifier is set to `"`.

4. **Click Next.**

The default file name is `Table1.txt`. You can change the name in the Export to File text box if you want.

5. Click Finish.

6. Click Close on the Access confirmation screen.

To test your newly exported file (`Table1.txt`, in this example), follow these steps:

1. Open Excel.

2. Open the text file (**Table1.txt**).

The Text Import Wizard opens.

3. Click Next.

4. Deselect Tab, select Comma, and then click Next.

5. Click Finish.

The data from the text-file data is now displayed correctly in your new spreadsheet.

Database administrators usually export data as a CSV text file (as you can do in the preceding example). This type of exported data fulfills the needs of most applications, including Excel.

Checking the icon

You can tell whether a table is imported or linked when you open an Access database. The icon next to the table name gives you a clue about whether the table is linked and which type of file it's linked to. An arrow next to a table's icon tells you that the table is linked data. Figure 3-4 shows some of the types of tables you might see in an Access database. From top to bottom, they are

- Access-linked table (Table1)
- Excel-linked spreadsheet (Table2)
- Text-linked table (Grades)
- Access Table (Sheet1)
- SharePoint List-linked table (Gradebook)

Sheet1 is the only table in this list that isn't linked. (The Table name is `Sheet1`: `Table`, which tells you that the data is an actual table within Access.) The origin of the table data doesn't matter because the data is now in an Access table.

Deleting a linked table

If you need to delete a linked table, the underlying data isn't changed. You receive a message telling you that only the link is being deleted, not the actual data. After you delete a linked table, you can't recover it. You must repeat the linking process to reestablish the link.

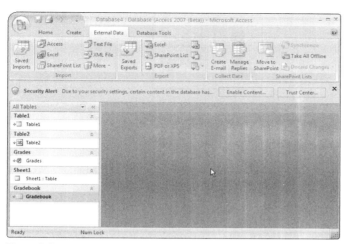

Figure 3-4: Multiple linked table types.

data dump: A generalized information export from a database. An export of an entire table is a type of data dump.

delimiter: A value separator in a file. A set of values can be separated by almost any type of character, but the most common are comma, tab, space, and quotation marks (single or double).

export: To collect, organize, and package information appropriately to be used by an external program.

external data source: A file created by another program that Microsoft Access can use as an attachable or importable supply of information.

import: To collect and modify information from an external data source so that the information is directly usable as an internal source of data.

link: An attachment to an external data source so that you can use the data but the source of the data remains external.

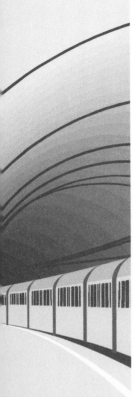

Practice Exam

1. **Why would you export data from Access?**

A) To share information with others

B) To be compatible with other applications

C) To make sure that everything is working

D) None of the above

2. **Which type of file do you create when you need to export data but don't know the application that will use it?**

A) Excel

B) Access

C) Text

D) PDF

3. **What's the default name for any file that's exported?**

A) `Table1.txt.`

B) `Table1.xlsx.`

C) There isn't a default name.

D) The name of the exported table.

4. **To use a SharePoint server, you must know:**

A) The name of the SharePoint server

B) The location of the SharePoint server

C) The URL of the SharePoint server

D) The design of the SharePoint server

5. **What's the greatest advantage of exporting to a text file?**

A) It's the easiest method of export.

B) It's the least intrusive method of export.

C) The exported file is smaller.

D) Almost any application can use it.

6. **Importing data into Access is an excellent way to:**

A) Get a lot of data into Access quickly.

B) Store data from someone else.

C) Exercise your Access skills.

D) Become familiar with other database programs.

7. **You must use caution when importing data into Access that will be appended to an existing table. Why?**

A) Appending data requires that you watch the data transfer bit by bit.

B) The names and number of columns in the external file must match the Access table exactly.

C) You can overwrite existing table data.

D) You must extract the external file in sections.

8. **Using a SharePoint Portal Server with Access is a great way to:**

A) Convert data

B) Reorganize data

C) Purchase data

D) Share data

9. **When importing data, Access automatically attempts to assign a primary key to the table. Why?**

A) This is a standard Access security feature.

B) It is a feature of good design.

C) To make it easier for you to keep track of how many records are imported.

D) This is an internal tracking mechanism for Access.

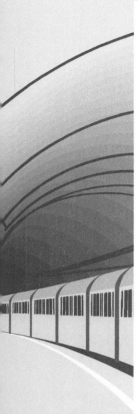

10. **What's one major advantage of linking to rather than importing data from external sources?**

A) Linked data is lower maintenance.

B) The process of linking data is easier than importing.

C) Exclusive edit locking.

D) Linked data is backed up more frequently.

4

Asking the Database for Data — Level I

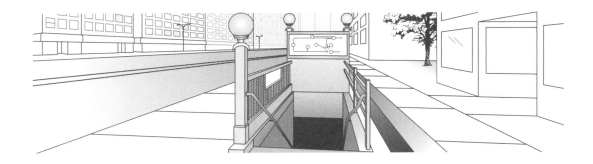

Enter the Station

Questions

1. What's a query?

2. What's a filter?

3. How do you round values?

4. How do you create calculated fields?

5. How do you perform calculations on data in columns?

6. What's summary data?

7. What are the aggregate functions?

Express Line

If you already are familiar with simple queries, then skip ahead to Chapter 5.

This chapter focuses on performing simple queries, first with the Query Wizard, then manually by using Query Design View. You can find out some simple techniques for getting the data you really need for a report, and you're introduced to aggregate functions.

Getting Information from a Database

After you have data in your database(s) (which you can figure out how to do in Chapter 2), at some point you need a way to see that data. When you need information from a database, you pose a question to that database. A question that's posed in database format is called a query. A *query* is a specially formed question that extracts information from a database. Using filters, it gets a report of only the data you want.

Consider this example: You're the administrator of a local high school (grades 9–12) and have constructed a database that has 1,200 currently enrolled student records in it. You want to know your 10th-graders' grades to give you a snapshot of their progress. The 10th-grade class has about 300 students. You have several options:

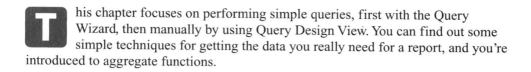 Print all the records in the database, look for the 10th-graders, and check their grades individually.

Print the information for all 300 10th-graders, read through the grades, and check them individually.

Print the number of students who have passing grades and the number who have failing grades.

You probably want to go with the last option, in this case. You can use a database to query and filter information quickly. At a glance, you know the exact number of 10th graders who are passing and the number who are failing. After getting this information, you could then print the failing students' complete information to send progress letters home to their parents. You'd be able to check this amount of student information individually. By using a filter, you can narrow down the number of *hits,* or positive matches, from 1,200 to about 30.

To fully grasp the concepts of *query, filter*, and *hit*, try the following exercise. Just follow these steps:

1. Go to your favorite Internet search engine.

I'm using www.google.com for this example.

2. Type the word Access **into the search field and click Search.**

I got 344,000,000 hits from my query.

3. **Type** "Microsoft Access" **(with quotes) into the search field and click Search.**

I got 18,900,000 hits by using "Microsoft Access" as my query keywords.

4. **Type** "Microsoft Access 2007" **(with quotes) and click Search.**

I got 9,980 hits by using the more specific search phrase.

The preceding steps show you the process of filtering by using keywords. When you type keywords into a search engine, you're actually creating a query that's being sent to a massive database, and the number of hits you get is the number of records from that database that match your criteria. The more specific a query, the fewer hits it returns.

Creating a Query

Instead of typing keywords into a search field as you do in an Internet search engine, in Access, you construct a query by using a wizard to help you find the information you need. This wizard assists you in creating the query with the necessary filters to extract only the data you want to see. The type of query you use in this chapter is a Select query. With a Select query, you're selecting the data you want to see in the query. This is the most common type of query.

The following examples illustrate simple Select queries. You need a sample table called Grade_10. You can either download the Chapter 4 material from this book's Web site or create a new table named `Grade_10` in your current database — and then enter the data from Table 4-1 into it. (The `ID` field, which isn't shown in Table 4-1, will be created for you automatically.)

Table 4-1   Grade_10 Table Data

First_Name	Last_Name	Grade
Ken	Shay	49
Tom	Evans	89
Sue	Cleary	95
Ed	Balster	56
Missy	Trumbull	74
Kevin	Taverner	88
Maria	Rinker	62

To use the Query Wizard, follow these steps:

1. Click the Create tab.

You should see four sections: Tables, Forms, Reports, and Other.

2. As shown in Figure 4-1, click the icon labeled Query Wizard.

The Query Wizard starts by opening the New Query dialog box.

3. Click OK to choose Simple Query Wizard.

The Simple Query Wizard opens with selections for Tables/Queries and Available Fields.

4. Select a Table (for example, Grade_10) from the Table/Query drop-down list.

The Available Fields list populates with the fields from the table you use (for example, the Grade_10 table).

5. Select fields from the Available Fields list (for example, select First_Name, Last_Name, and Grade from Grade_10), and then click the > button to send each field to the Selected Fields list, as shown in Figure 4-2.

The Selected Fields list will be in your final report.

6. Click Next.

7. Select Detail and click Next.

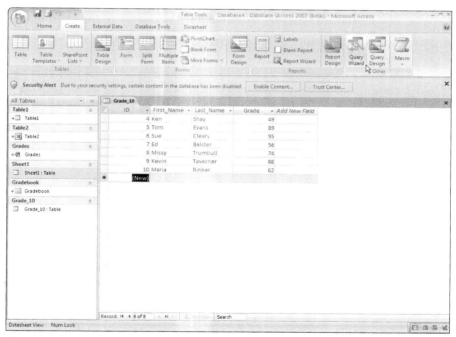

Figure 4-1: Use the Query Wizard to create a query.

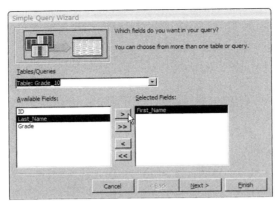

Figure 4-2: Select which fields you want in your query by using the Simple Query Wizard.

8. Click Finish.

Your query opens; it shows the fields you selected. This is a very simple query that differs from the original table by only one field. However, if you had a table with a dozen columns and thousands of rows, you would see a more significant change from table to query results. The example in this section requires more data in your table. Follow these steps to add that data:

1. Open table Grade_10 and change the name of the column Grade to Test1.

2. Add two more columns named Test2 and Test3.

3. Add the records for each student shown in Table 4-2.

Table 4-2   More Grade_10 Table Data

First_Name	Last_Name	Test2	Test3
Ken	Shay	67	51
Tom	Evans	92	85
Sue	Cleary	97	92
Ed	Balster	48	51
Missy	Trumbull	81	83
Kevin	Taverner	93	90
Maria	Rinker	77	66

4. Save the table.

Follow these steps to create a new query:

1. Click the Create tab.

2. Click the Query Wizard button.

3. Click OK in the New Query Wizard dialog box.

4. Select Table: Grade_10 from the Table/Query drop-down list.

5. Select all of the fields except ID and Test2 in the Simple Query Wizard, and then send them to the Selected Fields list.

To send all Available Fields to the Selected Fields list, click the >> button. To remove a field from the Selected Fields list, select it, then click the < button.

6. Click Next.

7. Click Finish.

You can select and deselect any field or any number of fields for a query. You can also change the order of the fields in a query by choosing them individually.

Sometimes you may want to select data in a different order than what the table gives you. With a query, you can present data in any order that you need.

For this example, the test scores are presented first, then last name, and finally first name. Follow these steps to create the query:

1. Click the Create tab.

2. Click the Query Wizard button.

3. Click OK in the New Query Wizard dialog box.

4. Select Table: Grade_10 from the Table/Query drop-down list.

5. From the Available Fields list, select Test1 and send it to the Selected Fields list.

6. Select Test2, Test3, Last_Name, and First_Name from the Available Fields list, and then send them to the Selected Fields list.

7. Click Next.

8. Click Next.

9. Click Finish.

The query presents your data in the order you specified. These simple queries are exactly that: simple. They illustrate the Simple Query Wizard and how to select fields for inclusion in the query results. You can also use these simple queries to figure out how to reorder fields for a customized view of your data. These query examples are fine for a very limited look at your data, but when you want to see a subset of records instead of all of them, you must use filtering criteria. Filtering is a way of narrowing your results. If you want to see every grade for every student (and sometimes you would), you can; more often, you want to see who's failing or who's in jeopardy of failing. Snapshots of data (a summary report) are very useful in many disciplines — not just for grades. Taking a preliminary snapshot of sales data before a quarterly report can prove extremely valuable to a CEO in preparing her presentation to nervous stockholders.

Adding Criteria to a Query

Selecting data with criterion-based filters is the whole point of a query — to see only the data you need. A criterion placed on a column of data narrows the returned results. And the more restrictive the criterion, the fewer results will be returned. For example, if you want to find which students are currently failing a class, you place a criterion of **<70**, which is a failing grade. The number of failing students would be considerably less than the total number of students (hopefully!).

The examples in this section use the Grade_10 table, which you can create in the section "Creating a Query," earlier in this chapter.

You need to find the 10th-grade students who failed Test1. To find these students, you must place the criterion of <70 on the Test1 column and then run the query to see the results. There isn't a wizard to create this criterion for you, so you have to do it yourself. Follow these steps:

1. **Click the Create tab.**

2. **Click the Query Design button.**

This step opens the Query Design View and the Show Table dialog box that presents you with a list of tables and queries available in your current database.

3. **From the Tables tab, select Grade_10 and click Add.**

The Grade_10 table tab appears in the Query Design View.

4. **Click Close on the Show Table dialog box.**

Your Query Design View should now look like Figure 4-3.

5. **To create a query from a table, double-click the field you want included in the query.**

The field appears in the Query Builder window (the lower window) of the Query Design View.

6. **Double-click First_Name, Last_Name, and Test1 to send them into the Query Builder window.**

Figure 4-3 shows several row headings, and the Query Builder window displays Field, Table, Sort, Show, Criteria, and or.

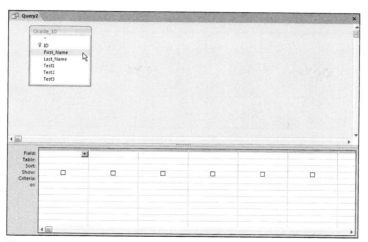

Figure 4-3: Table Grade_10 in Query Design View.

7. On the Criteria row under Test1, enter <70.

Figure 4-4 shows the correct entries.

The query is complete.

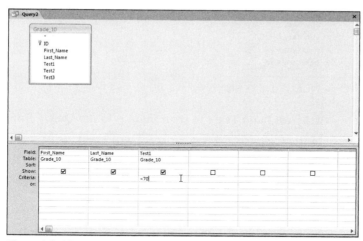

Figure 4-4: Adding criteria in the Query Builder window.

8. To *run* (execute) this query, click the Run button on the (Query Tools) Design tab.

The results from the query are shown in Table 4-3.

Table 4-3   Test1 Failing Grade: Query Results

First_Name	Last_Name	Test1
Ken	Shay	49
Ed	Balster	56
Maria	Rinker	62

This example query was successful because only those students whose scores are below 70 are shown.

For the following example, add Test2 and Test3 with the same criteria you use in the preceding example. Follow these steps:

1. **Go back to Query Design View by right-clicking the Query name then clicking Design View, as shown in Figure 4-5.**

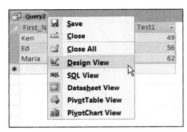

Figure 4-5: Use the right-click menu to return to Query Design View.

2. **Double-click Test2 and Test3 to send them into the Query Builder window.**

3. **Add <70 to the Criteria row under Test2 and Test3.**

4. **Execute the query.**

   You may have to click Query Tools above the Design Tab to make the Run button appear.

The results from the query are shown in Table 4-4.

Table 4-4   All Tests Failing Grade: Query Results

First_Name	Last_Name	Test1	Test2	Test3
Ken	Shay	49	67	51
Ed	Balster	56	48	51

Why did Maria Rinker's scores drop out of the results? The answer lies in how the query was created. By creating the query with the criterion of <70 for all three tests, the table is being asked to provide information for students whose test grades for *all three* tests are less than 70. This query is designed in such a way that it's asking the database for students who've failed Test1 and Test2 and Test3. Excluding data in this way is a common mistake when using databases. The data you have is legitimate, but you're also missing legitimate data. A student could have failed two of the three tests and have an overall failing grade, but because he didn't fail all three tests, he doesn't appear in the results. To correct this error, you have to create the query as a list of the students who've failed Test1 or Test2 or Test3. The OR query yields very different results.

By entering the criteria all in the same row of the Query Builder, you build the query as an AND query. To build this same query as an OR query, you must place the criteria on different rows. Now you know what the or row is for in the Query Builder. All the rows from Criteria downward are for criteria entries, with each row representing a different or value.

To create an OR query for the tenth-grade tests, follow these steps:

1. **Go back to Query Design View.**

2. **Under Test2, remove <70 and enter it on the line below its current location.**

3. **Under Test3, remove <70 and enter it two lines below its current location.**

Figure 4-6 shows you the correct entries.

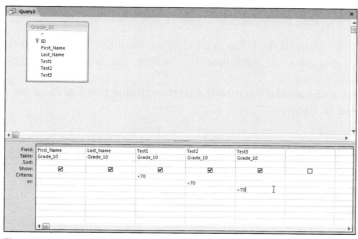

Figure 4-6: Building an OR query using multiple criteria rows.

4. **Execute the query.**

The query now returns the expected results — anyone who has ever failed a test is now included in the list. Does this list accurately reflect the number of failing students? You can tell by looking at the three students listed here that two of them are definitely failing the class. What about Maria Rinker? It's a little difficult to tell whether she's failing the class, although she has failed two of the three tests. The solution to this dilemma is in the following section.

Adding Calculations to a Query

You can add calculations to a database, just like you can in a spreadsheet. The most logical place to do calculations is in the query statement so that the calculated data is included when the data is output.

To solve the problem of needing summary data (presented in the preceding section), you have to use a calculation. The average of each student's grades yields a more useful result than his or her individual test scores. The *average* of a set of numbers is defined as the sum of the set of numbers divided by the number of items in the set. For this example, this calculation translates to

```
Average = (Test1 + Test2 + Test3)/3
```

You construct a calculated field in a query in a special way. Instead of entering the formula for the average directly into the Field area of the Query Builder, you use the following general syntax:

```
Label: (Calculation)
Average: (Test1 + Test2 + Test3)/3
```

Average is the name of the column label in the results. The calculation itself looks like an ordinary mathematical formula entry. To enter the calculation, follow these steps:

1. **Enter this calculation into the first available Field area in the query, as shown in Figure 4-7:**

   ```
   Average: (Test1 + Test2 + Test3)/3
   ```

2. **Click the Show box under the formula so that the information from this field is presented in the query results.**

3. **Execute the query.**

Step into the Real World

The appropriate place for calculations is in queries or reports. It's poor design to include calculated fields in a table. Because computers perform calculations with great speed, you shouldn't waste database space and resources on calculated fields.

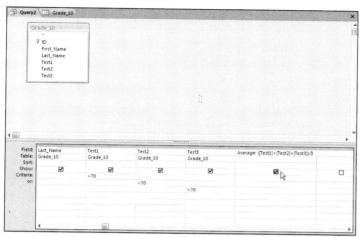

Figure 4-7: Enter the formula in the Field row.

The results from the query are shown in Table 4-5.

Table 4-5   Average Test Grade: Query Results

First_Name	Last_Name	Test1	Test2	Test3	Average
Ken	Shay	49	67	51	55.6666666666667
Ed	Balster	56	48	51	51.6666666666667
Maria	Rinker	62	77	66	68.3333333333333

All three students are failing this class, and the results from the query in the preceding section are accurate.

If you're looking only for averages to see who's failing the class, you can streamline this data by presenting only the average for each student. Follow these steps:

1. **Go back to Design View.**

2. **Deselect Show under Test1, Test2, and Test3.**

This step hides the data for the tests but uses those fields in the calculation of the average.

3. **Execute the query.**

The query results are shown in Table 4-6.

Table 4-6   Average-Only Query Results

First_Name	Last_Name	Average
Ken	Shay	55.6666666666667
Ed	Balster	51.6666666666667
Maria	Rinker	68.3333333333333

You can see the data more easily without all the clutter of the test scores. The numbers produced by calculations are sometimes a bit unwieldy, however, as you can see from the averages in Table 4-6. You can clean up these numbers significantly by using the Round function. Here's the function in its simplest form:

```
Round(Number)
```

You can be more specific by using this version of the function:

```
Round(Number, Accuracy)
```

Accuracy defines the number of decimal places the Round function uses. If you use

```
Round(30.9333)
```

The result is

```
31
```

If you use

```
Round(30.9333, 2)
```

The result is

```
30.93
```

For the purposes of this test-average example, use the simpler version of the Round function. To edit the formula, follow these steps:

1. Edit the formula for the average of the test scores and add the Round **function, as follows:**

```
Average: Round((Test1 + Test2 + Test3)/3)
```

2. Execute the query.

The results are shown in Table 4-7.

Table 4-7　　　　Rounded Test Average: Query Results

First_Name	Last_Name	Average
Ken	Shay	56
Ed	Balster	52
Maria	Rinker	68

The results using this new formula are much cleaner than those in Table 4-6, and quickly convey the desired information.

As you can see from this example, calculations in queries can be valuable assets in your data extraction and reporting activities. You can use any formula in field calculation that you can use in a spreadsheet program — from statistical calculations to very-high-level mathematical functions.

Summarizing Data

You can summarize your data in Access by using *aggregate* (summary) functions that are built into the Query Builder. These aggregate functions use data from the columns rather than data from the rows. So, if you want to know the average test score for Test1 in this example, you must use the aggregate function Avg.

Information Kiosk

Although summary and aggregate are used interchangeably, the preferred name for the functions — by many professionals and in the Access help — is aggregate. Aggregate functions deal with summary data such as sums, averages, and various groupings based on criteria you assign. People who regularly use spreadsheets are probably very familiar with these aggregate functions because you often sum or average a column of data in a spreadsheet.

To enable the summary functions, click the sigma symbol (Σ) labeled Totals on the menu bar in Query Design View. After you click the Totals button, a new row label (Total) appears in the Query Builder window.

The Total row offers several aggregate functions, as listed in Table 4-8.

Table 4-8   Total Row Functions

Name	Function
Group By	Subtotals data in a query
Sum	Total of a column
Avg	Average of a column
Min	Minimum value in a column
Max	Maximum value in a column
Count	Number of rows in a column
StDev	Standard deviation
Var	Statistical variance
First	First value in a column
Last	Last value in a column
Expression	Refers to an aggregate function in another query column
Where	Specifies a criterion to restrict a column's value

Transfer

The functions Group By, Expression, and Where are advanced functions. They're covered in Chapter 5.

A useful tool to use on the Grade_10 table is the Avg (Average) function. This function calculates the average value for a column of data. For the preceding examples, an average score for each test is good information to have. Standard deviation and variance (if you're already familiar with them) can help you measure the validity of your testing program. This book isn't a course in statistics, but if you're involved in measurement of any kind, you should employ statistics as part of your assessment and decision-making processes. Statistical analysis can give you insight into the validity of your measurements, whether they're student test scores, scientific data, or psychological assessments.

The following example uses the Avg function to find the average test score for Test1, Test2, and Test3. Just follow these steps:

1. **Create a new query by using the Query Design button on the Create tab.**
2. **Select the Grade_10 table, click Add, then click Close.**
3. **Double-click Test1, Test2, and Test3 to send them into the Query Builder window.**

4. If you don't see the Total row label in the Query Builder window, click the Totals (Σ) button on the menu bar to make it appear.

5. Click into the Total field and choose Avg from the drop-down list for each column.

Compare your Query Builder window with Figure 4-8.

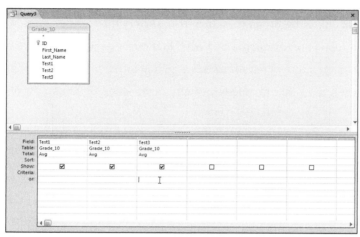

Figure 4-8: This Query Builder window uses the Avg function.

6. Execute the query.

Table 4-9 shows the query results.

Table 4-9   Test Averages Query Results

AvgOfTest1	AvgOfTest2	AvgOfTest3
73.2857142857143	79.2857142857143	74

The numbers are rather ugly, but they're accurate.

Transfer

In Chapter 7, I show you how to use the Round function to round these test-average values. You had a short introduction to the Round function in the section "Adding Calculations to a Query," earlier in this chapter, but to use the Round function for the averages in Table 4-9, you have to use the Expression aggregate function, which is discussed in Chapter 5.

aggregate: A summary function designed to produce calculations on columnar data.

criterion: The value or range of values in a query that creates filtered results.

filter: A restriction or constraint placed in a query designed to narrow the results.

hit: A search or query term that refers to a positive criteria match.

keyword: A term that produces search results when used as part of a query in a search engine.

query: A question directed toward a database to extract information.

round(ing): A mathematical function designed to shorten long numbers, making them easier to deal with by sight and in manual calculations.

Last Stop

Practice Exam

1. **What's the main purpose of a filter?**

A) To get as many hits as possible

B) To get 100 hits

C) To get no hits, then ease the filter restrictions

D) To get a small number of relevant hits

2. **What's the main purpose of a query?**

A) To show all of the data in the database

B) To show a few records

C) To show hits

D) To show specifically selected data

3. **What do aggregate functions do?**

A) They summarize data.

B) They correlate data.

C) They narrow search results.

D) They produce hits.

4. **What's a hit?**

A) A search criterion

B) A data summary

C) A positive result

D) A negative result

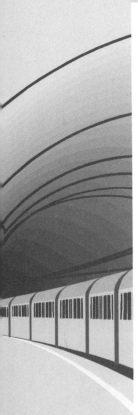

5. **Why would you want to use a rounding function?**

    A) It's better than a squaring function.

    B) It makes numbers easier to deal with.

    C) It creates more hits.

    D) It's a necessary part of a query.

6. **Why wouldn't you use calculated fields in a table?**

    A) It's poor design.

    B) It puts too much stress on a database.

    C) You always use calculated fields in a table.

    D) It takes too long to perform the calculations.

7. **What type of queries have you read about in this chapter?**

    A) Aggregate

    B) Select

    C) Preferred

    D) Narrow

8. **How can you narrow the number of hits returned from a query?**

    A) By using a criterion-based filter

    B) By using the Round function

    C) By using table-based calculations

    D) By using the Simple Query Wizard

9. **Why would you want to summarize your data?**

    A) Too many hits are returned on the data.

    B) Rounding doesn't work on summarized data.

    C) To make quick comparisons between columns.

    D) Access doesn't allow calculated fields.

10. **Which of the following are aggregate functions?**

    A) Max, Min, Round

    B) Max, Min, StDev

    C) Avg, Round, Min

    D) Avg, New, Min

Asking the Database for Data — Level II

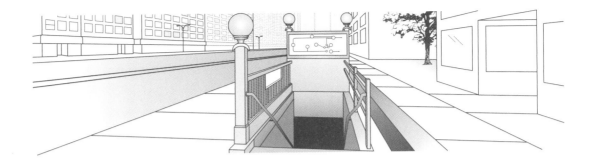

 # Enter the Station

Questions

1. What's an `Update` query?

2. How do you update data in other databases?

3. What's another name for an `Append` query?

4. How can you create a quick backup of a table?

5. How do you change data in a table?

6. How can you remove a single record from a database?

Express Line

If you're familiar with advanced queries, then skip ahead to Chapter 6.

This chapter extends your ability to create queries, showing you how to use queries beyond simple Select queries. Topics this chapter covers include using queries to create new tables, append (insert) data to a table, update data in a table, and delete data from a table. These types of queries actually write to the database and therefore are different from Select queries, which only look at data. Several examples in each section help to illustrate the concepts discussed in that section.

Using Queries to Write Data to a Database

Queries (as shown in Chapter 4) are powerful information-retrieval tools. You can also often use them to insert, update, and delete data and to create new tables.

i Information Kiosk

In the language of databases, SQL (Structured Query Language), the term *insert* is used rather than *append*. In this book, I use the two terms interchangeably to stay consistent with the language used in Access. Access translates your queries from the Query Builder into SQL behind the scenes. Chapter 13 covers this process — and how to use SQL.

Writing data to a database is much slower than *retrieving* (reading) information from it. You may not notice this difference for small single-user queries as you work through the examples in this book. Users of multi-user databases usually experience some lag when writing to a database but almost no delay when running Select queries.

This lag may happen because of such issues as security, slow hardware, and table locking. The most likely reason is *table locking*: Some database systems, such as Access, lock the table or records that they're writing to. This isn't an error; it's a feature that protects data from corruption and accidental overwrites by another user. You (or other users) can still read data from the table through Select queries, but only one query at a time can write to the table.

i Information Kiosk

Insert, Update, Delete, Make Table, and other queries are often called *statements,* not queries, because such statements don't ask for data.

For work in this chapter, you can either download the example Chapter 5 database from this book's Web site or start modifying the Chapter 4 database from Chapter 4. Follow these steps to create a new table:

1. **Create a new table in the same database with the** `Grade_10` **table, as shown in Table 5-1.**

Table 5-1   Grade_10b

First_Name	Last_Name	Test1	Test2	Test3
Jane	Doe	81	75	87
John	Lawson	69	56	71

2. **Save and name the table** `Grade_10b`**.**

3. **Close table Grade_10b.**

4. **Open a different database (old or new).**

5. **Create a new table and add the following fields to it:**

- `Last_Name`
- `Test2`
- `Test3`

6. **Save the table as** `Table_App`**.**

Appending Data

An `Append` query only inserts or adds data to a database. It doesn't overwrite any existing records.

For this exercise, you'll append the data from the Grade_10 table to the Grade_10b table. To create an `Append` query, follow these steps:

1. **Create a new query by clicking the Query Design button.**

The Show Table dialog box appears.

2. **Select Grade_10, click Add, and then click Close.**

3. **Send First_Name, Last_Name, Test1, Test2, and Test3 to the Query Builder by double-clicking each of them.**

4. **Click the Append button in the Query Type Group.**

The Append dialog box appears, showing a Table name drop-down list and selections for either the Current Database or Another Database. You want to append the records in this table.

5. **Select Current Database and then use the Table drop-down list to choose Grade_10b.**

6. **Click OK.**

The Append query has been constructed and is now ready to be executed.

7. **Click Run.**

A dialog box appears, telling you that you're about to append seven records.

8. **Click Yes.**

The Append query is complete. Open table Grade_10b. It should have nine records.

If you don't receive the message that you're about to append records, look in the bottom-left corner of the Microsoft Access window for this message: The action or event has been blocked by Disabled Mode. If you see this message, as shown in Figure 5-1, then you must enable writing to the database.

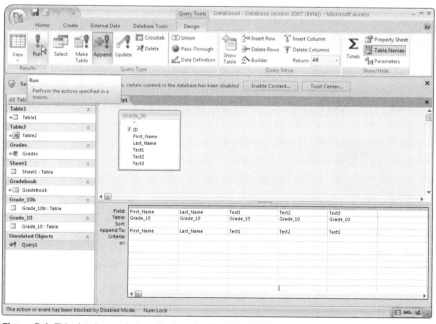

Figure 5-1: This database window displays the Disabled Mode warning in the bottom-left corner.

You can enable writing to the database in two ways:

- Enable content every time you open a new database. (This is the most secure method.)
- Set up a trusted location. (All databases within that location will be write-enabled.)

I prefer to set up a trusted location, but the following sections show you how to do both approaches.

The first method gives you temporary permission to write to a database. Each time you open the database, you must enable the content to be able to write to the database.

Information Kiosk

There's more to a database than the data you put into it. Database documents also have *executable* content (such as macros, Visual Basic for Applications code, and ActiveX controls) — useful code that is (unfortunately) also vulnerable to malicious code attacks. *Disabled content* is a new security feature in Access 2007: All database content is disabled by default. Before you can run the executable content, you must purposely enable it or create a trusted location. The main purpose of this new security is to protect your computer and other databases from malicious attacks.

Enabling Content

To enable content on a per-database basis, follow these steps:

1. Click the Enable Content button on the message bar, as shown in Figure 5-2.

The `Trust in Office` security alert appears.

Watch Your Step

Note the message in the alert: `If you trust the contents of this database and would like to enable it for this session only, click Enable this content.` If you are sure this database contains code that won't harm your program or computer, then it's okay to proceed.

2. Click the Enable this content radio button and then click OK.

Figure 5-3 shows the Security Alert.

This database is now trusted, and all its content is enabled for as long as the current session lasts.

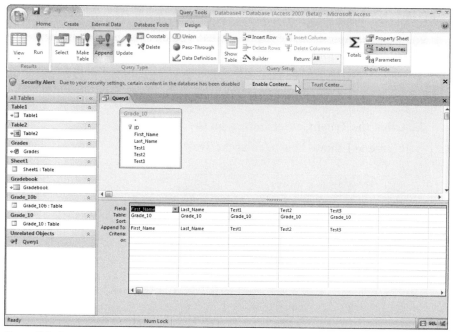

Figure 5-2: Use the Enable Content button on the message bar to enable database content.

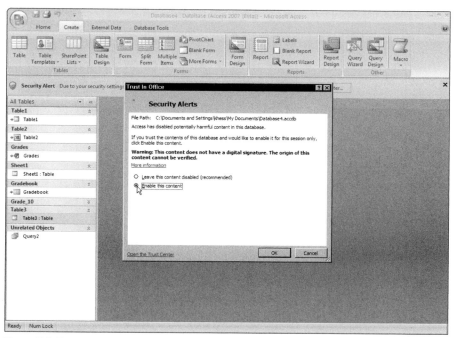

Figure 5-3: The Trust In Office Security Alert verifies that you want to enable content.

Trusted Locations

If you want all your databases to be trusted, you can put them all in the same folder and designate that folder as a trusted location. Doing so enables all content for all databases in that location.

To create a trusted location, follow these steps:

1. **Click the Trust Center button on the message bar.**

Figure 5-4 shows how to enter the Trust Center.

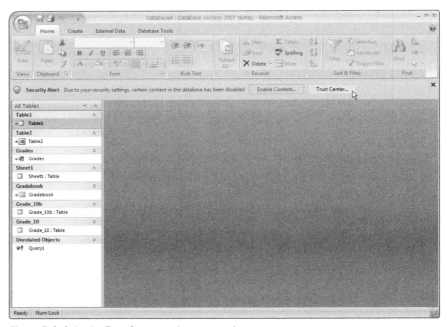

Figure 5-4: Selecting Trust Center on the message bar.

The Trust Center window opens.

2. **Select Trusted Locations (shown in Figure 5-5) and then click Add new location.**

A Browse dialog box opens.

3. **Browse to and select the folder you want to use as a trusted location for your databases.**

My Documents is the default location for databases.

4. **Click OK after you've chosen the location.**

Your Trust Center should now show the new trusted location, as shown in Figure 5-6.

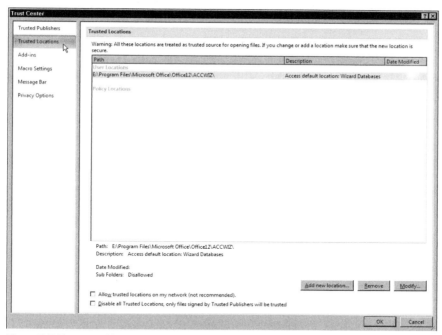

Figure 5-5: You can add a new trusted location in the Trust Center.

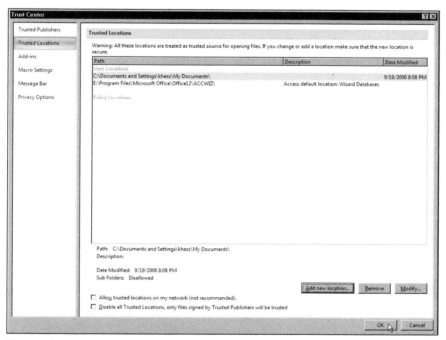

Figure 5-6: The Trust Center lists your trusted locations.

5. Click OK to return to the database window.

The message bar may still be warning you that the content is disabled. Don't worry; the next step takes care of that.

6. Exit the current database and reopen it to refresh the security settings.

You now have a trusted location where all databases are writable and all content is available and executable.

Appending Data

You can append records to a table in a database that's not already open. To do so, you must create a table in another database with matching fields from which to append the data. For instance, if you want to append records from the Grade_10b table into a different table in another database, you must create a table in the other database with fields such as First_Name, Last_Name, Test1, Test2, and Test3. You don't have to use all the fields in the Grade_10b table — only those you need for the new table — and you can add extra fields to the new table, but remember: Only those fields that match existing fields in the Grade_10b table will have data inserted into them.

An example can illustrate this feature. To append records from one database to another, follow these steps:

1. Open the database that has the Grade_10b table in it.

2. From the Create tab, click Query Design.

3. Select Grade_10b, click Add, and then click Close.

4. Select Last_Name, Test2, and Test3 from the table to create the Select query.

5. Click the Append button.

The Append dialog box appears.

6. Select the Another Database radio button, click Browse, and select the database in which you created your new table.

If the Table drop-down list doesn't show the name of your new table, type it into the Table field.

7. Click OK.

8. Click Run to execute the query.

You should receive a message that tells you that you're about to append nine rows.

9. Click Yes.

10. **Open the database where you created the new table.**

You should see the selected records from Table_10b (that is, Last_Name, Test2, and Test3) in your new table.

Updating Data

You can use Update queries to change data in a table, including more than one record at a time. An Update query is similar to the familiar Find and Replace utility in Microsoft Word, WordPad, or Notepad. You can't use an Update query to add new records to a table, but you can use one to add data to records.

Creating an Update Query

The test scores on Test1, Test2, and Test3 need to be curved so that the scores are adjusted upward. You want to change the highest grade on each test to 100 and adjust the others accordingly. Five points will be added to Test1, three points to Test2, and eight points to Test3. To make these grade changes in your database, follow these steps:

1. **Open the database containing the Grade_10 table.**

2. **Create a new query and select the Grade_10 table.**

3. **Close the Show Table window.**

4. **Select Test1, Test2, and Test3 for the** Select **query.**

5. **Click the Update button in the Query Type section of the Query Designer.**

An Update To row appears in the Query Builder window.

6. **Under the Test1 column, on the Update To row, type [Test1] + 5. In the Test2 column, enter** [Test2] + 3**, and in the Test3 column, enter** [Test3] + 8.

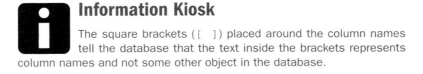

Information Kiosk

The square brackets ([ ]) placed around the column names tell the database that the text inside the brackets represents column names and not some other object in the database.

Your Query Builder window should look like Figure 5-7.

7. **Click Run to execute the query.**

A dialog box appears, stating that you're about to update seven rows of data.

8. Click Yes.

9. Open the Grade_10 table.

All the grades have been adjusted. Compare Table 5-2 (Original Data) to Table 5-3 (Adjusted Data).

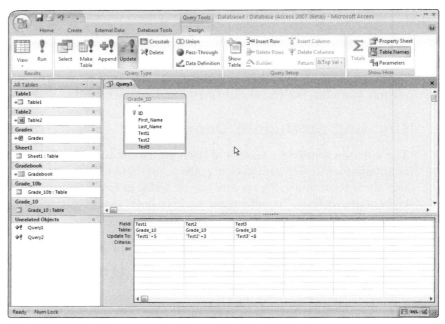

Figure 5-7: This Update query updates the criteria for the table's test scores.

Table 5-2   Original Data

ID	First_Name	Last_Name	Test1	Test2	Test3
1	Ken	Shay	49	67	51
2	Tom	Evans	89	92	85
3	Sue	Cleary	95	97	92
4	Ed	Balster	56	48	51
5	Missy	Trumbull	74	81	83
6	Kevin	Taverner	88	93	90
7	Maria	Rinker	62	77	66

Table 5-3   **Adjusted Data**

ID	First_Name	Last_Name	Test1	Test2	Test3
1	Ken	Shay	54	70	59
2	Tom	Evans	94	95	93
3	Sue	Cleary	100	100	100
4	Ed	Balster	61	51	59
5	Missy	Trumbull	79	84	91
6	Kevin	Taverner	93	96	98
7	Maria	Rinker	67	80	74

The preceding steps give you a very quick and easy way to change data — and making changes in this way is a very common task for database administrators. Data is in a state of constant change: People have children, change addresses, switch phone numbers, and so on. Updating data is a major part of managing a database, and you should factor in the time and ability needed to do it when you're operating a database.

The preceding example is very useful if you need to update all records in a table. To update a single record is a bit more complicated because you need to specify a criterion that isolates the record you want to update.

Changing a Single Record

Say you need to change the grade for Ken Shay's first test from 54 to 56. This is a single-record change. To update a single record, you must use a unique criterion; otherwise you may accidentally update multiple records. Last names often aren't unique; so specify the first name and last name when updating records that are name related. The best way to update such records is to use a truly unique criterion (such as a Social Security Number) because you may very well have two students in a class or school named John Jones or Mary Johnson.

To change a single record, follow these steps:

1. **Create a new query and select the Grade_10 table.**

2. **Select the Test1 column twice from the Grade_10 table.**

You have to select Test1 twice because you have two criteria: `First name` and `Last name`.

3. **Click Update if the Update To row isn't visible.**

4. **In the first Test1 column, enter 56 in the Update To row.**

5. In the Criteria row, enter [First_Name]="Ken".

6. In the Criteria row, under the second Test1 field, enter [Last_Name]="Shay".

7. Execute the query by clicking Run.

You receive a message that you're about to update one row.

8. Click Yes.

9. Open the Grade_10 table.

Ken Shay's Test1 score has been updated from 54 to 56.

Always use as many criteria as are needed to make sure that you update only one record.

Updating Data across Tables

After you curve grades and update Ken Shay's score for Test1, you must update table Grade_10b so that users of that table have the latest information.

To update information from one table to another, follow these steps:

1. Create a new query using the Grade_10 table and the Grade_10b table.

2. Click the `First_Name` field in the Grade_10 table and drag it onto the `First_Name` field of the Grade_10b table.

This action joins the two tables together at the `First_Name` field.

3. Click the `Last_Name` field in the Grade_10 table and drag it onto the `Last_Name` field of the Grade_10b table.

This step creates another join between the tables; this one uses the `Last_Name` field.

Information Kiosk

Joining two tables in this fashion basically sets the fields equal to each other if the two fields contain matching data. This protects the rest of the data in the table from being accidentally updated by stating that you only want data to be updated if `[Grade_10].[Last_Name]` is equal to `[Grade_10b].[Last_Name]`.

4. Double-click the `Test1` field (column) from the Grade_10b table to add it to the Query Builder window.

This is your destination table and the field that you want to update.

5. **If you don't see the Update To row in the Query Builder window, click the Update button.**

6. **In the Update To row, enter** [Grade_10].[Test1]**.**

This location is the source for the data you want to update. This field is for new data in an Update query. In the example in the preceding section, you used 56 as the new data.

Your query should look like Figure 5-8.

7. **Click Run to execute the query.**

A notice appears that tells you you're about to update rows of data.

8. **Click Yes.**

9. **Open the Grade_10b table to see the updated information.**

Now update Test2 and Test3 from the Grade_10 table to the Grade_10b table by following these steps for each remaining test.

To check your work, refer to Figure 5-9 for the correct setup.

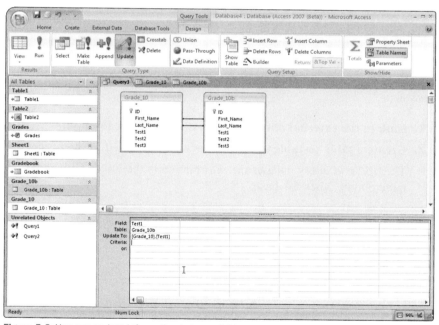

Figure 5-8: You can update information between tables.

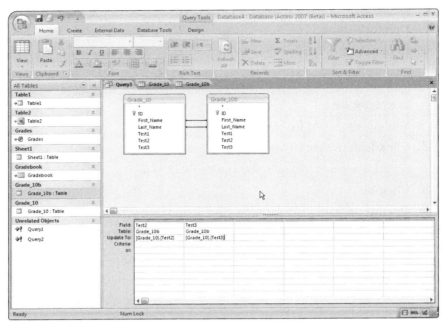

Figure 5-9: Updating Test2 and Test3 from the Grade_10 table.

Although there isn't a direct method to update data from one database to another, you can update data by using links and queries. The method is fairly simple — just follow these steps:

1. Link to the external database table that you want to update.

2. Create a table-to-table Update query, as described in the preceding steps.

The Update query updates the information in the linked table that's also contained in the other database.

Deleting Data

You can delete data from a database with a query. It's a great way to purge unwanted data very quickly. It's also a very efficient way to *lose* a lot of information unintentionally from a database; *be careful* when you use a query to delete information. A Delete query must be criterion-based; the criteria you specify determine which records are purged. Without specifying criteria, you can lose every record in a table.

You have two ways to use a Delete query to delete information:

⊙ Delete all records in a table by choosing the * (All fields) field in the query and the From action in the Delete row of the Query Builder.

⊙ Delete specific records by using criteria with the `Where` action in the Delete row.

Watch Your Step

Deleting data with a `Delete` query can cause a disaster by irreversibly deleting all the data in a table. Always use the `Where` action to specify criteria so you delete only the records that you want to delete.

Normally, you want to purge only a single record from a table, so you should use very specific criteria when purging data. Use a unique identifier, such as a Social Security number, student number, or even the number in the ID field. Because the example tables in this chapter have so few records, you can use `Last_Name` as a criterion for the following example.

Jane Doe has moved away, and you need to remove her record from the Grade_10b table. Follow these steps:

1. Open a new query and select table Grade_10b.

2. Select Last_Name from the list of fields in Grade_10b.

3. Click Delete in the Query Type group.

The Delete row and `Where` action appear in the Query Builder.

4. In the Criteria row, enter [Last_Name]="Doe".

Notification that you're about to delete one row from the specified table appears in a dialog box.

5. Click Yes.

6. Open the Grade_10b table.

The record for Jane Doe has been deleted.

To see just how much damage a mistake can do, create a query to delete all records from table Grade_10b with test scores below 70. Follow these steps:

1. Create a query and select table Grade_10b.

2. Select Test1, Test2, and Test3 from Grade_10b.

3. Click Delete in the Query Type group if you don't see the Delete row in the query.

4. **Enter** [Test1]<70, [Test2]<70, **and** [Test3]<70 **in the Criteria row in the appropriate column for each.**

This query deletes any record that contains a score of less than 70 for all three tests.

5. **Execute the query.**

6. **Open the Grade_10b table to see the results.**

Information Kiosk

Putting more than one criterion in the same row creates an AND query. This type of query requires that all criteria in the row be met in order to carry it out. To make this same query delete records that contain a score of less than 70 for *any* test, you must put the criteria on different rows. Figure 5-10 and Figure 5-11 show AND and OR criteria.

If you run the query in Figure 5-10, one row of data will be deleted; on the other hand, if you run the query in Figure 5-11, four rows of data will be deleted. The number of rows deleted could just as easily be 100 or 400 in a larger table. The bottom line is: Be careful.

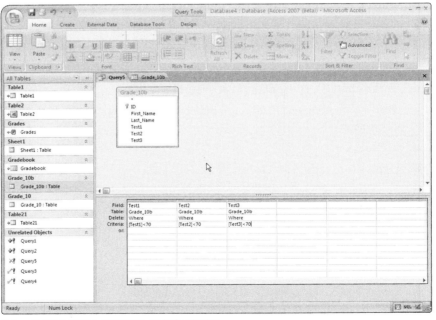

Figure 5-10: A Delete query with an AND criterion.

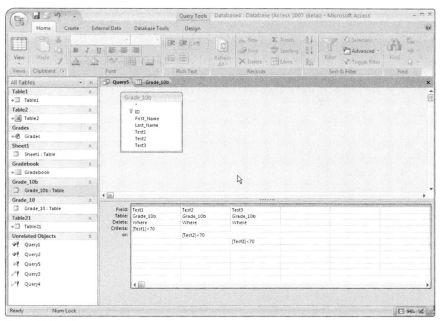

Figure 5-11: A Delete query with an OR criterion.

As you may have guessed by now, you can delete information from another database by using a `Delete` query. You perform a deletion in another database the same way you perform an update (as described earlier in this chapter): Link to the other database and then delete the records in the linked table.

Making New Tables

A `Make Table` query is a special case of the `Select` query. It's a `Select` query that creates a new table from the returned results. The new table can be either an exact copy of the table from which it's derived or a subset of the data from that table. The new table can duplicate the data in the old table or specify only part of that data.

Information Kiosk

A `Make Table` query is an excellent way to back up a set of data.

Copying a Table

For example, create a table named Grade_10_1 that's an exact copy of the Grade_10 table by following these steps:

1. Create a new query and select the Grade_10 table.

2. Select the * field for the query.

3. Click Make Table from the Query Type group.

4. When prompted for a name for the new table, enter Grade_10_1 **and click OK.**

5. Execute the query.

A notification dialog box appears, saying that you're about to paste seven rows of data into a new table.

6. Click Yes.

The table Grade_10_1 is created.

7. Open table Grade_10_1.

It's an exact copy of Grade_10.

Create a Table from a Subset of Data

Sometimes creating a table by using a subset of data from another table is both convenient and necessary. If (for example) you need to create a table of data that contains student names and the results of Test3 for a progress audit by your principal, follow these steps:

1. Create a new query and select Grade_10.

2. Select First_Name, Last_Name, and Test3 for the query.

3. Click Make Table from Query Type group.

4. When prompted for a name, enter Test3 **and click OK.**

5. Execute the query.

A notification dialog box appears, telling you that you're about to paste seven rows of data into a new table.

6. Click Yes.

Table Test3 is created.

7. Open Test3.

Student names and Test3 results from Grade_10 are displayed.

You can also create a table in another database by using this `Make Table` query method. When you're prompted for a name for your new table, the dialog box also has a drop-down list box. This list box displays a list of the available databases on your system.

Give it a try. Create a new table in another database by either selecting all or some of the data from a table in the current database.

Append query: Used for the insertion of new data into a current database.

Delete query: Used for the removal of entire records from a database.

Make Table query: A query that creates a new table from an existing table.

purge: Delete unwanted records from a database.

Update query: Used for the replacement of data in a database.

Last Stop

Practice Exam

1. **What's the basic query that only reads data?**

A) Select

B) Append

C) Update

D) Delete

2. **If you want to change data in a table, which type of query would you use?**

A) Select

B) Append

C) Update

D) Delete

3. **If you want to add data to a table, which type of query would you use?**

A) Select

B) Append

C) Update

D) Delete

4. **If you want to remove entire records from a table, which type of query would you use?**

A) Select

B) Append

C) Update

D) Delete

5. If you want to make a backup of a table, which type of query would you use?

A) Make Update

B) Make Table

C) Make Select

D) Make Append

6. To update or delete data in a table in another database, which type of query would you use?

A) Select

B) Append

C) Update

D) Delete

7. List the steps to update information in another database.

_____

_____

_____

8. Which type of query can be performed without enabling content or creating a trusted location?

A) Select

B) Append

C) Update

D) Delete

9. What would be the purpose of using a query to make an exact duplicate of a table?

A) It's good practice for querying a database.

B) It's a great way to update information.

C) It helps maintain the database.

D) It's a simple way to make a backup of a table.

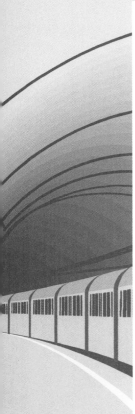

10. **By creating a trusted location, you perform this task:**

A) Trust all databases in that location.

B) Prevent editing of your databases.

C) Delete all databases in that location.

D) Limit yourself to using databases only in that location.

Using Forms to Enter Data

STATIONS ALONG THE WAY

- O Creating forms by using wizards
- O Customizing your data-entry forms
- O Using built-in navigation and search utilities
- O Navigating through records
- O Building your own navigation tools

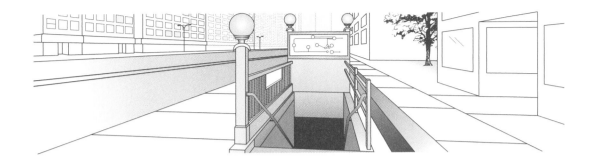

Enter the Station

Questions

1. How do you create a form?

2. Why does the form show data when created?

3. How can you change the color of a form?

4. Can you add navigational elements to a form?

5. Can you customize forms?

6. Is there a form editor that allows complete design control?

7. How does the built-in search utility work?

Express Line

If you know how to create and use Forms, then skip ahead to Chapter 7.

This chapter introduces you to forms that you can use to enter data into your databases. Forms are convenient and enjoyable to work with. You can use them to create an interface between users and the database that requires no database knowledge on the part of the user. You can use forms with tables and queries, and to update, edit, and delete data.

Creating Your First Form

Creating a simple form is as easy as clicking a button. In Microsoft Access, the process is automated to the point that you don't even step through a wizard. After you create a table, you can immediately create a data-entry form for others to use.

You can customize forms with labels, logos, buttons, and other tools. You can also limit what's shown in a form. You don't need to (and you probably shouldn't) show every column of data in a form to other users.

The examples in this chapter use the database I explain how to create in Chapter 5. If you didn't create this example, you can download it from this book's Web site.

To create a simple form, follow these steps:

1. **Open the database.**

   For this example, open the Chapter5 database.

2. **Select the table you want to work with (for example, Grade_10) by clicking it.**

   You don't have to open the table.

3. **Click the Create tab, then click Form.**

   Figure 6-1 shows the first step in creating a new Form.

A form named `Grade_10` is created and automatically populated with data from the Grade_10 table. Congratulations — you've just created a data-entry form that can be used to enter, edit, update, or delete data! This form allows a user to work with data in the Grade_10 table; however, you may want to customize this form to make it more elegant and professional-looking, as well as easier to use.

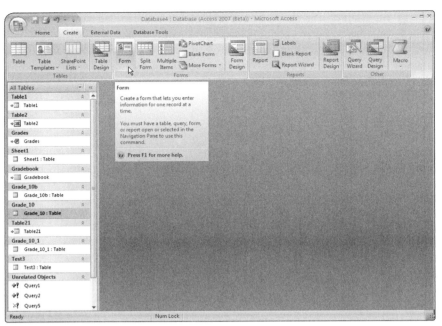

Figure 6-1: Preparing to create a form from the Grade_10 table.

Get started by getting rid of the ID field and shrinking the data-entry fields so they're sized to the type of data that you plan to put in them. You don't need the ID field because the database automatically generates it, and a user doesn't need to view, enter, or edit it. To customize the form, follow these steps:

1. **Click the ID box, then press the Delete key on your keyboard.**

This step removes the ID label and field from the form.

2. **Begin shrinking the data fields by clicking a field (for example,** First_Name**) to select it.**

3. **Move the slider at the bottom of the window all the way to the right if you can't see the right edge of the field, and place your mouse cursor over the bottom-right corner of the field until you see a two-headed arrow (as shown in Figure 6-2).**

4. **Click and drag the bottom-right corner to the left until the field is the size you want (about one-fourth its original size for this chapter's example), as shown in Figure 6-3.**

All the other fields shrink simultaneously.

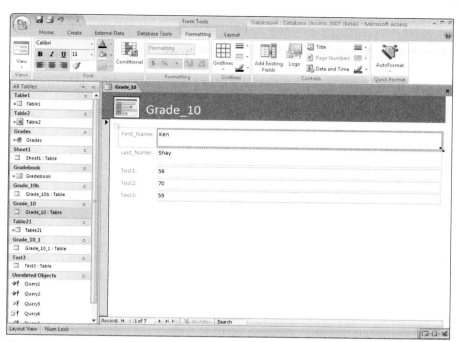

Figure 6-2: You can shrink the First_Name field to fit your data.

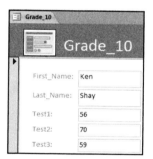

Figure 6-3: The final size of the data-entry fields.

Creating Professional-Looking Forms

The form now has a good clean look, and users can work with the underlying table data. Your company may have its own color scheme or in-house style that you want to comply with to make your application consistent with others. You may just have a flair for something more dramatic than plain vanilla. In either case, you can quickly customize your forms to give them that extra touch that looks like they were created by a professional designer.

Access gives you the Form Layout Tools tab to use for customizing your forms. When working with forms in Layout View, you see two tabs under Form Layout Tools: Format and Arrange.

Selecting a theme

To select a theme for your form, follow these steps:

1. **Select the Format tab.**

Figure 6-4 shows the Form Layout Tools tabs on the Ribbon.

2. **Click the AutoFormat button.**

A multiple-selection window opens, showing many different themes (color schemes) you can pick. I selected Trek from the list. Figure 6-5 shows how to select a new Theme.

Figure 6-4: The Form Layout Tools tabs give you access to Format and Arrange tools.

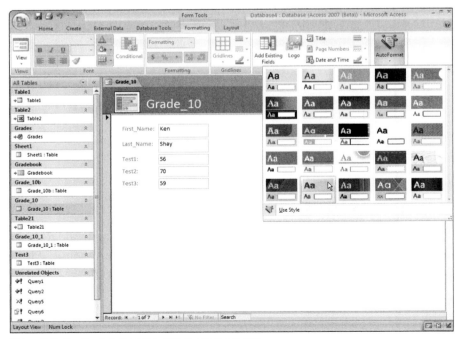

Figure 6-5: Use the AutoFormat button to select a theme.

Not only do the colors change, but you may notice that the fonts, fields, and number justification (alignment) have also changed.

 Transfer

You don't have to use a pre-built theme. You can alter individual form attributes yourself. Chapter 10 shows you how.

Customizing forms with controls

The Controls group in the Format tab gives you several options for customizing your forms. They are Add Existing Fields, Logo, Title, Page Numbers, and Date and Time.

Add Existing Fields lets you add fields to your form from the underlying table (Grade_10, in this chapter's example). If you want to add new fields to your table after the form is built — or reintroduce fields that you previously removed — then you can use Add Existing Fields to insert those fields into your form at any time. Just follow these steps:

1. **Click Add Existing Fields.**

A Field List window appears on the right side of the screen. All fields from the current table (in this example, the Grade_10 table) are shown.

2. **Double-click the ID field, and it's added to the form.**

The ID field is added to the bottom of the existing fields.

3. **To move the ID (or any) field, place your mouse cursor over the field until it becomes a four-headed arrow, as shown in Figure 6-6.**

4. **Click and drag the field to where you want it in the list, and then release.**

You can arrange the fields in any order you want. As discussed in Chapter 2, the order of columns in a table is irrelevant, so you may want to rearrange them into a more logical sequence, making data entry quick and efficient for the user. Having columns in a logical order also creates a more efficient (even enjoyable) data-entry experience for your users.

Adding a logo to your forms can help create a sense of cohesion between your applications and other corporate documents.

To add a logo to this form, follow these steps:

1. **Click Logo in the Controls group.**

2. **Browse to and select your logo, then click OK.**

The logo now appears on your page.

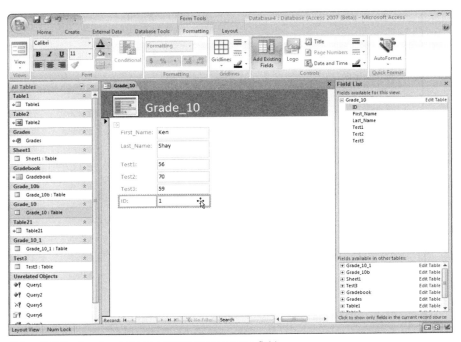

Figure 6-6: The four-headed arrow allows you to move a field.

Watch Your Step

There's no real limit to the size or type of graphic that you can use for a logo, but you should generally use a graphic that's no larger than 200 × 100 pixels. Larger graphics require scrolling, which isn't efficient during data entry.

You can also professionalize the look and feel of your application by titling your forms. A title can also help users prevent mistakes when they're entering data, assuring them that they're using the correct form.

Your form already has a title: Grade_10. The default title for any form is the name of the underlying table or query from which it was created.

To edit the title of your form, follow these steps:

1. Click Title.

For this example, the current title (Grade_10) is in edit mode.

2. Enter a Title (for example, 10th Grade Test Scores**) into the Title area and press Enter.**

This title provides you and your users an unmistakable identification for this form and the data for which it's used.

The final bit of customizing you can do on this form is a Date and Time entry. If your form has multiple pages, you can use the Page Numbers tool. The addition of a Date and Time entry helps users track their data-entry time (or just get an occasional reality check).

To add a Date and Time feature to your form, follow these steps:

1. **Click the Date and Time button in the Controls group.**

The Date and Time dialog box appears.

2. **Select Include Date and Include Time.**

3. **Select the Date and Time formats that you prefer and click OK.**

The Date and Time features that you select are placed in the form header.

4. **Save the form by right-clicking the tab above the logo and clicking Save from the menu that appears.**

5. **Name the form (for example,** Tenth Grade Test Scores**) and click OK.**

Figure 6-7 shows you the final version of my form from these exercises.

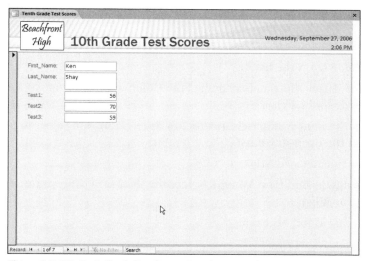

Figure 6-7: This Tenth Grade Test Scores form has some features added.

Creating a custom form

Now that you have some experience creating a form from the available themes and controls, it's time to create a fully customized form. You can still use any of the controls or themes to get started, but this section shows you how to make them truly your own.

To create a custom form, follow these steps:

1. **Click the table to select it.**

   This chapter's example uses the Grade_10 table.

2. **Click the Create tab, and then click Form.**

   A new form based on the table (the Grade_10 table, for example) is created with generic attributes (such as fonts and colors).

3. **Delete the ID field.**

4. **Change the fields to an appropriate size.**

   In the Grade_10 example, make the fields about one-fourth their original size.

5. **Click a column's label to select it.**

   For example, you can click the First_Name label.

6. **Right-click to bring up the menu, click Layout, and then Select Entire Column.**

7. **Right-click the highlighted column and then click Properties.**

   The Property Sheet appears on the right side of your screen. Take a look at all the properties you can customize for your forms.

8. **About halfway down the list, find Fore Color; click in that field, and then click the ellipsis (. . .) button.**

   A color palette appears.

9. **Select a color from the list.**

   If you select Black, the numbers in the Fore Color column change to #000000 (the hex code for black).

10. **Click into the Font Name field just below Fore Color and select the font you want from the drop-down list.**

    In this example, choose Arial.

11. **Two lines down, find Font Weight. Select the Weight setting you want from the drop-down list.**

    I went with Bold for this example.

You may have noticed that your changes take effect immediately upon selecting a property.

The labels that are taken from the table column names aren't particularly descriptive for a data-entry form. They're also a bit strange to look at — with underscores and no spaces to use for visual cues. To make your column labels more user-friendly, follow these steps:

1. **Click the field (for example, First_Name).**

The Property Sheet should now hold the properties for the selected field, such as First_Name, only.

2. **Click into the Caption field on the Property Sheet and replace any underscores with spaces or add spaces where they're needed.**

In the example, do the same for Last_Name.

3. **Repeat these steps for any remaining field names (for example, Test1, Test2, and Test3).**

You can, of course, use any descriptive text you want for the labels, but you should try to come up with something that needs no explanation for your users.

Some users think that the data fields' flat appearance means you can't select the fields for editing. To some, this look gives the form the feel of a report rather than a form. To change the appearance, follow these steps:

1. **Select the data field next to a column label (for example, First Name), right-click, select Layout, then Select Entire Column.**

2. **In the Property Sheet, a few spaces above Fore Color, select Special Effect and choose Sunken from the drop-down list.**

3. **Click anywhere on the body of the form to deselect the data column.**

You can see the change you made to the data fields.

Now, the data fields look more like the form elements on a Web page in which you enter data when filling out a form.

Color attributes on a form can be visually significant for your users. Choose colors for your forms that are easy on the eyes because some users must look at them for extended periods of time. If you need to use a corporate color scheme, limit those colors to the header and the logo areas of the form. The form body should be white, light gray, or some other light color that contrasts greatly with the field's background color and the data font. Avoid using too many colors on a form; it gives the form an unprofessional look.

To change form colors, follow these steps:

1. **Click the body of the form.**

The Property Sheet should change to Detail. If you don't see the Property Sheet, right-click the body of the form and then click Properties.

2. **Click Back Color and select a color.**

If you select Light Gray 2, for example, the Back Color field changes to #D8D8D8.

3. Click the form header.

The Property Sheet should change to `FormHeader`.

4. Click Back Color and select a contrasting color from the color palette.

For example, select Dark Blue 5.

5. Select the table's title (in this chapter's example, Grade_10) by clicking on it.

The Property Sheet should change to `Auto_Title0`.

6. Choose a color (for example, Dark Blue 5) to make the Back Color match the header Back Color.

This very attractive, easy-to-read form is suitable for public consumption. You can still make some improvements that will give the form an extra professional touch. You can add a logo, which the preceding section explains. Or you can adjust the look of the test scores so that they're *right-justified* (aligned with the right margin). It's a good idea to right-justify numbers so they're easier to read.

To right-justify numbers, follow these steps:

1. Click the data field (for example, Test1) to select it.

The Property Sheet should change to your selected data field (in this example, Test1).

2. Click the Text Align field (which you find about two-thirds of the way down the Property Sheet) and change it to Right.

For grades (which can range from 0 to 100), justification isn't absolutely necessary, but it's a good idea to right-justify numeric fields.

In the final example in this section, you add a Date and Time feature to the form. You then change some of the properties of that feature. To make these changes, follow these steps:

1. Insert a Date and Time feature into your form.

2. Select the Date field on the form.

3. If the Property Sheet is still visible, move it to the left side of the form.

If the Property Sheet isn't visible, right-click the Date and Time feature, and then click Properties.

4. Find the Fore Color property and change the color to white or some other color that contrasts with the background color.

5. Select the Time field and change its color.

6. Change the title, add a logo, and save the form.

My final version of this form is shown in Figure 6-8.

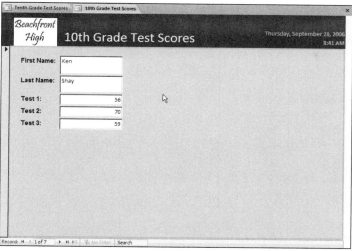

Figure 6-8: A gussied-up version of the 10th Grade Test Scores form.

Navigating the Form

Form navigation is probably the least intuitive of all form actions. For some reason, programmers haven't put making an intuitive navigation control particularly high on their to-do list of improvements. In the following sections, I show you how to navigate your own forms and how to add navigational elements that take the guesswork out of navigation for your form users. You also get an introduction to viewing the form in its production state (Form View), in layout design format (Layout View), and in raw design format (Design View). I also cover the built-in search control.

Record navigation

Simple record navigation has been added to Access itself, but this navigation is a bit difficult to find and use because the controls are so small. The built-in record-navigation utilities are at the bottom-left of your form and titled `Record:`. The form from the example in this chapter (10th Grade Test Scores) shows record 1 of 7. Figure 6-9 shows your choices for navigating records.

Figure 6-8 shows all the controls for navigating form records, including the New (blank) record control. Creating your own controls for your forms can make navigation easier — and make new records easier to create — for your users. You can find out how to create your own form controls in the "Design View" section, later in this chapter.

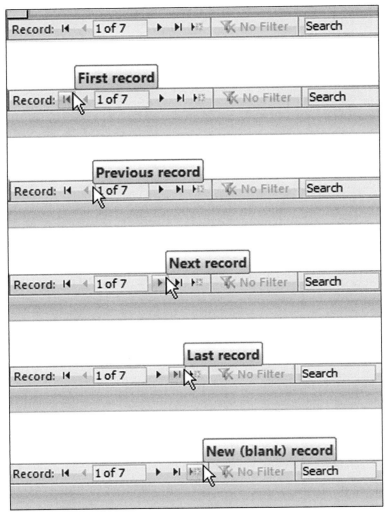

Figure 6-9: You can use built-in record navigation in Access.

The one control that's suspiciously missing from the built-in list of controls is one that would delete records. If you want to allow your users to delete a record, you can create a control for that purpose when you create the other controls for your forms.

Tab order

You probably don't give much thought to *tab order* — the order in which you fill out fields when you enter data into a form — unless you're designing your own forms. For the forms you create in this chapter, the tab order is First Name, Last Name, Test 1, Test 2, and Test 3. That's because the tab order of the fields in a newly created form is, by default, the same order in which you place those fields on the form as you create it. If you insert new fields or rearrange the fields, then you must check the tab order to make sure that it's still intuitive for your users.

Watch Your Step

When creating forms, take care to establish a field order and tab order that are intuitive and also correspond to the data source. If (for example) the data source is a paper form that lists Last Name, First Name, Address, and so on, then your form should conform to the same field order. This consistency makes the form quicker and easier for users to fill out. It can also prevent transposition errors that take time to clean up later.

Tab order is determined by a property named Tab Index. The index number begins at 0 for the first field, the next field has a Tab Index value of 1, and so on. You can alter the tab order by changing the Tab Index number.

To look at tab order and the Tab Index property, open one of your forms in Layout View and follow these steps:

1. **Right-click the body of the form, then click Layout View.**

2. **Click the data field (for example, First Name) to select it.**

3. **Right-click the data field, and then click Properties.**

   The Property Sheet opens. If you need to view more of your form, move the Property Sheet to the right side of the form so you can see your fields.

4. **Click the Other tab on the Property Sheet.**

   The tab controls are about two-thirds of the way down the list. You see Auto Tab, Tab Stop, and Tab Index.

5. **Click a field (for example, Test 2).**

   The Tab Index for Test 2 is 3.

6. **Change the Tab Index to a number after the Tab Index of the control you want to tab from.**

   If you change the Test 2 Tab Index to 4, the Tab Index for Test 3 is automatically changed to 3.

7. **To see the effect of changing the Tab Index, right-click the body of the form and click Form View.**

8. **Press the Tab key on your keyboard.**

   The cursor appears in the first data field (the First Name field, in this chapter's example) with the name highlighted.

9. **Continue to press the Tab key and watch carefully as the cursor moves from field to field.**

In this example, the cursor moves from First Name to Last Name to Test 1 to Test 3 and finally to Test 2.

10. **Change the Tab Index of the field selected in Step 5 back to its original number.**

You would change Test 2 back to the Tab Index of 3. The Tab Index for Test 3 will automatically change from 3 to 4.

Auto Tab (Yes/No) is the property that automatically sends the cursor to the next field after the field has reached its preformatted mask limit. This advanced feature of Access isn't covered in this book. Tab Stop (Yes/No) determines whether or not the field is included in the tab order. The default is Yes because normally you want to include all fields in the tab order of the form.

Record search

Access includes a record-search utility for form data. The utility is at the bottom of the form near the record-navigation utilities. Figure 6-10 shows the Search field.

Figure 6-10: You can use this built-in form-search utility to make a quick search.

This search utility is a quick search and isn't based on anything database related. It's more of a *heuristic* search (in which you enter your search criteria and get an approximate match based on a minimal amount of information).

To illustrate the built-in record-search utility, search for the student records for Maria Rinker in the example 10th Grade Test Scores table. Just follow these steps:

1. **Open any of your forms.**

2. **Click into the Search field.**

3. **Type the letter m in the search field.**

The record for Tom Evans appears, and the m is highlighted to show your search match. But this isn't the match you want — you're searching for Maria Rinker's record.

4. **Add an a into the search form after the m.**

The record for Maria Rinker now appears.

5. **Clear the search field by backspacing over the ma.**

Now search for the records for Tom Evans by following these steps:

1. **Type the letter** e **into the search field.**

The record for Ken Shay appears.

2. **Add a** v **into the search field.**

You now have the record for Tom Evans.

Access searches all fields for the search criteria when you use this built-in search utility. In actual practice, this process is slow and frustrating. In Chapter 13, I share another method of searching through database records. And in the section "Custom navigation controls," later in this chapter, you can build your own search utility for your forms.

Form View

You'll switch between views of your forms while you're in the design stages of building, rearranging, and adding to your forms. Form View is the view you use when you want to see the production look and feel of your forms, the actual view that your users see when they use your forms.

Always look at your forms in Form View and test all of the functionality you've built into them. Testing and tweaking the form for public use almost assures that your users will be happy with the new form.

In Form View, you can't change any design elements of the form. You can use the form only as if you're the end user.

Layout View

You've been spending most of your time in this chapter in Layout View. This view lets you make property changes — and most design changes — in a WYSIWYG (What You See Is What You Get) environment. Layout View is nice when you need to create a form quickly or just get an idea of what you want the form to look like. It provides some flexibility for design.

Watch Your Step

But Layout View has many limitations. You experience one of them when resizing the fields in the section "Creating Your First Form," earlier in this chapter. All fields are resized together — which isn't desirable if you want to use field size to limit data input (for instance, using a very small field for the test score and a much larger one for last name). Sometimes, when fields are too large, it confuses the person entering data (*Yikes. Does the field need more data? Is the data I'm entering incorrect?*). Make the field fit the amount of data you want entered into it.

Design View

Design View is the view in which you can make any and all kinds of changes to the form. Design View gives you the most creative freedom in designing a form. In this view, you can also alter the tab order very efficiently and ungroup the fields so that you can edit them individually.

At first, you may be intimidated by the Design View's stark appearance, but in time, you'll spend all of your design time in this view.

The following examples show how to alter the tab order and how to ungroup form fields so you can edit them individually.

To alter the Tab Order property, follow these steps:

1. **Open a form and select Design View from the right-click menu.**

2. **Right-click the background, then select Tab Order from the menu that appears.**

The Tab Order screen displays instructions for altering the tab order of fields, as shown in Figure 6-11.

3. **Click the gray rectangle to the left of the field name to select it, then drag it to the desired position in the tab order.**

4. **Click OK to accept your choice.**

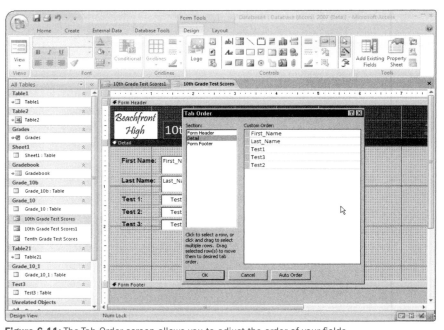

Figure 6-11: The Tab Order screen allows you to adjust the order of your fields.

If you get confused or need to start over, click Auto Order to return the tab order to the default.

You can alter tab order in this way more intuitively than by changing the Tab Index number because the numbers don't correspond directly with the field number. Many people prefer to use the Tab Order screen to view and change tab order.

To ungroup the field list on a form, follow these steps:

1. Click and drag a box around all the fields to select them all.

All the fields are highlighted.

2. Right-click the fields, select Layout, then click Remove.

The field highlighting changes.

3. Shrink the individual field, as shown in Figure 6-12.

If you're using the sample database, you can select the data field for Test1, shrink the field (as shown in Figure 6-11), and then Shrink Test2 and Test3 to match Test1.

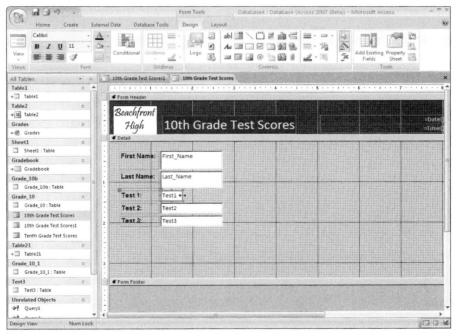

Figure 6-12: Shrinking an individual field.

4. Save the Form by right-clicking the Title tab and selecting Save in the menu that appears.

5. Right-click the Title tab again and select Form View from the menu.

Custom navigation controls

The really fun part of designing your own forms is the excitement of putting controls on the form to automate, enhance, and further professionalize them. As with all design elements, the fewer the better. You don't want your forms to be without any special design elements (such as buttons, logos, and special fonts), but you also don't want them to look like they were designed by someone with no clue about design. Keep your designs simple, clean, and utilitarian.

Custom navigation controls are a great way to add useful elements to your forms. They should also be a standard part of all forms. Be consistent in the placement, size, and structure of your elements from form to form; all the forms should give the impression that they're part of the same application.

To add navigation features to your form, follow these steps:

1. **Open a form in Design View.**

2. **Click the Design Tab under Form Tools.**

3. **Locate the Button control in the Controls grouping, as shown in Figure 6-13, and click it.**

4. **Move your mouse cursor onto the form.**

Your cursor changes into a button with a plus sign (+) near it. This cursor is telling you that you've selected the Button control. The plus sign shows you where you'll start your button drawing.

5. **Click to begin drawing the button, drag the mouse cursor diagonally down and to the right to create a small rectangle, and then release the mouse button.**

The Command Button Wizard starts as soon as you release the mouse button. This wizard steps you through creating your new Button control. Record Navigation is the first category shown in the wizard.

6. **Under Actions in the Record Navigation category, select Go To First Record and click Next.**

This screen lets you select a picture for your button. The default picture (Go To First) has been selected for you.

7. **Select a picture (or accept the default selection) and click Next.**

You're prompted for a name for your control. (I'd suggest something simple, such as Next.)

8. **Type the name for the button into the Name field, then click Finish.**

9. **Repeat Steps 3 through 8 to create any remaining buttons (for example, Go To Last Record, Go To Next Record, and Go To Previous Record).**

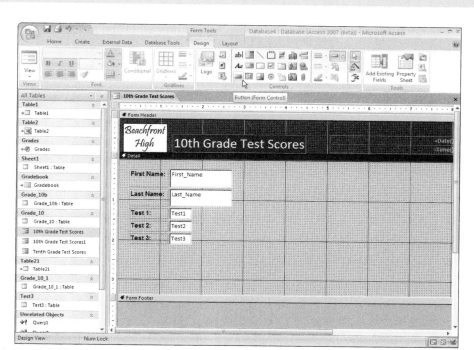

Figure 6-13: Use the Button control to add a button.

10. **Create a new button.**

The Command Button Wizard opens.

11. **Select Categories→Record Operations→Actions→Add New Record.**

12. **Click Next twice and name the button (for example,** New**).**

13. **Click Finish.**

14. **Create one last button that can delete a record.**

15. **Save your form and then view it in Form View.**

I've arranged my buttons so that users can easily navigate from record to record and create a new record. Deleting a record takes a bit of effort (to prevent accidental deletion) because of its placement. You can arrange your buttons in any way that makes you feel comfortable; I find these placements are suitable for most users. My final form is shown in Figure 6-14.

To add a more useful and complete search utility to your forms, follow these steps:

1. **Open your form in Design View.**

2. **Click Design under Form Design Tools.**

3. **Click the Button control to start the Command Button Wizard.**

4. Select Categories → Record Navigation and then Actions → Find Record (if these aren't already selected).

5. Click Next.

6. Change the selection from Picture to Text and enter Search into the Text field.

7. Click Next.

8. Name the command Search and click Finish.

9. Save the Form and switch to Form View.

10. Click the Search button.

The Find and Replace utility opens.

11. Enter a name (for example, Tom) into the Find What field and click Find Next.

For this example, the record with Tom Evans's data is displayed.

Using this utility, you can also find text or numbers that have been entered by mistake and correct them with the Replace utility. This is a much better search tool than the built-in tool because it lets you search in different directions, search whole words, and also lets you find and replace words or numbers.

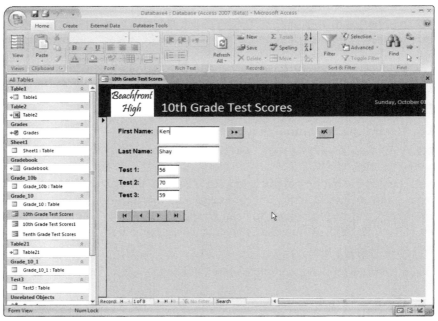

Figure 6-14: The final form.

button: A form control that automates or performs some operation. A New Record button is an example of a button that allows the user to create a new database record.

element (as in design element): Any part of a design, such as a button, field, color, or title.

form: A collection of elements that you use as a data-entry interface to a database.

navigation: The paging of records, either one by one or many at a time, performed with the assistance of record controls.

property: An attribute or quality of a field, label, or control. Size is a font property.

theme: A selection of colors, fonts, labels, and other design elements that you put together to give your database and its forms one consistent look.

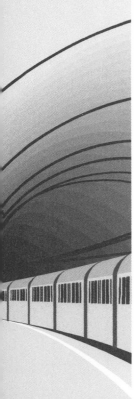

Last Stop

Practice Exam

1. **Why is it important to customize your forms with colors, fonts, and navigational elements?**

A) It's not important.

B) It gives the form a more professional look and feel.

C) You have to customize forms to use them.

D) Forms can't be customized.

2. **What's the purpose of tab order?**

A) Tab order assists the user when entering data.

B) It generates additional data.

C) It prevents spelling errors during data entry.

D) It's useful only for entering data into numeric fields.

3. **What's the default tab order?**

A) Text fields first, then numeric fields.

B) The order in which the fields were created.

C) There is no default — you must set tab order explicitly.

D) Numeric fields first, then text fields.

4. **Which of the following is a good design scheme for a form?**

A) A lot of colors and fonts, and large data-entry fields.

B) One color, very large fonts, and correctly sized data-entry fields.

C) A few colors, normal fonts, and correctly sized data-entry fields.

D) A few colors, normal fonts, and no data-entry fields.

5. **Why do you need to resize data-entry fields?**

A) You don't; they automatically resize themselves.

B) So that data entry is less confusing for users.

C) You only need to resize text fields; numeric fields are sized properly automatically.

D) To keep the default tab order.

6. **To create a Button control, you must be in:**

A) Form View

B) Layout View

C) Design View

D) Table View

7. **To fully test your forms before allowing users to use them, you must be in:**

A) Form View

B) Layout View

C) Design View

D) Table View

8. **What lets you change attributes of fonts, fields, and background colors for a form?**

A) Record Search

B) Form View

C) New Record

D) Property Sheet

9. **Which attribute lets users make sure they're using the correct form for data entry?**

A) The color

B) The title

C) The field

D) The tab order

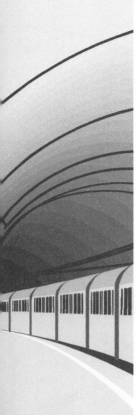

10. **Which two items are sometimes added to give a form a more professional look and feel?**

A) A Date and Time feature and a logo.

B) A bright yellow background and a white title.

C) A wide variety of fonts and a very large logo.

D) A generic title and very small fonts.

Presenting Data with Reports

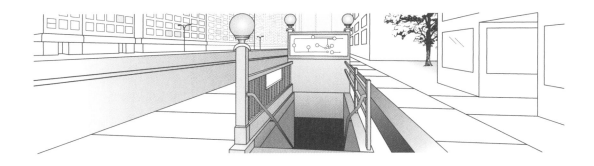

 # Enter the Station

Questions

1. How do you create a basic report?

2. How do you create a report based on two or more tables?

3. Can you add summary data to a report?

4. Can you add fields that aren't in a table to a report?

5. How do you summarize column data?

6. How do you summarize data in rows?

Express Line

If you already understand how to create and use reports, then skip ahead to Chapter 8.

This chapter focuses on the creation and customization of reports. Here's where you can figure out how to create a quick, basic report based on a single table or query. Examples illustrate customizing and designing reports. You're also given an overview of the impact of summary data and summary functions. The chapter concludes with how to add new expression-based fields to a report.

Creating Your First Report

A report is an organized, *read-only* view of data; usually it's for the presentation of database data to people who don't use the database. Reports don't involve data entry or changing data; they're only for generating a snapshot of data that already exists in the database. They're generally built to look at trends, totals, or other summary data. Reports are often printed for presentation in meetings, or saved and e-mailed to a group of interested parties. Some database administrators allow *report-only* access to their data, which means users can generate reports — through wizards or the use of *canned* (pre-built) reports — without having to know anything about databases, the structure of the database, or even data entry. Reports are a great way to allow users who aren't familiar with the database to view its data in a non-intrusive way.

You can build a report from tables or queries. The queries or tables from which you build a report are the *record source*. A report must have a record source from which to pull its data.

The examples in this chapter use the Chapter 6 database. If you didn't completely update that database in Chapter 6, you can download the database from this book's Web site.

Selecting a record source and creating a report

Creating a report is much like creating a new form; you choose your source, and then create the report from it. Access builds a report that's generated directly from your data. You can edit the report after you create it in much the same way you edit a form.

To create a report based on a table, follow these steps:

1. Click the table (for example, Grade_10 Table) to select it.

2. Click the Create tab.

3. Click Report.

The report is presented to you in Layout View, and you can edit it if you want.

4. Delete the ID field from the report.

5. Change the column headings to make them more easily read by users.

Change First_Name to **First Name** and Test1 to **Test 1**, for example.

6. **Change the Title (for example, to** 10th Grade Test Scores**).**

7. **Shrink the fields so they're more fitting for the data in them.**

   You can shrink or expand individual report fields as needed.

8. **Insert a Logo into the report, if you want.**

9. **Choose a color scheme from the AutoFormat drop-down list.**

   In this example, I chose the theme named Aspect. My final report is shown in Figure 7-1.

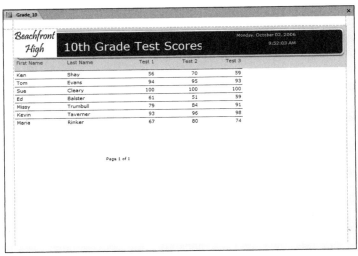

Figure 7-1: My 10th Grade Test Scores report.

10. **Name the report (for example,** 10th Grade Test Scores**) and save it.**

Watch Your Step

Naming an object is different from titling it. The *title* exists only on that form or report; it's simply a label. *Naming* a form, report, or other database object (on the other hand) gives it a unique name *in the database*. Access gives any new object a generic name, but you should always rename objects so they're individualized and specific to their intended purpose.

Step into the Real World

You create the report by using names and grades in this example, but in actual practice, you should keep the ID field (or other unique identification code) confidential, and not use names if other personnel will see the report.

As you can see, the process of creating and editing a report is like creating and editing a form. Reports have Report View (the equivalent of a form's Form View), Layout View, and Design View, but reports also have a Print Preview because many reports are printed and distributed. Access's Print Preview is like the Print Preview in Microsoft Word or other programs that you may have used. It shows you exactly how the report will look when printed. You can access these different views from the right-click menu.

Design basics for reports

I don't cover cosmetic design explicitly in this chapter because a large portion of Chapter 6 is dedicated to that topic. The same rules apply for reports as for forms:

- Keep the design simple and clean.
- Maintain a low-key background to prevent eye strain.
- Make the text and background colors in high contrast with one another.
- Restrict font choices to ones that are easy to read.
- Restrict the number of different fonts to one or two per report.
- Use normal sizes for fonts — use large or bold only for special emphasis.
- Restrict the number of colors to a tasteful few.
- Use Print Preview and print a sample report. What looks good on-screen may not have the same impact in print.

Reports, unlike forms, can have multiple pages. Don't over-restrict yourself and clutter a report to keep it to one page. Multi-page reports are normal.

Creating a Report by Using the Report Wizard

Using the Report Wizard is less restrictive than using the automatic report generator that's simply based on an underlying table or query, as demonstrated in the section "Selecting a record source and creating a report," earlier in this chapter. The wizard steps you through the creation of a report and lets you customize features along the way.

When using the Report Wizard, you select your record source(s) within the wizard. When the wizard is finished, your report is presented in Print Preview.

To create a report with the Report Wizard, follow these steps:

1. **Click the Create tab and, under the Reports grouping, click Report Wizard.**

The Report Wizard launches, prompting you to choose your record source(s) from its drop-down list.

2. **Select the table (for example, Table: Grade_10) from the list.**

3. **Send the fields (for example, First_Name, Last_Name, Test1, Test2, and Test3) to the Selected Fields column and click Next.**

   This screen asks for any grouping levels. (In this example database, Grade_10 data isn't formatted for any groupings.)

4. **Click Next.**

5. **Sort fields and choose either ascending or descending sort order.**

   For this example, select Last_Name from the drop-down list. Ascending is the default selection for sort order.

6. **Click Next.**

7. **Select the report format that you want.**

   For this example, Select Tabular under Layout and Portrait under Orientation. Also check the box that reads: Adjust the field width so all fields fit on a page.

   You can present the data in the Grade_10 table example in a tabular format because that's historically how a grade book is arranged. But you could also choose Portrait orientation for printing because you have only five columns of data to present. You can also adjust the field width so that all fields fit on a page because you have only five fields. You must experiment with your reports to find out when to use Landscape orientation and when not to adjust the field size. Some of these decisions are personal preference and some are just good design.

8. **Click Next.**

   You're now prompted for a style (theme) for your report.

9. **Select a style and click Next.**

   I chose Aspect for my report. You're shown a preview of the style when you select it from the list.

   The final screen asks for a name for the report and whether you want to preview the report or modify it.

10. **Name the report (for example, 10th Grade Custom Report), select Preview the report, and click Finish.**

The report is complete, and it's presented to you in Print Preview mode. Examine the report carefully — top to bottom — to see whether it meets your expectations. If you like the report, print or close it. If you need to edit a feature, use the right-click menu to select Layout View or Design View and make your changes. Always use Print Preview to see how your changes affect the look of the report.

Creating a report from multiple record sources

You can create a report from multiple record sources. When choosing multiple record sources, you usually choose tables. Typically, you create a query-based report from a single query because queries can be based on multiple tables.

For the examples in this section, you need a new database and two new tables. You can either download the database from the book's Web site or follow these steps to create the database:

1. Create a new database.

2. Create a new table and enter the data shown in Table 7-1.

Table 7-1   Literature Test Data

First_Name	Last_Name	Test1	Test2	Test3
Linda	Jones	90	94	91
Bob	Smith	80	88	79
Roberta	Martinez	89	92	95
Gilbert	Nash	77	79	68
Lee	Davis	82	77	71

3. Save this table and name it Literature.

4. Create a second new table and enter the data shown in Table 7-2.

Table 7-2   Algebra Test Data

First_Name	Last_Name	Test1	Test2	Test3
Linda	Jones	88	79	82
Bob	Smith	77	74	80
Roberta	Martinez	69	85	87
Gilbert	Nash	90	88	91
Lee	Davis	64	70	59

5. Save this table and name it Algebra.

Creating a relationship between two tables

Before jumping right into the Report Wizard, you must analyze the data that you want to report. The two tables in this example (Literature and Algebra) are related to one another by the First_Name and Last_Name fields. If you want to include information from both tables in a report, then you must *acknowledge* (create) this relationship.

Transfer

You can read more about relationships between tables — an advanced topic — in Chapter 9. This chapter gives you just an abbreviated introduction.

Watch Your Step

If you don't create the relationship between the tables, you can't proceed with the Report Wizard. You receive a warning message that no relationship exists between the two tables, and you must either create the relationship or back up and remove fields from your report that don't require a relationship.

To acknowledge the relationship between the Algebra and Literature tables, follow these steps:

1. Click the **Database Tools** tab.

2. Click the **Relationships** button.

For this example, the Show Table dialog box appears with the Algebra and Literature tables.

3. Select **Algebra and click Add, then select Literature and click Add and Close.**

Both tables are now shown in the Relationship Builder window.

4. Click **First_Name in the Algebra table, drag it onto the** First_Name **field in the Literature table, and release.**

The Edit Relationships dialog box appears, displaying the relationship you just created between Algebra.First_Name and Literature.First_Name.

Below the First_Name entry for each table, there's a drop-down list that displays all fields in each table.

5. Select **Last_Name for each table and click Create.**

Figure 7-2 shows the entries.

When you click Create, the relationships are created between the two tables. Basically, by creating these relationships, you're telling any query or report based on the two tables that you want to look at records from each table in which the first and last names match each other.

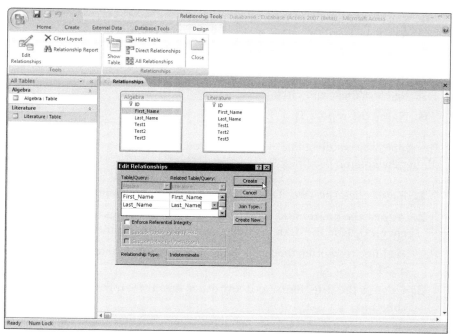

Figure 7-2: Relationship between the Algebra and Literature tables.

Building a report based on two record sources

After you acknowledge the relationship between the two tables, which I cover in the preceding section, you can proceed with the Report Wizard. For this chapter's example, follow these steps:

1. **Click the Create tab, then click Report Wizard.**

2. **After the wizard launches, select the Algebra table and send First_Name, Last_Name, Test1, Test2, and Test3 to the Selected Fields list.**

3. **Select the Literature table from the drop-down list and send Test1, Test2, and Test3 to the Select Fields list.**

   The names of the fields change as you select them. `Test1` from the Algebra table becomes `Algebra.Test1` and the `Test1` field from the Literature table becomes `Literature.Test1`. Fields in different tables that have the same name must be kept separate from each other by expanding their names to their explicit field names. The *explicit field name* is a designation that uses `Table_Name.Field_Name`, removing any confusion.

4. **Click Next twice.**

5. **Select Sort Ascending on the Last_Name field. Click Next.**

6. **Select Block layout, Landscape orientation, and select the Adjust field width so all fields fit on a page check box. Click Next.**

   This example uses Landscape orientation because of the number of fields on the report.

7. **Select Aspect and click Next.**

8. **Name the report** Two_Tables **and click Finish.**

The report is accurate but not very pretty. You can make the report easier to read by editing the column headings. Follow these steps:

1. **Right-click the Two_Tables tab and click Layout View.**

2. **Adjust the names and sizes of the column headings so that each is sized correctly (for the data in each column) and readable.**

   Feel free to shorten the test column names (to such abbreviations as **Alg. Test 1** and **Lit. Test 1**).

3. **Change the title, fonts, and any other layout features that you want at this time.**

Advanced reporting features

In this section, you can find out how to use some of the advanced reporting features of Microsoft Access 2007, including advanced editing features, summary functions, and adding new fields that aren't table related.

Without these advanced features, your reports would have only raw data displayed in very standard ways. Reports are meant to inform and convey information in a clear, easy-to-read format. Well-designed reports should also deliver information in an at-a-glance way so readers can quickly find the data they need without hunting and deciphering or having to ask many explanatory questions.

Altering the structure of a report

If the column header fields (such as First Name and Last Name) are too high in the report header, you can move them by using Design View. The following example demonstrates how to use Access's advanced editing features to remedy this problem. I use my Two_Tables report, shown in Figure 7-3, in this example. Follow these steps:

1. **Open the report (for example, Two_Tables).**

2. **Right-click the open report's tab (for example, the Two_Tables tab) and click Design View.**

   Instead of selecting the fields themselves and moving them (which doesn't work, by the way), you need to edit the underlying structure of the report.

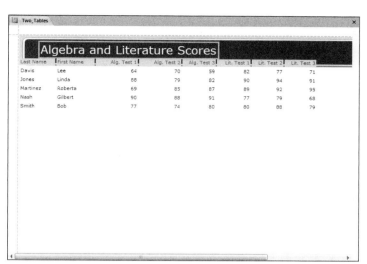

Figure 7-3: My Two_Tables report needs some editing.

3. **Move your mouse cursor over the Page Header bar until it changes into a drag bar with a double-headed arrow. Click to select the Page Header bar.**

Refer to Figure 7-4.

Figure 7-4: Move the Page Header bar to make it larger.

4. **Drag the cursor down until you can see the whole header graphic, plus some extra space for a border.**

5. **Switch to Layout View or Print Preview to see the results of your edit.**

Figure 7-5 shows my results for this example.

Changing other report properties

After you move the page header down, as described in the preceding section, you may notice the gray default background color of the header. You can change the background color of the page header, detail (body), page footer, or report footer of the report.

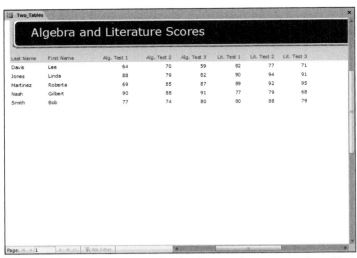

Figure 7-5: My Two_Tables report's headers have much more room after editing.

Information Kiosk

The page footer is a specific footer for the current page. For example, the page footer might display Page 6 of 10. The report footer appears on each page throughout the report. The report footer can include information such as the title, author, purpose, or company name.

Changing the background color of any part of a report follows the same basic steps as the following example.

To change the background color of the header, follow these steps:

1. **Return to Design View.**

2. **Right-click the page header's background and select Properties from the menu that appears.**

The Property Sheet opens, showing the properties of the Page Header section.

3. **Select Back Color and use the ellipsis button (. . .) to open the color palette.**

4. **Select the Back Color that you want and click anywhere on the report for the color change to take effect.**

5. **Switch to Layout View or Print Preview to see the change.**

Nothing teaches quite as well as experience. Try the following structural and property changes (one at a time) on your own — and remember to look at each change in Layout View or Print Preview before making other changes:

- Change the Detail Back Color to Light Gray.

- Change the column header and font colors to Black.

- Make the Detail section larger (see the Page Header example in the preceding section).

- Change the size of the column-header font.

Adding summary functions to a report

Summary functions are those functions that have a mathematical calculation associated with them. Summary functions include Sum, Average, Variance, Total, Standard Deviation, and so on. You can also create your own summary functions as expressions. *Expressions* are functions that perform mathematical operations on a set or series of fields. Expressions can perform calculations on rows, columns, or randomly selected fields anywhere on the report. Column-oriented calculations are built into Access as controls. I give some examples of row and column calculations in the following sections.

Built-in summary functions

The purpose of many reports is not only to show data in a nice, easy-to-read format but also to summarize data for decision-making. A list of 30 or 40 numbers can mean very little if the report has several columns. An average or sum of the numbers in a column, however, can be the key to a quick decision based on that column of numbers. For example, you may look at a list of grades for an end-of-semester assessment but not actually know who is failing or passing. An average provides this information at a glance.

Transfer

Summary functions are also discussed in Chapter 4, where you can find out about queries.

To add column averages to each test score in the example database, follow these steps:

1. **Open the Two_Tables report in Layout View.**

2. **Click the Alg. Test 1 column to select it.**

3. **Right-click the column to bring up the right-click menu, select Total Algebra_Test1, and then click Average.**

    The average score for Algebra Test 1 is calculated and placed at the bottom of that column of numbers.

4. **Add averages to the rest of the columns for this report by following Steps 2 and 3 for each column.**

You may find that an average for each exam is a very useful piece of information. It helps you decide how difficult or valid an exam is, and you can compare statistics between exams. It doesn't give you individual student information, however. For that kind of information, you must create a new field and add an expression (which can be a calculation or function) to the field.

Calculated fields, as they're called, are quite common in such reports. You can create any type of function that you want for a set or series of fields. Access understands a very wide array of mathematical operators, functions, and constants.

Adding a new field to a report

In the example in this section, you add a field for each set of exams that calculates the average score for each student per subject. You thus add two columns to the report: **Avg. Algebra** and **Avg. Literature**. (I made up those names; you can use any designation you want for them.)

Adding a calculated field to an Access report is like adding a calculation to a spreadsheet. You must explicitly provide the function with the cell locations to get the correct calculation.

To add a new field to a report, follow these steps:

1. **Open the report (for example, Two_Tables) in Design View.**
2. **Select the Design tab under Report Design Tools.**
3. **Click the Text Box control from the list of controls.**

    Figure 7-6 shows the Text Box control.

Figure 7-6: With the Text Box control, you can create a Text Box.

    Your mouse cursor changes into a text box with a plus sign (+) — that's your drawing guide.

4. **Draw a text box in the Detail section of the report.**

    This field has no column header.

    You can find the column header to the left of the text box you just created and behind the other text boxes. It's highlighted.

5. Grab the header and drag it to the left until you see the placement line. Release the mouse button.

The text box now has the same format as the others on the report. Figure 7-7 shows the details.

6. Bring up the Property Sheet by right-clicking the Text Box and selecting Properties from the menu that appears.

7. When you open the Property Sheet, you may have to use the drop-down list to select the text box you just created.

The new text box is named `TextXX`, where `XX` is the number identifier. The label for the text box is `LabelXX`.

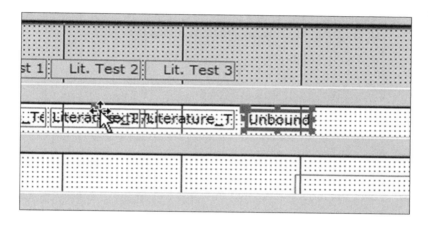

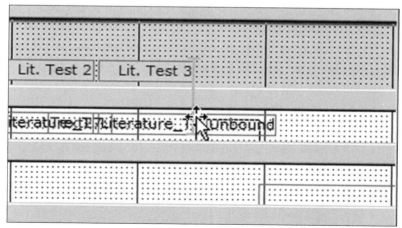

Figure 7-7: You can find and move a column header in Access.

8. **Select the Data tab on the Property Sheet and click into the Control Source field. Enter a formula into the Control Source field, like this:**

```
=Round((([Algebra_Test1]+[Algebra_Test2]+[Algebra_Test3])/3)
```

You can build an expression such as this with the Expression Builder (the ellipsis [. . .] button in the Control Source field), but you'll probably make fewer mistakes by entering the formula directly. Often I write the formula in Notepad and then copy and paste it into the Control Source field. For very long formulas, I can use Notepad more easily than the Control Source field because I can visualize the entire formula in Notepad.

In general, the same rules that apply for creating a query in a report also apply for creating an expression:

- Begin the expression with the equal sign (=).
- Use square brackets ([ ]) around field names.
- Use parentheses to isolate a single calculation (the addition of a series of numbers) and with functions (Round(*expression*)), for example.

I added the Round function to match the other numbers (to make them whole numbers) on the report. It makes the report look cleaner and easier to interpret.

9. **Click the Other tab to change the name of the Text Box from TextXX to something more descriptive (for example, Alg_Avg).**
10. **Select the label for the text box in the drop-down list on the Property Sheet.**

When you select the correct label, it becomes highlighted on the report.

11. **Select the Format tab and change the Caption to something descriptive (for example, Algebra Avg).**
12. **Switch to Layout View and adjust the size of the label so that you can read it.**
13. **Select the label and the data of the field, then select the Bold format button to make the text bold.**

Bold text makes the averages stand out on the report.

14. **Change the Text Align of the numbers to Right justification.**

For this example, follow Steps 3 through 14 to add the Literature Avg. field on your own. Figure 7-8 shows my final report.

Algebra and Literature

Last Name	First Name	Alg. Test 1	Alg. Test 2	Alg. Test 3	Lit. Test 1	Lit. Test 2	Lit. Test 3	Algebra Avg.	Literature Avg.
Davis	Lee	64	70	39	82	77	71	64	77
Jones	Linda	88	79	82	90	94	91	83	92
Martinez	Roberta	69	83	87	89	92	95	80	92
Nash	Gilbert	90	88	91	77	79	68	90	75
Smith	Bob	77	74	80	80	88	79	77	82
		77.6	79.2	79.8	83.6	86	80.8		

Figure 7-8: My final report includes average test score summary data.

ascending sort: A to Z ordering for alphabetical data.

control source: A property that contains a reference to a field or expression.

descending sort: Z to A ordering for alphabetical data.

expression: A formula or calculation in a control source that produces numeric data usually based on functions and other fields in a table, tables, or a query.

Print Preview: A printer-ready view of a report.

read-only: A condition in which no data can be changed or altered in any way. You can only look at (read) the data.

relationship: A connection in which a field in one table contains the same information as a field in another table. This equality creates a relationship between the two tables.

Report View: A production layout view that shows exactly how a report will look on the computer.

text box: A form or report control that can contain text, expressions, or other data.

Last
Stop

Practice Exam

1. Which view gives you the most creative freedom and lets you fully edit a report?

A) Report View

B) Layout View

C) Design View

D) Print Preview

2. Which view gives you an exact preview of the way the report will look when a user views the report?

A) Report View

B) Layout View

C) Design View

D) Print Preview

3. Which view gives you an exact preview of the way the report will look when printed?

A) Report View

B) Layout View

C) Design View

D) Print Preview

4. When adding a new field to a report that's not table-bound, how do you bind the field to the table?

A) Add an expression to the field that references table fields.

B) Correctly name the field within its Property Sheet.

C) Place the field on the report, which binds the field to the table.

D) Bind the field to the table automatically by using Design View.

5. **Which type of summary function is built into Access?**

A) Row-oriented

B) Column-oriented

C) Report-oriented

D) Design-oriented

6. **What action do you take if you have too many columns on your report to be viewed on one page in Portrait mode?**

A) Remove some columns from the report.

B) Change the orientation of the report to Landscape mode.

C) Re-create the report from scratch and hope it turns out better this time.

D) Re-create the report and use a query rather than tables.

7. **What must you do before you can create a report based on multiple record sources?**

A) Create a report based on a single record source.

B) Create a form based on the record sources.

C) Create a relationship between the two tables.

D) Create a table-bound field.

8. **Reports are great for presenting what type of data?**

A) Summary

B) Well-designed

C) Averages

D) Expression-based

9. **What's the quickest way to create a new report based on a single record source?**

A) Create a blank report and edit it manually.

B) Use the Report Wizard.

C) Create a form, and then base the report on the form.

D) Create a basic report.

10. **What's the purpose of using summary data on a report?**

    A) It makes the report easier to create.

    B) It makes the data easier to find and interpret.

    C) It makes the report longer.

    D) It makes the report more convincing to read.

CHAPTER 8

Putting SharePoint Services to Work

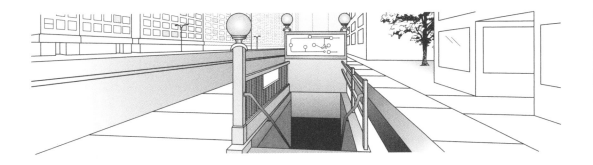

 # Enter the Station

Questions

1. What is SharePoint?

2. What are the advantages of using SharePoint?

3. Why should you move your database data to a SharePoint site?

4. How do you work with tasks?

5. Is it possible to set up a trouble-ticket system in SharePoint?

6. How do you work with SharePoint if you aren't connected to the server?

Express Line

If you are already an experienced SharePoint user, then skip ahead to Chapter 9.

In this chapter, you're introduced to SharePoint Portal Services. SharePoint is a collaboration and shared workspace server that integrates quite nicely with Microsoft Access. You can find out about the different types of lists and get some examples of each. You can also figure out how to deal with data in an offline mode and how to create a shared workspace for meetings or events.

Thinking in Terms of Remote Data

For some time now, Microsoft has had the plan to make local data (the kind stored on your hard drive) and remote data (stored anywhere in the world) transparent to one another. By *transparent,* I mean that the data you access, use, store, or deal with in any way may or may not be stored locally — but is readily available and usable anyway. In fact, you can store some of the data you use locally (on a local server in your network) or on a remote server thousands of miles away. SharePoint provides this kind of portal.

SharePoint Portal Services (SPS) and Windows SharePoint Services (WSS) work together to provide users with

- A Web-based interface
- An integrated database service for storing large amounts of data
- Many templates for lists, contacts, events, links, tasks, and more
- A shared document area
- A shared picture area
- Discussion boards
- A survey area
- The ability to create custom sites
- The ability to add special content

Originally, SPS was meant to be used in an intranet (internal network) setting to allow businesses to share documents, ideas, and information among employees. But SPS has become a way for companies to share information with their clients as well. Some companies run multiple SharePoint sites for different purposes — keeping some information strictly internal, providing separate services to their clients, and even offering some services to anonymous Internets users. Some entrepreneurial ventures charge a monthly fee for using their SPS, as you can read about in Chapter 3.

Information Kiosk

SharePoint Portal Services have replaced the Data Access Pages of Access. Data Access Pages were HTML pages that Access built to let users manipulate data through Internet Explorer. If you're using an .mdb file created in an older version of Access in Access 2007, you can view data in those pages, but you can't take any other actions (edit, delete, or insert).

Chapter 3 covers SharePoint Portal Services as an External Data Source, which this chapter revisits briefly as a reference point for further discussion. I use the terms *SharePoint* and *SPS* interchangeably in this book to make the text less wordy. I also present SPS from a user's perspective, not from an SPS administrator's point of view. This way, you get the view of SPS that you're most likely to deal with yourself. If you're the administrator, you can find several good books available on the topic.

Setting the scene

The examples in this chapter build upon the examples from Chapter 7. (You can download a copy of the Chapter7 database from this book's Web site). The examples require a background setup. The following is a list of items that are shown as examples in this chapter to get you started:

- The SharePoint site on your network is located at http://sharepoint.
- The user name for these examples is Teacher, and the password is Access. This Teacher account lets you view and edit data.
- A student account has been set up to see what the site looks like to a read-only user. The user name is Student, and the password is Access.
- You're a 10th-grade teacher, and you use the SharePoint system to post such information as grades, homework assignments, class photos, announcements, and events for your students and parents to use.

Though there is much more to SharePoint, the examples in this chapter cover only Access-related services and features.

Transfer

If you don't have a SharePoint server to use for these examples, you may want to skip this chapter for now or until you sign up for a trial or install one of your own.

Moving information to SharePoint

Moving your data to the SharePoint site is very simple. You can move the data in two ways:

- Move all data to the SharePoint site. Tables are created as lists, and links to those lists are created back to the current database.

- Save a copy of the database to the SharePoint site and create shortcuts to your Access forms and reports.

There are some advantages to moving your data to the SharePoint site:

- If you use a laptop, you probably can access your SharePoint site from anywhere.

- Updates are immediately available to all readers.

- Your network administrators are more likely to perform backups on a server than on each individual workstation.

To move a database to SharePoint, follow these steps:

1. **Open the database (for example, the database that contains the Algebra and Literature tables that you can create in Chapter 7).**

2. **Click the External Data tab.**

3. **Click the Move to SharePoint icon.**

    The Move to SharePoint Site Wizard is launched, prompting you for the location of your SharePoint server. I've set one up for these examples at `http://sharepoint`. This is an SPS server that I set up on my network for this chapter; you can't connect to it.

4. **Deselect the *Save a copy of my database . . .* check box and click Next.**

    You see a progress bar and messages informing you of what's being done as your data is transferred over to the SharePoint site. After the data is fully transferred, a message informs you that the process is complete. You may receive a message that says there were issues with the transfer and to click the Details button for details of the errors. Most of the time, the message says only that Access made a backup of your database.

5. **Click Finish.**

Information Kiosk

SharePoint lists are the same as Access tables. When moving database data to SharePoint, tables are converted to lists, and SharePoint lists are linked as tables in Access.

6. Open the linked tables (for example, Literature and Algebra) and see that they contain the same data as before the transfer (with some exceptions).

All of the actual data is intact. The ID field is missing, and new fields have been added to comply with SharePoint's versioning system. Figure 8-1 shows the Literature table as a SharePoint list.

On the SharePoint site, these tables are now lists. Figure 8-2 shows the Literature list on the SharePoint site.

Copying the database to SharePoint

For the example in this section, you perform the same actions that you do in the preceding section, but this time you place a copy of the database on the SharePoint site, rather than just a copy of the tables.

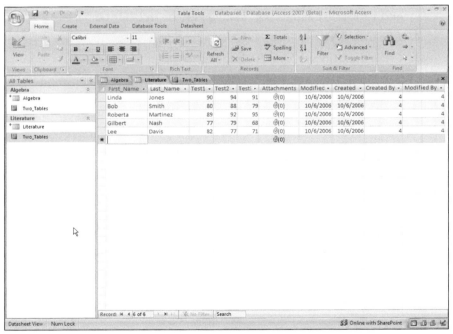

Figure 8-1: The Literature table after converting to SharePoint.

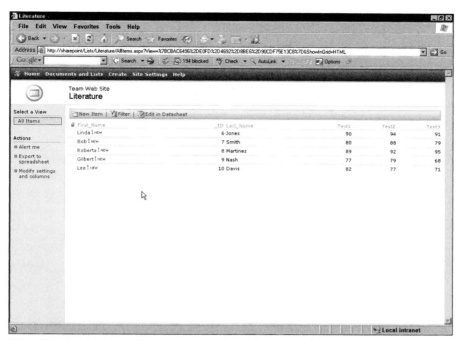

Figure 8-2: The Literature table appears on the SharePoint site as a list.

To copy the database to SharePoint, follow these steps:

1. Change the name of the backup database from the preceding section.

My database was named `Database6.accdb`, and a backup named `Database6_Backup.accdb` was created when I moved the original to SharePoint. Rename the database you use in the preceding section to **Chapter8.accdb**.

2. Open the Chapter8 database.

3. Launch the Move to SharePoint Site Wizard by clicking the Move to SharePoint button under External Data.

4. Enter the SharePoint site name (for this example, http://sharepoint**) and click the box _Save a copy of my database to the SharePoint site and create shortcuts to my Access Forms and Reports_.**

5. Click Browse to Select a Document Library to save your database.

A Browse window opens on the SharePoint server. Figure 8-3 shows the locations where you can save documents.

Shared Documents is the default library for sharing files. I created the library named `Databases`.

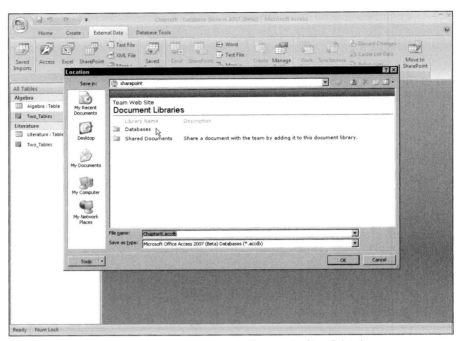

Figure 8-3: Select a document library to save your database to the SharePoint site.

6. Double-click the Library (for example, the Databases library) and click OK.

You return to the SharePoint Site Wizard. The database you selected is shown on the wizard. Figure 8-4 shows the first step in the Move to SharePoint Site Wizard.

7. Click Next.

The database loads to the SharePoint site. You see a progress indicator and receive several messages to let you know what's going on. When the process is complete, a message tells you that your tables have been successfully shared.

8. Click Finish.

For this example, the modified Chapter8 database is the current database in Access.

In my version of Access 2007, my tables remain intact (even the ID field) and only one field (Attachments) was added.

9. Open the SharePoint site in which you saved a copy of the database and click the database copy (for example, click Chapter8). Click Open when prompted.

A new instance of Access 2007 launches, opening with the database from the SharePoint site. You're notified that this is a read-only copy of the database and that certain content has been disabled.

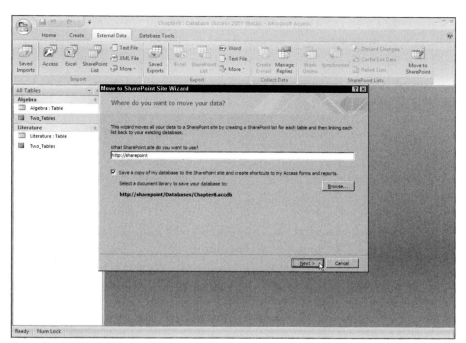

Figure 8-4: The SharePoint Site Wizard is ready to move data.

10. **Open the tables and report (for example, open Two_Tables).**

They look exactly the same as your local copy.

You can update or edit your local copy of the database, then synchronize it with the online copy.

To update the Chapter8 database by adding a new student record, follow these steps:

1. **Open the local copy of the Chapter 8 database.**

2. **Open the Algebra table and add the record shown in Table 8-1.**

Table 8-1 New Algebra Record

First_Name	Last_Name	Test1	Test2	Test3
Alice	Hansen	82	85	83

3. **Save the table.**

This step is optional, but it's good practice to always save your work.

4. Open the Algebra list on the SharePoint site to see that Alice's info has been updated.

5. Open the Chapter8 database on the SharePoint site.

It now has Alice's information as well.

If you look at the Two_Tables report in either copy of the database, Alice's information isn't included in the report. The answer to why Alice doesn't appear in the reports lies in the relationship between the two tables. As Chapter 7 shows, the relationship that you set up requires that the First_Name and Last_Name fields in both tables match exactly. If they don't, then you don't see the records.

To see Alice Hansen in the report, follow these steps:

1. Open the local copy of the Chapter8 database and add the record shown in Table 8-2 to the Literature table.

Table 8-2   New Literature Record

First_Name	Last_Name	Test1	Test2	Test3
Alice	Hansen	99	92	92

2. After you enter this record, open the Two_Tables report and see Alice's information inserted into the table in the correct order and with averages.

Watch Your Step

If you enter records into tables but they don't show up in the report, check the spelling of the fields that are supposed to match. If the two fields don't match exactly, then they won't show up in a report or query based on the equality of the fields.

When Alice's information appears on the Two_Tables report in the preceding steps, the column averages become very long numbers. To round the averages to the nearest whole number, follow these steps:

1. Open the report in Design View.

Locate the report footer.

2. Enclose each Avg function in the report footer in a Round( ) function.

In this example, the expression looks like this for Alg. Test 1:

```
=Round(Avg([Algebra_Test1]))
```

3. Save and view the report in Report View.

Using SharePoint to store a copy of the database maintains better consistency of the original database design rather than just moving tables to a SharePoint site. The lists look more like the tables you originally created (the ID field remains intact, for example). The SharePoint site administrator can provide you with the security you need for your databases and lists.

Information Kiosk

There are four types of SharePoint users: administrators, Web designers, contributors, and readers. If unauthorized users can read your database, they can make a local copy of it — essentially stealing your database, structure, and all the data in it. Give your administrator a list of people who need access to such resources as your databases and lists. You can make public information public and keep private information private. Generally speaking, most administrators opt for providing the least invasive privileges possible on files and directories unless you provide reasons why they should loosen up.

Changing information in an existing object, such as a table or report, is immediately reflected in the SharePoint's copy of the database. If you create or remove an object, you must upload the changes to the SharePoint site by using the Publish to SharePoint Site button, as shown in Figure 8-5.

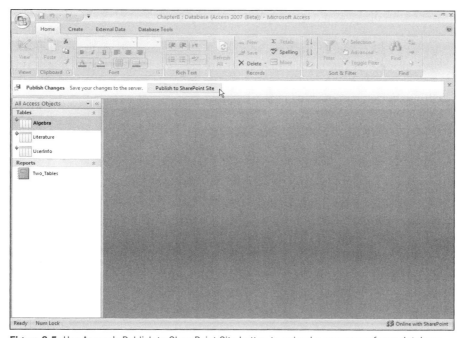

Figure 8-5: Use Access's Publish to SharePoint Site button to upload a new copy of your database.

Working Offline with SharePoint Data

Many people work remotely these days. Remote users may not always be connected to a network that has access to the SharePoint server, but you can work offline with your SharePoint data. The second example in the preceding section sets this scenario perfectly.

To work with SharePoint data offline, you must

- Save a copy of the data to the SharePoint site.
- Have a local copy of the database.
- Explicitly disconnect from the SharePoint site.

Preparing to work offline

To take your database offline, use the following steps. (As an example, you can open the database from the last example in the section "Copying the database to SharePoint," earlier in this chapter.)

1. **Click the External Data tab.**

2. **Click the Work Offline button in the SharePoint Lists group.**

   You receive messages that the data is being taken offline. The icons for your tables (SharePoint-linked lists) change. Compare the table icons in Figure 8-6 with the table icons in Figure 8-5.

After you take your data offline, two new buttons are available to you in the SharePoint Lists group: Synchronize and Discard Changes. Under Discard Changes, you have two choices: Discard All Changes, and Discard All Changes and Refresh. The Work Offline button has changed to Work Online.

Synchronizing offline data with the SharePoint server

The Synchronize utility attempts to connect to the SharePoint server so it can upload your offline changes and download any changes made to the server copy while you were disconnected. If there are data conflicts, you have the option of discarding or retrying your changes. If you don't have the option of retrying your changes, you have to discard your changes.

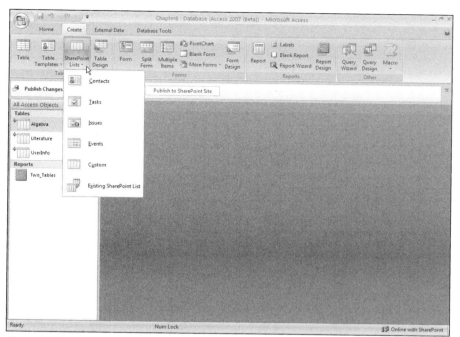

Figure 8-6: You can access SharePoint data offline through the SharePoint Lists group.

To add and synchronize data in this chapter's example database, follow these steps:

1. Add the record from Table 8-3 to the Algebra table in the Chapter8 database.

Table 8-3   Add A New Algebra Record

First_Name	Last_Name	Test1	Test2	Test3
Don	Fenton	80	80	82

2. Add the record from Table 8-4 to the Literature table in the Chapter 8 database.

Table 8-4	Add A New Literature Record			
First_Name	**Last_Name**	**Test1**	**Test2**	**Test3**
Don	Fenton	83	86	90

When you add new records in offline mode, the ID numbers appear as negative numbers. The record for Don Fenton has an ID of -1. An additional record would have an ID of -2, and so on. These negative numbers indicate that you're offline and the records aren't synchronized.

3. **Click the Synchronize button.**

4. **Open the Algebra and Literature lists to check that the changes have been synchronized.**

5. **Open the Two_Tables report to see that Don Fenton's grades have been added correctly to the report.**

Synchronize connects to the SharePoint site, updates the information, then disconnects. You're now working offline again.

When you're connected to your corporate network or a permanent network connection that allows access to your SharePoint server, you can click the Work Online button to reconnect permanently with the SharePoint site. The table icons change back to the standard linked list icons.

6. **Open the Algebra and Literature tables from the Chapter8 database on the SharePoint site to see that the local database and the online database are truly synchronized.**

Revisiting SharePoint Lists

Other than simple tables, you can create other lists by using Access, including contact, task, issue, event, and custom lists. (Chapter 3 introduces you to SharePoint lists when you use external data sources.) When you create a custom list, a new empty table is created for you. Because you have a lot of experience with creating new tables, these examples skip custom lists.

Contact, task, issue, and event lists are automatically generated tables set up for Access and SharePoint. These lists are part of the beauty of SharePoint. Access and SharePoint are very tightly integrated for such services. When users of these lists update them on SharePoint, the data is automatically and readily usable by an Access database. You can perform queries and reports on these lists. The users never know where the actual data is kept. The following sections cover each type of list to give you an idea of how using Access with SharePoint is far more powerful than using either of the two alone.

Creating a new contact list

Contact lists are among the most-used database objects. Almost everyone uses a contact list of some sort — from an old Rolodex to the newest integrated enterprise application. Many database-oriented books begin by building a contact database as the classic example for a database.

To create a new contact list, follow these steps:

1. **Click the Create tab.**

2. **Click the SharePoint Lists drop-down menu and select Contacts.**

You're prompted for a SharePoint site to connect to and a name for the new list.

3. **Enter the name of the new list (for example, Clients) and click OK.**

The new list opens and prompts you for information.

4. **Enter the information you want to store in your new list.**

For the Clients example, you can enter the information from Table 8-5.

Table 8-5 Contact List Data

Last Name	First Name	E-mail Address	Company	Job Title	Business Phone	Home Phone	Mobile Phone	Fax Number	Address	City	State	Postal Code	Country	Web Page	Notes
Stevens	Mary	marys@ example .com	XYZ, Inc.	President	817-555-1234	817-555-1727	817-555-6609	NA	400 N. Main St.	Lakeside	TX	77665	USA	www. xyzinc .com	Widget supplier, 10% discount.

The information is automatically uploaded to the SharePoint site. You can enter more Clients contacts by following the steps in the preceding list.

The following section shows how to work with data in a list.

Working with a new list

On the SharePoint site, you can access the new list on the Documents and Lists page. To access the Clients List, follow these steps:

1. **Click Documents and Lists on the top navigation bar or Lists in the left navigation pane.**

2. **Click Clients.**

Figure 8-7 shows the location of the Clients list on the SharePoint site.

If you used Table 8-5 for sample data in the preceding section, you see part of the client entry for Mary Stevens when you select the Clients list. Table 8-6 shows the entry in the Clients list.

Figure 8-7: You can select Clients on the SharePoint Documents and Lists page.

Table 8-6   The Mary Stevens Entry

Last Name	First Name	Company	Business Phone	Home Phone	E-mail Address
Stevens	Mary	XYZ, Inc.	817-555-1234	817-555-1727	marys@ example.com

You entered a lot of information for Mary Stevens in the preceding section, but only a small part of it shows up in her entry. The entry has been reduced to the *quick view,* which shows the information that's most often sought for a contact.

3. To see the full entry for Mary, place your mouse cursor over the Last Name entry, Stevens.

A drop-down menu and hyperlink appear.

4. Click the hyperlink (Stevens).

You now see the whole record for Mary Stevens (shown in Figure 8-8).

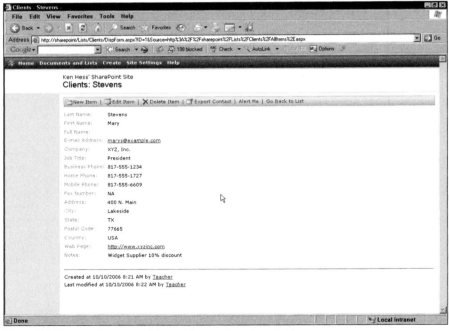

Figure 8-8: You can view a complete contact record on SharePoint.

The complete contact record contains hyperlinks for both the e-mail address and the Web site, giving you easy access to more information. On this page, you have several options; you can edit, delete, or export the record. You can also add a new record to the Clients list, set up an e-mail alert, or go back to the original Clients list.

Setting up an e-mail alert for a list

A very interesting and useful feature of SharePoint is the ability to set up e-mail alerts for any object that you create or upload to a site. You can set up an e-mail alert to notify you of any changes made to an object that you own.

Watch Your Step

E-mail alerts can get quite annoying if many changes are made on an object that you own. Use a bit of discretion when setting up these alerts. This feature is intended to alert you to any *unexpected* changes to your lists, databases, or other files.

When you set up your account on the SharePoint site, you received an e-mail address. You receive the alerts at this e-mail address unless you change where SharePoint sends the alerts (which you can do by following the steps in this section).

To set up an alert for a list (such as the Clients list), follow these steps:

1. **Click Go Back to List.**

2. **Click the Alert Me link in the left navigation pane under Actions.**

   The default e-mail address to which all alerts will be sent appears. You can change it by clicking Change my e-mail address.

   The other item that you can change on this page is the *alert frequency,* which means how often SharePoint sends the alerts. How often you receive notification is up to you, based on how critical your data is and how often you want to get e-mail.

3. **Select how frequently you want to receive the alerts and click OK.**

   You receive an e-mail message informing you that you've successfully set up the e-mail alert. The object (for example, the Clients list) is named in the e-mail notification.

You can test the alert by changing a piece of data in the SharePoint list (for example, change the client's first name from Mary to Marie in the Clients list). You should receive an e-mail notifying you of the change. A link to the object and the record that was changed is provided in the e-mail so you can inspect the change(s) immediately. The person who changed the record is identified in the e-mail as well.

Creating a personal or public task list

A task list, either personal or public, is a nice addition to the Access-SharePoint partnership. You can create reports, searches, and queries from a task list. If the task list is public, then many users can place tasks in it and maintain milestones for a common project. It provides a nice project management tool by allowing users to create reports. If you're very organized, you can use a personal task list to track your progress through training or on a project, or even to track projects that you've assigned to members of your team.

Whether a task list is public or private depends on the permissions placed on it by the administrator.

To create a new task list, follow these steps:

1. **Click the Create tab.**

2. **Click the SharePoint Lists drop-down menu and select the list (for example, Contacts).**

You're prompted for a SharePoint site to connect to and a name for the new list.

3. **Enter the name of the new list (for example, To Do) and click OK.**

The list opens and prompts you for information. For example, you can enter the information from Table 8-7 into the To Do list.

Table 8-7   To Do List Data

Title	Priority	Status	% Complete	Assigned To	Description	Start Date	Due Date
Technical Documentation of New Application	(1) High	In Progress	15.00%	Ken Hess	Create a 50-page technical document with screen-shots for the New Application.	10/9/ 2006	12/15/ 2006

When you press the Enter key during data entry, some of the fields are almost self-filling. You accomplish this by using a Combo Box in the Display Control property field; Chapter 10 shows you how. The pop-up calendar (called a Date Picker) is a nice feature that you can add by using a Date/Time data type rather than a Text data type when you create the table.

Going public or keeping it private: A word on permissions

When you create any list, it's automatically publicly accessible. You must notify the administrator of the site to alter the permissions for the list:

- If it's a personal task list, ask the administrator to add you as the owner, give you full permissions to the list, and remove all other users.

- Public lists may need adjustments to limit which users are allowed to use the list.

> ### Information Kiosk
>
> For public SharePoint servers, administrators alter the permissions for the entire server to the owner only by default. You must grant your own permissions to others if you want to give them shared access to your lists. Intranet (local network) sites usually aren't as security restrictive, but it really depends on the administrator(s) and on corporate policy.

Using your new task list

A task list gives you some options not available in a contact list. This example gives you a quick overview of those features. To use a Task List, follow these steps:

1. **From the Documents and Lists page, click a list (for example, To Do).**

If you use this chapter's example, the To Do task list opens in the All Tasks View which displays all of the tasks. In the left navigation pane, you see All Tasks, My Tasks, Due Today, Active Tasks, and By Assigned To.

2. **Click each one of the selections to see how the view changes.**

You may have to add more tasks to see much difference.

This is the standard setup for tasks in SharePoint, but you can edit the content, layout, and structure if you're the owner of a list.

Creating a problem issues list

Most groupware application systems such as SharePoint include a trouble-ticket system for handling various problems within a company, a Web site, or service offering. The issue list is perfectly set up for this activity.

Creating and using an issue list is like creating and using a task list, which I discuss in the preceding sections. After you create it, an issue list presents you with the familiar left navigation pane that has links for All Issues, My Issues, and Active Issues for tracking purposes.

Setting up a meeting event system and workspace

I am very impressed with the quality and advanced abilities of the event list. This section explores some of them.

You can (for example) use the event list to create a recurring meeting for your team with a common workspace — where you can place an agenda, manage attendees, share documents, and post objectives. Follow these steps to create an event list:

1. **Click Create, SharePoint Lists, then Events.**

2. **When prompted for a name, enter it (for example,** Weekly Staff Meeting) **and click OK.**

   The new list opens in Access (in the form of a table), awaiting input. Ordinarily, I suggest entering information directly into the table, but SharePoint has a much more user-friendly interface for working with events.

3. **Click Documents and Lists on the top navigation bar or Lists from the left navigation bar.**

4. **Locate and click the Name (for example,** Weekly Staff Meeting**).**

   The Events page opens in All Events by default. If you need to look at a calendar, you can find one in the left navigation pane.

5. **Click New Item.**

6. **Enter the Title (for example,** IT Staff Meeting) **into the Title field.**

   Don't add or adjust dates at this time.

7. **Enter the Description (for example,** Weekly IT Staff Meeting and Round Table Discussion) **into the Description field.**

8. **Click the Recurrence radio button to specify how often you need the event to occur (None, Daily, Weekly, Monthly, or Yearly).**

   If you want the meeting to recur indefinitely, then make sure you select No end date.

9. **Select the Begin time and the End time.**

10. **Click the check box next to Workspace to create a new meeting workspace for this event list.**

    Figure 8-9 shows a completed New Item form for an example meeting and workspace.

11. **Click Save and Close to save the new event list.**

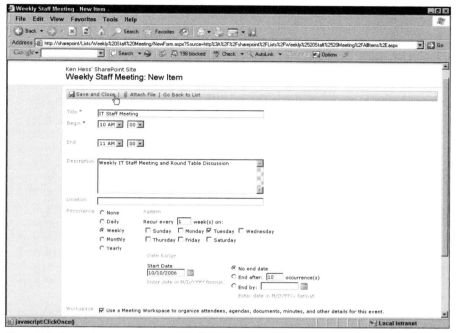

Figure 8-9: I'm ready to save my new event list.

12. **Click OK on the New Meeting Workspace page.**

You're prompted for your user name and password before the site creates this new workspace.

13. **Enter your user name and password and then click OK.**

The user name and password you enter here must have sufficient permissions to create a new workspace.

You're presented with a Template Selection page, in which you can choose the type of meeting workspace you want to use. The options are: Basic Meeting Workspace, Blank Meeting Workspace, Decision Meeting Workspace, Social Meeting Workspace, and Multipage Meeting Workspace.

14. **Select Basic Meeting Workspace from the list and click OK.**

SharePoint creates your new workspace. I suggest using the SharePoint interface for adding, editing, and navigating events of any kind. The SharePoint interface includes more options than Access for creating and using events. Figure 8-10 shows you an example completed workspace.

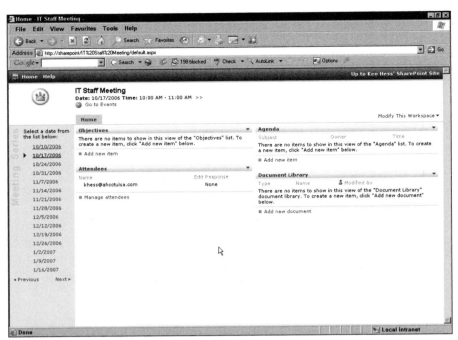

Figure 8-10: This IT Staff Meeting workspace is ready to use.

intranet: A network that's not exposed to or accessible from the public Internet.

list: A table of data on a SharePoint site.

offline: Disconnected from the SharePoint site.

online: Connected to the SharePoint site.

synchronize: Copy data to and from a SharePoint site to keep both copies of the data exactly the same.

workspace: A collaboration area in SharePoint in which users can share documents, agendas, objectives, and other information. Only people on the user list have access to this area.

Last Stop

Practice Exam

1. **Why might you need an offline mode for SharePoint?**

A) To conserve resources.

B) In case you need to change a large amount of data.

C) You should always disconnect before creating new lists.

D) You may need to work in a place where the SharePoint server isn't available.

2. **What's the best reason for making a list or database private?**

A) Security.

B) To conserve space.

C) All lists should be private.

D) Lists should never be private.

3. **Why would you set up an e-mail alert for a file or list?**

A) To track any changes that occur on the file

B) To prevent anyone from stealing the file

C) To know who's looking at the file

D) To make sure the file doesn't grow too large

4. **After creating a new event, why should you use SharePoint to edit the event?**

A) Permissions don't allow you to use Access to edit the event.

B) You shouldn't. Access is the best way to edit an event.

C) SharePoint has a more user-friendly, richer interface for editing events.

D) SharePoint is more stable than Access for handling events.

5. **True or false: It's necessary to publish all changes to a database after that database is shared on a SharePoint site.**

A) True

B) False

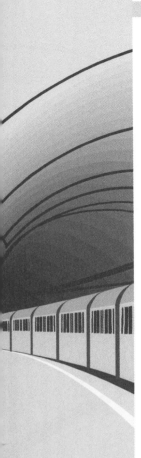

6. What happens when you synchronize SharePoint data?

A) Only lists are updated.

B) Only databases are updated.

C) All data is updated in both lists and databases.

D) Only the local copy downloads changes.

7. A Table in Access is converted to what kind of object in SharePoint?

A) Database

B) Workspace

C) Event

D) List

8. True or false (explain why): SharePoint lists are initially read-only.

_____

_____

_____

9. True or false (explain why): Someone can steal your data without being able to edit it.

_____

_____

_____

10. What is one advantage to moving your database(s) to a SharePoint site?

A) Your network administrators are more likely to perform backups on a SharePoint site.

B) SharePoint sites are more stable than Access.

C) It takes less effort to manage a SharePoint server than to manage Access.

D) It makes the database(s) smaller.

Managing Relationships

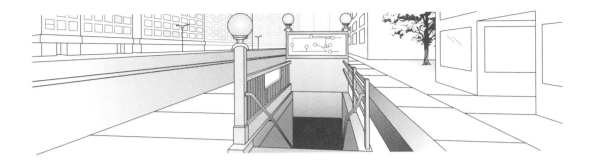

Enter the Station

Questions

1. What's the Relational Data Model?

2. Why is the Relational Data Model important?

3. Who created the Relational Data Model?

4. What types of relationships does Access support?

5. Why should you use relationships?

6. What does referential integrity mean?

7. Why are table relationships an element of good design?

Express Line

If you are already familiar with Table to Table relationships, then skip ahead to Chapter 10.

This chapter focuses less on Access and more on a central database concept: The relationship. Relationships are the foundation of all modern databases. I cover the Relational Data Model, giving you some basic guidelines. This chapter emphasizes design elements and best practices and introduces the concepts of referential integrity, normalization, and normal forms. By following the examples in this chapter, you can design a new database from beginning to end.

Entering the Relational Data Model

Back in 1970, IBM employee E.F. Codd wrote the Relational Data Model in a paper titled "A Relational Model of Data for Large Data Banks." This landmark paper presented 12 rules that must be followed to make a database a Relational Database Management System (RDBMS).

Even more than 35 years later, no database system complies with all 12 rules. He later expanded these original 12 rules to an outstanding 333 in 1990. Because the original 12 are an ambitious lot, it's doubtful that any RDBMS will ever comply with 333 rules.

The following list summarizes Codd's 12 basic rules and assesses how Access 2007 complies with them:

1. *All information is represented in relational tables.*

   This is the basic definition of a relational database, and Access is a relational database.

2. *All data is accessible using the table name, primary key value, and column name.*

   Access is fully compliant. Any Access query allows the use of the table name, primary key value, and column name.

3. *Support missing information as NULL values regardless of data type.*

   Access is fully compliant. It allows NULL values.

4. *The relational schema itself is represented in tables and is accessible in the same way as other database information.*

   Access has system tables (system objects) that contain this information.

5. *A relational query language must be provided that supports data definition, view definition, data manipulation, integrity constraints, authorization, and transaction support.*

   Access supports a large subset of the SQL language, but not views, transactions, or stored procedures.

6. *Basic support for view updatability.*

Access doesn't support views in the strict database definition of a *view*. Access does, however, support Make Table queries — which are essentially views — and they're updatable.

7. *Table-at-a-time retrieval and update operations are provided.*

Access complies with this rule as it relates to not only retrieving data but also inserting, deleting, and updating data.

8. *The access or storage techniques used by the DBMS should not affect the user's ability to work with the data.*

Access complies with this rule by design. I'm not sure how a DBMS wouldn't comply with this one.

9. *Changes to storage and retrieval should not adversely affect the user.*

This is very similar to Number 8, and Access is compliant.

10. *The database language should support integrity constraints that restrict the data that can be entered into the database and modifications to the data.*

Almost no DBMS fully complies with this one. Access complies up to a point, but most vendors give precedence to a well-designed database.

11. *The database language must be able to manipulate distributed data on other computer systems.*

Access easily complies with this rule. Access can connect to many other data sources, and its abilities aren't limited by these connections.

12. *Protection must prevent subversion of database relational structure and integrity.*

Access complies with this rule. This rule is like Number 10, except it deals with individual records rather than whole-table data.

The following list summarizes the 12 rules into something more understandable and compact that you can really use:

- Uniqueness of names and rows
- Foreign keys
- Data integrity
- Relationships
- Normalization

Putting the Relational Data Model into practice

A database that's correctly designed will automatically have the characteristics that make it a true relational database. A database doesn't have to comply with all the rules of creating a relational database. You can just put data into a table and extract it at will. Unique rows aren't necessary. You don't even have to have a primary key in a table. A database doesn't have to have any tables that are related to each other. You've created databases that don't have any table-to-table relationships.

So what's the point of all this relationship information and the Relational Data Model if you don't have to follow the rules? The answer lies in the needs of the designer, the needs of the users of the data, and the intended purpose of the database. Some databases don't need to follow the rules and would be hindered if they did. The purpose of this chapter (and of the whole book) is to show you how to comply with the rules when appropriate, follow best practices, and build and maintain well-designed databases. By following the rules of a well-designed database, you build the following qualities into your databases:

- Data integrity
- Speed
- Scalability
- Predictability
- Compatibility

Figuring out how to create well-designed databases can also help you take your learning to the next level, job, or DBMS. These rules aren't just for Access but all databases.

Sometimes a table is just a table

A *table* is just a collection of data that's organized into rows and columns. A *relation* is a table that has the following characteristics:

- A single value per cell
- A single data type per column
- Unique rows
- Columns with unique names
- Independence from the order of columns or rows

Fortunately, Access has built-in constraints that attempt to maintain each table as a relation. Each column within a table must have a unique name. You can't name two columns the same. Access also automatically begins each table with an ID column to make each row unique by adding a primary key.

Watch Your Step

Access allows you to delete the ID field. You receive a warning that you're about to delete the primary key and that you must be in Design View to remove that field. You also receive a warning when you delete the ID field in Design View, but you're allowed to remove it. Never delete a primary key unless you have a very good reason (such as using a list of data without a need for indexing or unique values). Without a primary key, rows may not be unique and can't participate in any relational operations in the database.

It's possible (and sometimes best) to change the name of the Primary Key column. I usually advise students to leave them as ID because it is easy to remember that you have a column named ID in each table. Stick to a predictable naming convention to make relationships easy to remember and maintain.

Cultivating a Relationship

A table-to-table relationship, like all parts of the Relational Data Model, is a mathematical definition that refers to equality. I don't go into the mathematics of any aspect of the Relational Data Model — you only need to worry about the qualitative definitions and descriptions in this context.

A *table-to-table relationship* is defined as how records in one table reference records in another table. Each relationship is between two — and only two — tables. Relationships are based on the primary key/foreign key (PK/FK) connection between two tables. A primary key in one table can reference foreign keys in many other tables, but each relationship exists between only two tables. A visual representation can help clarify the concept.

Figure 9-1 shows Primary Key/Foreign Key relationships.

Figure 9-1 shows three tables: Students, Exams, and Subjects. Each table is related by PK/FK pairs. As you can see in the figure, Students and Subjects aren't directly related to one another; they're indirectly related through the Exams table.

The primary key for each table is the ID column. The Exams table contains two foreign keys: Student_ID (paired with the primary key, ID, in the Students table) and Subject_ID (paired with ID in the Subjects table).

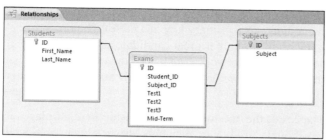

Figure 9-1: These table-to-table relationships show the Primary Key/Foreign Key connection.

Types of relationships

Access supports three relationship types: one-to-one (1:1), one-to-many (1:∞), and many-to-many (∞:∞).

One-to-one relationships

A *one-to-one relationship* is where exactly one record in one table matches exactly one record in another table.

Transfer

Chapter 7 shows the one-to-one relationship when dealing with reports that have multiple record sources. You set a relationship between two tables to allow the wizard to continue. You set up a relationship between First_Name in the Algebra table and First_Name in the Literature table, and Last_Name in the Algebra table and Last_Name in the Literature table. These two relationships are both one-to-one.

In a 1:1 relationship, if the records in the affected columns don't match, then those records aren't included in the query, report, or control. In pseudo-mathematical terms, you've set an instance of equality between the two tables. This isn't a great example of a 1:1 relationship, but it illustrates the concept. A typical 1:1 relationship involves primary keys from two different tables.

One-to-one relationships aren't very common, and you should generally avoid them. Usually, if you have a 1:1 relationship, you should redesign at least one table. The exception is databases that deal with financial transactions; many of those have 1:1 relationships.

One-to-many relationships

The one-to-many relationship is the most common relationship type. This relationship is defined as one record in a table that references many records in another table. Looking at the three tables in Figure 9-1, the Subjects table lists the available subjects. Each subject is used many times in the Exams table because each class has probably 25 students, and each student takes multiple subjects.

You've probably ordered several products from one company, and you have a Customer ID (a great candidate as a primary key in a table). The order you place has an Order ID associated with it — another great candidate as a primary key. Each item has its own ID, and so on. Each order you place has its own Order ID, but you always have the same Customer ID; therefore your Customer ID and all of the Order IDs are in a one-to-many relationship.

You can see other instances of the one-to-many relationship in other places in your daily life — checking accounts, credit card accounts, driver's licenses, Social Security numbers, student IDs, and just about anything else that has a unique number and multiple records associated with it.

Many-to-many relationships

A many-to-many relationship can cause problems in any table-to-table relationship. For example, look again at Figure 9-1, and imagine that you had only two tables — Exams and Subjects. You'd have many subjects, many exams for each subject, students with many exams for each subject, and multiple subjects for each student. It would be very difficult to collect *all* the exams in *each* subject for a *single* student. Fortunately, you can use three tables to remove any many-to-many relationships. The data is rearranged; in this example, Exams is set up as a linking table to remove the many-to-many conundrum that exists without the third table. A *linking table* is a table that acts as a bridge between two other tables by having foreign keys from the other two tables. A linking table is also called a *junction table*.

To avoid this headache in the first place, you should avoid many-to-many relationships. Access does support them, but you only make your data more difficult to deal with if you include many-to-many relationships in your database. Although such relationships have found their way into some databases, I can't think of any instance in which they are more appropriate than troublesome. Always create a linking table to connect two tables that have a many-to-many relationship. You have to rearrange data, but in the end, you have a more efficient database that's more immune to inconsistency. The section "Designing the Database," later in this chapter, walks you through developing a multi-table database from a single table of data.

Normalizing a Database

Normalization of a database is a process that involves breaking a collection of data apart and reassembling it into tables that

- Are related by primary key/foreign key pairs
- Contain no redundant data
- Contain only one type of data
- Have columns that are indivisible

Chapter 3 introduces you to the PK/FK pair concept for referencing data in other tables. Getting rid of redundant data is easy to do — just make sure that no two tables contain the same information. For instance, it would be redundant to have First_Name and Last_Name data in two different tables. Through the use of PK/FK pairs, you can remove the need for this information to exist in two different tables. Each table should contain only one type of data, such as customers, cities, exams, subjects, orders, or products. A table needs to have columns that are indivisible. An example is a column that holds names. If you have only one column that holds names, then it must contain first and last names. This format works okay until you need to sort by last name or to use a first name in a mail-merge situation. There are other applications in which having the whole name in a column causes a problem. You can divide a column that holds names into first names and last names. The indivisibility of a column is an extremely important aspect of designing and normalizing a database.

The normal forms

An aspect of database design and the process of normalization involves *normal forms,* different levels of normalization that can describe a database. Codd described six levels of normalization (1–6). You usually don't need more than the first three levels to create a fully normalized database. If your database complies with Third Normal Form (3NF), then you can feel comfortable that your database is normalized.

Table 9-1 lists the relevant normal forms and their prerequisites.

Table 9-1   Normal Forms and Their Prerequisites

Prerequisites	Zero Normal Form (0NF)	First Normal Form (1NF)	Second Normal Form (2NF)	Third Normal Form (3NF)
Primary key	Yes	Yes	Yes	Yes
Single-entity data	Yes	Yes	Yes	Yes
No repeating groups (arrays)		Yes	Yes	Yes
Indivisible columns		Yes	Yes	Yes
Each column depends on the primary key			Yes	Yes
No partial dependencies exist			Yes	Yes
No column depends on any other column				Yes

Normalization is a progressive process. Your database must comply with the preceding normal form to move on to the next.

Zero Normal Form

Formally, a Zero Normal Form (0NF) doesn't exist, but some database designers, such as me, decided that before you can consider a database for First Normal Form, you must fix the data so that you can make it conform to First Normal Form. These fixes are the prerequisites for attempting to place your database into First Normal Form:

- All tables must contain a unique identifier (primary key).
- Tables must contain data for a single subject.

First Normal Form

To qualify for First Normal Form (1NF) normalization, your tables must

- Comply with Zero Normal Form.
- Have no repeating groups of data in any cell.
- Ensure that each column is indivisible.

Second Normal Form

Many people get into trouble with this normal form. Those people have a fear of splitting tables into smaller tables and creating more PK/FK pairs. Often, a single table becomes three new tables because you need to create the linking table to rid you of any many-to-many relationships. Second Normal Form (2NF) is only somewhat relevant when you have a multi-column primary key — a primary key that contains more than one field. To create a muli-column primary key, highlight multiple fields in a table's Design View and click the Primary Key button.

To take your database to 2NF, you must follow these guidelines:

- Comply with the First Normal Form.
- Each table column must depend on the whole key (primary key).
- No column can partially depend on any other non-key column.

Third Normal Form

The Third Normal Form (3NF) is the highest level that most databases should ever aspire to. It's sufficiently normalized to make the database usable, durable, and consistent.

Your database is in 3NF if

 Your database is in 2NF.

 Each non-key column depends only on the primary key.

I don't really go through this progression from form to form in a stepwise manner, laboring over whether or not each table is compliant with this normal form or that normal form. I just figure out how the data I have is related. I split tables, create PK/FK pairs, split tables again, and examine each table along the way. I normalize by knowing the rules and reworking the data rather than beating the data into a particular normal form.

Denormalization

Because there are six levels of normalization, some database designers think they must go to the highest degree. I'm not sure if they do this for bragging rights or some other agenda, but most database administrators consider 3NF complete. Those who normalize to the highest theoretical degree sometimes find that their databases are unmanageable and slow. It's possible to over-normalize your data.

If you find yourself, or a database, in this position, you may have to figure out how to *denormalize* the database. This process is far more difficult than normalization because you must combine tables and remove PK/FK pairs. The process may also involve the difficult task of reworking forms, reports, and other applications to match the new database structure.

Referential Integrity

To understand referential integrity, look at the three tables in Figure 9-1, and then suppose a student moves away and you delete the student from the Students table — but you still have her exam scores in the Exams table. The Subjects table isn't affected by the Students table change — but the exam scores for the now-nonexistent student become orphaned without a Student_ID to refer to the ID field in the Students table. These orphaned records just take up space in the Exams table and slow down queries. The integrity of the reference is broken.

You can avoid this situation by enforcing referential integrity in a relationship. You can also select Cascade Delete Related Fields and Cascade Update Related Fields to delete and update related fields. (Enable Cascade Update/Delete in your relationships to remove the possibility of orphaned records.)

Checking Cascade Update changes the values in the foreign key fields if the values in the primary key fields change. Checking Cascade Delete deletes related records if the primary record is deleted. Be careful using the Cascade Delete option as you can inadvertently delete many records you might not intend to. For example, if you delete a customer that has many orders with your company, you can easily delete all their orders if Cascade Delete is checked.

To enforce referential integrity on a relationship, follow these steps:

1. **Create a relationship between two fields by dragging the Primary Key field onto the Foreign Key field and release.**

The Edit Relationships dialog box opens, as shown in Figure 9-2.

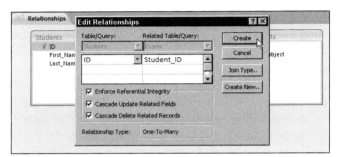

Figure 9-2: The Edit Relationships dialog box.

2. **Select Enforce Referential Integrity, Cascade Update Related Fields, and Cascade Delete Related Fields, as shown in Figure 9-3.**

3. **Click Create.**

After you create the relationships with referential integrity, you can now see the type of relationship (1:∞) in the relationship diagram, as shown in Figure 9-4.

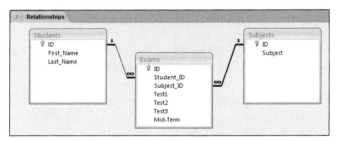

Figure 9-3: Editing relationships to enforce referential integrity.

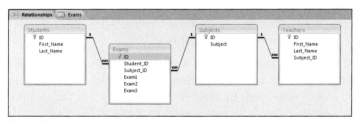

Figure 9-4: The paths between the tables show you the relationship type.

Designing the Database

The following sections show you how to create a project based on the material earlier in this chapter. You can create and design a grade-book database for a small high school. Although this example is a very real-world project, I'm purposely limiting the scope in the example to avoid confusing you with too much unnecessary data. You can discover plenty about normalization and referential integrity with this simple project.

The problem

You have to create a grade-book database for your school that can serve as the school's student information database. This database will be used to produce transcripts, create report cards, and place SharePoint status reports online. The database, at a minimum, should contain

- Student information
- Teacher information
- Subjects
- Grades

You just create the database in the exercise in the following sections. If you wanted, you could also include forms and reports, which would expand this project into a very lengthy undertaking. (Chapters 6, 7 and 10 cover forms and reports.)

The solution

Before opening Access and creating a database, tables, and relationships, analyze this problem on paper. I go through this exact process when I'm designing a new database. I always start by writing down on paper the information I need to enter into the database.

I've already separated out the information I think should go into this database. Table 9-2 puts that information into a familiar form with some sample data.

Table 9-2　　　　**Sample Grade-Book Database Data**

Student	Teacher	Subject	Exam1	Exam2	Exam3	Current Grade
Ann Davis	G. Smith	Art	79	82	72	78
Paul Jones	L. Lee	Chemistry	88	80	82	83

You could create a new database at this point and name it Grades; create one table and name it Gradebook; create columns for such tables as Student, Teacher, and Subject; and begin entering data into the Gradebook table. You could even perform queries on Gradebook to get all of Paul Jones's grades into a single report and place that report online. You could also do this same grade book and report in a spreadsheet program. The beauty of a database is its rich reporting and multi-user capability. Because this example database is relatively simple, you may be tempted to use a spreadsheet. But think of the bigger, more realistic picture — you can build a database that will maintain all of the grades for all of the current students.

You have many questions to answer when taking on a project such as this example for real. Fortunately, all of the questions have the same answer: a database. Just because your task here is to simply account for a small portion of data doesn't mean that you shouldn't use a well-designed scalable database solution.

From the description of the problem (and my ongoing rant that you should use a database with multiple tables), you may decide that you should begin by creating four tables. Though you should really begin by writing down your needs for such a database, my best advice is to start by creating four tables — one for each kind of data (Students, Teachers, Subjects, and Grades).

Because this is a lengthier example than any other in this book, I'll break it up into parts. And remember that the number of columns in this example is far more limited than an actual database.

First steps

1. **Create a new database named Chapter9.**

2. **Create four new tables named Students, Teachers, Subjects, and Grades.**

The Grades table will hold the bulk of the information for the database. The other tables will be fairly static. Grades will be a linking table, as well. Now you need to decide on the columns for the tables and the limits of the data they'll contain.

Column as you see 'em

Follow these steps to create columns for your tables:

1. **Open the Students table and add the following columns:** First_Name **and** Last_Name.

2. **Open the Teachers table and add the following columns:** First_Name, Last_Name, **and** Subject_ID.

3. **Open the Grades table and add the following columns:** Student_ID, Subject_ID, Exam1, Exam2, **and** Exam3.

Be sure to change the data type of the Student_ID, Subject_ID, and Exam fields (columns) to Number. If you don't, you can't create a relationship or perform calculations by using those fields. You can only create relationships between matching data types.

4. **Open the Subjects table and add a** Subject **field.**

5. **Create relationships between the Primary and Foreign Keys for each table. Enforce referential integrity and use Cascade Update and Delete for each relationship.**

When you finish, your relationship diagram should look like Figure 9-5.

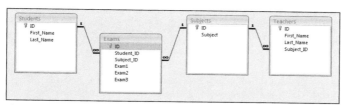

Figure 9-5: You can see the table relationships in your Chapter 9 database.

Testing

At this point, you have a very well-designed database. It's 3NF compliant (check it against the definitions in the section "Third Normal Form," earlier in this chapter). Does the database sufficiently solve the problem? You must enter some data and run some queries to know for sure. Follow these steps:

1. **Enter the data from Table 9-3, Table 9-4, Table 9-5, and Table 9-6 into the corresponding database tables.**

Table 9-3   Students Table

First_Name	Last_Name
Ann	Davis
Paul	Jones

Table 9-4   **Subjects Table**

Subjects
Algebra
Geometry
Composition
Literature
History
Geography
Political Science
Art
Drama
Music
Physical Education
Biology
Chemistry
Physics

Table 9-5   **Teachers Table**

First_Name	Last_Name	Subject_ID
Gene	Smith	8
Leslie	Lee	13

Table 9-6   **Grades Table**

Student_ID	Subject_ID	Exam1	Exam2	Exam3
1	8	79	82	72
2	13	88	80	82

2. Save and Close the tables.

3. Create a new query in Design View.

4. Add all four tables to the Query Builder.

5. Select the fields (Student First_Name, Student Last_Name, Subject, Exam1, Exam2, and Exam3).

6. Run the query.

The results should look like Table 9-7.

Table 9-7   Query Results

First_Name	Last_Name	Subject	Exam1	Exam2	Exam3
Ann	Davis	Art	79	82	72
Paul	Jones	Chemistry	88	80	82

7. Add the following calculation to the query to calculate Current Grade:

```
Current Grade: Round(((([Exam1]+[Exam2]+[Exam3])/3))
```

8. Run the query.

For this example, the Current Grades should be 78 and 83, respectively.

This database can support queries and calculations.

For more practice, try expanding this database on your own to include class schedules and grade level (Freshman, Sophomore, Junior, and Senior; or 9, 10, 11, and 12).

denormalization: The process of recombining tables and data because you normalized to a higher degree than you needed to.

linking (junction) table: A table that connects two other tables to eliminate many-to-many relationships between the original two tables. They're connected by using PK/FK pairs.

continued

 **continued**

normal form: Criteria for changing the structure of a database so that the tables are relations and data defects are minimized.

normalization: The process of rearranging data and splitting tables into ones that contain specific data, primary keys, unique column names, and no redundant data.

referential integrity: Connecting and enabling tables in such a way as to prevent orphaned records from remaining in a database after their parent records have been deleted.

Last Stop

Practice Exam

1. True or false (explain why): Normalization is a lengthy and unnecessary process.

_____

_____

_____

2. True or false (explain why): Databases should be normalized to the highest possible degree.

_____

_____

_____

3. Generally speaking, which normal form is sufficient for most database implementations?

A) 0NF

B) 1NF

C) 2NF

D) 3NF

4. What's the purpose of enforcing referential integrity?

A) To speed up processing of generalized data

B) To prevent orphaned records in the database

C) To prevent over-normalization of a database

D) To maintain a higher level of normality

5. **What's a benefit of normalization?**

A) Speed

B) Accuracy

C) Longevity

D) Compatibility

6. **What component of a table do you need to have before attempting to normalize a database to the First Normal Form (1NF)?**

A) A primary key

B) A secondary key

C) A normal key

D) A denormalized key

7. **How can you resolve a many-to-many relationship?**

A) Add more records.

B) Create another many-to-many relationship.

C) Create a junction table.

D) Remove a junction table.

8. **True or false (explain why): All relations are tables.**

_____

_____

_____

9. **Which of the following relationship types is the most common?**

A) 1:1

B) 1:∞

C) ∞:∞

D) 1:0

10. **Which of the following is not a true normal form?**

A) 0NF

B) 1NF

C) 2NF

D) 3NF

Advanced Form Creation and Use

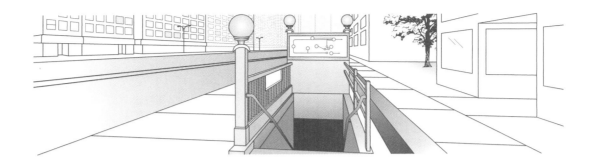

 # Enter the Station

Questions

1. How do you add Tool Tips to forms?

2. Can you open a form from another form?

3. How do you create a list from a query?

4. How do you prevent users from adding choices to a list?

5. How do you allow users to add a choice to a list?

6. Can you put information or messages into the status bar?

7. Can you remove the scroll bars from a text box?

Express Line

If you are familiar with advanced form elements, then skip ahead to Chapter 11.

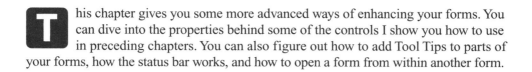

This chapter gives you some more advanced ways of enhancing your forms. You can dive into the properties behind some of the controls I show you how to use in preceding chapters. You can also figure out how to add Tool Tips to parts of your forms, how the status bar works, and how to open a form from within another form.

Advanced Form Construction

Entering data into tables that have complex relationships can be difficult. You must pay attention to the order in which you enter data so all your fields have the correct references. Creating advanced forms to display and enter data properly is sometimes very frustrating because the table relationships make the database compliant with the Relational Data Model.

After you create the forms and can correctly enter data into the various tables, your database will be efficient and easier to use. This chapter includes several examples of advanced form controls.

Don't be put off by the term *advanced*. To me, it means working with aspects of form controls that are more complex than text fields. You can figure out advanced form controls through a mixture of wizards and manual editing in this chapter.

For a deeper look at the power of forms and reports, there are several books available that just cover forms and reports. The examples in this chapter use the Chapter9 database that you can create in Chapter 9. This database works well for the examples in this chapter because it has four tables that contain data — and relationships between tables. You can either download a copy of the Chapter 10 database from this book's Web site or rename the Chapter9 database by following these steps:

1. **Open the Chapter9 database.**

2. **Click the Microsoft Office icon, select Save As, and select Access 2007 Database.**

3. **Name the database** Chapter10 **and click Save.**

Form Wizardry

For the examples in this section, you use the Form Wizard. The Form Wizard is extremely valuable for creating advanced forms because it lets you select fields from multiple tables or queries. The controls, bindings, and expressions are created for you. I'm very impressed with the Form Wizard in Access 2007 because it seems to have some intelligence built in to it.

Occasionally you must still fix a form control manually because of complex table relationships, but the wizard is generally an effective tool. Always begin with the

Form Wizard and then make any changes manually, instead of diving into a blank form in Design View.

Creating a new student form

You can create a new student form relatively simply because the only information you need is first and last names. Increasing the level of difficulty, you also want the ability to add classes for the student, and each class has a teacher associated with it. What started as a simple form quickly becomes a form that must reference three different tables: Students, Subjects, and Teachers. The best way to approach a problem with this level of complexity is to break it down into smaller parts. To create the Student Information Form, follow these steps:

1. **Open the Chapter10 database.**
2. **Click the Students table in the left navigation pane to select it.**
3. **Click the Create tab, then click Form.**

   The Student Information Form is created for you.
4. **Shrink the name fields and delete the ID column and subform from the form so only the name fields remain.**

   Access adds the subform (a form within a form) to display data from related tables.
5. **Switch to Design View and add a button control to the form. Make the Button action** Record Operation, Add New Record.
6. **Save and close the form.**

   Figure 10-1 shows my Student Information Form.

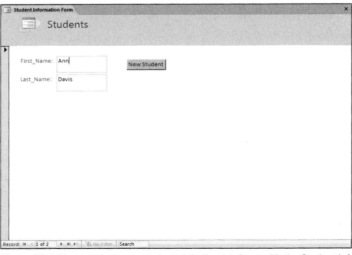

Figure 10-1: You can enter new students into the database with the Student Information Form.

Creating a new teacher form

To create a new teacher form (Teacher Information Form) in Database10, follow these steps:

1. **Click the Teachers table to select it.**

2. **Click the Create tab, then click Form.**

    The Teacher Information Form is created for you.

3. **Delete the ID and Subject_ID fields from the form.**

    You will replace the Subject_ID field with a Subject list.

4. **Switch to Design View and shrink the name fields to so they're not too wide for the data.**

5. **Grab the footer pane and move it down.**

    This step gives you more room in the Detail part of the form.

6. **From the Form Design Tools area above the form, select Combo Box.**

7. **Draw a rectangle for the combo box below the Last Name field.**

    The Combo Box Wizard is launched and prompts you to make a selection for a record source.

8. **Select *I want the combo box to look up values in a table or query* and click Next.**

9. **Select the Subject table and click Next.**

10. **Select the Subject field, send it into the right pane (Selected Fields), and click Next.**

11. **Select Subject and Ascending for sorting. Click Next.**

    Hide key column should be checked.

12. **Click Next.**

13. **Select *Store that value in this field*, select Subject_ID from the list of fields, and click Next.**

14. **Name the control Subject_List and click Finish.**

15. **Create a button that allows you to create a new teacher record.**

16. **Save the form as Teacher Information Form.**

Your Teacher Information Form is now ready to use. You can add a new teacher to the list by following these steps:

1. **Switch to Form View.**

2. **Click the New Teacher button (or whatever you named it).**

    You're presented with a blank record.

3. **Enter the information in Table 10-1 for the new teacher.**

Table 10-1   Sample Teacher Record

First Name	Last Name	Subject
Stacy	Blair	History

4. Click Add Teacher.

5. Open the Teachers table to see that your record has been added with the correct Subject ID.

You chose Subject from the combo box, but you recorded the Subject ID into the Teachers table.

6. Close the Teachers table and add two more records, as listed in Table 10-2, by following Steps 1 through 4 for each record.

Table 10-2   Sample Teacher Records

First Name	Last Name	Subject
Leo	Dumbrowsky	Music
Alva	Jarvitz	Physics

7. Open the Teachers table to view your entries.

Figure 10-2 shows my Teacher Information Form.

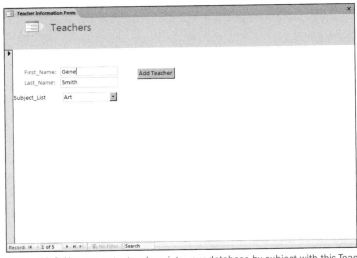

Figure 10-2: You can enter teachers into your database by subject with this Teacher Information Form.

Putting the Data Together in a Form

After you complete the exercises in the preceding sections, you now need to create a form in which you can assign classes to students. To create the form is relatively easy and I give you a somewhat unorthodox approach that's a quick and simple way of doing it.

Create a form that assigns classes to students by following these steps:

1. **Click the Exams table in the left pane to select it.**

2. **Click the Create tab, then click Form.**

   The form is created for you.

3. **Switch to Design View and remove all the fields from the form.**

   This step gives you a blank form that's already formatted with a header, detail section, and footer. This method creates a blank form with some basic attributes that you need without going through all the steps to create one from scratch.

4. **Create a combo box by selecting Combo Box from the Controls group.**

   The Combo Box Wizard is launched and prompts you to make a selection for a record source.

5. **Select *I want the combo box to look up values in a table or query* and click Next.**

6. **Select the Students table and click Next.**

7. **Select Last_Name and First_Name, and then click Next.**

   You select the name fields for this combo box in reverse order because you see only the first column (last name) in the combo box when it's closed.

8. **Select Last_Name, select Ascending, and then click Next.**

9. **Click Next.**

10. **Select *Store that value in this field,* select Student_ID from the list of fields, and click Next.**

11. **Use Student: for the label and click Finish.**

   The ID in the combo box is Student_ID. The data is stored in the Student_ID — the source of the data is shown in the combo box on the form.

12. **Switch to Form View and check the behavior of the list by using the Combo Box drop-down list.**

Watch Your Step

When you open a form, the current record appears in a combo box that is vulnerable to inadvertent changes. In Chapter 11, you can find out how to avoid this problem. For now, use a New Record button to remove the possibility of changing the default record.

13. Switch back to Design View.

14. Create a combo box below the Student combo box.

This combo box is for the Subject list.

15. Select *I want the combo box to look up values in a table or query* and click Next.

16. Select the Subjects table and click Next.

17. Select Subject and click Next.

18. Select Subject, Ascending, and click Next.

19. Click Next.

20. Select *Store that value in this field,* select Subject_ID from the list, and click Next.

21. Use Subject: for the Label and click Finish.

22. Switch to Form View and use the combo boxes.

23. Add a New Record button to your form and name it Assign Subject.

24. Save the form as Assign Subjects Form.

Using the Assign Subjects Form to assign subjects to a student

To use the Assign Subjects form, follow these steps:

1. Open the Assign Subjects Form in Form View.

2. Click the Assign Subject button to go to a new record.

3. Use the Student combo box to select Ann Davis.

4. Use the Subject combo box to select Music from the list.

5. Click the Assign Subject button to go to a new record.

6. Open the Exams table to see that a new entry for Ann Davis appears.

Your Exams table should look like the entries in Table 10-3.

Table 10-3   Sample Exams Table

ID	Student_ID	Subject_ID	Exam1	Exam2	Exam3
1	1	8	79	82	72
2	2	13	88	80	82
3	1	10			

Here `Student_ID 1` is `Ann Davis`, and `Subject_ID 10` is `Music`. There are no exam entries for Music because Ann has just been assigned to this class.

Figure 10-3 shows my Assign Subjects Form.

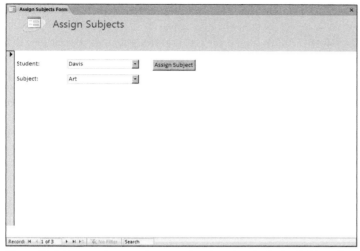

Figure 10-3: I can assign a student to a class by using the Assign Subjects Form.

Enter Grades by using the Gradebook form

You can design a form that lets you select a student and a subject, and then enter grades for that student in that subject. The form design is a little complicated, but the Form Wizard takes care of the complexity for you. Follow these steps to create the Gradebook form:

1. **Click the Create tab, select More Forms, then select Form Wizard.**

   The Form Wizard launches.

2. Select the Students table and send Last_Name and First_Name to the Selected Fields pane.

3. **Select the Subjects table and send the Subject field to the Selected Fields pane.**

4. **Select the Exams table and send Exam1, Exam2, and Exam3 to the Selected Fields pane. Click Next.**

5. **Accept the defaults (sorting by Students and *Form with subforms*). Click Next.**

6. **Select Datasheet and click Next.**

7. Click Next.

8. Name the form Gradebook **and the subform** Gradebook subform; **click Finish.**

The form is created and opens in Layout View.

9. Change the sizes of the name fields and the subform to the appropriate proportions.

The name fields have the annoying scroll-bar feature automatically added to them. The scroll bars have no effect, and you should remove them.

To remove the scroll-bar feature from fields, follow these steps:

1. Switch to Design View.

2. Select a field (for example, Last_Name), right-click the field, and click Properties to open the Properties Sheet.

About halfway down in the list, you see Scroll Bars. The selection is set to Vertical.

3. Change Vertical to None.

4. Repeat Steps 2 and 3 for each field (for example, First_Name).

5. Add the navigational elements (buttons) to the form for First, Previous, Next, and Last Records.

You don't need to add a New Record button. The subform allows adding scores.

Figure 10-4 shows my Gradebook form.

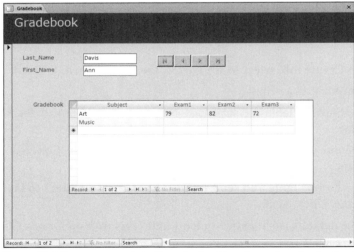

Figure 10-4: You can see a student's grades in all her classes by using the Gradebook form.

Form Enhancement and the User Experience

The users of your database are your customers, and they're the consumers of your services. You must make sure that their satisfaction is one of the top priorities when you're creating database applications.

The form enhancements in the following sections run the gamut from "absolutely required for data integrity" to "those nice-to-haves" to the somewhat esoteric. I prefer to give the user the richest experience I can; the following sections show you how to do the same.

Scrolling through data

Access automatically adds scroll bars to text boxes. This feature can be really helpful, or it can be a big annoyance (as it is in the preceding section). For text that stretches beyond two lines, scroll bars are a great enhancement. If you have only one line of text, those scroll bars can confuse the person entering data. When it comes to scroll bars, use them only if you need them — otherwise, remove them. Scroll bars do have one definite advantage — they can save you screen space. Make the text box large enough to show the user that it has multiple lines of text but small enough to conserve screen space. Even at a screen resolution of 1024×768, the screen gets quickly crowded with too many options, fields, navigational features, and other bits of information.

An example of a text box that needs scroll bars is a Comments field in which someone can enter comments or noteworthy information about a subject, such as a student, product, or service. A Description field for a course is another good example in which you'd use a text box with scroll bars.

To implement a Comments field for teachers to use, follow these steps:

1. **Create a new table and enter** Student_ID, Teacher_ID, **and** Comments.
2. **Change the data type to** Number **for Student_ID and Teacher_ID, and change the data type to** Memo **for the Comments field.**
3. **Save the table as** Comments.
4. **Create an automatic form by selecting the Comments table and clicking Form.**
5. **Switch to Design View, remove all but the Comments field; then make the Comments field large enough to hold several lines of text and wide enough for a sentence length of about eight words.**
6. **Create a combo box on the form.**
7. **Select** *I want the combo box to look up values in a table or query* **and click Next.**
8. **Select the Students table and click Next.**

9. Select Last_Name, First_Name, send them to Selected Fields, and click Next.

10. Select Last_Name, select Ascending, and then click Next.

11. Select *Store that value in this field,* select Student_ID from the list, and click Next.

12. Name the combo box Student and click Finish.

13. Go through the same procedure for a Subjects list combo box, store the value in the Subject_ID field, and name the combo box Subject.

14. Switch to Form View and make an entry for each student.

    Now the Comments field has scroll bars.

15. Save the form with a name (Teacher Comments, for example).

Automating by using buttons

Chapter 6 shows that you can use buttons to navigate records. Buttons can perform many operations and automate some tasks for you. Opening a form is one of these operations. It's often convenient to have quick access to one form while you use another form. You can use macros to perform this task (which I talk about in Chapter 11), but for this example, you use a wizard that creates the form-opening macro for you. Follow these steps:

1. Open the Gradebook form in Design View.

2. Create a button on the form.

    The Command Button Wizard opens.

3. In the Command Button Wizard, select Form Operations, then select Open a Form. Click Next.

4. Select the Teacher Comments form and click Next.

5. Select *Open the form and show all the records,* and then click Next.

6. Select Text, enter Add Comments into the text field, and then click Next.

7. Name the button Comments and click Finish.

8. Switch to Form View and click the Add Comments button.

    The Teacher Comments form opens and displays the first record.

Try adding a New Record button on the Teacher Comments form on your own.

Opening a form by context

The ability to edit information that's related to your location on the form is a new feature of Access 2007. On the Teacher Comments form, for example, say you're about to comment on a student, but you realize that you haven't entered the student into the database yet. You can hunt through the list of forms, find the one you need, and edit it — or you can use a context-based edit to enter the information.

You should include this very useful feature where you think it's appropriate. You can use this feature only in a combo box or list box. To open a form to edit values in a drop-down list, follow these steps:

1. **Open the Teacher Comments form in Design View.**
2. **Select the Student combo box, right-click the combo box, and select Properties.**
3. **Click the Data tab, click into the List Items Edit Form field, and select Student Information Form from the list.**
4. **Switch to Form View.**
5. **Click the Student combo box to see the list of students.**

   You also see an Edit icon below the list.

6. **Click the Edit icon to open the Student Information Form.**

Limiting your users (or not)

If you have a list of choices for a particular item on a form, you can limit your users to that list of choices. You may want to limit the list of choices or possible responses to

- Remove choice confusion.
- Maintain data integrity.
- Allow direct comparisons of responses.

You may want users to give their own responses to questions if their responses aren't represented on your list. The list can act as a guide for their answers, but no choice on the list may match exactly to their circumstances. Be aware of the following limitations before you allow users to insert their own responses:

- Only combo boxes are supported.
- The contents of the combo box must be based on a query.
- Users can accidentally add incorrect responses to the list.

Information Kiosk

If you need to allow users to enter their own responses into a database, include an Other choice in the combo box and add a text box below the combo box in which the user can write his response to the question.

The following example illustrates how to create and use an editable list in a combo box:

1. **Create a query that selects the list of subjects from the Subjects table.**
2. **Create a blank form by clicking the Create tab and selecting Blank Form.**
3. **Close the Field List window.**
4. **Switch to Design View.**
5. **Create a combo box on your blank form.**
6. **Select** *I want the combo box to look up values in a table or query* **and click Next.**
7. **Select Queries, select the query created in Step 1, and click Next.**
8. **Send Subject to the Selected Fields column and click Next.**
9. **Select Subject, then Ascending, and click Next.**
10. **Click Next.**
11. **Select** *Store that value in this field:,* **select Subject, and click Next.**
12. **Label the combo box (for example,** Subject:**) and click Finish.**
13. **Switch to Form View.**
14. **Type a subject (for example, Graphic Design) into the Subject field and press the Enter key.**
15. **Click the Combo Box drop-down list.**

    Look at the list. You've overwritten one of your entries. Can you figure out which one? The correct way to add a new entry is to navigate to a new record by using the navigation bar at the bottom of the form.

16. **Click the New Record button at the bottom of the form to go to a new record.**
17. **Type a subject (for example,** Calculus**) into the field and press Enter.**

Your new entry doesn't immediately show up in the list. Press the F5 key to perform an update and then look at the list again.

In Chapter 11, you can find out how to avoid the problem of someone overwriting a list choice by opening a form without a record already showing in it. You can design the form so the form initially opens to a new record.

You can use some add-ons to further professionalize a form. You should add some of these features to every form you create, but other special features are optional. It's up to you and your users to decide which optional ones you add.

Adding Tool Tips to a form

Generally, little pop-up descriptions that you see when you place your mouse pointer over an on-screen item are called Tool Tips, but in Access, they're called ControlTip Text. These Tool Tips are similar to *context-sensitive help,* in which help is provided to correspond to your mouse's location on a form. Whatever they're called, they can really help you save space on a crowded form by supplying contextual instructions to the user that appear only when needed. The user doesn't have to refer to a manual, call for help, or try to guess at the meaning of a field or button.

You should always add Tool Tips to all buttons, fields, and lists that you place on a form. Follow these steps to create custom Tool Tips:

1. **Open the form (for example, Gradebook) in Form View.**
2. **Place your mouse cursor over any navigation button you created, and the Tool Tip text pops up, explaining the button's use.**

   The Tool Tip text for these button is automatically created.

   Figure 10-5 shows Tool Tip text for the Next Record button.

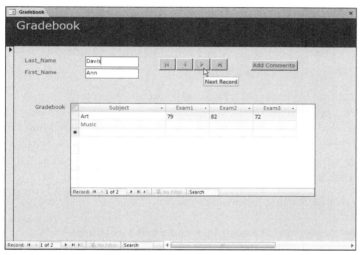

Figure 10-5: The Tool Tip text explains that this button takes you to the next record.

3. **Switch to Design View.**
4. **Select the Add Comments button, right-click the button, and click Properties.**
5. **Click the Other tab on the Property Sheet.**
6. **Click the ControlTip Text field and enter a description (for example, Open the Teacher Comments Form) into it.**
7. **Switch to Form View and place your mouse cursor over the button to see your handiwork in action.**

I suggest that you add Tool Tips for every field on a form. As a courtesy, also add Tool Tips to fields that the user can't edit. Figure 10-6 shows a helpful Tool Tip.

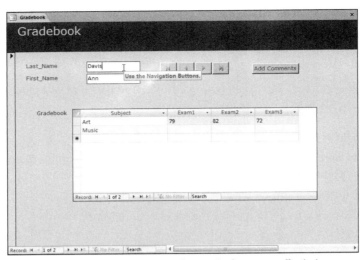

Figure 10-6: This Tool Tip helps the reader use the form more effectively.

Supplying a default entry

Instead of giving the user just a blank space in a field, you can supply a prompt as a guide. For instance, if you want the user to enter only last names into a field, you can supply a few words to let the user know that. A prompt is often kinder than a Tool Tip that says, "Enter a Last Name." The default entry prompt can serve as a gentle guide for the user without insulting her intelligence. The prompt applies just enough pressure to get the data you want.

To supply a default entry, follow these steps:

1. **Open the form (for example, Gradebook) in Design View.**

2. **Select the field (for example, Last Name), right-click the field, and click Properties.**

3. **Click Data on the Property Sheet.**

4. **Type the default value (for example,** Last Name**) into the Default Value field.**

   Access surrounds your entry with quotation marks.

5. **Switch to Form View and click New Record on the navigation bar at the bottom of the form.**

In the preceding example, your Last Name prompt now appears in the Last Name field. Compare the default value to the blank First Name field. Does the default value give you more of a sense of the type of data that's expected for that field?

Checking your status

Supplying information in the status bar is a bit esoteric, in my opinion. I'm sure some people out there swear by it, but I've never found it particularly necessary. If you want to give the user some extra bit of information, though, the status bar may be exactly what you're searching for.

The *status bar* is the strip of space along the bottom of the Access screen that provides extra information. You can view it most easily when you have Access maximized on your screen. The status bar text that you enter shows up in the bottom-left corner of the program. Follow these steps to add status bar text:

1. **Open the form (for example, Gradebook) in Design View.**
2. **Select the field (for example, Last Name), right-click the field, and click Properties.**
3. **Click the Other tab on the Property Sheet.**
4. **Locate the Status Bar Text field and type a helpful description of the data you want in the field into it (for example,** Last Names Only Please**).**
5. **Switch to Form View.**
6. **Select the field that you select in Step 2 again and look at the bottom-left corner of your screen.**

   For this example, you should see `Last Names Only Please` in the status bar.

context/context-based/context-sensitive: Said of a helpful hint or bit of information that appears where the cursor is on a form, report, Web page, or other document.

status bar: The area of a program, typically on the bottom strip, that displays helpful information about a field that requires an entry or other manipulation.

Tool Tip: A pop-up bit of text-based information that can assist the user of a form, report, Web page, or other document. In Access, it's called ControlTip Text.

Last Stop

Practice Exam

1. True or false (Explain why): Maintaining data integrity is a good reason to limit a user's possible responses to a read-only list of choices.

_____

_____

_____

2. You should remove scroll bars from text boxes because:

A) Users may be confused by them.

B) They aren't necessary.

C) They take up too much space.

D) Both A and B.

3. Status-bar messages are useful if:

A) You need to save space on a form.

B) You think you should use them because they exist.

C) You need to supply some bit of extra information to the user.

D) You want to supply a default entry.

4. What should you always supply for every field, button, or other control on a form?

A) A status-bar message

B) A Limit to List property

C) A navigation button

D) ControlTip Text

5. Which data type would you use for user feedback on a form?

A) Comment

B) Memo

C) Text

D) Field

6. Why would you provide a default entry for a field?

A) It makes the form easier to navigate.

B) It's easy to do.

C) Access requires it.

D) It provides a prompt for the user.

7. Tool Tips are also called:

A) Context-sensitive help

B) ControlTip Text

C) Control Advice

D) Default Entries

8. Buttons can perform which of the following?

A) Navigating a record

B) Opening a form

C) Automating some tasks

D) All of the above

9. Which property lets you open a form from another form by using a combo box?

A) Limit to List

B) Open Form

C) List Items Edit Form

D) Status Bar Text

10. When you open a saved form by using the left navigation pane in Access, which view are you in?

A) Form View

B) Layout View

C) Design View

D) Print Preview

Automating Access with Macros

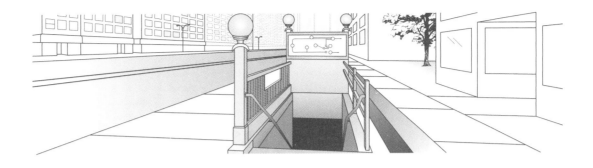

 # Enter the Station

Questions

1. Why should I use macros?

2. How do I create a Switchboard?

3. Can I run external applications and programs from within Access?

4. What's the best type of macro to use?

5. What's the difference between embedded and stand-alone macros?

6. How do I automatically open a form in Access?

Express Line

If you already know how to use macros, then skip ahead to Chapter 12.

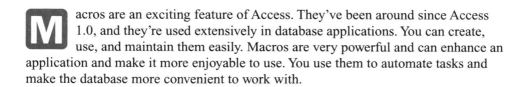

Macros are an exciting feature of Access. They've been around since Access 1.0, and they're used extensively in database applications. You can create, use, and maintain them easily. Macros are very powerful and can enhance an application and make it more enjoyable to use. You use them to automate tasks and make the database more convenient to work with.

Adding Macros to Your Toolkit

A *macro* is a simple chunk of programming language that's used to automate tasks inside Access. Macros are used to perform actions. They can open or close forms, reports, queries, and tables. You can maximize and minimize windows, display messages, run other macros, and produce filtered reports. You can have a macro close your database or even have one close Access for you. Although you can use macros in many ways, this chapter simply gives you an introduction to the most common macro types and their application to real-life situations.

I like macros. They're great timesavers — and they give you convenient ways of doing some repetitive tasks. I think the biggest advantage is that you don't have to know how to program in a programming language to use macros. That gives macros a very broad appeal. Their biggest drawback is that you may not be able to transfer them from one version of Access to another. Today, you're using macros in Access 2007, but when you want to upgrade to Access 2010 (or whatever the next version will be named), your macros may not work in the new version — you may have to rewrite most, or all, of them.

Information Kiosk

Macros execute in a classic *top-down* fashion, which means that the first action in the list executes first, and each subsequent action executes sequentially down the list until the last action is executed.

The following lists give the advantages and disadvantages of using macros in Access. The decision whether to use macros is really up to you, but I think they're an invaluable asset that is so easy to use and integrate into your Access-based applications.

Advantages:

- They have a real programming language behind them: Visual Basic for Applications (VBA).
- You don't have to know VBA to use macros.
- Wizards exist to help you create some macros.
- They're easy to build and use.

Disadvantages:

- Macros may not translate correctly from one version of Access to another.
- They're sometimes difficult to troubleshoot.
- They're relatively limited in what they can do, as compared to Visual Basic *modules* (programs written in Visual Basic for Applications).

Anatomy of a Macro

A macro has these few key components:

- **Action:** The true purpose of the macro, this component opens a form.
- **Arguments:** The parameters of the action; for example, the name of the form to open.

  Every macro must have an action and an argument.

- **Condition:** An optional filter or limitation; for example, [Exam1] < 70.
- **Comment:** An optional note on what action the macro performs.

  It's good practice to include comments for any program. It helps future administrators and users figure out the purpose of a program. You don't need to make your comments lengthy or elaborate. They can be as simple as, "This macro opens the Gradebook form."

- **Name:** Refers to the name of a macro in a macro group.

Optionally, a macro can have Conditions and Comments.

Types of Macros

You can create two types of macros:

- An *embedded macro* is part of a form or report, often as a command button that performs some action.

  You create an embedded macro in Chapter 10 when you create the Add Comments button on the Gradebook form.

A *stand-alone macro* defines an action, or actions, and isn't part of a form, report, or control. It's listed in the left navigation pane as an independent database object. It can be *called* (executed) from a form, report, or control. (Embedded macros aren't independent database objects and therefore don't show up in the navigation pane.)

Building the Classic Switchboard

Since the early days of Access, a Switchboard has been almost an essential part of any application. If you built an Access-based application, you automatically built a Switchboard to use with it. A *Switchboard,* for those of you who grew up in the Internet Age, is basically an index page which you use to navigate to all of your other forms and reports. It's a form that usually contains only buttons that open your various forms and reports. It also usually has an Exit or Quit button that closes Access or, at least, your current database. The Switchboard is typically set up to open when you open the database so you only have to choose the form, task, or action that you want from the Switchboard list.

All the steps in this chapter are based on a copy of the Chapter10 example database, renamed as Chapter11.

If you created the Chapter10 database, open it and save it as **Chapter11**.

If you didn't create the Chapter10 database, you can download the Chapter11 database from this book's Web site.

You can build your Switchboard manually or by using a wizard. Because I prefer to use the tools that Access provides, I use the Switchboard Manager under Database Tools. To create a Switchboard using the Switchboard Manager, follow these steps:

1. **Open the database (for example, Chapter11).**
2. **Click the Database Tools and locate the Switchboard Manager button in the Database Tools group.**
3. **Click the Switchboard Manager button to open the Switchboard Manager.**

   You receive a message that tells you there's no valid Switchboard in the database and prompts you to create one.
4. **Click Yes to create the Switchboard.**

   A Switchboard Manager Wizard appears, as does a Switchboard form and a Switchboard Items table.

   Figure 11-1 shows the main Switchboard Manager dialog.

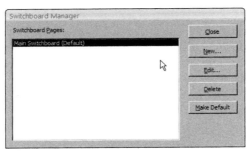

Figure 11-1: You can create a new Switchboard by using the Switchboard Manager Wizard.

The Switchboard is created and ready to edit. You can close the Manager at any point and come back to it later by repeating Steps 2 and 3.

Creating Switchboard entries

Switchboard entries are command buttons that perform some action by using macros. Generally, you use Switchboard entries to open forms or reports.

If you're following this chapter's example, you have plenty of forms to place on the Switchboard in this database. Follow these steps for each form in the database (for example, Gradebook, Teacher Comments, and Student Information Form):

1. Open the Switchboard Manager.

2. Click Edit on the Switchboard Manager.

Watch Your Step

This initial set of steps doesn't work the way you may expect. Your first response might be to click New on the first page of the Switchboard Manager, but that just creates another form (a Switchboard page). If you compare the Switchboard to the `index.html` page of a Web site, then a new Switchboard page is the same as another HTML file separate from the `index.html`. By editing the Main Switchboard page, you're placing command buttons on that page that can navigate to your forms and reports. These command buttons are equivalent to hyperlinks to other HTML pages on a Web site.

You can change the default name (`Main Switchboard`) of the Main Switchboard on this page.

3. Click New.

4. **Enter the name of this entry into the Text field (for example, enter** Gradebook).

5. **Click the Command drop-down list and select Open Form in Edit Mode.**

You could use Add mode in this step, but some people feel more comfortable in Edit mode when a table already has data. Add mode is a bit hard to get used to because it looks like it's the first record in the table each time it's opened. You might prefer Add mode when you want users to add records without being able to view old records in the table. For example, if you want the user simply to enter data without regard for any other records, then you'd use a form in Add mode.

6. **In the Form drop-down list, select the form (for example, Gradebook) and click OK.**

7. **Click Close twice to close the Switchboard Manager.**

8. **Open the Switchboard form in the left navigation pane.**

Figure 11-2 shows the Switchboard you just created.

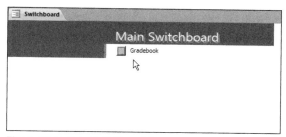

Figure 11-2: Main Switchboard Form.

Information Kiosk

A Switchboard is a form. You can switch to Design View and edit the form manually if you want. The preferred method is to use the Switchboard Manager, but you may want to edit such form elements as the form's layout, colors, and fonts. You can do that only from Layout or Design View.

9. **Try out your new Switchboard by clicking the appropriate button (for example, Gradebook).**

The selected form opens in Edit mode.

Figure 11-3 shows my Main Switchboard after adding all of the forms in the Chapter11 database.

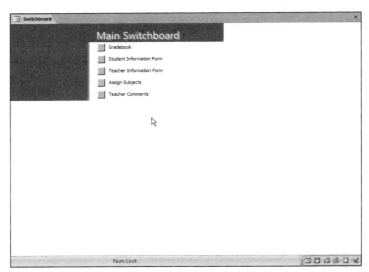

Figure 11-3: I've added all Chapter11 database forms to the Main Switchboard.

Adding an Exit button

You always want an Exit button on your Switchboard. This button closes your database without closing Access.

 Transfer

The section "Finishing touches," later in this chapter, shows how to close Access by using a button on the Switchboard.

 Step into the Real World

Rules exist for everything, including Switchboards. It's considered poor Switchboard design to put form and report buttons on the Main Switchboard. You should, instead, create a Form Switchboard, a Report Switchboard, an Administrative Switchboard, and Exit buttons. If you have only a few forms and reports (three or fewer of each), you can put them on the Main Switchboard if you want. Keep the Main Switchboard clean and professional-looking. You don't want too many choices on the Main Switchboard, forcing users to scroll down to get to them.

To create an Exit button (for example, a *Close the Gradebook* button), follow these steps:

1. **Open the Switchboard Manager.**
2. **Click Edit.**
3. **Create a new Switchboard item by clicking New.**
4. **Enter an action for the button (for example,** Close the Gradebook**) into the Text section.**
5. **Select Exit Application in the Command section and click OK.**
6. **Click Close to exit the Edit Switchboard Page dialog box.**
7. **Click Close to exit the Switchboard Manager.**
8. **Open the Switchboard form.**
9. **Click the button you just created (for example, Close the Gradebook).**

    Your application closes, but Access remains open.

Building Macros

In the following sections, you can find out how to create embedded and stand-alone macros. You already have some experience creating embedded macros, but this section gives you more practice building them.

Macros provide a quick and elegant solution to even the newest user of Access. Whether you embed them in a control or use a list of stand-alone macros, I hope you find them as indispensable as I do.

Macros, whether embedded or stand-alone, share some basic characteristics:

- They are named objects.
- They can have multiple steps.
- They can be interactive.

Embedded macros

New users seem to be most intimidated by embedded macros because these macros don't stand alone. They're somewhat hidden from view, and their purpose is also a bit obscured by design. The following sections remove the mystery that surrounds embedded macros.

Automated export

A very practical application of an embedded macro is to create a button that runs a query, then exports that query output to an Excel spreadsheet. Users commonly request that they have the ability to export data they see on the screen to a spreadsheet.

To automate an export (for example, the Teachers and Subjects tables in the Chapter11 database), follow these steps:

1. **Create a new query by using a table (for example, Teachers and Subjects).**
2. **Select the fields (for example, First_Name and Last_Name from the Teachers table, and Subject from the Subjects table).**
3. **Execute the query to be sure that it gives the results you want.**
4. **Save the query with a name (such as** Teacher_Subjects**).**
5. **Open the form (such as Teacher Information) in Design View.**
6. **Create a new button on the form.**
7. **When the Command Button Wizard launches, click Cancel.**
8. **Right-click the new button and click Properties to open the Property Sheet.**
9. **On the Format tab, change the Caption to a descriptive name, such as** Export to Excel**.**

    You may need to change the size of the button so it correctly displays the name.

10. **On the Event tab, click the Ellipsis (. . .) button in the OnClick field.**

    The Choose Builder dialog box appears.

11. **Select Macro Builder and click OK.**

    The Macro Builder opens.

12. **From the Action drop-down list, select RunCommand.**

    The Action Arguments pane changes to display the Command field.

13. **In the Command field, select ExportExcel.**

14. **In the Comments section, enter a description of what the macro does, such as** Exports Teachers and Subjects to an Excel file**.**

15. **Close the Macro Builder and click Yes on the prompt to update the control.**

16. **Switch to Form View and click the Export to Excel button.**

    A destination dialog box opens, prompting you for a location to which to save the new Excel file. You can change the location and file name as needed.

17. **Select** *Open the destination file after the export operation is complete* **and click OK.**

    The new file opens in Excel.

Watch Your Step

When your new Excel file opens, you may see incorrect column names, though the column names were correct in your query. The column names may change because the spreadsheet column names come from the Teacher Information Form labels. To change the column names in the exported Excel file, go back into the Access form in Design View, open the Property Sheet for the control, choose the Other tab, and change the Name property to the correct column name, then click the Export to Excel button again.

18. **Close the final export dialog box in Access.**

Information Kiosk

Embedded macros have a valuable extra feature: They're saved as part of the object they're bound to. If a form is copied to another database, the embedded macro travels with the form to its new location.

Creating an embedded macro help file

The embedded macro in this section provides extra information to a user. You can provide some online help to your users through the use of message boxes. A Message Box is a pop-up dialog box that you create and customize. This isn't the only way to provide help within your application, but it's a quick and easy method for you to provide quick instructions or information. Follow these steps to create a Message Box:

1. **Open the form (for example, Teacher Information Form) in Design View.**

2. **Create a button on the form and cancel the Command Button Wizard.**

3. **Open the Property Sheet for the new button.**

4. **Select the Event tab and click the Ellipsis (. . .) button in the OnClick field to launch the Builder Chooser.**

5. **Select Macro Builder and click OK.**

The Macro Builder opens for you.

6. **Under Action, select MsgBox from the drop-down list.**

Step into the Real World

As a matter of preference and good design, I move my Export to Excel button to the form footer and the Help button to the form header. Figure 11-4 shows my form. Arranged this way, the form appears less cluttered.

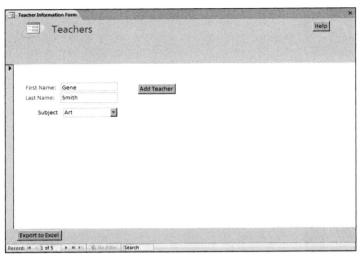

Figure 11-4: The embedded macros aren't in the way on this Teacher Information Form.

7. **Enter information into the Message field in the Action Arguments pane.**

   For example, you could enter, "This form is for entering new teacher information into the database. A subject should be assigned to each teacher. For further assistance, please contact the Database Administrator at extension 360."

   You can enter up to 255 characters into the Message field.

8. **Select No for Beep.**

   Selecting Yes causes the computer to beep when the message box appears.

9. **Select Information for Type of message box.**

10. **Enter the form name (for example, Teacher Information Form Help) for Title.**

11. **Close the Macro Builder and select Yes when prompted to save and update the property.**

12. **Select the Format tab and enter Help in the Caption field.**

13. **Switch to Form View and click the Help button.**

Stand-alone macros

You can create a stand-alone macro in two ways:

- Create a new macro by using the Create tab.

- Create a macro as an embedded macro, and then do a Save As and name the macro.

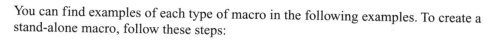

You can find examples of each type of macro in the following examples. To create a stand-alone macro, follow these steps:

1. **Click the Create tab and then click Macro to launch the Macro Builder.**
2. **Select OpenQuery from the Actions drop-down list.**
3. **In the Query drop-down list in the Action Arguments pane, select a query, such as Teacher_Subjects.**
4. **Select Print Preview from the View drop-down list.**
5. **Select Read Only from the Data Mode drop-down list.**
6. **Save the macro with a descriptive name, such as Teacher_Subjects_Macro.**

   After you save the macro, it appears in the left navigation pane.
7. **Execute the macro to see the results.**

The major difference between stand-alone macros and embedded macros is that you can execute the stand-alone macro independent of any form, report, or control. The x macro is an independent object in the database.

To use a stand-alone macro, follow these steps:

1. **Open a form (for example, the Teacher Information Form) in Design View.**
2. **Create a new button and cancel the Command Button Wizard.**
3. **Open the Property Sheet for the button and select the Event tab.**
4. **Click the drop-down list in the OnClick field and select the macro, such as Teacher_Subjects_Macro.**
5. **Click the Format tab and enter Print Preview into the Caption field.**
6. **Adjust the size of the Print Preview button so that you can read the whole caption.**
7. **Switch to Form View and try out your new button.**

Your macro has executed the query (for example, Teacher_Subjects) and presented the results in Print Preview mode.

To create a stand-alone macro similar to the way you created an embedded one, follow these steps:

1. **Open a form (for example, the Teacher Information Form) in Design View.**
2. **Create a button in the form footer and cancel the Command Button Wizard.**
3. **Open the Property Sheet for the button and click the Event tab.**

4. Click the Ellipsis (. . .) button and select Macro Builder.

5. Select RunCommand from the Action drop-down list.

6. Select ExportText from the Command drop-down list in the Action Arguments pane.

7. Enter a comment in the Comments field, such as Exports the Teacher Information to a text file.

8. Click the Save As button, name the Macro (for example, Teacher_Info_Text_Export), and click OK.

9. Click Close and click Yes on the save and update message.

10. Click the Format tab on the Property Sheet and enter a caption (for example, Export to Text) in the Caption field.

11. Adjust the size of the button to display the caption (for example, Export to Text).

12. Switch to Form View and click the button (for example, Export to Text).

13. Select *Open the destination file after the operation is complete,* and then click OK.

14. Click OK to accept the default Windows encoding on the Encode As dialog box.

    The text file opens in Notepad.

15. Close the final export dialog box and Notepad.

Your macro now appears in the left navigation pane. This means the macro is stand-alone, and you can use it over and over again in many applications on forms and reports.

Knowing whether to use an embedded or stand-alone macro

Many new users ask me, "Should I use an embedded or stand-alone macro — and why?" The answer is relatively simple — either one you want, generally speaking. There are situations in which you may prefer one type of macro over the other. For instance, if you want to create a macro for use on multiple forms or buttons, then certainly stand-alone is the type you want — especially if you want to perform an operation outside a form, report, or button. Stand-alone macros can be executed in the same way as any program, with only one limitation: They must be executed inside Access.

You should use embedded macros if you need to create a one-off document for some purpose. Embedded macros are also advantageous if you plan to copy a form or report to another database because they will be copied with the form or report.

Multi-step macros

A *multi-step macro* is a single macro that performs multiple actions. Each step is executed sequentially. Multi-step macros can be either embedded or stand-alone.

Creating a multi-step macro is easy. Just think of what you want the macro to do and create an action for it. For instance, the example in this section shows how to create a three-step macro that

- Beeps
- Warns you that you're about to export data
- Exports the data to a text file

To create a multi-step macro, follow these steps:

1. **Click the Create tab, then click the Macro button.**
2. **Select Beep from the Action drop-down list.**
3. **Select MsgBox from the Action drop-down list in the next row.**
4. **Enter the following (or equivalent message) into the Arguments field:** You are about to export data to an external file. This may be a violation of corporate security. Please check with your manager if you are unsure.
5. **Select No for the Beep.**
6. **Select Warning! for the Type.**
7. **Enter Export File Warning for the Title.**
8. **Select RunCommand from the Action drop-down list in the next row.**
9. **Select ExportText from the Command drop-down list in the Action Arguments pane.**
10. **Save the macro as** 3Step_Export.

At this point, you can't successfully run the macro because you don't have any data to export. The macro executes to the point of sending the message to the screen, but it errors out on the export. This macro must be associated with a form in order to work. The advantage of this macro is that you can place it on any form to export the data because it's not specific to any data set.

To prove the value of this generic macro, create buttons on two different forms that each use the same macro. Just follow these steps:

1. **Open the Student Information Form in Design View.**
2. **Create a button and use the Command Button Wizard.**

3. Select Miscellaneous in the Categories list and Run Macro under Actions.

4. Click Next.

5. Select a macro (for example, 3Step_Export) and click Next.

6. Select Text, enter Export as Text into the Text field, and click Next.

7. Name the button Export and click Finish.

8. Switch to Form View and click the Export to Text button.

   Your computer beeps and you see your warning message.

9. Click OK on the warning message.

10. Select *Open the destination file after the export operation is complete* and then click OK.

11. Click OK on the Encode As dialog box.

12. Click Close on the final export dialog box and view your file.

13. Close the Student Information Form.

Now, create the same button on the Teacher Information Form by following the instructions in this section. That button produces a text file export of Teacher Information data.

Macro Groups

A *macro group* is a related group of macros that are saved as a single file. Some database administrators have many macros that clutter the navigation pane. Macro groups alleviate the clutter and better organize your ever-growing list of macros.

Macro groups are different from multi-step macros because each macro in a macro group is actually a stand-alone macro, but a multi-step macro is a single macro that executes several actions in a stepwise fashion. Each macro in a macro group can be a multi-step macro.

When you choose a macro from a macro group, it's named with the group name followed by the macro name, like this:

GroupName.MacroName

 Watch Your Step

Good naming helps keep macro groups organized, as it does in any other database object. Give the group a descriptive name, such as Export_Macros, rather than a generic name, such as Macro_Group1. Each macro in the group needs to have a very descriptive name, as well. Use action names, such as Export_to_Text and Export_to_Excel, rather than cryptic names, such as ExText or Export1.

Although the macro group shows up in a list of available macros when you're using a macro within a control, you can't use the entire group. You must select an individual macro from the list.

Here's an example:

Group Name	Export_Macros
Macro Name	Export_Macros.Export_to_Text
Macro Name	Export_Macros.Export_to_Excel

In the examples in the following sections, you create this group and add the macros to it.

Creating a macro group

To create a macro group, follow these steps:

1. Click the Create tab, then click Macro to open the Macro Builder.

2. Click the Macro Names button.

The Macro Name column appears. You must name each individual macro that you create.

3. Enter Export_to_Text in the first row under the Macro Name column heading.

4. Use the Action drop-down list to select RunCommand in the row that you use in Step 3.

5. Select ExportText in the Command field of the Action Arguments pane.

6. On the row below Export_to_Text, enter Export_to_Excel.

7. Use the Action drop-down list to select MsgBox in the row that you use in Step 6.

8. Enter the following (or equivalent) into the Message field: You are about to export your data to an Excel file.

9. Select Yes for the Beep field.

10. Select Information for the Type.

11. Enter Export Data Notification in the Title field.

12. On the row below Export_to_Excel, select the RunCommand Action from the drop-down list.

You don't need to put a name on this row because you're still creating the same macro.

13. Select ExportExcel in the Command field from the Action Arguments drop-down list.

14. Save the macro group as Export_Macros.

15. Close the Macro Builder.

This macro doesn't execute by itself. You must choose one of the macros in the Export_Macros group by creating a control that refers to one of them.

Using a macro within a macro group

The example in this section demonstrates how to use a control to select one of the macros in a macro group. Follow these steps:

1. Open the Gradebook form in Design View.

2. Create a button and use the Command Button Wizard.

3. Select Miscellaneous from Categories, select Run Macro from Actions, and click Next.

The list of available macros appears.

4. Select Export_Macros.Export_to_Excel and then click Next, as shown in Figure 11-5.

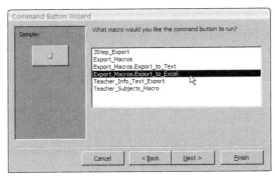

Figure 11-5: Use the Command Button Wizard to select a macro.

5. Click Next to accept the Run Macro picture.

6. Name the button ExportExcel and click Finish.

7. Switch to Form View and click your new button.

You hear the beep, and the pop-up message box appears.

8. Click OK on the message box.

The exported information opens in Excel. Excel contains only the student names because the data is pulled from the form and doesn't include information from the subform.

9. Close Excel and the final export message.

Finishing Touches

The following sections of this chapter alone are well worth the price of this book. These finishing touches, as I call them, truly demonstrate the elegance and power of macros.

The macro applications in the following sections further professionalize your database applications. They're exciting additions to any application that you create. After you see them in action, you'll understand my passion for them.

Close Access

Your database doesn't absolutely need the Close Access macro action, but I think it adds a professional touch. And you'll see it in any professionally created Access-based application. Follow these steps to create an Exit (Close Access) button:

1. **Open the Switchboard form in Design View.**
2. **Create a button in the form header and cancel the Wizard.**
3. **Open the Property Sheet for the button and click the Event tab.**
4. **Click the Ellipsis (. . .) button, select the Macro Builder, and click OK.**
5. **Select RunCommand from the Action drop-down list.**
6. **Select Exit from the Command drop-down list in the Action Arguments pane.**
7. **Click Close, and then click Yes on the prompt to save and update the On Click event.**
8. **Enter** Exit **into the Caption field on the Format tab.**
9. **Enter** Exit **into the Name field on the Other tab.**
10. **Save the form.**
11. **Switch to Form View.**
12. **Click the Exit button.**

    Access closes.

Closing Access in this way prompts the user before the program actually closes if the database contains unsaved objects. You can close Access without saving, but it's always best to allow users to save their work before exiting.

RunApp

RunApp is the macro action that lets you launch programs that are external to Access from within Access. This is an extremely useful feature of Access and has been part of its programming from very early on. This feature lets you create a micro-environment for the user that's so complete, she may never need to exit Access after opening your application.

If you use many external applications, I suggest creating a separate Switchboard page for external applications and including a button that makes the Switchboard accessible from every page of your application.

Watch Your Step

You must enter the complete path to the application you want to launch. If you want to launch Microsoft Word from within Access, you must tell Access where to find the executable program explicitly. For Microsoft Word on my computer, the path is `C:\Program Files\Microsoft Office\OFFICE11\winword.exe`. To find the path to the program you want, search for that program. The complete path appears in the search window. Remember to include the name of the program at the end of the path (for example, `winword.exe`).

Information Kiosk

You can find most of the programs your users will probably want to use within Access in one of two places: `C:\Windows` or `C:\Program Files`.

In the following example, you provide your users with the Windows calculator. After you see how to do this, you can provide buttons to launch all of your favorite programs from within Access. To create a button that launches the Windows Calculator, follow these steps:

1. **Search for the** `calc.exe` **program on your computer.**

This is the Windows Calculator's program file. You can find it in `C:\Windows\System32`, so the full path to the program is `C:\Windows\System32\calc.exe`.

2. **Open the Gradebook form in Design View.**

3. **Create a button and cancel the wizard.**

4. **Open the Property Sheet for the button and click the Event tab.**

5. **Click the Ellipsis (. . .) button in the OnClick field, select Macro Builder, and click OK.**

6. **Click the Show All Actions button.**

It looks like nothing happens, but the Action drop-down list has several hidden actions. The Show All Actions button un-hides these options.

7. Select **RunApp** from the now-longer list of Actions.

8. In the **Command** field, enter C:\Windows\System32\calc.exe.

9. Close the Macro Builder and click **Yes** on the Update and Save prompt.

10. In the Property Sheet, enter Calculator **into the Caption and Name fields.**

11. Adjust the size of the button to show the word `Calculator`.

12. Save the form and switch to Form View.

13. Click the Calculator button.

The Windows Calculator launches and appears on your screen.

 Information Kiosk

The programs you launch from within Access aren't bound to Access in any way. There's no difference between a program launched inside or outside of Access. Use them, minimize them, close them, and reopen them as you would normally.

AutoExec

In the pre-Internet dark ages of the early 1990s, it took me months to figure out how to create this particular macro, AutoExec. After I got it, it became part of my permanent bag of tricks.

This macro automatically executes when you open any database that contains it. Its name, AutoExec, comes from the old DOS days when you had a start-up file called AUTOEXEC.BAT. Autoexec is simply an extension of that familiar naming convention. To create an AutoExec macro, follow these steps:

1. Click the **Create** tab, then click the **Macro** button to launch the Macro Builder.

2. Select **OpenForm** from the Action drop-down list.

3. Select **Switchboard** from the Form Name drop-down list in the Action Argument pane.

You can ignore the other options.

4. Save the macro as AutoExec.

 Information Kiosk

The capitalization of AutoExec is traditional, but it doesn't matter to Access. The file works with any capitalization (or none), such as autoexec or Autoexec.

5. Close the Macro Builder.

6. Close the database.

7. Open the Chapter11 database.

The Switchboard should be ready for use.

Watch Your Step

Be careful what actions you place in a start-up (AutoExec) macro. If you inadvertently put in an action that exits the Switchboard, database, or Access itself, you may find it very frustrating to work around since you can't get into the database to fix it. Fortunately, there's a workaround. When selecting the database you want to open, hold down the Shift key until the database opens. This simple step bypasses any start-up options, including AutoExec macros.

action: The function that a macro performs.

arguments: The parameters that guide a macro's action.

AutoExec: A stand-alone macro that is executed when the database is opened.

embedded macro: A macro that's part of a control, form, or report. It has all the attributes of a stand-alone macro but doesn't show up in the navigation pane under Macros.

macro: A program used to automate repetitive or laborious tasks.

macro group: A logically grouped (usually by function) set of programs used in automation.

stand-alone macro: A macro that can execute on its own to produce some desired action. Stand-alone macros are listed in the navigation pane.

Switchboard: A form that's specially constructed to act as a central reference for other forms, reports, and programs in an Access database. It's analogous to an HTML index file.

Visual Basic for Applications (VBA): The language of macros and modules in Microsoft Access and other Microsoft Office products.

Last Stop

Practice Exam

1. **Macros are minimally composed of:**

A) Conditions and parameters

B) Conditions and actions

C) Actions and switches

D) Actions and arguments

2. **An argument is a(n):**

A) Action

B) List of parameters

C) Condition

D) Array of numbers

3. **The main reason for constructing and maintaining a Switchboard is:**

A) User convenience

B) Data integrity

C) To allow the use of macros

D) To organize your data

4. **True or false (explain why): A multi-step macro and a macro group are the same thing.**

_____

_____

_____

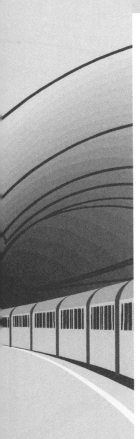

5. **Macro groups are created mainly for what reason?**

A) Data integrity

B) To reduce clutter

C) To make data easier to enter

D) To associate dissimilar functions

6. **Macros execute in what type of fashion?**

A) In bursts

B) After all tables have been closed

C) Side-out

D) Top-down

7. **True or false (explain why): You can launch external programs from within Access by using macros.**

_____

_____

_____

8. **One of the advantages to creating and using macros is:**

A) They improve table structure.

B) They increase overall stability of the database.

C) No knowledge of VBA is required.

D) The database is more easily normalized.

9. **What's the one requirement for using the RunApp macro action?**

A) A database in Third Normal Form

B) A full path to the program

C) A thorough knowledge of VBA

D) A macro group

10. **What's the main purpose of using macros in an Access database?**

A) Design

B) Stability

C) Automation

D) Selection

Making Access Templates Work for You

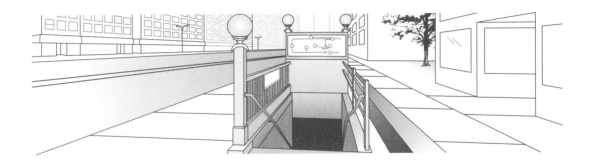

Enter the Station

Questions

1. What's a template?

2. How do I get templates from Microsoft?

3. Why should I use a template?

4. What different types of templates are available?

5. What should I look for when evaluating a template for use?

6. How do I create my own database templates?

Express Line

If you know how to use Access templates, then skip ahead to Chapter 13.

This chapter gives you an overview of database templates and their place in your company or personal life. You can find out how to evaluate a template for use. And a step-by-step tutorial shows you how to create your own templates from existing databases.

Employing Access Templates

Access offers you several diverse choices when it comes to templates. There are templates for business applications, personal interest, and education, just to name a few. A *template* is a complete database application created with no (or very little) data to give you a ready-to-use solution to common needs like tracking contacts or basic accounting. You can download a template from Microsoft, another vendor, or community developer sites; or you can create your own template to use or share with others.

Using a template doesn't reflect on your ability, or inability, to create a great application in Access. Templates are solutions to common problems. If you find a great template for a Contact Management application, then why spend hours building one from scratch? You can change a template to meet your needs. You can also use a template as a guide for your own databases. One way to get to know databases, database structure, and good design is to observe what others have done.

If you're planning to use a template and must alter it in some way to fit your own needs, make a copy of the original and work on that copy. I don't want to discourage you from making changes, but they sometimes can be disastrous. Study the template's relationship diagram carefully to understand how the tables interact with one another before you make any changes. You should also check the Property Sheet when working with forms, reports, and controls to make sure you change all the properties (fonts, colors, and so forth) for your new template. You may want to enter some dummy data into the template you're changing so that you know how the changes affect the data.

Browsing the Templates

When you first open Access, the entire middle pane of the page is dedicated to Featured Online Templates. This list of Access 2007 templates available for download from Microsoft is subject to change over time, so check it often for new additions. The list is currently broken down into four categories:

- Business
- Education
- Personal
- Sample

Under each of the categories is a list of related database application templates:

- Business
  - Assets
  - Business Account Ledger
  - Contacts
  - Customer Service
  - Events
  - Issues
  - Lending Library
  - Marketing Projects
  - Projects
  - Sales Pipeline
  - Tasks
- Education
  - Faculty
  - Students
- Personal
  - Contacts
  - Home Inventory
  - Lending Library
  - Nutrition
  - Personal Account Ledger
- Samples
  - Northwind 2007

i Information Kiosk

To use any of the online templates from Microsoft, you must be a valid user of the Microsoft Office product with which you're working. A dialog box appears the first time you attempt a download to notify you of the check. After you're validated, you can download one or all of the database templates during your session.

The Northwind 2007 Database

To select and download a template from the list of templates, follow these steps:

1. **Select the Sample category.**

   You want to download the Northwind 2007 database from Microsoft.

2. **Click the Northwind 2007 icon to begin the download process.**

   You're prompted in the lower-right area of the screen to download the file with the filename `Northwind 2007.accdb`. See Figure 12-1.

3. **Click the Download button to begin the download process.**

4. **Click OK on the Windows Genuine Advantage dialog box.**

   The file downloads after your Office license has been validated. The default download location for the file is My Documents.

5. **After it downloads, open the Northwind 2007 database.**

6. When prompted to log in, select Andrew Cencini — or any name from the list — from Select Employee drop-down list and click Login.

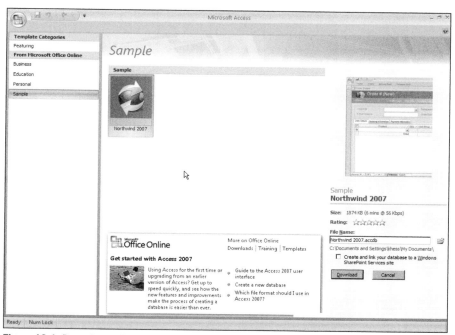

Figure 12-1: Preparing to download the Northwind 2007 database.

The Northwind database has been around since the very first version of Access. It used to be the only example database that came with Access.

Northwind Traders is a fictional company with products, suppliers, orders, customers, and employees. It contains 20 tables and many queries, reports, forms, macros (including the AutoExec macro), and modules. *Modules* are actually Visual Basic for Applications (VBA) programs created to perform tasks that may be too complicated for macros.

The Northwind database is very complete. Take a look at the relationship diagram (Chapter 9 has the details of how to view the relationship diagram) to see the number of one-to-many relationships and how the tables relate to each other. The diagram is too large and complex to show in this book, but you can study it for yourself. When you look at it, identify the primary key/foreign key (PK/FK) pairs in the tables. You can rearrange the tables for a better view of the tables, columns, and relationships.

Figure 12-2 shows the relationships related to the Orders table. As you might expect, a company such as Northwind Traders needs to track orders and anything related to those orders. So the Orders table is central to this database, just as the Gradebook table is central to the database you create to manage grades for a high school in Chapter 9. The tables that aren't directly connected to the Orders table are connected indirectly to it.

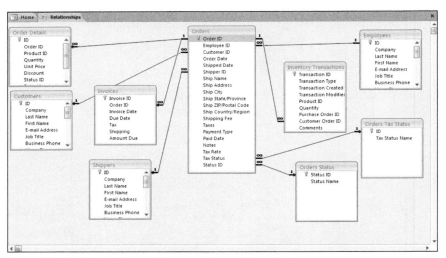

Figure 12-2: The Orders table and its connections (relationships).

You need to intimately understand the relationships in your databases, whether or not you create those databases. At some point, you may need to edit, or add to, a table, and you must be aware of any consequences of those changes.

Watch Your Step

Never assume that a database has been correctly designed just because it's available commercially or comes from a reputable company. Check the column types and each relationship to make sure they're correct. You don't want to find out after entering hundreds or thousands of orders that your database has a glitch you easily could have fixed before you entered any data.

The Northwind database has a clean and clever form design. The reports are well thought out, and the application includes every aspect of a larger Access implementation. It's a real application written entirely in and for Access.

The other Access templates offer special opportunity for database study, but none are as complete and business-oriented as the Northwind database. When you can design and implement a database such as Northwind, you can truly call yourself an Access guru.

Business templates

Anyone trying to figure out Access is probably doing it for a business purpose of some sort — whether it's to take part in some mandatory training, upgrade skills, or move away from spreadsheets and word-processing documents. The business templates may well serve a purpose you're looking to fill. They're generic enough to fit many scenarios but are very practical and ready to use.

This book doesn't cover all of the templates for this category, but the following sections talk about the ones that are the most immediately useful.

Assets

Many companies are in dire need of asset management. The companies have no means of determining such essential information as what assets they have, how much those assets are worth, when they should replace the assets, or warranty information.

Single- or limited-use items aren't really considered assets, but computer equipment, copy machines, cash registers, signs, desks, chairs, tables, and any item that could fall under the category of *capital equipment* is considered an asset.

Assets are different from inventory. *Inventory* includes the products that are brought in to a business to be resold in some way. Most companies have some sort of inventory tracking system (good or bad), but those same companies have little or no asset control. This is why you sometimes see auditors come through your offices to count, catalogue, and cryptically label assets.

Any business should use an asset management system to track costs, depreciation, warranties, repairs, and disposal. For example, you may have a computer system that requires regular maintenance or occasional upgrades. Those charges must be associated with that asset so that you can tell if one of your systems is constantly in need of repair or maintenance — that way, you may decide just to replace that system instead of wasting money on fixes. Without a good asset-management system, you aren't aware of this issue until a $1,500 desktop computer has cost you $7,000 to maintain. It obviously would be more cost-effective just to replace it.

You also need a good set of reports in your asset-management system so that your accountant can depreciate the assets and remove them from asset inventory after you dispose of them. Any business that doesn't use an asset-management system is probably losing a lot of money.

You can be the company savior by implementing an asset-management system and improving it over time. The Assets database template that you can find in the business templates list is a pretty good one, although it lacks many features of a professional asset-management system.

Download the Asset database from the business templates list and open it.

When the database opens, the Asset List form opens automatically.

You won't find an AutoExec macro for this database because the designer decided to use Access's start-up options. You can use either an AutoExec macro or Access's start-up options to open a form automatically when an Access database is opened.

To use, view, or edit start-up options, follow these steps:

1. **Click the Office icon and select Access Options.**

2. **Select Current Database in the left navigation pane.**

Refer to Figure 12-3 for this example. After this, you're ready to change options for the current database. The following sections show you how.

Application options

You can change the title bar from `Assets: Database (Access 2007) Microsoft Access` to whatever you want by entering text into the Application Title field. Follow these steps:

1. **Enter Company Assets into the Application Title field.**

2. **If you want an Application icon, you can browse your computer, select the icon, and place it here.**

The Display Form prompt asks you to select the form that you want to launch when the database opens. Asset List is the default selection for this database.

You can choose the option to Compact on Close. You should consider this maintenance option if the database is very busy. You can also perform a compact and repair manually on a regular basis. You can find more information on maintenance in Chapter 16.

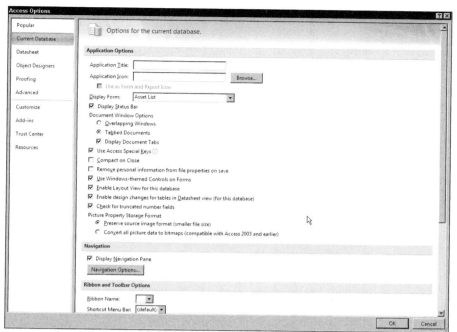

Figure 12-3: You can adjust database options in the Current Database.

The rest of the options in the following sections are self-explanatory.

Navigation

You can control the appearance of the navigation pane so your users don't see confidential database objects.

To completely hide the navigation pane, deselect the Display Navigation Pane check box.

To display the navigation pane but change the objects that appear, follow these steps:

1. Click the Navigation Options button.

Using the options on this screen, you can hide one or both tables or allow users to see forms and reports but hide tables, macros, modules, and queries (or any other combination). Figure 12-4 shows Navigation Options.

2. Select Object Type and deselect the check boxes for Tables, Queries, Macros, and Modules, as shown in Figure 12-5.

3. Click OK.

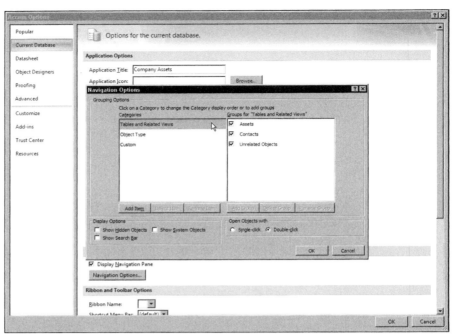

Figure 12-4: You can change which objects are visible in the Navigation Options screen.

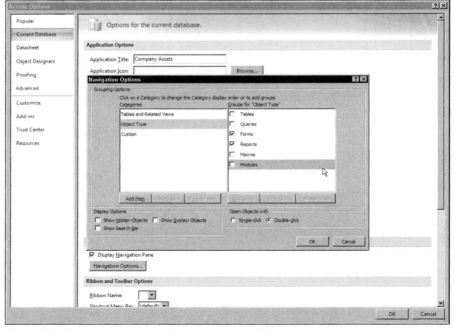

Figure 12-5: Deselect the database objects you want to hide.

Ribbon and toolbar options

The Ribbon and Toolbar Options affect the user experience by limiting or enhancing the Access Ribbon and toolbars. You can use custom ribbons and toolbars in your databases by disabling the default ones and creating new ones. Chapter 17 has details on enhancing the Ribbon but customizing ribbons and toolbars is beyond the scope of this book.

Watch Your Step

If you deselect Allow Full Menus or Allow Default Shortcut Menus (or both) and you can't get these options back by using the Microsoft icon, then close the database and reopen it while holding down the Shift key on your keyboard. This process allows you to see all objects and reset the ribbon and toolbar options.

Accepting and undoing changes

After you change individual options, you can accept all of your changes by clicking OK. You may receive a message that you must close and reopen the database to see your changes.

If you use the example in the section "Navigation," earlier in this chapter, you can see only forms and reports in the navigation pane after you close and reopen the Assets database.

To view all database objects again, follow these steps:

1. Click the Microsoft Office icon, select Access Options, select Current Database, and then select Navigation Options.

2. Select Object Type and reselect all of the objects in the list.

3. Click OK to close the Navigation Options dialog box.

4. Click OK to close the Access Options window.

All database objects should be visible again.

Customer service

The Customer Service database is a full-blown customer-service-and-response application that can track customer issues, issue resolution, and response times. It also includes a knowledge base of issues and their resolutions.

The Report Center in the Customer Service database has very good report capability. You get charts that give you an at-a-glance check on issues that are overdue, days active, status, and category. These reports measure how well your customer service issues are being resolved.

The only criticism I have for this database is that it gives you no way to charge a client for an issue. Customer service is usually free to a point, but you may have service contracts to bill against or even a charge per incident. In any case, if you decide to use this database, you may want to add a Fees table and Fee fields for related forms. You should also add a report that can track those fees for each customer and has the ability to invoice from the application.

On the other hand, your Accounting department may decide to use records of resolved cases and handle billing from that end. They may request a report and invoice clients in that fashion.

This database doesn't have an AutoExec macro. The author of this database used the start-up options that you can examine in the section "Assets," earlier in this chapter. You don't have any particular advantages or disadvantages when using a macro rather than the start-up options; they're just different ways of doing the same thing — opening a form when the database is opened. An AutoExec macro gives you the opportunity to make several things happen upon entering the database, and the Current Database options alone give you other flexibility. You can also use the Current Database Application options with an AutoExec macro, but you can open an initial form with only one or the other — not both.

Information Kiosk

If you need to open multiple forms when you open a new database, use an AutoExec macro. The form that's opened last will be the one that users see first. The other forms will be available on tabs. The start-up options described earlier in this chapter only allow you to open one form.

Sometimes, you want to open a status report and a data entry form when you open a database. For instance, in the case of the Customer Service application, you may want to open the "Overdue Cases" report or the "Open Cases by Assigned To" report. The Customer Service Representative or the Technical Support person should be told about overdue and assigned cases when he enters the database without having to manually open the report.

Some customer support teams may even want to place status reports on a SharePoint server so the client can check the status of her tickets without having to call in. This kind of shared tracking is one way to minimize calls to your business and raise customer satisfaction.

This database (Customer Service) contains only five tables. A database that performs complex tasks, such as this database, doesn't need 20 or more tables. You can do quite a lot with only a few tables.

Take a look at the relationship diagram shown in Figure 12-6.

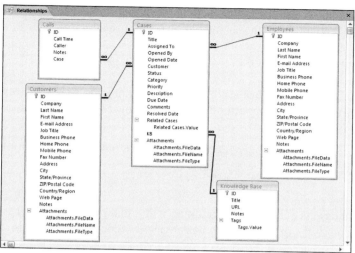

Figure 12-6: This is a customer-service database relationship diagram.

I've rearranged and expanded the tables in the Customer Service database relationship diagram so you can clearly see all of the relationships involved. The Cases table is the main table to which all others attach. The Cases table is the central table because customer service cases are the focus and purpose of the database.

When building your own database, you must figure out the main purpose of your database and make the main data table reflect that central theme. Refer to the customer-service database design often for its clean and complete design and for its simplicity. Don't think simple design means lack of ability. This relatively simple database could be a great asset to your company.

Other Business templates

You may want to check out these other Business templates: Business Account Ledger, Sales Pipeline, Projects, and Marketing Projects.

In the following sections, I very briefly introduce you to these other Business templates.

Business Account Ledger

Even if you're not an accounting person by any stretch of the imagination, this very simple Business Account Ledger database can get you started by keeping a computer record of your transactions. The database has only two tables: Account Transactions and Categories.

Account Transactions is the data table, and Categories is a *lookup table* (a table that only contains choices to select from in a list) for different types of transactions. This template, although useful in a limited way, is provided to introduce you to more calculations involving forms and reports. If you look at the forms and reports in this database in Design View, you can see how the designer uses the summary functions for the calculations.

Sales Pipeline

This simple Sales Pipeline database is designed to work business sales leads. It has only three tables (Customers, Opportunities, and Employees) and centers around the Opportunities table.

The power of this database isn't necessarily in its design but in the use of forms and reports to provide tracking, follow-up, and forecasting.

Projects

The Projects database is a database for tracking individual projects, as well as all projects. And, thankfully, project costing has also been added to the database for each project.

This database has four tables (Tasks, Common Tasks, Employees, and Projects). You may guess that the Projects table is the central table in the database, but in reality, the Employees table is central, as the relationship diagram shows you.

Although this is a Projects database, a project has an owner — and the project is centered on the person who owns it. If the project has no owner, it's an orphaned project and can't make any progress. Therefore, the project owner is as important as the project itself.

This database is a lightweight project-management and tracking application. You probably couldn't use it for any project-management tasks that require multiple deadlines, milestones, or complex interdependent projects.

Marketing Projects

The Marketing Projects database is really an expansion of the Projects database. This database uses a slightly different logic than the Projects database, however. It has five tables (Employees, Deliverables, Common Deliverables, Vendors, and Projects).

This database is concerned with deliverables related to marketing, such as services, products, and meetings. Therefore, the focus shifts from employees to deliverables.

In this database's relationship diagram, this change in focus from the Projects database is represented by the design and the inclusion of the deliverables to the customer.

A small company could use the Marketing Projects database to manage deliverable-type projects, but it must be on a small scale. This database gives you good examples of forms and reports with and without calculations in them. It also has excellent examples of some advanced queries for appending and updating data.

Personal templates

The Personal templates are database templates that you may find useful in your personal life. They're also useful from a design standpoint. Look behind the scenes in Design View to see how the designer performed a task or created a certain look. Most of these databases are copies of, or very similar to, the Business templates, so I don't cover them here. Two of the Personal templates are unique and complex enough that they deserve closer examination: Nutrition and Lending Library.

Nutrition

The most unique, and my favorite, amongst the Personal templates is the Nutrition database. This database, although very useful in its own right, is also a great example of a simple database that's well-designed and has some interesting characteristics not found in the other Personal templates.

When you open the Nutrition database, it greets you with the profile builder shown in Figure 12-7.

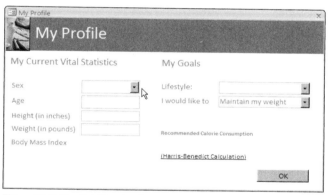

Figure 12-7: The Nutrition database presents you with the My Profile form.

After you fill out this form and click OK, you're presented with the Today's Report form. This form has a lot of information on it. You can find links that prompt you to enter your current weight, foods that you have eaten, recipes, and exercise data. You also see helpful links to the USDA Food Database and USDA nutrition sources. Two charts show your progress. (Charting is an advanced aspect of Access that isn't covered in this book.)

The Today's Tip adds an extra value to this form. Every time you open the form, you get a random tip and a link to the USDA's MyPyramid page that also has daily tips. The designer of this form used an advanced lookup function and a random number generator to pull a random tip from the database. If you want to add random tips to your own forms, just copy the formula.

The relationship diagram for this database is very interesting. You can see it in Figure 12-8.

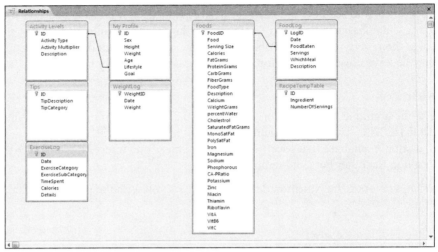

Figure 12-8: The relationship diagram for the Nutrition database.

This relationship diagram has eight tables and only two relationships. This database proves that you don't absolutely have to connect every table in a database. Sometimes, you need tables that themselves need no relationships. The relationships are one-to-many, but the 1 and ∞ don't appear in the diagram because referential integrity isn't enforced.

Information Kiosk

You can figure out what kind of relationship exists between two tables, even when the symbols aren't shown in the relationship diagram, in two ways. Double-click the relationship line to make the Edit Relationships dialog box appear, showing the relationship type and the affected columns. ID columns (primary keys) hold unique values and are always on the one side of a one-to-many relationship.

This database also includes a Delete query and an Append query. The Delete query empties the RecipeTempTable by using a DeleteRecipeTempTable macro. This database doesn't have any reports because everything is accomplished by using forms. Reporting is done directly on the form. This type of design works when you don't need reporting for external sources. An *external source* is a meeting, an e-mail distribution, a monthly report to a manager, and so on. You probably won't need a report from this data. If you want a report to give to a personal trainer, you can create one.

Lending Library

The Lending Library is both a Business and Personal template. When you think of a lending library, books probably come to mind. But people borrow all kinds of things, not just books. I've loaned out CDs, tools, cameras, laptop computers, a tent and camping gear, and even a heating pad. (I wish I'd used a Lending Library database to help me keep track of the borrowed items that my friends and relatives never seem to return.)

Ignoring my personal angst, the Lending Library database provides a great learning tool. The relationship diagram may look a bit confusing, and so does the table design. I'm not sure that you need such detail in a personal database. For Contacts, you probably don't need more than First_Name, Last_Name, and Phone unless you don't know the individual(s) to whom you're loaning things. The Assets table is also a bit detailed for a personal item. The Transactions table, however, is perfect just the way it is.

This database, in its current state, is more appropriate for business lending activity. For a business situation, you might add a column to the Contacts table named Security and use that column to store a credit card number.

You should create your own version of this database for personal use and decide how you can improve on its design and quality.

Evaluating a Template

You evaluate a template for business differently than a template for personal use. You should consider several common items when evaluating a template for any purpose.

Here are some attributes to consider when evaluating a template (in no particular order):

- Licensing
- Simplicity
- Design
- Customizability
- Applicability

Licensing

Licensing is a very important aspect of using any template. Many templates are shared on the assumption that you'll evaluate the template for a period of time, then pay for the use of the template or delete it from your computer. You can also find many templates that are free for personal use or for evaluation. Most templates require some sort of payment when a commercial (for-profit) entity uses them.

Ask the creator of the template how the template is licensed if you can't find licensing information clearly stated on the Web site or in the database itself. Please don't use a template for personal or business use without knowing the licensing information.

The following is an excerpt from Microsoft's Web site, under `License Agreement for Community Templates`, that talks about template licensing, including the templates discussed in this book:

> The Microsoft Service Agreement and this license agreement apply to templates that you download from this site. Please read them. If you do not agree to these terms, do not download a template. You must have a validly licensed copy of Microsoft Office to use these templates. The templates include content in or provided with the templates.

Use. You may download, copy, and use the templates in documents and projects that you create. You may distribute those documents and projects non-commercially. If you wish to use the templates for any other purpose, go to `www.microsoft.com/permission` to learn whether that use is allowed.

No Warranty. Microsoft provides this site for members of the Microsoft Office community to share document templates. These members are not Microsoft employees or representatives. Because of this, we do not promise that the templates will work for your purposes. We also do not promise that they are free from viruses, bugs, or other defects.

Simplicity

When evaluating a new template for use in either a personal or business setting, be sure that the template is simple enough to use with little or no training. This is especially true when evaluating a template for business use. Users become frustrated with any program that's difficult to use or time-consuming to understand. Those users may abandon the template for an old familiar spreadsheet or Notepad in short order. Be prepared to provide training for users of any new template that you evaluate. Also, be aware that requests may come your way to customize the template to suit the needs (and whims) of your user base. Check the template's licensing to be sure that you're allowed to make those changes.

Don't buy off on a template that you can't change to meet your needs unless you've contacted the template designer to customize it for you herself. Personal use templates don't need to follow the rules of simplicity so strictly, but you may become frustrated if you must spend several hours fumbling through a template or basically rewrite the whole thing to meet your needs.

Design

The basic design of a database is important. The first place I look when examining a new database is the relationship diagram. You can see how the designer connected the tables, what level of normalization to expect, and whether any referential integrity exists.

Form and report design are far less important than the back end (the tables). You need to know that the database can withstand extensive use without having any data integrity issues or odd behavior when you remove a record. You can always tweak or redesign a form or report, but redesigning a database is sometimes so much work that it's easier to start from scratch, using an idea or two from the template.

Design is less important in a personal database than a business database, but you still have valuable information as a personal user. The bottom line is that there's just no substitute for good design in any setting.

Customizability

Customizing a template is related to licensing. The license agreement must permit you to change or customize the database. Some designers don't allow customers to change the database because those changes may compromise the integrity of the database — and, in turn, damage the designer's reputation.

The Microsoft licensing statement doesn't explicitly mention altering the templates, although it does say that you can "use the templates in documents and projects that you create." This statement at least implicitly gives you the ability to use all or part of a template in your own project. To be sure, check with Microsoft at www.microsoft.com/permission or http://support.microsoft.com/contactus.

You must have some idea of what you're looking for in a template before you even begin searching for one. You need to find a template that's licensed correctly, simple to use, well-designed, customizable, and applicable to your needs.

Step into the Real World

Don't use a template that you can't change. A designer could design a database application template for every customer that works without the customer having to make any changes. You may have to pay extra for the ability to customize a template for your own use.

For example, say you're looking for an inventory control database to manage your company's entire inventory for a medium-sized company that gets a lot of local traffic and has a large mail-order business. You need a database that meets all of the preceding criteria, plus it also must work for your business, specifically. Everyone has given you their opinions as to what this database needs, and you've come up with the following checklist.

At a minimum, you need

- Inventory management
- Accounting for over-the-counter sales
- Accounting for Internet sales
- Automated label printing for outgoing shipments
- Bar-code labeling for incoming products
- Automated reorder reports
- Accounting for returns and restocks
- Automated overstock reports
- The ability to do discounted and combined shipping

Knowing the criteria for a template narrows your search. The goal is to find something as close to perfect as possible for your needs and then either compromise on some points or discuss modification and customization.

A personal database doesn't have less stringent requirements, but the price per feature that you're willing to pay may be significantly lower than for a business database.

Checking under the hood

After you decide to evaluate a template, use the evaluation period to its fullest. Typically, you have 30 days to evaluate a product or program. If the database hasn't been *obfuscated* (encrypted) or crippled in some way, begin your evaluation by looking at the back end. Look at the table design, relationship diagram, forms, and reports. Have at least one other person assist in the evaluation from a user's point of view.

The following checklist can assist you in evaluating a database for usability:

- Enter data into every data entry form.
- Use every report.
- Delete some data.

- Export data.

- Print out such productivity information as reports, labels, and forms.

- Look at the relationship diagram and make sure you know how the tables are related.

- Examine the tables' structures, column types, and number of tables to make sure there aren't tables you don't need and the columns match the data you plan on filling in.

- If the database is networked, have several people connect to and use it.

- Try to identify any potential trouble spots or bottlenecks in the application.

- Review any priorities, needs, wants, or complaints with the evaluation team.

- Discuss the results of the evaluation team meeting with the vendor.

- Ask for references from the vendor's current clients and follow up with them all.

You may receive a crippled version of the database for evaluation. If you can't fully evaluate the database with the demo version, contact the vendor and ask for a live demo or a production database for this evaluation.

I've seen too many companies (and individuals) get locked into a solution that doesn't really work for them. They bought a product based on marketing tactics — not on features, performance, or applicability to their needs.

Creating Your Own Templates

If you want to gain fame and fortune, you can create your own templates to share with others (for free or at a price). If you want to create and distribute your databases as full, installable applications, you should purchase the Access Software Development Kit from Microsoft, although you can always just supply the database as a template, such as the ones in earlier sections in this chapter.

A template is just an empty database application that you create, including all forms, reports, tables, macros, queries, and modules.

Follow these guidelines when creating your own templates suitable for distribution:

- Test all aspects of the application using real data to ensure everything works.

- Have multiple users try out the application individually and simultaneously, if the template can network.

- Distribute a runtime version of Access (a minimal version of Access that only runs the database but allows no editing) with your application in case a potential user doesn't have Access.
- Provide navigational elements on forms and reports.
- Provide some documentation (instructions, licensing, and help files) with your template.
- Decide on a license type for your template.
- Empty the tables of all data before distribution.

You should empty the data out of the tables before you present the database as a template to be shared or sold. (The section "Copying tables without copying data," later in this chapter, shows how to copy tables without keeping the original data.) The only exception is when you use the template as a demonstration database.

The example databases in this chapter are good guides for your own templates. The Northwind 2007 database is a sample database, but it's also a demonstration of the power of Access database and needs data entered into it to reveal its power. The other templates contain no data, but they all have a start-up form prompting you for input.

The following sections create a template from a database that has forms, reports, queries, data, and macros. You can create a template from the Gradebook database in Chapter 11. (You can also download a copy of the Gradebook database from this book's Web site.)

Starting the database

Follow these steps to begin copying the database as a template:

1. Create a new blank database and name it (for example, name it MyTemplate1**).**

This database will be the new template.

2. When MyTemplate1 opens, close Table1 to delete it.

You need to import all of the queries, forms, reports, macros, modules, and any tables from the Chapter11 database. You can import the Subjects and Switch-board tables with the other objects (such as Tables). You need to empty the other tables before importing them, so don't worry about importing them at this point.

3. Click the Access button in the Import group.

The Import Objects dialog box appears.

4. On the Tables tab, select Switchboard and Subjects.

Hold the Control (Ctrl) key down to select multiple tables while selecting each table.

5. Click the Queries tab and click Select All.

6. Repeat the selection step for the Forms, Queries, and Macros tabs.

7. Click OK.

   All selected objects are imported into the database (for example, the MyTemplate1 database).

8. Close the new template database (for example, MyTemplate1).

9. Open the original database (for example, Chapter11) and close the forms that automatically open.

10. Click the External Data tab.

   At this point, you're ready to export the remaining tables from the original database (for example, Chapter11) to the new template database (for example, MyTemplate1). You must export data one object at a time. The following section shows you how.

Copying tables without copying data

After you create the new template database, which the preceding section explains, you need to copy tables from the original database without copying the original data.

Repeat the following steps for each table you want to export (for example, repeat these steps for the Comments, Exams, Students, and Teachers tables in the Chapter11 database):

1. Click the table (for example, Comments) to select it.

2. Click More in the Export group and select Access Database from the drop-down list.

3. Click Browse, then locate and select the database created in the preceding section database (for example, MyTemplate1).

4. Click OK.

   The Export dialog box appears.

5. Keep the object name (for example, Comments), select Definition Only, and click OK.

   This step exports the table structure without the data; the AutoNumber column is reset to 1.

6. Click Close on the Save Export dialog box.

If you used the examples, the Chapter11 database structure is completely exported into the MyTemplate1 database. The Comments, Exams, Students, and Teachers tables in MyTemplate1 are empty, but the Switchboard and the lookup tables (if any) have retained their data.

relationship diagram: A graphical representation of the tables in a database and the connections between them.

template: A ready-to-use database solution containing little or no data.

Practice Exam

1. True or false (explain why): You can export all objects in a database to another database at once.

_____

_____

_____

2. True or false (explain why): You can import all objects in a database to another database at once.

_____

_____

_____

3. What must you check before altering a database template that you downloaded from a Web site?

A) Design

B) Applicability

C) Licensing

D) Data integrity

4. When evaluating a template, you should:

A) Pay for the template up front to avoid any issues.

B) Thoroughly test the template.

C) Make needed changes to the template.

D) Copy the parts of the template that you like to another database.

5. When would you need to export a table instead of importing a table to create a template?

A) When security is the highest priority

B) When security is of no concern

C) When tables need to retain all of their data

D) When tables need to be emptied of their data

6. What should you check when evaluating any template?

A) References from current users

B) The amount of data already in the database

C) The number of macros

D) The designer's credentials

7. When is it okay to put data into data tables and leave the data in a template that you create?

A) When evaluating a template.

B) When supplying a database as a demonstration database.

C) When creating a database for general use.

D) It's never okay to leave data in a template.

8. Aside from using a template in a business or personal situation, templates also offer value for:

A) Customization

B) Copying

C) Selling

D) Teaching

9. True or false (explain why): It's okay to change a template that you download from the Internet, change it, and sell it as your own.

_____

_____

_____

10. If you create a template that you want to share freely, what information should you still include in the template?

A) Business applications

B) Licensing and copyright

C) Your contact information

D) A note about donations

SQL: The Structured Query Language

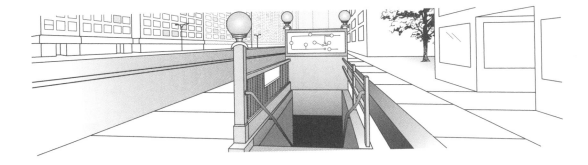

 # Enter the Station

Questions

1. What is Structured Query Language?

2. Is SQL really a language?

3. What's the correct way to pronounce SQL?

4. Why does SQL have sub-languages?

5. How do I switch from the Query Builder to SQL View?

6. How do I enter a SQL query in Access?

7. How do I know that my changes have taken place?

Express Line

If you know SQL, then skip ahead to Chapter 14.

The language of relational databases is SQL (Structured Query Language). You can interface directly with table data by using this language. SQL has three *sub-languages,* or logical separations based on their actions. SQL is an action-oriented language that's interactive in nature. In this chapter, you can find simple SQL queries and their equivalent structure in the graphical Query Builder.

Introducing SQL: The Language of Databases

SQL is the language of relational databases. All modern relational databases understand SQL to varying degrees. Access translates queries that you create in the Query Builder into SQL for you. The translation process happens automatically. I frequently switch between actual SQL and the Query Builder to get a query just right. Access provides both because some users with more of a programming mentality like to use SQL in its raw form and other users are more visual, designing queries from that standpoint in the Query Builder. You can work in either way in Access.

You should know SQL because Access can connect to external data sources for information. Access uses a non-standard subset of ANSI (American National Standards Institute) SQL that may produce errors when it queries a database other than Access, such as an Oracle database. You may assume that anyone who works with databases understands SQL.

The correct way to pronounce SQL is *ess-que-ell,* although many pronounce it *sequel.* I'm guilty of using the pronunciations interchangeably. Fortunately, there's only one way to write SQL, and you don't hear me pronounce it at all. You hear it pronounced both ways even among database administrators.

SQL is considered a language because it has the two main elements that define a language:

- **Syntax:** Order of of words and spelling
- **Semantics:** Meaning

Step into the Real World

Some people argue that SQL isn't a true language because it's non-procedural and has no constructs for looping, variables, and other constructs that define a computer language. Whether or not it's a traditional computer language doesn't really matter to me. That's for the academic-types to decide — what they call it won't affect the language, how it works, or anything else, for that matter.

SQL is an *action language,* which means that each time you enter an SQL command, you're demanding some action from the database. In Chapters 4 and 5, you can read about queries in which you ask for data from tables. You may also pose statements to the database that return no results at all but still call for an action. For example, a statement can insert a new row of data, update a record, or delete a record completely. Most people call any dialog with a database a query. But a query returns an answer (results) and a statement doesn't.

Information Kiosk

Knowing SQL is an essential database skill; you can duplicate any SQL statement by using the graphical tools in Access.

Data Types

Column data types are important in databases because they determine

- What type of data a column can contain
- What type of manipulations you can perform on the data

Information Kiosk

Some data types aren't interchangeable and lose their special characteristics if you switch one for the other. For instance, if you change a Number data type to a Text data type, you can't perform mathematical operations on that data. You don't necessarily need to store numeric data in Number data-type columns. If you have a Zip code column, don't create it as Number data-type column. Use a Text data type for Zip codes because you won't be adding, subtracting, multiplying, or dividing this data.

The Access column data-type definitions are

- Text
- Memo
- Number
- Date/Time
- Currency
- AutoNumber

Yes/No

○ OLE Object

○ Hyperlink

○ Attachment

Table 13-1 shows the data types, the type of data stored, and any restrictions.

Table 13-1   Access Data Types

Data Type	Data	Restriction
Text	Text/Numbers	255-character limit
Memo	Text/Numbers	2 GB or 65,535 characters
Number	Numeric	Field size restriction
Date/Time	Dates/Times	Dates and Times
Currency	Monetary	None
AutoNumber	Unique numbers	Auto-generated
Yes/No	–1/Yes or 0/No	Boolean
OLE Object	Images/Documents/Other	Inefficient way to store files, 2 GB limit
Hyperlink	URL Information/Links/Files	1 GB limit
Attachment	Any file type	New and best way to store files

SQL Sub-Languages

Under the umbrella of SQL, you find three sub-languages. These sub-languages are simply groupings based on the actions they perform in a database:

○ **Data Definition Language (DDL):** Creating, deleting, and changing database objects.

○ **Data Manipulation Language (DML):** Selecting, inserting, updating, and deleting data.

○ **Data Control Language (DCL):** Granting or revoking access to database objects.

Each sub-language contains its own keywords that define the actions that language performs. A *keyword* is an action word that commands the database to do something specific. These keywords can't be used for any other object in a database. This will become clearer in this discussion.

You may see these sub-languages split up in different ways, but these separations are widely accepted by the practicing database community. This chapter covers each of the keywords within each sub-language in detail. Not all of the keywords work in Access, but you should still get to know the few keywords you can't use in Access because of their importance to SQL, overall. You may know many of these keywords from the chapters covering queries. In those exercises, you perform Append (insert), Update, Delete, and Select queries. Those terms originated with SQL query keywords.

Transfer

You can read about Access queries in Chapters 4 and 5.

Table 13-2 lists the query types and their SQL keyword equivalents.

Table 13-2   Query Types

Query Type	SQL Keyword
Select	SELECT
Make Table	SELECT . . . INTO
Append	INSERT
Update	UPDATE
Crosstab	TRANSFORM
Delete	DELETE

Data Definition Language statements start with these keywords:

- CREATE
- DROP
- ALTER

Data Manipulation Language statements start with these keywords:

- SELECT
- SELECT . . . INTO
- INSERT
- UPDATE
- DELETE
- TRANSFORM

The Data Control Language statements start with these keywords:

- GRANT
- REVOKE

The SQL sub-languages contain more keywords than these. Some keywords are shared between the different sub-languages. I'll show you some of these keywords throughout the chapter.

Information Kiosk

SQL keywords appear in all caps to distinguish them from other words in a sentence, and table and column names in SQL queries and statements.

Syntax definitions

Any computer language has syntax definitions for commands. You see the command and a list of options, then an explanation of those options. You may be daunted when you first look at syntax definitions if you don't know *how* to look at them. This section provides a guide to those definitions so you'll never fear them again.

SQL syntax definitions adhere to the following structure:

- SQL keywords are in all caps.
- Optional keywords are enclosed in square brackets [ ].
- Table and column (field) names are in lowercase letters.
- Anything enclosed in parentheses must be enclosed in parentheses in the SQL statement, as well.

- An ellipsis (. . .) means that there's a continuation of some kind (you can read the ellipsis as *et cetera*).

- A comma followed by an ellipsis (, . . .) means that you may have multiple entries of the same type.

- Curly brackets { } (not shown in the following example) contain alternative required options. See the syntax for the DROP keyword in the section "DROP," later in this chapter, as an example.

The following syntax definition is for the REPLACE keyword, which is a valid keyword in some SQL implementations (Access doesn't recognize REPLACE, so it's a great example):

Syntax definitions are displayed on multiple lines, but SQL commands aren't written that way. Using multiple lines for a syntax definition makes the definition easier to read and understand. These syntax definitions may become very long — covering a full page or more — and can be somewhat difficult to decipher if you don't have the preceding list to assist you.

Data Definition Language

The Data Definition Language (DDL) is concerned with creating, deleting, and changing database objects. It's called Data Definition because these keywords *define* the landscape of a database. By using the DDL keywords, you create databases, tables, views, indexes, and so on. Any database object that you create by using the CREATE keyword may also be deleted by using the DROP keyword. DROP is the SQL way to delete a database object.

Watch Your Step

You may be confused by having to use DROP to delete a database object and DELETE to delete columns or rows of data, but the two terms are meant to distinguish between the types of objects that you're deleting. Imagine the disaster if you had only one keyword to delete objects and data — you could DELETE an entire table when you only wanted to DROP a few records from the table.

CREATE

You use the CREATE keyword in an SQL statement to create a database or database object. You can't create a database by using the CREATE keyword in Access, but you can in most other RDBMSs (Relational Database Management Systems).

CREATE TABLE

After you create a database, creating tables is the next step in building a data-filled database. Creating tables can be a very complex task with SQL, but it's a skill worth knowing. The difficult part of creating a table is determining the data type and the column size for each column.

Here's the syntax for the CREATE TABLE statement:

```
CREATE [TEMPORARY] TABLE table
    (field1 type [(size)] [NOT NULL] [WITH COMPRESSION
| WITH COMP] [index1]
    [, field2 type [(size)] [NOT NULL] [index2] [, ...]]
    [, CONSTRAINT multifieldindex [, ...]])
```

You use SQL to build the examples in this chapter, with the exception of the database itself. Follow these steps to create a database in Access:

1. **Create a new database and name it (for example,** Chapter13**).**
2. **Close Table1 to delete it.**
3. **Click the Create tab.**
4. **Click the Query Design button and close the Show Table dialog box.**
5. **Right-click the Query1 tab and select SQL View.**

   You see a blank page that has the word SELECT highlighted in the upper-left corner.
6. **Use the Backspace key to remove SELECT from the SQL Query window.**
7. **To create an example table, enter the following SQL statement into the SQL Query window:**

   ```
   CREATE TABLE Customers (ID Counter Primary Key,
   First_Name text(50), Last_Name text(50), Phone
   text(12));
   ```
8. **Execute the query.**

   The Customers table appears in the left navigation pane.

Here are the functions of each part of the example CREATE TABLE statement in Step 7 of the preceding numbered list:

- **CREATE TABLE Customers:** This part of the statement tells Access that you're creating a table named Customers.

- **ID Counter Primary Key:** The first field (column) is named ID. "Counter" tells the database that this is an AutoNumber field, and "Primary Key" means that the field must be unique and can't be NULL or have no value.

- **First_Name text(50):** First_Name is the next field in the Customers table, and this statement defines that field with the text data type and a size limitation of 50 characters. I chose 50 simply to save space in the database. A text data type can be as large as 255 characters. You enclose the size parameter in parentheses.

- **Field Separator:** The field separator is the comma. Each field (column) definition is separated by a comma.

- **Parentheses:** The field (column) definitions are enclosed in a set of parentheses.

- **Semicolon:** The semicolon at the end of the CREATE statement tells Access that it has reached the end of the SQL statement. The semicolon is analogous to the period at the end of this sentence.

To continue populating this example with tables, repeat Steps 7 and 8 of the preceding numbered list for each of the following statements:

```
CREATE TABLE Orders (ID Counter Primary Key,          ←
Customer_ID integer, Item text(100), Description memo);

CREATE TABLE Suppliers (ID Counter Primary Key, Company ←
text(50), Address text(50), City text(30), State       ←
text(2), Zip text(10), Contact text(100));
```

Chapter 2 shows how to create tables and change the data type for a column in Datasheet and Design Views, so I don't review those processes here. In all of the other sections in this chapter, I demonstrate both the SQL and graphical method for each example.

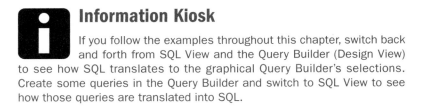

Information Kiosk

If you follow the examples throughout this chapter, switch back and forth from SQL View and the Query Builder (Design View) to see how SQL translates to the graphical Query Builder's selections. Create some queries in the Query Builder and switch to SQL View to see how those queries are translated into SQL.

CREATE VIEW

A *view* is a virtual table that's based on a select query. A view simply retrieves records from one or more tables, just like a query. A view is virtual in the sense that it holds no data and therefore takes up minimal space in a database.

Here's the CREATE VIEW syntax:

```
CREATE VIEW view
    [(field1[, field2[, ...]])]
    AS selectstatement
```

Transfer

Although you can't formally create a view in Access, I show how to simulate a view in Chapter 5. The "Make Table" query is a "view."

CREATE INDEX

An *index* is a special database object that's designed to speed access to data by creating references to the actual data. The index, rather than the actual data, is searched because the index is smaller and concerned with only one field (column) at a time.

Here's an example of a type of index that may better illustrate the point: Say you have a storage server that holds 300 GB (gigabytes) of data on it. When you want to find something, you open a search window, type in your search criteria, and click Search. After a very long time, the document you're looking for appears in the search window. Instead of following this procedure every time, you can create an index to search instead of looking through each file on the storage server. You create a file that's actually a list of all the other files, and you search that list from now on. The searches go much faster than before.

This book has an index that you can use to search for a topic much faster than flipping through each page to find what you're looking for. The Index in a book supplies you with a pointer (page number) to the item you want. A library also has an index, called a *card catalog,* that provides a pointer (a location in the library through the Dewey Decimal system) to the publication you want.

Your index provides a manageable way to refer to the actual data, speeding your search.

Here's the syntax for CREATE INDEX:

```
CREATE [ UNIQUE ] INDEX index
    ON table (field [ASC|DESC][, field [ASC|DESC], ...])
    [WITH { PRIMARY | DISALLOW NULL | IGNORE NULL }]
```

An index can either be unique (no duplicates allowed), such as a primary key, or it can be a regular index that allows duplicate values. This makes the index less efficient, but having any index is usually better than having no index at all. You should index all key fields. Primary keys are automatically indexed, but foreign keys aren't. You must create that index manually.

To create an index for a Foreign Key field in the Orders table, follow these steps:

1. **Enter a CREATE INDEX statement in the Query window, like this:**

```
CREATE UNIQUE INDEX custid_idx ON Orders (Customer_ID);
```

Always give your indexes a descriptive name. In this step's example, custid_idx is the name of the index.

2. Execute the query.

It looks like nothing happens, but the query's executed on the Orders table.

3. To see this example, open the Orders table in Design View, click the Customer_ID field, and look in the Field Properties window.

Figure 13-1 shows the Orders table in Design View.

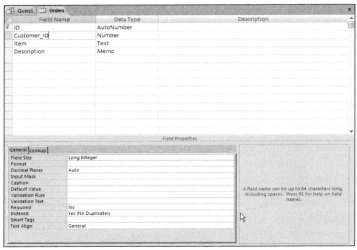

Figure 13-1: In the Field Properties window for Customer_ID, Indexed is set to "Yes (No Duplicates.)"

Find the Indexed row in the Field Properties window. The property for the Indexed row reads `Yes (No Duplicates)`, which is equivalent to the SQL statement keyword UNIQUE.

To see more information on indexed fields, click the Indexes button on the toolbar while you're in Design View. The Indexes window gives you more details about the indexes on the fields in your table.

DROP

DROP permanently deletes or removes a database object from a database.

The DROP keyword has this very straightforward syntax:

```
DROP {TABLE table | INDEX index ON table | PROCEDURE    ↩
procedure | VIEW view}
```

To remove an index (such as the one you create in the preceding section) by using the DROP keyword, follow these steps:

1. **Open a new query in SQL View.**
2. **Enter a DROP INDEX statement into the Query window, like this:**

   ```
   DROP INDEX custid_idx ON Orders;
   ```

3. **Execute the query.**
4. **Check that the index has been removed by looking at the table in Design View.**

If you forget the index name, then follow these steps:

1. **Open the Orders table in Design View.**
2. **Click the Indexes button on the toolbar.**

   The index names appear in this window.

To delete an entire table, follow these steps:

1. **Open a new query in SQL View or reuse an open query.**
2. **Enter a DROP TABLE statement to remove a table, like this:**

   ```
   DROP TABLE Customers;
   ```

3. **Execute the query.**

   The Customers table is removed from the left navigation pane.

 Watch Your Step

When you delete a database object with an SQL statement, no confirmation window pops up and asks, "Are you sure?" If you remove a table (by any method), all of the data in that table is also removed from the database, and you have no way to retrieve it.

ALTER TABLE

ALTER TABLE is actually a part of the ALTER keyword syntax. ALTER TABLE is the only ALTER syntax that works in Access. In other SQL implementations, you see the ALTER keyword and syntax for DATABASE, TABLE, VIEW, PROCEDURE, and so on. This is the ALTER TABLE syntax in Access:

```
ALTER TABLE table {ADD {COLUMN field type[(size)]
    [NOT NULL] [CONSTRAINT index] |
    ALTER COLUMN field type[(size)] |
    CONSTRAINT multifieldindex} |
    DROP {COLUMN field I CONSTRAINT indexname} }
```

With ALTER TABLE, you can easily add or remove columns from tables. If you always seem to forget an important column when creating a table, fortunately, you can use a simple remedy.

To add a column to a table, follow these steps:

1. **Open a new query in SQL View.**
2. **Enter an ALTER TABLE statement in the Query window, like this:**
   ```
   ALTER TABLE Suppliers ADD COLUMN Email text(60);
   ```
3. **Execute the query.**
4. **Open the Suppliers table to see that your column has been added.**

Information Kiosk

If you follow the example in these steps, look at the table in Design View under Field Properties — you can see the Field Size is 60, as designated in the SQL statement.

For practice, try removing the column you add to the Suppliers table in the preceding steps.

Data Manipulation Language

As the name implies, the Data Manipulation Language (DML) lets you manipulate data in a variety of ways. You can use this language to look at data selected from one or many tables; create a new table by selecting data into it; and insert, update, delete, or transform data.

INSERT

INSERT is the keyword you can use to write data to a table or multiple tables. In Access, you achieve this process by using an Append query. Although you can enter multiple records, as shown in the syntax definition, it's far more common to use the single-record method and repeat the INSERT statement through some kind of looping mechanism.

Here's the syntax for a multiple-record Append query:

```
INSERT INTO target [(field1[, field2[, ...]])]
    [IN externaldatabase]
    SELECT [source.]field1[, field2[, ...]
    FROM tableexpression
```

Here's the syntax for a single-record Append query:

```
INSERT INTO table [(field1[, field2[, ...]])]
    VALUES (value1[, value2[, ...])
```

The example in the following steps requires you to recreate the Customers table that you drop in the section "DROP," earlier in this chapter. If you need to recreate a table, follow these steps:

1. **Create a table with the CREATE TABLE statement.**

The CREATE statement for the Customers table is

```
CREATE TABLE Customers (ID Counter Primary Key,      ↵
First_Name text(50), Last_Name text(50), Phone       ↵
text(12));
```

2. **Execute the query.**

The table appears in the left navigation pane.

3. **For each record you want to add in a table, enter an INSERT statement and execute the statement.**

The following INSERT statements populate the Customers table in this example:

```
INSERT INTO Customers (First_Name, Last_Name,        ↵
Phone) VALUES ("Bob", "Smith", "918-555-1234");
INSERT INTO Customers (First_Name, Last_Name,        ↵
Phone) VALUES ("John", "Lee", "918-555-2234");
INSERT INTO Customers (First_Name, Last_Name,        ↵
Phone) VALUES ("Linda", "Jones", "918-555-3234");
INSERT INTO Customers (First_Name, Last_Name,        ↵
Phone) VALUES ("Alice", "Hill", "918-555-4234");
```

An explanation of the INSERT statements follows these steps.

4. **Open the Customers table to see that the records were correctly inserted.**

An INSERT statement has a straightforward syntax that consists of three parts:

- **INSERT INTO table (for example,** `INSERT INTO Customers`**):** This part of the statement informs Access that you want to insert information into the Customers table.

- **Field list (for example,** `(First_Name, Last_Name, Phone)`**):** Lists the fields into which you want to insert data. You usually include all of the fields here, but you can include only one if you want to insert data into only one field.

- **Values list (for example,** `VALUES ("Bob", "Smith", "918-555-1234")`**):** The values list must match the field list in number and type. If you have two fields listed in the field list with a certain data type, you must have two fields in the values list with the same data type.

I left out the ID field in my example statements, even though the ID field is required because it's a primary key. The omission is on purpose. You can omit the ID field because it's an AutoNumber field (Counter) whose value Access handles for you. If you use any other data type for the primary key, you must supply a unique value for the field manually.

SELECT

SELECT is the standard way to pull data from a database. Selecting data is the most basic way to interact with a database, and SELECT is by far the most used keyword in SQL. To select data from a database, you must have

- Access to the database
- A database client that's connected to the database
- Permissions to read data

Selecting data from a database requires the least effort from a database administrator and is the basic way that most people interact with data. Actions that you can perform by using SELECT queries include

- Looking up a price
- Searching for a phone number
- Validating an ID

 Information Kiosk

Having SELECT permission to a database is sometimes called *read-only access.* This permission means that you may read (look at) data, but you can't write anything new to the database.

Here's the syntax for SELECT:

```
SELECT [predicate] { * | table.* | [table.]field1
    [AS alias1] [, [table.]field2 [AS alias2] [, ...]]}
    FROM tableexpression [, ...] [IN externaldatabase]
    [WHERE... ]
    [GROUP BY... ]
    [HAVING... ]
    [ORDER BY... ]
    [WITH OWNERACCESS OPTION]
```

Because SELECT is such a complex keyword, I use only some very simple examples in this chapter.

The following example shows you how to get all of the data from a table exactly as it was inserted. This approach isn't a good example of proper SQL, but I give it to you for quick queries and for testing purposes. To use SELECT in a query, follow these steps:

1. **Open a new query and switch to SQL View.**
2. **Enter a SELECT statement, like this:**

```
SELECT * FROM Customers;
```

3. **Execute the query.**

If you're following the examples in this chapter, you see results like Table 13-3.

Table 13-3   Sample SELECT Results

ID	First_Name	Last_Name	Phone
1	Bob	Smith	918-555-1234
2	John	Lee	918-555-2234
3	Linda	Jones	918-555-3234
4	Alice	Hill	918-555-4234

You can also select individual columns in any order you want. Just follow these steps:

1. **Enter a SELECT statement into the Query window, like this:**

```
SELECT Last_Name, First_Name FROM Customers;
```

2. **Execute the query.**

The results of this example are shown in Table 13-4.

Table 13-4   Selected Results

Last_Name	First_Name
Smith	Bob
Lee	John
Jones	Linda
Hill	Alice

When you create a query in SQL View, the equivalent query is also created in Design View in the Query Builder. The same is true for queries created by using the Query Builder — any query you create with the Query Builder appears in its SQL format in SQL View.

Watch Your Step

When switching to SQL View from Design View, you may find that the SQL seems a bit more complex than a query that you would enter yourself. You see square brackets [ ], parentheses, and the keyword AS in SELECT statements that are generated automatically by Access.

To see the query in the Query Builder, follow these steps:

1. With the SELECT statement still in the SQL Query window, switch to Query Design View to see how the query looks from that perspective.

2. Execute the query and compare the results with those you received when you executed the SQL statement.

Information Kiosk

Using the * in SELECT statements is discouraged because when you use *, the database has to scan across every column and down every row in the table. If the table is very large, this scanning could take some time. Always select only the columns you need for a query. Rarely do you ever need all the columns in a table for a query.

To use SELECT to isolate a single record, you need to use a query that contains the WHERE clause. The WHERE clause isolates records based on some criteria that you set. Usually, the criterion is a column (field) that's set to a value.

Here are some examples of WHERE clauses:

🔘 WHERE Last_Name = "Hill"

This retrieves all of the records where the value in Last_Name is Hill.

🔘 WHERE ID = 2

This retrieves all of the records where the value in ID equals 2. Because ID is a primary key field, this criterion will retrieve a maximum of one record.

To use a WHERE clause in a query, follow these steps:

1. **Enter a SELECT statement into the Query window, like this:**

```
SELECT First_Name, Last_Name WHERE Last_Name ="Hill";
```

2. **Execute the query.**

For this example, the record for Alice Hill appears.

As another example, try the same query with the WHERE clause: WHERE ID = 2.

SELECT . . . INTO

SELECT . . . INTO is the way Access executes a Make Table query. This method also somewhat simulates a View (virtual table) in Access. You can also use SELECT . . . INTO to create a new table of data from another table or multiple tables by using a SELECT statement.

Here's the syntax for the SELECT . . . INTO keyword:

```
SELECT field1[, field2[, ...]]
INTO newtable
[IN externaldatabase]
FROM source
```

To create a new table by using SELECT . . . INTO, follow these steps:

1. **Enter a SELECT . . . INTO statement into the Query window in SQL View, like this:**

```
SELECT Last_Name, First_Name INTO Names FROM Customers;
```

2. **Execute the query.**

3. **Click Yes when prompted to append rows of data into a new table.**

The new table (for example, Names) appears in the left navigation pane.

The AS keyword, mentioned in the "SELECT" section, adds a bit of creativity to the column names if you need it. The AS keyword creates an alias for a column name. For instance, if you want to select the first and last names from the Customers table but want to use `Fore` and `Sur` rather than `First_Name` and `Last_Name` for the column names, then you use the AS keyword alias.

To use the AS keyword with a SELECT statement, follow these steps:

1. **Enter a SELECT . . . INTO statement into the Query window in SQL View, like this:**

```
SELECT First_Name AS Fore, Last_Name AS Sur INTO    ↵
Olde_Names FROM Customers;
```

2. **Execute the query.**

3. **Click Yes when prompted to append rows to a new table.**

   For this example, the Olde_Names table appears in the left navigation pane.

4. **Open the new table (for example, Olde_Names) to view the data.**

   For this example, your results should look like those in Table 13-5.

Table 13-5 **Sample AS Results**

Fore	Sur
Bob	Smith
John	Lee
Linda	Jones
Alice	Hill

UPDATE

You can use the UPDATE keyword to change or correct data in a table. The syntax is very simple, but this statement can have devastating results if you don't construct it carefully. The contents of an entire column can be updated to the same value by a malformed UPDATE query. This is the syntax for the UPDATE keyword:

```
UPDATE table
    SET newvalue
    WHERE criteria;
```

Say you find that, Alice Hill's name is actually Alice Hall. You can use the UPDATE keyword to solve this issue. The only problem is finding a way to update just the one record for Alice and not any others. You use the WHERE criteria part of the UPDATE statement to uniquely identify a record. If you can, use the ID as the WHERE criteria because the ID is unique to the record.

To use UPDATE to change a single record, follow these steps:

1. **Enter an UPDATE statement into the Query window, like this:**
   ```
   UPDATE Customers SET Last_Name = "Hall" WHERE ID = 4;
   ```

2. **Execute the query.**

3. **Click Yes to verify the update.**

4. **Open the table to confirm the change.**

   For this example, open the Customers table to see that the record for Alice has been updated.

By omitting the WHERE clause, you're telling Access to update the entire column to the SET value. The following example demonstrates this technique. To see how this works, follow these steps:

1. **Enter an UPDATE statement into the Query window, like this:**

   ```
   UPDATE Customers SET Phone = "918-555-1234";
   ```

2. **Execute the query.**

3. **Click Yes to verify the update.**

4. **Open the Customers table to observe the change.**

   For this example, each customer's phone number is now 918-555-1234.

 Information Kiosk

Access has a nice built-in warning system for updates and appends. It notifies you that you're about to update or append a certain number of records, and you must click Yes to continue or No to cancel. If you're updating one record and you receive a warning that says four records will be updated, click No and try the query again.

DELETE

DELETE removes data, not objects, from a table. If improperly written, this type of query can empty the contents of an entire table. You can actually use DELETE to empty a table purposefully. Using DELETE in this way is the same as omitting the WHERE clause in the UPDATE statement.

Here's the syntax for the DELETE keyword:

```
DELETE [table.*]
    FROM table
    WHERE criteria
```

Say that Alice Hall is no longer a customer, and you need to purge her record from the system. The following steps perform the task:

1. **Enter a DELETE statement into the Query window, like this:**

   ```
   DELETE FROM Customers WHERE ID = 4;
   ```

2. **Execute the query.**

3. **Click Yes to confirm the deletion.**

4. **Open the table to see that Alice's record has been removed.**

Emptying a table is probably easier than you think — and maybe easier than it should be. To empty a table, follow these steps:

1. **Enter a query into the Query window, like this:**

```
DELETE FROM Customers;
```

2. **Execute the query.**

3. **Click Yes to confirm the deletion.**

4. **Open the table (for example, Customers) to see that you have no data.**

Pay attention to the confirmation dialog boxes that Access provides to make sure that the action (DELETE, in this case) is what you really want to do. Use this safety net to prevent yourself from deleting data you want to keep.

TRANSFORM

TRANSFORM is an SQL keyword that's unique to Microsoft Access. You use it to create Crosstab queries and Pivot tables. I'm providing TRANSFORM to make you aware of its existence, but I don't cover the SQL part of it in detail because you can use this procedure more effectively by using the graphical tools. The TRANSFORM keyword, Crosstab queries, and Pivot tables are too advanced to fall into the scope of this book.

The SQL syntax for TRANSFORM is

```
TRANSFORM aggfunction
    selectstatement
    PIVOT pivotfield [IN (value1[, value2[, ...]])]
```

Data Control Language

Access 2007 databases don't support user-level security, but older database versions do. I'm including the keywords in the Data Control Language (DCL) as definitions only so you can use them to manipulate user-level security in older Access databases. (Also, they're still a part of basic SQL, so you should be aware of them.)

 Transfer

You can get a thorough look at Access security features and issues in Chapter 15.

DCL includes transactional keywords such as BEGIN, ROLLBACK, and SAVE-POINT. Access doesn't support transactions in DCL, so I'm omitting the keywords that define them from this discussion.

GRANT

The GRANT keyword bestows privileges (such as SELECT, UPDATE, DELETE, and INSERT) on database objects to a user or users.

The GRANT keyword has the following syntax:

```
GRANT {privilege[, privilege, ...]} ON
    {TABLE table | OBJECT object| CONTAINER container }
    TO {authorizationname[, authorizationname, ...]}
```

REVOKE

REVOKE is the SQL opposite of GRANT. REVOKE removes privileges on a database object from a user or users.

The syntax for REVOKE is

```
REVOKE {privilege[, privilege, ...]} ON
    {TABLE table |OBJECT object|CONTAINTER container}
    FROM {authorizationname[, authorizationname, ...]}
```

index: A database object that's created to speed searches by pointing to (referencing) the actual data in a compact and organized form.

keyword: An SQL word that performs some action on tables and data.

semantics: The perceived meaning of a set of instructions in a language.

SQL: Acronym for Structured Query Language; the organized set of keywords you use to manipulate database data.

syntax: The order and spelling of words in a language.

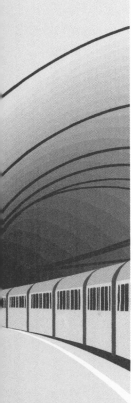

Practice Exam

1. The Data Manipulation Language is responsible for which of the following actions?

A) Creating database objects

B) Changing database objects

C) Speeding up data access

D) Removing data

2. Which of the following keywords removes a table from a database?

A) DELETE

B) DROP

C) REMOVE

D) REVOKE

3. Which SQL keyword is used more than any other?

A) APPEND

B) SELECT

C) INSERT

D) TRANSFORM

4. Which of the following is necessary to isolate a single record in a SELECT query (statement)?

A) SELECT

B) WHICH

C) WHERE

D) SET

5. SQL is a language because it has _____ and _____.

A) Client, server

B) Fore, Sur

C) DML, DDL

D) Syntax, semantics

6. It's possible to completely empty a table with which keyword.

A) UPDATE

B) DELETE

C) REVOKE

D) SELECT . . . INTO

7. Which of the following keywords would you use to change the spelling of a person's name in a table?

A) SELECT . . . INTO

B) SELECT

C) ALTER

D) UPDATE

8. Which keyword would you use to create an index on a column?

A) ALTER

B) UPDATE

C) SELECT

D) INDEX

9. The SELECT . . . INTO keyword is one way to:

A) Create a new table with data already in it.

B) Create an index on a column.

C) Update a person's name in a table.

D) Empty a table.

10. **What would you use to remove a column from a table?**

A) REMOVE COLUMN

B) ALTER COLUMN

C) ALTER TABLE

D) ALTER INDEX

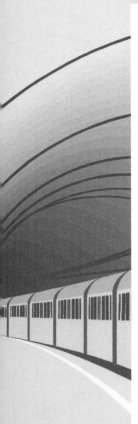

Connecting with ODBC

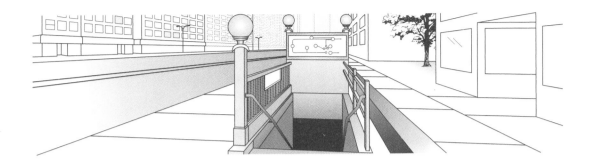

 # Enter the Station

Questions

1. What is ODBC?

2. Why do you use ODBC?

3. What's a DSN?

4. How can you connect to non-Microsoft databases by using ODBC?

5. How can you connect to SQL Server by using ODBC?

6. Can you connect to file-based databases by using ODBC?

Express Line

If you already know about ODBC connections, then skip ahead to Chapter 15.

This chapter introduces you to connecting to other databases by using ODBC (Open Database Connectivity). ODBC is a universal method for connecting to foreign databases. Using Access, you can connect to a wide array of foreign databases and use the data as if it were local. This chapter includes several methods of connecting to databases by using ODBC.

Open Database Connectivity

ODBC is one of Access's finest features. It makes connecting to other RDBMSs (Relational Database Management Systems) a snap. ODBC is the capability to connect to databases on remote database systems like they're local to Access.

Access can connect to any foreign database system for which someone has created a driver for this purpose. Access installs some drivers and others you have to download. In this chapter, I demonstrate how to connect to three different database systems: Microsoft SQL Server, MySQL, and SQLite. I work with these three very popular and diverse systems on a regular basis. They represent the full gamut of connectivity options you have in ODBC when connecting to foreign database systems.

Because ODBC operates under the assumption that all databases speak and understand SQL, those databases should be able to communicate with each other on some level. This cross-database connectivity is extremely valuable if, for example, your organization uses SQL Server as its enterprise database solution but your staff are more comfortable with Access. Access can happily act as an SQL client for just about any database. Access can also connect to many different types of databases simultaneously, and the end user has to know only how to use Access.

You can use Access as an SQL client to connect to other RDBMSs by using ODBC. This approach solves many issues for corporations and users alike. The issues that Access resolves include these:

- Access is inexpensive.
- Many people already have experience with Access.
- Training is inexpensive and readily available.
- Access is such so widely used as a DBMS (Database Management System) client that it's almost universal.
- Access has rich form and report capability.
- Access has an intuitive graphical interface.

Access also has its downside as a client interface. The following list includes often-given arguments against using Access as an SQL client interface:

- It uses a very small implementation of SQL.
- It's a *heavy* client, meaning it requires installation and has a very large *footprint* (installation size).
- It works only on Windows systems.
- It requires training to use its advanced features.
- It isn't free.
- Some vendors supply their own client software or use a Web-based client interface, both of which may be better than using Access.

Access works well as a client because of its features, interface, and ease of use. But you must evaluate each database implementation individually to test Access's viability as a client for that system.

Making the Connection to SQL Server

Microsoft SQL Server is Microsoft's entry into the enterprise-level database-server market. It's the next logical step in upsizing from Access. You can even access an SQL Server Upsizing Wizard from the Database Tools tab in Access.

Making the leap from Access to SQL Server doesn't mean that you must, or should, dump Access. Access is a great companion to SQL Server for two reasons: It can connect readily to SQL Server databases, and Access has impressive form and report features that make it a perfect partner to SQL Server. In fact, SQL Server database administrators (DBAs) often *prototype* (build and test) their databases in Access before migrating them to SQL Server.

Information Kiosk

To connect through ODBC to an SQL Server database, you need to know a user name and password for a database on that SQL Server system. Contact your SQL Server DBA for a test database that you can use for these examples. You can also download MSDE (Microsoft Desktop Engine) to your computer and set up your own test environment. MSDE is a Desktop version of SQL Server that you can download and use for free.

Unless you're using MSDE or another local version of SQL Server, this book assumes that you'll be connecting to SQL Server over the network. The following example is based on an over-the-network ODBC connection to SQL Server. If your copy of SQL Server is local (on the same computer as Access), you can find instructions on how to connect to that later in this chapter.

Creating the DSN

A DSN (Data Source Name) is a connection string that contains the information necessary to connect a database client to a database server by using ODBC. The DSN may be a file that contains all of the connection parameters. The DSN connection information may also be stored in your computer's Registry or in the client program.

The DSN usually consists of the following pieces of information:

- A unique name for the DSN: _____

  The DSN must have a unique name on the host on which it's created. The name can be anything you want, as long as it conforms to standard system naming rules, but it should be descriptive.

- The hostname or IP Address of the database server: _____

  The hostname or IP address of the database server is the identifying name or numerical address of the server that holds the database to which you're connecting.

- A user name and password: _____

  You must use a user name and matching password to make the connection. The user name must have sufficient privileges to connect over the network or locally to the database.

- A TCP/IP port number (if different than the default): _____

  The TCP/IP port number is valid only in RDBMSs with client/server architecture. File-based systems generally don't use this scheme.

- The database name and a table name: _____

  The database and table names are specified in the connection string to attach directly to that resource.

- The driver name: _____

  The driver name is sometimes included in the connection string in the DSN.

- Optional parameters: _____

  Depending on the RDBMS you're connecting to, there you may have to supply optional parameters in the connection string.

The following examples are different DSN connection strings for different RDBMSs:

Microsoft SQL Server:

```
ODBC;DRIVER=SQL Server;SERVER=10.0.1.240;UID=sa;APP=2007 Microsoft    ↩
Office system;DATABASE=Books;TABLE=dbo.Titles
```

MySQL Server:

```
ODBC;DATABASE=Books;DSN=mysql-books;OPTION=0;PORT=0;SERVER=10.0.1.250;    ↩
TABLE=Titles
```

SQLite database:

```
ODBC;DSN=SQLite-Books;Database=D:\SQLite\Books.db;StepAPI=0;Timeout=;    ↩
NoWCHAR=0;TABLE=Items
```

To create an ODBC connection to a Microsoft SQL Server database, follow these steps:

1. **Open a new blank database in Access.**
2. **Name the database (for example,** Chapter14**) and click Create.**

   The database opens, showing a blank Table1.
3. **Close Table1 to remove it.**
4. **Click the External Data tab and click the More button in the Import group.**
5. **Select ODBC Database in the drop-down list.**

   The Get External Data — ODBC Database dialog box opens.
6. **Select** *Link to the data source by creating a linked table* **and click OK.**

   You're now presented with the Select Data Source window shown in Figure 14-1.

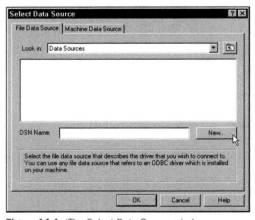

Figure 14-1: tThe Select Data Source window.

7. Click the New button.

The Create New Data Source window opens.

8. Scroll to the bottom of the list, select SQL Server, and click Next.

9. Enter a name for the DSN into the field (for example, SQL_Svr_Books) and click Next.

10. Click Finish.

The Create a New Data Source to SQL Server window opens. The Data Source Name field is grayed out because you supply that in Step 9.

11. Enter a description into the Description field (for example, "Books Database on SQL Server").

Clicking the Server drop-down list browses your network for SQL Servers, which may or may not be found.

12. Select your SQL Server from the list or enter the SQL Server name or IP address in the dialog box and click Next.

For example, I enter the IP address of the SQL Server (10.0.1.240) on my network.

13. Select the method that you want to use to authenticate to the SQL Server.

I always use a separate user name and password. So I choose the following option: *With SQL Server authentication using a login ID and password entered by the user.*

14. Enter the user name and password for SQL Server authentication and click Next.

15. Select the check box labeled "Change the default database to" and select a database (for example, Books) from the drop-down list, click Next, and click Finish.

You're presented with a window showing a summary of all of your connection parameters. The screen displays three buttons: Test Data Source, OK, and Cancel. You always need to test your data source to make sure all the information you entered for the DSN is okay, and to verify connectivity between the client (Access) and the server (SQL Server).

16. Click the Test Data Source button.

On-screen messages show you the connection process going on; finally a message appears that says TESTS COMPLETED SUCCESSFULLY!

17. Click OK three times to finish the wizard and return to Access.

The following section shows how to connect to the ODBC data source (SQL Server database).

Linking the tables

After you finish the ODBC Wizard and return to Access, which I describe in the preceding section, you're prompted for a password for the ODBC connection. Follow these steps to connect Access to the SQL Server database (Books):

1. Enter the password and click OK.

The connection is made, and the database you specified in the ODBC connection string appears in the Link Tables window with its tables displayed. Figure 14-2 shows the available tables on the SQL Server.

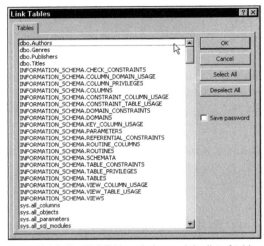

Figure 14-2: The Link Tables window and the list of tables from the Books SQL Server database.

ℹ Information Kiosk

Microsoft SQL Server table names begin with the letters dbo. These letters tell you that these tables are user-created — differentiating them from the system tables. System table names begin with sys and INFORMATION_SCHEMA. The user can't directly alter the system tables.

2. Select the four dbo tables and click OK.

When you click OK, the Link Tables Wizard launches and begins to connect to the tables, one by one. As you can see in Figure 14-3, the wizard prompts you to select the primary key (Unique Record Identifier) for each table.

3. Select the ID field and click OK.

You're prompted to identify the primary key for each table to which you're linking.

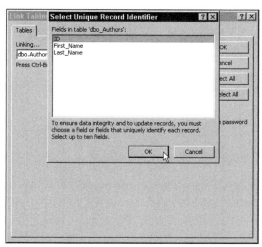

Figure 14-3: Select each table's primary key from the Select Unique Record Identifier dialog box.

All selected tables are now linked to your current database (in my Books example). Because you specified a primary key for each table, you can perform queries on the data just as if the tables were local to Access.

Watch Your Step

The permissions you have on an SQL Server database are con-
trolled by the DBA from SQL Server. You have the specified permissions that DBA has granted you.

Exploring MySQL through ODBC

MySQL is considered the world's most popular open-source database. It's not a Microsoft product. It's an *open-source* product, which means the company that created it (MySQL AB) lets you download the source code for MySQL along with the program itself. This is a new trend and business model for companies worldwide. You can read more of the story at www.mysql.com.

MySQL is like SQL Server (which you can read about in the preceding sections) in several ways. Both are

- Enterprise-level database solutions
- Commercially supported
- Compliant with SQL standards

- Client/server style databases
- Greatly concerned with security and data integrity

Both SQL Server and MySQL offer multiple versions of the same product for different uses.

The steps in the following sections are an example of how you connect to non-Microsoft database sources by using Access. You use a very similar process when you want to connect to other client/server architecture databases (such as Oracle, Sybase, PostgreSQL, and Informix).

The example in the following sections assumes that you have a MySQL Server on your network and a user name and password adequate to connect and use a database through the network in the MySQL Server.

Setting up the ODBC data source

Before you connect to MySQL, you must do some preliminary work. This method of connection is a little different than connecting to SQL Server, but this section shows you the standard way to connect to a foreign RDMBS. To set up the ODBC data source, follow these steps:

1. **On your Desktop, select Start → Programs → Administrative Tools → Data Sources (ODBC).**

The ODBC Data Source Administrator opens. Figure 14-4 shows the ODBC Data Source Administrator and its options.

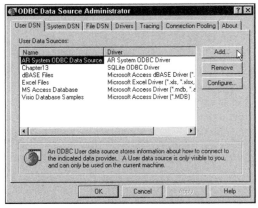

Figure 14-4: You can create a new data source (DSN) in the ODBC Data Source Administrator.

2. Select the System DSN tab and click Add.

Scroll all the way down to the bottom of the list to find the MySQL driver labeled MySQL ODBC 3.51 Driver.

3. Select the MySQL ODBC 3.51 Driver and click Finish.

The MySQL ODBC driver isn't listed by default. You must download it from www.mysql.com and install it. After you install it, it shows up in the list.

When you click Finish, the MySQL Add Data Source Name Applet is launched, as shown in Figure 14-5.

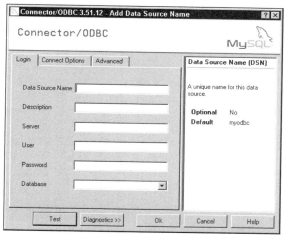

Figure 14-5: Create the DSN by using the MySQL Add Data Source Name Applet.

4. Table 14-1 lists the connection information that you need to enter and suggests some sample data.

Table 14-1   MySQL Connection Information

Login Information	Sample Data
Data Source Name	MySQL–Books
Description	ODBC Connection to Books
Server	10.0.1.250
User	dbuser
Password	password
Database (drop-down list)	Books (from drop-down list)

When you enter the information in Table 14-1, the drop-down list populates with the available databases the user can access.

5. Click OK.

The DSN has been added to the list of available System DSNs in the ODBC Data Source Administrator.

6. Click OK to close the ODBC Data Source Administrator.

The following section shows how to connect to the MySQL server.

Connecting to the MySQL Server

When you have created a DSN, the next order of business is to use it to connect to a MySQL Server. To do so, follow these steps:

1. Click the External Data tab and click the More button in the Import group.

2. Select ODBC Database in the drop-down list.

The Get External Data — ODBC Database dialog box opens.

3. Select *Link to the data source by creating a linked table* and click OK.

The Select Data Source window appears.

4. Click the Machine Data Source tab.

5. Scroll down and select the DSN you created (for example, the steps in the preceding section create "MySQL–Books") and click OK.

A list of tables from the ODBC-connected database (for example, the Books database used earlier in this chapter) appears in the Link Tables window, as shown in Figure 14-6.

Figure 14-6: The Link Tables window shows tables from Books on the MySQL Server.

6. **Select the tables you want to link to and click OK.**

In my example, I select Agents, Authors, Editors, Publishers, and Works from the list. You're prompted to select the primary key in each table as you link them so they can be updated by using Access.

All selected tables are now linked to the current database.

Accessing SQLite by Using an ODBC Connection

Like Access, SQLite is a *file-based* RDBMS, which means it's not a client/server application. SQLite is open-source software, available free of charge. You can download it, use it, create commercial applications with it, and sell those applications without paying any money to anyone. This makes SQLite ideal for anyone who needs a versatile database that can be used for almost any purpose.

SQLite is a small, useful desktop database but it lacks many features that would enhance its chances of widespread adoption. For example, it has only a command-line interface (although some available third-party tools can give it a graphical interface).

You can find out more about SQLite at www.sqlite.org.

The download version is labeled something like *sqlite-2_x_x.zip for Windows* or *Win32*.

After downloading the zip file, unzip it into the C:\Windows folder on your computer.

The following sections demonstrate how Access can connect to diverse data sources. To connect and use an SQLite database you only need to access the SQLite database file from a file share or on your local computer. I've downloaded and installed the SQLite ODBC drivers necessary to make this connection. They aren't included with Windows.

Use the following link to download the current version (sqliteodbc.exe):

www.ch-werner.de/sqliteodbc

After you download the file (sqliteodbc.exe), locate it, and double-click it to install the SQLite ODBC drivers on your computer.

Follow the on-screen instructions to complete the installation.

Creating the SQLite ODBC connection

You can create the SQLite DSN from within Access.

Watch Your Step

The ODBC connection in this section is made with SQLite version 2.X. SQLite version 3.X is available, but many vendors don't support it yet. I've been able to create ODBC connections with only SQLite version 2.X databases. Your success depends on the availability of the newer ODBC drivers for version 3.X.

To create the SQLite DSN, follow these steps:

1. **From within Access, click the External Data tab and click the More button in the Import group.**

2. **Select ODBC Database in the drop-down list.**

   The Get External Data — ODBC Database dialog box opens.

3. **Select *Link to the data source by creating a linked table* and click OK.**

   The Select Data Source window appears.

4. **Click the Machine Data Source tab.**

5. **Click the New button.**

6. **Select System Data Source and click Next.**

7. **Scroll all the way down the list of data sources until you see SQLite ODBC Driver, select it, click Next, and then click Finish.**

   The SQL ODBC DNS Configuration window appears. The following section shows how to link tables to this DSN.

Linking to the SQLite tables

After you create the DSN (as shown in the preceding section), you can link to the tables in an SQLite database. Follow these steps:

1. **Enter a database name (such as SQLite–Books) into the Data Source Name field.**

2. **Click Browse and navigate to the location of the database (for example, the Books database), select it, and click Open.**

3. **Click OK to accept the information and click OK again to close the Select Data Source window.**

   The Link Tables window opens, displaying the available tables.

4. **Select the tables you want to link to and click OK.**

   I chose all three tables in my example: Customers, Items, and Orders. The tables are linked one table at a time. You're prompted for the primary key for each table as it's linked.

connection string: A list of parameters used to identify a foreign database, a path to the database, a TCP/IP port, a driver name, a table name, a user name, and other parameters needed to access a foreign database through ODBC.

DSN: Data Source Name; comprised of a connection string and a driver to make a connection to a foreign database.

MySQL: An open-source database system that's useful as a desktop database, a workgroup database, and an enterprise solution.

ODBC: Open Database Connectivity; a standard that describes how dissimilar databases can connect to and communicate with each other through SQL.

open source: A type of computer program that's usually delivered with its source code so that the worldwide community can make changes and improvements.

SQLite: An open-source database system that's small and free, and which can be used on a variety of platforms (operating systems).

Last Stop

Practice Exam

1. **ODBC is an acronym that stands for what?**

A) Open Database Clustering

B) Open Database Connectivity

C) Open Data Connection

D) Open Data-Bound Collection

2. **To use ODBC to connect to a foreign database, what must you have in place?**

A) ODBC drivers for the foreign database

B) A backup plan

C) A simplified protocol for maintaining data integrity

D) A client/server model

3. **A DSN connection string usually contains which of the following pieces of information?**

A) Database, protocol, and connection

B) Database, table, and driver name

C) Table, TCP/IP port, and structure

D) Table, structure, and driver name

4. **Open Source means:**

A) The software is free.

B) The software is very inexpensive.

C) The program code is available.

D) The program is unsecured.

5. When linking tables through ODBC, you're prompted for what before each table is linked?

A) The table structure

B) The primary key

C) The secondary key

D) The table key connection

6. Access can make an ODBC connection to SQL Server very easily because:

A) Access can't connect to SQL Server through ODBC.

B) Both Access and SQL Server use the same drivers.

C) SQL Server support is built into Access and Windows.

D) The DSN already exists.

7. True or false (explain why): You may connect only to databases that have a client/server architecture.

_____

_____

_____

8. True or false (explain why): A DSN can be created only from within Access.

_____

_____

_____

9. When you connect to a foreign database through ODBC, you can work with the tables from those databases the same way you would if they were:

A) Local

B) New

C) Integrated

D) Separate

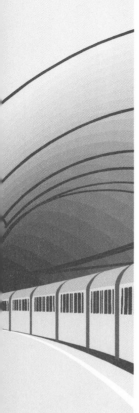

10. **Using ODBC is advantageous because:**

A) It's inexpensive.

B) It shows that you have advanced Access expertise.

C) It lets you connect to a wide array of foreign databases.

D) It's proprietary.

Securing Access Databases

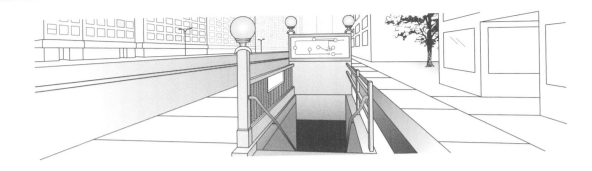

 # Enter the Station

Questions

1. What's user-level security?

2. Why doesn't Access 2007 support user-level security?

3. What types of security does Access 2007 support?

4. How can I protect my databases on a network?

5. What's a trusted publisher?

6. How can I prevent users from changing the design or code in a database?

Express Line

If you're already familiar with securing Access databases, then skip ahead to Chapter 16.

This chapter focuses on the advances and changes in security for Microsoft Access 2007 over previous versions of Access. User-level security has been replaced with trusted locations, operating-system permissions, and other advanced methods. This chapter also includes sections on how to prevent users from changing design and code in your databases.

Exploring Access 2007 Security

Security is one of the biggest concerns in businesses of all sizes. Breaches, exploits, network break-ins, hacks, and hack attempts have increased dramatically in the past few years. Software companies such as Microsoft are scrambling to address those security concerns in a timely and cost-effective manner. Many companies have even hired security experts to address their problems and remain abreast of the latest developments in security and hacker techniques.

Microsoft has made great strides in security for its applications, services, and operating systems. With the introduction of Access 2007, much has changed in the way Access handles security: Access now handles user access to directories and from an operating-system perspective, and handles application security inside the application itself.

Information Kiosk

Access 2007 no longer supports or provides a mechanism for user-level security. This new version has no Workgroup Administrator application (which was available in previous versions of Access). Access 2007 honors user-level security if you open a database from an older version of Access in Access 2007. If you convert an older Access database to the Access 2007 format, however, the security settings will be stripped from the older version.

Handling User-Level Security

In Access 2007, user-level security is handled on the server where the database is stored. The permissions on the database determine such permissions as who can open it or make changes. If you're the server administrator, you can set permissions on the database file, the containing folder, or the shares (files or directories made available on the network) set up to allow network access to the database. User and group permissions at the level of the operating system are your strongest defense against unauthorized use.

Information Kiosk

In older versions of Access, user-level security was handled by the Workgroup Administrator application and a Workgroup information file. This file was checked when Access started, and the user was prompted for a password.

Using operating-system security

The best way to manage permissions on files, folders, and shares is to use access groups. For example, say you have three people in your research workgroup who need to use and modify a database that's on a network server. You, or the administrator, create a new group named Research and add the appropriate personnel to the group. The Research group is set up with file, folder, and share permissions necessary to allow the group to access the database appropriately.

Figures 15-1 through 15-7 show a hypothetical setup of file, folder, and share security settings.

Watch Your Step

The figures and instructions in this chapter are taken from a Windows Server (Windows Server 2003) and therefore don't look the same as a Windows Desktop (Windows 2000, Windows XP, or Vista) computer. Configuring security on your network might be different.

Adding share permissions

To show how to add share permissions, I created a folder on the server named `Databases` in which the databases I want to share will be stored. To share a network folder, follow these steps:

1. **Right-click the folder and select Sharing and Security.**

   Figure 15-1 shows this first step in configuring security for the folder.

   The Folder Properties dialog box appears.

2. **Select** *Share this folder.*

   The default share name is always the same as the folder name. You can change this name if you want.

3. **Click the Permissions button.**

   Doing so begins the process of setting security on the shared folder. Figure 15-2 shows the Sharing tab of the Folder Properties dialog box.

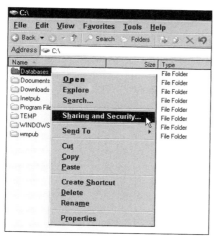

Figure 15-1: Select Sharing and Security from the folder's right-click menu.

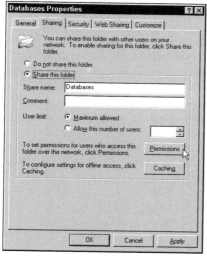

Figure 15-2: Share a folder in the Sharing tab.

4. Modify the default permissions if necessary.

Figure 15-3 shows the original permission settings for a new folder: Everyone — Read. This means any new folder you create is automatically set up with Read permission for Everyone. By default on this network, when you create a new folder, everyone can look at files in that folder, but nobody can change the files. Before you can change this default behavior, you must add the new permissions to the share, in the dialog box shown in Figure 15-3.

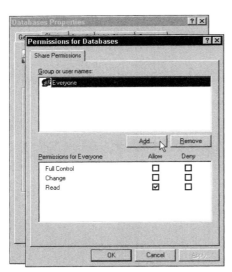

Figure 15-3: You can adjust permissions in the Share Permissions dialog box.

As a typical example, you can add the Research group to the Share Permissions list, specify this new group's permissions, and remove the Everyone group from the Share Permissions list.

Setting share permissions

After you add groups to the share permissions, you must set permissions for the physical folder that contains the databases. Figure 15-4 shows the check boxes you use to set permissions.

For my example, here's what you need to know:

- I've selected the folder's Security tab.

- I've added the Research group to the permissions.

- I've given Full Control to both the Research and Administrators groups by checking *Allow for all permissions*.

- I've removed the Everyone group from the folder permissions.

- I've set permissions for both the network folder share and for the actual physical folder that will contain the databases for the Research group.

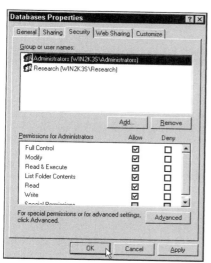

Figure 15-4: You can adjust security settings for each group in the Security tab.

You don't have to set permissions to the database file(s) explicitly after you place them in the Databases folder. They receive inherited permissions from the folder that contains them. The permissions on any database file placed in the Databases folder have Full Control for Administrators and the Research group without any intervention from you or the administrator.

Connecting to the shared folder

To connect to the shared folder (for example, Databases) from a workstation, follow these steps:

1. **Open My Computer, click Tools, then click Map Network Drive.**

   The Map Network Drive dialog box appears, and the first unused drive letter on your computer appears in the Drive drop-down list as the default network drive. You can change this drive to another unused drive letter if you want. Figure 15-5 shows how to set the drive letter in the Map Network Drive dialog box.

2. **Enter the name of the server and the share to which you want to connect, like this:**

   `\\servername\sharename`

   In my example, I use `\\10.0.1.240\Databases`, as shown in Figure 15-6.

3. **Select the** *Reconnect at logon* **check box and click Finish.**

   You're prompted for a user name and password for the share. Only the administrator or a member of the Research group can connect to this share.

Figure 15-5: You can set the drive letter in the Map Network Drive dialog box.

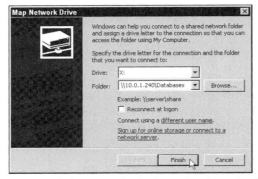

Figure 15-6: Connect to the database share by setting the folder.

4. **Enter a user name and password and click OK.**

For example, I enter the user name `bsmith`, type in the password for `bsmith`, and click OK, as shown in Figure 15-7.

Figure 15-7: Enter your user name and password in the protected-share password prompt.

The drive is mapped, and the Databases folder opens to show its contents.

Password-Protecting the Database

You can set a password on a database that a user needs to enter in order to open that database. This password is above and beyond any other server-related security that the server administrator places on the database file. Setting a password in this way also encrypts the database, which means the database file can be opened only with Access 2007. If you forget the database password, you can't open the database. Some third-party tools may be able to retrieve the password for you, for a fee.

Encrypting a database

Encryption is a reversible process, as you can see in the following section. The encryption scheme is far stronger in Access 2007 than in older versions of Access and therefore has a much higher level of security. Even if an encrypted database is copied from its original location, it can't be opened without the password that was set during encryption.

To hinder a brute-force attack on your database, use a password that has the following characteristics:

- Make the password at least ten characters long (longer is better).
- Use both capital and lowercase characters.
- Use numbers and alternate characters.
- Use a password that's difficult to guess but easy to remember.
- Use a password that's not based on a word you can find in the dictionary.

These general guidelines apply to passwords that you set for any purpose — not just encrypting a database. After you decide on a password, distribute it to the other members of the Research group but no one else.

To encrypt a database with a password, follow these steps:

1. **From within Access, click the Microsoft Office icon and click Open.**

Your default location opens, displaying a list of databases.

2. **Select the database you want to open by clicking it.**

3. **Click the Open button to reveal a drop-down list (as shown in Figure 15-8) and select Open Exclusive.**

4. **Click the Database Tools tab, and then click Encrypt with Password in the Database Tools group.**

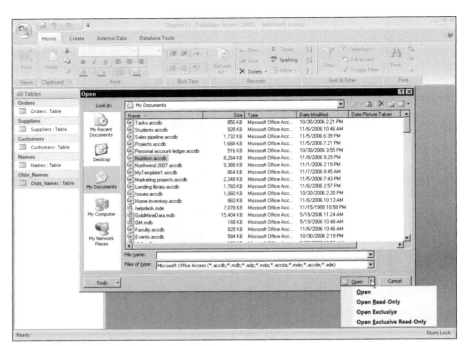

Figure 15-8: Opening the database in Exclusive mode.

The Set Database Password dialog box opens, prompting you for a password and to verify the password.

When you type the password, it appears on-screen only as asterisks, so be very careful when typing.

5. **Enter the password (for example,** Ch!5t@Por9**) in the Set Database Password dialog box, and enter it again to verify it. Click OK.**

The database is encrypted, and the Encrypt with Password option changes to Decrypt Database.

6. **Close the database.**

7. **Open the database again.**

You're prompted for the password.

8. **Enter the password (in this example,** Ch!5t@Por9**) and click OK.**

The database opens normally.

 **Information Kiosk**

A database that has been encrypted with a password is indis-
tinguishable from an unencrypted database until it's opened.
Externally, the database looks like any other database. Its icon, name,
extension, and size all remain constant.

Decrypting a database

The process of decryption restores a database to its original state and removes the password placed on it.

To decrypt a database and remove the password, follow these steps:

1. **With the encrypted database open, click the Database Tools tab and select Decrypt Database.**

2. **Enter the password (for example,** Ch!5t@Por9**) in the Unset Database Password prompt and click OK.**

The database is now decrypted, and the password has been removed.

Enabling Trusted Computing

A new aspect of Access 2007 is *trusted* computing — a new concept that enhances security because it requires you to explicitly enable either

- **Trusted locations:** By default, all locations are untrusted. You can set up a trusted location so that all its content is trusted.

- **Trusted content:** By default, all executable database content is disabled. Content may be trusted on a *per-use* (session) basis.

Trusting content for the current session

When a database is opened in a normal (untrusted) location, you see the Security Warning message bar, shown in Figure 15-9.

Figure 15-9: This Security Warning notifies you of disabled content.

To enable executable content for the current database, follow these steps:

1. **Click the Options button on the Security Warning message bar.**

The Microsoft Office Security Options dialog box appears. The Security Alert in this dialog box warns you that this database contains potentially harmful content. If you know the origin of this database, it's okay to enable it.

2. **Click** *Enable this content* **and then click OK.**

The Security Warning disappears, and all executable content is now available to you while you have this database open.

3. Close the database.

4. Reopen the database.

The Security Warning message bar appears again.

Setting up a trusted location

In Chapter 5, you can set up a trusted location so that you can write to the database in that chapter's examples. This section approaches that same concept from a security perspective.

To set up a trusted location, follow these steps:

1. From within Access, click the Microsoft Office icon and then click Access Options.

The Access Options window opens, displaying a left navigation menu that includes the following options: Popular, Current Database, Datasheet, Object Designers, Proofing, Advanced, Customize, Add-ins, Trust Center, and Resources.

2. Select Trust Center from the menu.

3. Click the Trust Center Settings button.

The Trust Center window opens. The left navigation menu contains the following items: Trusted Publishers, Trusted Locations, Add-ins, Macro Settings, Message Bar, and Privacy Options.

4. Select Trusted Locations from the menu.

5. Select the option Allow Trusted Locations on my network (not recommended).

Microsoft doesn't recommend this option because other people who have access to this trusted location can copy databases to it that may contain harmful content. You can solve this problem with another security feature that's demonstrated in the following section, "Creating signed databases."

6. Click the *Add new location* button in Trusted Locations.

A Microsoft Office Trusted Location dialog box opens.

7. Click the Browse button.

8. Click the My Computer icon in the Browse window.

9. **For this example, select the Databases shared folder on the drive letter that you choose (for example, X:) and click OK.**

   The path (for example, `X:\`) now appears in the Path field of the Trusted Location dialog box.

10. **Click OK to accept.**

Creating signed databases

A *signed database* is a database that contains a security certificate that verifies the database's content is safe. Of course, some unsavory people out there distribute a signed database that has virus code in it to harm the files on your computer. You have to trust the publisher of the database and the content that publisher is distributing to you. If you don't know the publisher of the content, then don't trust the content.

Signing and packaging a database in this fashion is a clever way to distribute content that's certified safe to use. By becoming a trusted publisher of content, you're letting the user know that you're responsible for the content and its actions. For an Intranet situation, you can adopt the policy to use only databases with content signed by a certified publisher.

Using the SelfCert tool

The SelfCert tool creates a security certificate that you can use to sign your databases. You can find this tool in the program directory with the other Office 2007 executables. Mine is located in:

`C:\Program Files\Microsoft Office\Office12`

The name of the file is `SELFCERT.EXE`.

To create a signed database, follow these steps:

1. **Locate the file** `SELFCERT.EXE` **and execute it by double-clicking it.**

   The Create Digital Certificate dialog box opens, prompting you for a name for the certificate. Read the entire dialog box for this tool to get detailed information on digital certificates and how to become certified for signing databases for commercial use. Figure 15-10 shows the Create Digital Certificate dialog box.

2. **Name the certificate (for example,** Chapter15-cert**) and click OK.**

   You receive a message that you successfully created the certificate.

3. **Click OK.**

   The message and the SelfCert Tool disappear. The creation of the certificate is complete.

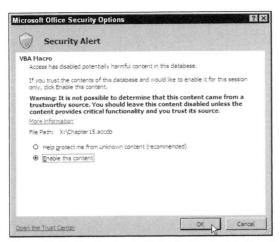

Figure 15-10: Use the Create Digital Certificate dialog box to create a signed database.

Creating the signed package

After you create the certificate, which you can read about in the preceding section, you can create the signed package, which includes the database and the signed certificate. Follow these steps:

1. **Open the database that you want to package for distribution.**

2. **Click the Microsoft Office icon, click Publish, and then click Package and Sign.**

The Select Certificate dialog box appears.

3. **Select the certificate you want to use to sign the database (for example,** Chapter15-cert**) and click OK.**

The Create Microsoft Office Signed Package window appears, prompting you for a location to save the package.

You can change the name of the package in the File Name drop-down list if you want, but the extension is `.accdc`.

4. **Select a folder in which to save the package and click OK.**

I suggest you choose a shared network location that has restrictive permissions limiting the groups that can use the package.

The package is created in the location that you specify in Step 4 of the preceding list, and it's ready for deployment. A signed package has a different icon than does a standard Access database. Figure 15-11 shows the dialog box for a packaged database.

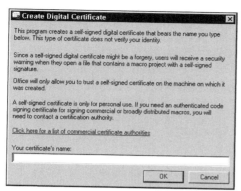

Figure 15-11: Microsoft Access uses this dialog box to create a certificate for a database.

Extracting and using the signed package

The signed package is located on a network share for others to extract and use. To use the database, you have to extract the package and accept the certificate. Follow these steps:

1. **From within Access, click the Microsoft Office icon and then click Open.**

2. **Select the location of the package by using the *Look in* drop-down list.**

   You don't see the package, but it's there.

3. **Select Microsoft Office Access Signed Packages (*.accdc) from the *Files of type* drop-down list.**

   The package is now visible.

4. **Select the package and click Open.**

   You're presented with the Microsoft Office Access Security Notice dialog box.

5. **Click *Trust all from publisher*.**

 Watch Your Step

Select *Trust all from publisher* only if you know the person or company that's providing the package to you. Trusting all packages from a particular publisher can have devastating results if the package is faked or contains virus code.

The Extract Database To dialog box appears, requiring a location to which you save the Access database file.

6. **Select a location in the Extract Database To dialog box and click OK.**

   The Access database opens and is ready to use.

Removing a trusted publisher

If you add a publisher that you no longer want to trust, you can remove that publisher from your list of trusted publishers. Follow these steps:

1. **Click the Microsoft Office icon and then click Access Options.**
2. **Select Trust Center from the left navigation menu.**
3. **Click the Trust Center Settings button.**
4. **Select Trusted Publishers.**
5. **Select the publisher that you no longer want to trust.**

    The certificate that you created (in my example, Chapter15-cert, as shown in Figure 15-12) is selected.

Chapter15.accdc

Figure 15-12: You can remove a publisher from your list of Trusted Publishers.

6. **Click Remove to delete the selected publisher from the list of trusted publishers.**

Using File Extensions for Security

Access 2007 arrives with a new extension (.accdb) that clearly differentiates it from all older versions of Access (.mdb). The .accdb extension carries many new, non-security-related features, which I talk about in the following sections.

ACCDE

The .accde extension is an execute-only mode for an Access database. The execute-only mode strips away the ability of a user to change any code or design aspects of the database.

It's equivalent to the .mde extension in older versions of Access.

To create an execute-only (.accde) version of a database, follow these steps:

1. **Open the database you want to convert.**
2. **Click the Database Tools tab, then click the Make ACCDE button.**

3. Select a location in the Save As dialog box for the `.accde` file, then click Save.

The database is now saved with the `.accde` extension.

4. Open the converted database.

5. Click the Create tab to see how many of the options are no longer available.

This isn't a disabled mode, and the user can work with all aspects of the database (such as macros, forms, reports, and VBA code). But users are locked out of making certain changes.

ACCDR

The `.accdr` file extension is a locked-down version of a database. (It's new to Access 2007.) The locked-down mode is called *runtime,* which means the database is fully functional from a user perspective but many design options aren't available to the user.

This example works best if the database you use has forms, reports, and macros in it. You can use the `Chapter15.acceb` file from this chapter's examples.

To create the runtime version of a database, follow these steps:

1. Locate the database you want to convert to runtime.

You can convert either an `.accde` or `.accdb` file.

 **Information Kiosk**

For maximum security, the original database file should be in the `.accde` format. If the original database is an `.accdb` file, users can change the runtime file back to an `.accdb` file, with full access to the code and design.

2. If you don't want to convert your only copy of the original database, make a backup copy now.

3. Rename the database with the `.accdr` file extension.

4. Open the `.accdr` file to see how locked down the application is.

Notice how you can navigate through forms and open reports, but you can't see the Navigation Pane to get access to the database objects directly. This is how a locked-down application operates.

certificate: A file that signs a file or application electronically, to mark it as being from a trusted source, as a means of security.

decrypt: To change a file from an encrypted mode to standard mode. This process requires a password.

encrypt: To change a file in such a way that its content is hidden or not accessible by standard means. This process requires a password.

file extension: The part of a file name that tells the operating system what type of file it's dealing with. The extension is after the dot in the file name.

locked-down: A security mode for a file that prevents users from tampering with certain aspects of that file.

runtime: A security mode for an Access database that's functional but allows no editing of design or code.

signed (signed package): A file associated with a certificate which verifies that file's publisher and content as safe to use.

trusted location: A folder that's been set up as safe from which you can launch executable content with confidence that it won't harm your computer.

trusted publisher: A source of content (whether person or company) you approve to distribute executable content to your computer in an unprotected manner.

Practice Exam

1. When is it appropriate to trust a publisher's signed content?

   A) Always

   B) Never

   C) Only if you pay for the content

   D) If you trust the publisher

2. True or false (explain why): After you trust it, a publisher or source of content may never be "untrusted."

_____

_____

_____

3. Changing a file extension to what makes it vulnerable to editing by a user?

   A) `.accdb`

   B) `.accde`

   C) `.accdr`

   D) `.accdt`

4. Which file extension designates the file as encrypted and password protected?

   A) `.accde`

   B) `.accdx`

   C) `.accpe`

   D) None of the above

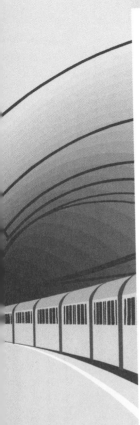

5. If you forget the password for an encrypted database, you may:

    A) Call Microsoft for assistance

    B) Forget about opening your database

    C) Try to find a third-party application or service to assist you

    D) Both A and C

6. True or false (explain why): Network drives aren't secure and therefore shouldn't be used as trusted locations.

_____

_____

_____

7. When using file, folder, and share permissions to secure a location:

    A) Use groups to set access.

    B) Use individual user accounts to set access.

    C) Grant full control to everyone.

    D) Grant read-only access to everyone.

8. When selecting a password for a database, you should:

    A) Use the company name.

    B) Use the name of your city.

    C) Use a non-dictionary word.

    D) Use a word from a thesaurus.

9. You can create a certificate to sign a package simply with the:

    A) Cert tool

    B) Sign tool

    C) GroupCert tool

    D) SelfCert tool

10. Access 2007 doesn't support user-level security from older versions of Access. What has taken this security's place?

A) Trusted locations

B) File, folder, and share permissions

C) Signed certificates

D) All of the above

Maintaining Access Databases

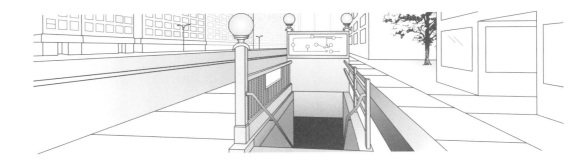

 # Enter the Station

Questions

1. How do I maintain my Access databases?

2. What is the Compact and Repair tool?

3. Why do I need to compact and repair my databases?

4. Can I automate database maintenance?

5. How do I perform a backup?

6. How can I share my databases with users of older versions of Access?

7. Can I save tables, queries, forms, reports, and macros as other types of objects?

8. How can I make my Access databases more efficient and prolong their life?

9. How can I move my databases to SQL Server but still use Access as a front end?

Express Line

If you're already familiar with maintaining Access databases, then skip ahead to Chapter 17.

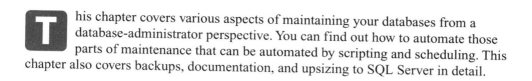

his chapter covers various aspects of maintaining your databases from a database-administrator perspective. You can find out how to automate those parts of maintenance that can be automated by scripting and scheduling. This chapter also covers backups, documentation, and upsizing to SQL Server in detail.

Maintenance Tools

Access provides its own set of tools to perform some necessary and routine maintenance and documentation. I group these tools together in this section because of their related actions and their grouping within Access.

To locate the maintenance tools, follow these steps:

1. **Click the Microsoft Office icon.**

2. **Select the Manage option.**

The options to manage the database appear to the right: Compact and Repair Database, Back Up Database, and Database Properties. These utilities assist you in keeping your databases healthy, backed up, and properly documented. This chapter shows you how each utility is used inside Access, and how to automate these processes so you don't need to perform them manually. You should know both methods because you occasionally must perform this maintenance manually.

The Compact and Repair tool

You'll probably become very familiar with the Compact and Repair tool. It's the ultimate Access utility and could quite possibly be worth the price of Access all by itself.

As you use a database and make changes to it, it becomes fragmented and somewhat enlarged, making the database inefficient and susceptible to corruption. Corruption can occur for many reasons, but the most common are

- Closing the database abnormally
- A physical disk corruption where the database is stored
- Failure to perform regular maintenance — allowing the database to become severely fragmented

You need to compact and repair databases on a regular and routine basis to prevent most problems that occur due to fragmentation and corruption.

Repairing an open database

When the Compact and Repair tool is launched on an open database, the database is copied to a temporary file and then the empty spaces and fragmentation are removed from the temporary file. The temporary database is also checked for internal errors and inconsistencies. If errors exist, they're analyzed and repaired (if possible). After this process is complete, the original file is removed and the temporary file is renamed to the original.

To repair an open database, follow these steps:

1. **Open the database in Exclusive mode.**

2. **With the database you want to repair open, click the Microsoft Office icon, click Manage, and then select Compact and Repair Database.**

The database momentarily closes and the cursor changes to an hourglass while the compact and repair is being done. The database reopens after the process is complete.

Repairing a closed database

If you have Access, you can repair any database(s) with this tool without having to open those databases. Follow these steps:

1. **Click the Microsoft Office icon, click Manage, then click Compact and Repair Database.**

A Browse dialog box named Database to Compact From opens to your default database location, displaying all `.mdb` and `.accdb` databases.

2. **Select the database you want to compact and repair, then click Compact.**

You're prompted for a new name for the database. Access provides the first available database name for you in the form of `DatabaseX.accdb`, where X is the first available number.

You can change the name to anything, including the original name of the database you're compacting and repairing. You're prompted to overwrite the original database with the newly compacted one if you don't change the name.

3. **Enter the name you want for the compacted and repaired database and click Save.**

Automating the compact and repair process

You can automate the compact and repair process to alleviate the need for continuous human intervention in this sometimes lengthy and tedious procedure. If you have only one database with which you're working, automation can be overkill. But as the number of databases under your control grows, you'll be glad that you have this ability.

This procedure works equally well for one database as it does for dozens. It involves writing a script that identifies the database you want to compact and repair. Each database to be repaired requires its own line in the script. After you complete the script, you must set up a schedule for it by using the Task Scheduler. The Task Scheduler launches the script at the time you specify, and the whole process is performed unattended when no one is likely to be using the databases.

To write a script to automate the compact and repair process, follow these steps:

1. **Click Start, click Run, and type** notepad **into the Run field.**

2. **Click OK.**

Windows Notepad opens.

3. **Enter the following single line into Notepad (including the quotation marks):**

```
"C:\Program Files\Microsoft Office\OFFICE12\
MSACCESS.EXE" "C:\Documents and Settings\khess\
My Documents\Database1.accdb" /compact
```

The /compact switch at the end of the line tells Access to perform a compact and repair on the specified database. A /repair switch also exists, but it's only to maintain compatibility with old scripts that use it. The /compact switch performs both functions.

The quotation marks are necessary because there are spaces in the folder names (such as Program Files and Microsoft Office).

If you want to repair more than one database, copy the line you enter in Step 3, paste it onto the next line, and change the name of the database.

4. **Save the script as** repairdbs.cmd **to the My Documents folder.**

The .cmd file extension tells Windows that this is a script file that will be executed at the command line. The command line is analogous to a DOS Window, for those of you who remember that far back.

Watch Your Step

When saving a file in Notepad, the file extension defaults to .txt and will append that extension to whatever file name you choose. To avoid this feature, select All Files in the File Type drop-down list in Notepad before saving the script.

To set up a scheduled task to run your script, follow these steps:

1. **Click Start → Programs → Accessories → System Tools → Scheduled Tasks.**

The Scheduled Task applet opens. Figure 16-1 shows the Scheduled Tasks window.

2. **Double-click Add Scheduled Task to start the Scheduled Task Wizard and click Next.**

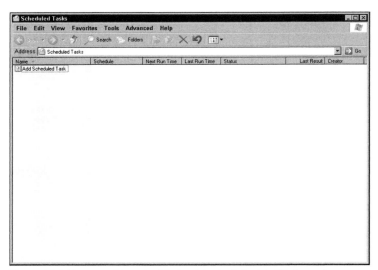

Figure 16-1: You can add a scheduled task in the Scheduled Tasks applet.

3. Click the Browse button and navigate to the folder where you saved your script.

4. Select the script and click Open.

5. Name the task Repair Databases, select Daily, and click Next.

6. Select a Start time for the task.

Choose a time when no one is working on the databases but before any nightly backups begin.

7. Select Every Day, a Start Date, and click Next.

The wizard prompts you for a user name and a password to run the task as that user. The wizard defaults to your user name.

8. Enter the user name and password for the user account that you want to execute this task.

9. Click Finish.

10. Close the Scheduled Tasks applet.

Your task is listed in the Scheduled Tasks applet and will execute at the specified time without intervention.

Backing up

The most important, yet the most neglected, part of any maintenance scheme is backing up and restoring databases. Most often, stringent backup-and-restore plans go into effect just *after* a major data-loss event.

Creating a backup plan

The following list gives you a simple backup plan that you can easily and inexpensively implement:

- Make nightly backups of all important data.
- Use removable media (such as tape, CD-R, CD-RW, DVD, or flash drive) to store backups.
- Rotate the media often and move a full backup to an offsite location.
- If you can't use removable media for any reason, copy files to a network share on another computer.
- Keep several days (preferably an entire week) of backups available in case of disaster.
- Use mirrored drives, when possible, to minimize drive-failure mishaps.
- Appoint someone to manage the backup plan.

Backing up an Access database

You can perform a manual backup in Access easily. Follow these steps:

1. Click the Microsoft Office icon, click Manage, then click Back Up Database.

A Browse window named Save As appears. The location is open to your default database storage location. Select a different location for the backup database.

The name of the backup is given as follows:

`Database_Name_YYYY-MM-DD.accdb`

YYYY is the four-digit year, MM is the two-digit month, and DD is the two-digit day.

2. After you find the location you want, click Save.

You're returned to your original database, not the backup.

Making a simple file-copy backup

This method of making a backup has nothing to do with Access. It's a simple file copy of a database from the default database location to some alternate location. Follow these steps:

1. Open the My Documents folder and locate the file or files you want to copy.

2. Select the files by clicking them.

Hold down the Ctrl key while selecting files to select more than one.

3. Right-click the highlighted files and click Copy.

4. Browse to an alternate location (preferably a shared network drive).

5. Right-click into the folder where you want to save the file(s) and click Paste.

The file(s) are copied to the new location.

Automating a backup

In addition to a formal backup routine, such as using a program to back up your files and folders, you can automate your own backups. This process is much like scripting the compact-and-repair procedure, which you can read about in the section "The Compact and Repair tool," earlier in this chapter. Follow these steps:

1. Open Notepad by clicking Start, clicking Run, entering notepad into the Open field, and clicking OK.

2. Enter the following line into Notepad:

```
Copy "C:\Documents and Settings\khess\My
Documents\Database1.accdb" X:\Backups
```

In this example, `X:\Backups` is a mapped network drive `X:` and a folder named `Backups`. The text in quotes is the database you want to copy and the folder after the quotes is the location of the backup. You must change this command to fit your network drive and folder names.

3. Choose File, then click Save As to save this file as **daily_backup.cmd.**

4. Set up a Scheduled Task to execute the **daily_backup.cmd** every night at 11:00 p.m.

Setting a scheduled task is described in the "Automating the compact and repair process" section. To save all of your databases to that same shared folder, you can use the following command:

```
Copy "C:\Documents and Settings\khess\My
Documents\*.accdb" X:\Backups
```

The asterisk (*) means any file name.

Database properties

Database properties aren't directly concerned with maintenance, but the Database Properties tool is located with the maintenance tools discussed in this chapter.

Access databases have various properties associated with them that provide valuable information to the database administrator. Some of these properties are

⊙ The complete path to the database

⊙ The created, last accessed, and last modified dates

- The title, author, and other miscellaneous information about the database creator
- A list of all database objects (such as tables, forms, and reports)
- Custom properties that may have been added to the database

From a maintenance standpoint, the created, modified, and last accessed dates are the most important properties because they give you the age of the database and the last time it was used. These dates can help you archive, delete, or update databases appropriately.

File-Oriented Tools

You can consider the following two utilities related because you can save a database onto a network share or SharePoint server, or just as another version. You can also use the Save As utility to save a specific database object as another type of object. Each of these utilities operates at the file level.

Publishing to a document management server

The document management server used in this example is SharePoint. If you're using SharePoint, you only have to select the SharePoint server (by name or IP address) to be directed by a wizard to save your database to the server.

Information Kiosk

Other document management servers have different methods of uploading files into a shared area, but the most common method is by network share. Another very popular method is through a Browse/Upload utility in a Web browser.

The following procedure isn't the same as publishing a table to a SharePoint server. Publishing the database uploads the file to the server to be shared with those who have access to the database. Users can't open the database on the SharePoint server. They must download the database to their local machines or network shares to use it.

To publish a database to a server, follow these steps:

1. **Open a database that you want to upload to the SharePoint server.**

I chose the Issues database.

2. **Click the Microsoft Office icon, Publish, then Document Management Server.**

The Publish to Web Server browse window opens, as shown in Figure 16-2.

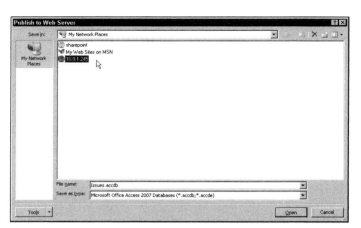

Figure 16-2: Choosing a server in the Publish to Web Server window.

3. **From this window, select your SharePoint server and click Open.**

My SharePoint Server appears as an IP address (10.0.1.245).

4. **At the login prompt, type in a valid user name and password and click OK to make the connection.**

5. **Select the folder you want to place the database in and click Open.**

I chose Databases, as you can see in Figure 16-3.

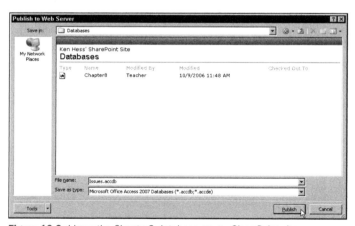

Figure 16-3: I have the Chapter8 database on my SharePoint site.

6. **Click Publish to upload the database to the selected folder.**

After the database has been saved, you're returned to your open database. A new message bar now appears in your database. Figure 16-4 shows the Publish Changes message bar.

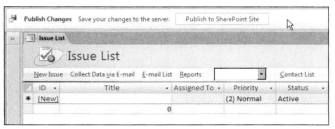

Figure 16-4: Publish changes from the Issue List.

You can upload any changes you make to the database without a wizard by clicking the Publish to SharePoint Site button. When you click the Publish to SharePoint Site button to update a database, you see the same window as shown in Figure 16-3.

Because the database already exists in the selected folder, you're prompted to overwrite the existing file.

Save As

The Save As utility has multiple purposes:

- Save Object As
- Find Add-ins for other file formats
- Save in Access 2007 format
- Save in Access 2002–2003 format
- Save in Access 2000 format

Save Object As

The Save Object As utility lets you save database objects, such as tables, queries, forms, reports, macros, and modules, as different types of objects.

The following list describes what other types of objects from which you can save the original object:

- Tables can be saved as tables, queries, forms, and reports.
- Queries can be saved as queries, forms, and reports.
- Forms can be saved as forms and reports.
- Reports can be saved only as reports.
- Macros can be saved as macros and modules.
- Modules can be saved only as modules.

To save a table as a query, for example, follow these steps:

1. **In your open database, select a table by clicking it.**

2. **Click the Microsoft Office icon, then click Save As and Save Object As.**

The Save As dialog box opens with the default name `Copy of Table_Name` (where `Table_Name` is the name of the table you select in Step 1). The default object is always the same kind of object as the original object.

3. **Change the object type in the As field to Query and click OK.**

The table is saved as a query named `Copy of Table_Name` and opened.

Finding add-ins for other file formats

You must download any available add-ins for other file formats from Microsoft or another company. These add-ins allow you to save your database objects in other file formats, such as PDF or XPS.

To obtain and install an add-in for additional file formats from Microsoft, follow these steps:

1. **Click the Microsoft Office icon, click Save As, and then click *Find add-ins for other file formats.***

Access Help opens, displaying three links to more information.

2. **Click the *Install and use the Publish as PDF or XPS add-in from Microsoft* link.**

This link moves you down the page in the Access Help window.

3. **Click the *Microsoft Save as PDF or XPS Add-in for 2007 Microsoft Office programs* link.**

This link opens your Web browser to a Microsoft download page (Download Details: 2007 Microsoft Office Add-in: Microsoft Save As PDF or XPS).

4. **Click the Continue button.**

To download files from Microsoft, you have to let the Microsoft Web site validate your Office products. If your Office products are genuine (legal), then the Download button for this add-in appears. If your software isn't genuine, a Get Genuine page opens.

5. **Click the Download button.**

6. **Click Run on the File Download dialog box.**

7. **Click Run on the Internet Explorer warning message. You can trust this program since you're at the Microsoft site.**

8. **Click the Accept box, then click the Continue button.**

9. **Click OK on the Installation is Complete message.**

10. **Close your browser.**

    The Save As options now include PDF and XPS.

11. **In an open database, select a table by clicking it.**

    A table that has data in it works best for this example so you will see the data.

12. **Click the Microsoft Office icon, select Save As, and then select PDF or XPS.**

    The Publish as PDF or XPS dialog box opens and prompts you for a name and other options.

13. **Enter the name and location for the file in the Save As dialog box or click Save to accept the defaults.**

14. **Select the file type (PDF or XPS).**

15. **Select "Open file after publishing and Optimize for Minimum size."**

16. **Click Publish.**

    The PDF file opens, displaying the column names and data from the table you select in Step 11.

Access 2007 format

This is the standard format for saving your Access databases when using Access 2007. This option saves a copy of your current database.

Access 2002–2003 format

This option saves a copy of your current database in the Access 2002–2003 format so that you can open the files in those older versions of Access. The file extension is `.mdb`.

Access 2000 format

When you choose this option, the current database is saved in Access 2000 format so you can open the files in Access 2000. The file extension is `.mdb`.

Analysis and Performance Tools

I talk about the performance tools only for the serious database administrator who wants to generate a huge amount of recorded detail on the structure, attributes, and properties of the objects in the database. The performance tools give you an idea of performance problems or potential bottlenecks, but they aren't the ultimate in analytical tools.

Database Documenter

The Database Documenter provides an exhaustive analysis of a database object. It analyzes each item in the object separately and prints out every attribute of each item in tabular form.

How detailed is the Documenter, you ask? For example, in the Issues database, the Contact Details form is 43 pages long; the Contacts table details run to 12 pages.

To generate documentation for a database object, follow these steps:

1. **Open a database.**

2. **Click the Database Tools tab.**

3. **Click the Database Documenter button in the Analyze group.**

The Documenter dialog box opens, as shown in Figure 16-5.

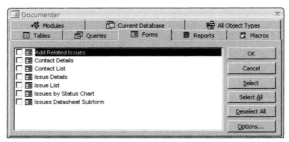

Figure 16-5: You can analyze your database by using the Database Documenter.

4. **Select the Tables tab, select the table you want to document (for example, Contacts), then click OK.**

The table analysis appears in Print Preview mode. You can view the document as is, save it, or print it.

The options for saving this information are

- Microsoft Word document in Rich Text Format
- Regular text (Notepad)
- PDF or XPS document
- Access database
- XML file
- Snapshot Viewer
- HTML document

To save the information in one of the available formats, follow these steps:

1. **From the Print Preview tab's Data group, Select the format in which you want to save the information (for example, Microsoft Word).**

   The Export File Wizard opens, prompting you for a location and name for the file.

2. **Accept the default location (My Documents) and the name (for example, `doc_rptObjects.rtf`).**

3. **Click *Open the destination file after the export operation is complete* and click OK.**

   The file is exported and opened in the format you choose in Step 1 (for example, Microsoft Word).

4. **Switch back to Access, and click Close on the dialog box.**

Watch Your Step

If you change any aspect of a database object after you print or save the information about your database, you must run the Database Documenter again to reflect the changes.

Performance Analyzer

Before you deploy a public database application, you should run that application through the performance-analysis utility. Using the Performance Analyzer ensures that you avert any serious issues in your application that could affect performance after users begin entering and using data.

To use the Performance Analyzer, follow these steps:

1. **Open a database (`Issues.accdb`).**

2. **Click Analyze Performance in the Analyze group.**

   The Performance Analyzer utility opens, as shown in Figure 16-6.

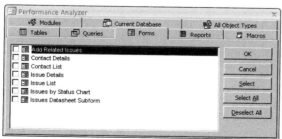

Figure 16-6: The Performance Analyzer lets you know what might be slowing down your database.

3. **Click the Tables tab, select both tables, and click OK.**

If Access has no performance suggestions, the message shown in Figure 16-7 appears.

Figure 16-7: The Performance Analyzer has no suggestions.

If the Performance Analyzer does have performance issues with the object(s) you select, a window similar to the one shown in Figure 16-8 appears.

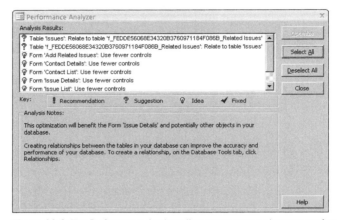

Figure 16-8: The Performance Analyzer lists some ways to improve performance.

The Performance Analyzer has three possible levels of suggestions for improving database objects if it finds problems:

- Recommendation — the analyzer believes fixing these items will have a major effect on performance.

- Suggestion — the analyzer believes fixing these items might slightly improve performance.

- Idea — the analyzer believes these items affect performance slightly, and fixing them might improve the performance.

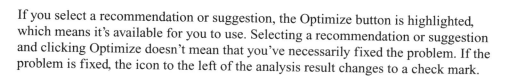

If you select a recommendation or suggestion, the Optimize button is highlighted, which means it's available for you to use. Selecting a recommendation or suggestion and clicking Optimize doesn't mean that you've necessarily fixed the problem. If the problem is fixed, the icon to the left of the analysis result changes to a check mark.

Analyze Table Wizard

The Analyze Table utility is actually a wizard that steps you through the process of table optimization by prompting you to split tables to remove redundancy. This process of normalization is covered in Chapter 9.

To fully appreciate how this utility looks at the data in your table and decides how it can be split up and normalized, use the Customers table. If you don't have this table in your database, create and save a table with the data from Table 16-1.

Table 16-1   Customers Table Sample Data

First_Name	Last_Name	Address	City	State	Zip
John	Doe	123 S. Main	Oneville	TX	77777
Jane	Davis	246 N. Elm	Twoville	OH	34567
Don	Smith	789 E. Pine	Threeville	MN	67890
Jill	Doe	567 W. 4th	Fourville	LA	12345

Fixing the table

To have Access analyze and fix the Customers table, follow these steps:

1. **Close the table if it's open.**
2. **Click the Database Tools tab, then click Analyze Table.**
3. **Click Next twice after the Table Analyzer Wizard starts to skip the introductions.**
4. **Select the Customers table and click Next.**
5. **Click Yes, let the wizard decide to let the wizard figure out which fields should go into which tables, and click Next.**

   A notice appears, saying Access doesn't recommend splitting this table.
6. **Click OK on the message.**

   The next step in the wizard appears that prompts you to select the redundant data fields, shown in Figure 16-9.

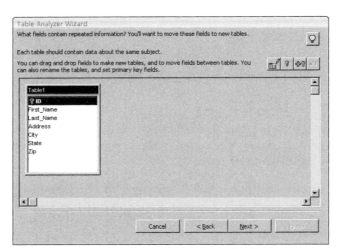

Figure 16-9: The Table Analyzer Wizard lets you split tables.

The redundant fields in the Customers example table are City and State. The following section splits these fields into other tables.

Splitting the table

To split a table, follow these steps:

1. **Click a redundant field (for example, City), drag it to the empty space to the right of the table being split, and release.**

The new table is created, and you're prompted to name it.

2. **Name the new table (for example, Cities) and click OK.**

3. **Repeat Steps 1 and 2 for each additional redundant field.**

For the Customers example, use the State field to create a table named States.

If you're following the Customers example, your Table Analyzer Wizard screen should look like Figure 16-10.

4. **Click Next.**

If you're following the Customers example, you may receive a warning about unrelated fields in the States table. Click OK on the warning.

The final step in the wizard prompts you to create a query to mimic the original table, so any forms, reports, or other objects aren't affected by splitting the table. I recommend doing this in case you need to see what the original table looked like before you split it.

5. **Click "Yes, create the query" and click Finish.**

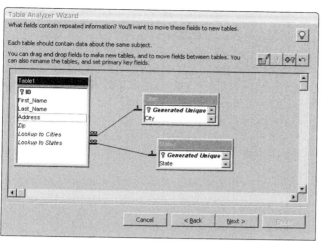

Figure 16-10: The redundant data appears in new tables.

For the Customers example, the tables States and Cities are created and the Customers table is renamed Customers_OLD. A new, normalized table named Table1 is created. The Customers query is created and executed. The names of the fields in the query change: The names Cities and States have changed to Lookup to Cities and Lookup to States in Table1.

Upsizing Tools

The developers of Access realize that as databases grow, the need to upsize becomes a very real issue. Access tries to make this process a little less painful for users.

You need to upsize when

- Your user base has increased beyond the capacity (2 GB) of a regular Access database.

- You need to decrease network traffic because of slowness *(latency)* with your network.

- The database has become so large or complex that Access is no longer sufficient to quickly add, modify, and retrieve data.

- You need a higher level of security for your databases.

Database Splitter

The Database Splitter does exactly what the name says; it splits the database so that tables are saved to one database (the back-end database) and other objects (such as forms and queries) are saved to another database (the front-end database).

Splitting a database can solve several problems if you operate in a multi-user environment:

- Network traffic is decreased.
- You can develop the front end (forms, reports, and queries) more easily while keeping the data available to users.
- It can extend the life of Access in your organization.

Splitting a database is an easy and free solution to the problem of upsizing a database. Upsizing to another solution, such as Microsoft's SQL Server, can be expensive. SQL Server itself isn't expensive for its power, but the training and time needed to understand the system may cost you a lot more than figuring out how to use Access.

To split a database, follow these steps:

1. **Open the database you want to split.**

2. **Click the Database Tools tab and click Access Database in the Move Data group.**

The Database Splitter Wizard launches, as shown in Figure 16-11.

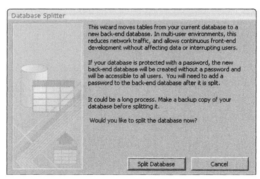

Figure 16-11: The Database Splitter Wizard puts your tables in one database and the other objects in another.

3. **Click Split Database.**

You're prompted for a name and location for the back-end database. The default name is Database_Name_be. You may want to accept the default so that you can easily determine which database is which.

4. **Click Split.**

A message appears saying that the database was successfully split.

Watch Your Step

Make a backup of any database before splitting it. Splitting a database can take a very long time, and may not go as planned.

5. Look at the list of tables in your database after the split.

The table icons have changed, and if you hover over one of them with your cursor, you can see the full path to your split database. You can use the database normally. If you place the back-end portion of the database on a network drive, you can distribute the front-end database to the other users.

SQL Server

The next logical step after splitting databases, which I talk about in the preceding section, is upsizing to a real client/server solution, such as Microsoft's SQL Server. Access 2007 makes this transition easy for you by providing the SQL Server upsizing tool.

There are two ways to connect to an SQL Server from Access:

- **ODBC (Open Database Connectivity):** If you use an existing SQL Server database, you must connect to the server with ODBC.

- **Simple authentication or a trusted connection:** If you create a new SQL Server database, you simply authenticate with a user name and password that has permission to create new databases on the SQL Server.

Upsizing an existing database

If you use an existing SQL Server database, you must connect to the server with ODBC, which I describe how to do in Chapter 14. You can use the same ODBC connection for this example.

To upsize your database by using an existing database on SQL Server, follow these steps:

1. Open the database you want to upsize.

I'm using the Projects database from the Microsoft templates.

2. Click the Database Tools tab, then click SQL Server in the Move Data group.

3. Select *Use existing database* and click Next.

The Select Data Source dialog box opens, prompting you to select your SQL Server data source for this connection.

4. Select the data source (such as `SQL_Svr_Books.dsn`, which you can create in Chapter 14) listed on the File Data Source tab and click OK.

5. Enter the password associated with the Login ID (user name) displayed in the SQL Server Login prompt and click OK.

6. Select all the tables listed in the Available Tables list, send them to the Export to SQL Server list, and click Next.

7. Click Next to export the tables and the data.

8. Select **Create a new Access client/server application, Save password and user ID**, and click Next.

   A warning appears to ask if you really want to save the password to a file, and it tells you the password will be saved unencrypted.

Information Kiosk

When you ask to create a new Access client/server application, the wizard creates a new project named `ProjectsCS.adp`. (The default name for the new project is `Database_NameCS.adp`, where `CS` stands for client/server and `adp` is the extension for Access Database Project.)

9. Click Yes on the warning.

   A dialog box appears, prompting you to either *Open the new ADP file* or *Keep the Database file open*.

10. Select *Open the new ADP file* and click Finish.

    The Upsizing Wizard moves your tables and data to the SQL Server. After the Upsizing Wizard finishes, an Upsizing Wizard Report appears. For the example Projects database, the report is 16 pages long.

11. Print, save, or discard the report.

    After you close the report, the Access project file (for example, `ProjectsCS.adp`) is opened in Access and ready to use.

Upsizing to a new database

The example in this section demonstrates how to create a new SQL Server database to which you'll upsize your existing Access database.

For this example, you can use the Nutrition database from the Microsoft Template databases.

To upsize an Access database to a new SQL Server database, follow these steps:

1. Open the Access database you want to upsize.

2. Click the Database Tools tab and select SQL Server from the Move Data group.

3. Select *Create new database* and click Next.

   The Upsizing Wizard launches after searching your local network for an SQL Server.

4. **Select the SQL Server in the drop-down list at the top of the Upsizing Wizard dialog box.**

   If the SQL Server isn't in the list, enter the name or IP address of the SQL Server in the drop-down list.

5. **Enter a user name and password to make the connection to the chosen SQL Server.**

   A default name for the new database is presented as `Database_NameSQL`.

6. **Name your database or accept the default name, then click Next.**

7. **Select all of the tables in the Available Tables list, send them to the Export to SQL Server list, and click Next.**

8. **Click Next to send the tables and data to the SQL Server.**

9. **Select *Create new Access client/server application, Save password and user ID,* and click Next.**

   A warning against saving an unencrypted password to a file appears.

10. **Click Yes on the warning.**

11. **Select *Open the ADP file* and click Finish.**

    An Upsizing Wizard Report appears. Save this report in case there are any questions about the process later.

12. **Close the Upsizing Wizard Report.**

    The new project launches (in this example, NutritionSQL), ready to use.

automation: The process of creating scripts and schedules to perform a task without human intervention.

back up: The process of creating a copy of a database to some location other than the default location. You should keep backups on removable media, such as tapes.

maintenance: The activities associated with keeping a program or data in a healthy state.

upsizing: Moving data to some other format to provide better access, increased speed of data through the system, or support for more users.

Practice Exam

1. **True or False (explain why): Backing up databases is a necessary activity.**

_____

_____

2. **You need to upsize a database when:**

A) You buy SQL Server and want to use it.

B) You need greater database security.

C) You need to buy a newer version of Access.

D) You've heard that SQL Server is better than Access.

3. **You should use automated maintenance because:**

A) It moves the responsibility of the task to a computer.

B) It provides a nice upsizing path.

C) It shows an innovative approach.

D) It improves database access.

4. **You should analyze performance on databases:**

A) Before you create them

B) After you create them but before you enter any data

C) Before you deploy them to users

D) Before you buy a new version of Access

5. **When should you perform backups?**

A) When you think about it

B) Weekly

C) Daily

D) Daily when no one is using the databases

6. You can upsize to SQL Server by using:

A) Backups

B) Regular maintenance

C) ODBC

D) A split database

7. What two things should you try before upsizing to SQL Server?

A) Performance analysis and database splitting

B) Performance analysis and database documentation

C) Database splitting and backups

D) Performance analysis and backups

8. You can save a table as which of the following?

A) Table

B) Query

C) Form

D) All of the above

9. Why would you want to save a table as a PDF file?

A) It's a standard add-in from Microsoft.

B) It's a very common file type.

C) It creates a client/server application.

D) All of the above.

10. What particular aspect of a table are you looking for when considering splitting that table into two or more tables?

A) Easy backups

B) Easy maintenance

C) Aggressive data entry

D) Redundant data

Exploring Your Options

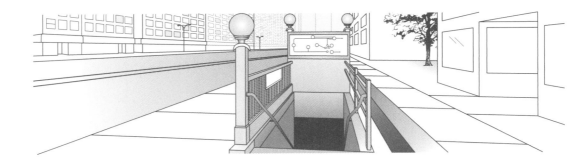

Enter the Station

Questions

1. What are the most popular options in Access?

2. How can I change the title of my current database?

3. How do I get technical support?

4. Can I customize Access's menus or add items to the toolbar?

5. Do I need to change all of the options in the Access Options window?

6. Which options affect just my copy of Access?

Express Line

If you're familiar with Access Options, then skip ahead to Chapter 18.

T his chapter covers Access options in detail. The chapter focuses on customizing and enhancing your database and gives suggestions for some of the more important choices. You can find out about popular options, current database settings, support options, and enhancing the Quick Access toolbar.

Access Options

This chapter focuses entirely on Access options and their effects on your Access databases. You don't need to change any of the options, but you should be aware of them. Most of the examples in earlier chapters in this book don't make any significant changes to any of the options.

This chapter covers the options in the order they appear in the navigation pane, from the top down. I don't talk about every single option, though — only the most useful.

To get to the Access Options window, follow these steps:

1. **Click the Microsoft Office icon.**

2. **Click Access Options, as shown in Figure 17-1, to open the Access Options window.**

Figure 17-1: The Access Options button opens the Access Options window.

Figure 17-2 shows the most popular options in Access.

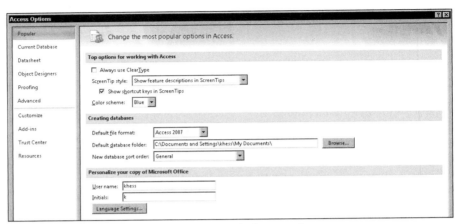

Figure 17-2: Popular lets you change the most popular Access options.

Microsoft asks for a lot of user feedback in its product launches and has gathered a large amount of data over the years related to application usage and user preferences. Microsoft has used this information in redesigning Microsoft Office 2007.

Top options for working with Access

The choices in this list are the ones that Access users change most often and consider to be the most important:

- **Always use ClearType:** This selection can enhance the way your applications appear, especially if you're using a laptop or other type of LCD screen.

- **ScreenTip style:** Here you have three options:

    Show feature descriptions in ScreenTips: This is the default selection.

    Don't show feature descriptions in ScreenTips: Feature descriptions give you more details of the feature than just showing you one or two words.

    Don't show ScreenTips: Not all users need them.

- **Show Shortcut Keys in ScreenTips:** This option shows the keyboard shortcut equivalent to navigating to and clicking the button for a feature. Figure 17-3 shows an example of a ScreenTip and keyboard shortcut.

- **Color scheme:** The choices are Blue, Silver, or Black. The default is Blue, and it's the color scheme used in the figures throughout this book.

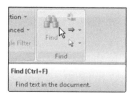

Figure 17-3: This ScreenTip tells you the keyboard shortcut for Find.

Creating databases

The settings in this section tell Access how you want files saved, the default location for opening and saving files, and the default language which determines the sort order of items in your databases. These settings are as follows:

Default file format: You can choose to save your databases in Access 2007, Access 2002–2003, or Access 2000 format. If you're the only person lucky enough to be using Access 2007 in your environment, you should change this selection to make your databases compatible with others in your organization. The default selection is Access 2007.

Default database folder: This folder is the location in which your databases will be saved or opened by default. When you open Access, this location lists your most recently opened databases. You can change this location, but you also must change the new location to a trusted location. Trusted locations are covered in the section "Trusted locations," later in this chapter.

New database sort order: Sort order is based on the language in which you're working. General is the default sort order for English-language databases. Choosing another language changes the sort order by basing it on the alphabet of the selected language.

Personalizing your copy of Microsoft Office

The settings in this section define your copy of Microsoft Office as being owned by you or another user. These settings are:

User name: You can type your name in this field. This information will be used for default entries throughout Microsoft Office.

Initials: This setting is just another way of identifying the creator of a database.

Language settings: You can select your editing language for Access — the language in which you interact with Access. This setting doesn't affect sort order in your databases.

Current Database

Options changed in the Current Database area apply only to the database you're currently using. These changes don't affect any other database, open or closed. These attributes are saved with the affected database.

Application Options

The Application Options section is shown in Figure 17-4.

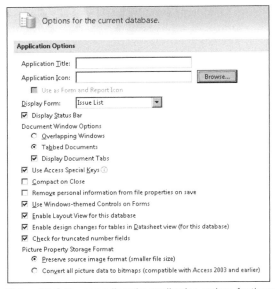

Figure 17-4: You can adjust the application options for the current database.

The settings in this section define settings and usability features for the database you're currently using. Here are the settings and how to use them:

Application Title: Enter the working title of your application here. This title appears in the application's title bar. I entered `Corporate Support Issues` for the title of the Issues database, one of the Microsoft Template databases.

Application Icon: You can browse to an icon file that you want to use as the application's icon. This icon appears when you minimize the application.

- You can also use the Application Icon as the icon for the forms and reports in your database. Select the Use Form and Report icon check box to use the Application Icon for the forms and reports.

- I chose an icon that I created for the Application icon field, and selected Use as Form and Report icon. You can see the effect on forms and reports in Figure 17-5.

Figure 17-5: The Issue form and report have their own custom icon.

Display form: A drop-down list of forms from which you can select one to open when you open this database. You can select "(none)" if you want to control startup forms by using a macro.

Display status bar: Turn on or off the status bar at the bottom of the application, which is similar to the title bar at the top of the application.

Document window options: You can choose from Overlapping Windows or Tabbed Documents. If you choose Tabbed Documents, you can choose whether to Display Document Tabs. You should try both options to see which you like better. I prefer tabbed documents with the Display Document Tabs option selected.

Use Access special keys: Check this box if you like to use keyboard shortcuts to perform actions in Access. You can see the keyboard shortcuts in ScreenTips if you select that feature in the Popular section of Access Options.

Compact on close: Selecting this option compacts and repairs the database when you close it. You should select this option only if you're the only or last user of the database.

Remove personal information from file properties on save: Your database is saved without the personalized name and initials that you can set in the preceding section.

Use Windows-themed controls on forms: Choose this option if you want your forms to have controls with the same look and feel as the ones in your Windows interface.

Enable Layout View for this database: Select whether you want to see the Layout View option when using this database.

Enable design changes for tables in Datasheet View (for this database): This option allows you to make changes in the Datasheet View for all objects in your database.

Check for truncated number fields: When this option is selected, numbers appear as hash marks (#####) when the column is too narrow to display the entire value. De-select this option to show the partial number in the column.

Picture property storage format: The picture-storage options you select depend on whether you must share your databases with users who have older versions of Access. The options are

- Preserve source-image format (which gives you a smaller file size)
- Convert all picture data to bitmaps (a file format compatible with Access 2003 and earlier)

Navigation

The Current Database options not covered in the preceding section are shown in Figure 17-6:

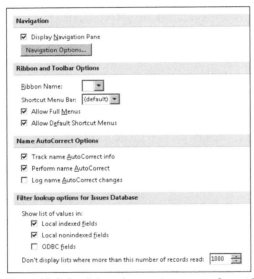

Figure 17-6: Scroll down the page to see more Current Database options.

Display Navigation Pane: Select this option to display the left navigation pane in Access. If this option isn't selected, you can't browse database objects.

Navigation Options: This button opens a dialog box containing several options for customizing the navigation pane. The options in the Navigation Options dialog box are

- *Tables and related views:* Show or hide specific tables in the database.
- *Object type:* Select the objects (such as tables and forms) that you want to show or hide.
- *Current database navigation:* Specific categories and groups for the current database (for example, Issues).

You can also show or hide system objects and hidden objects, and the search bar and change how objects are opened or launched (by using either a single or double click).

Ribbon and Toolbar Options

The ribbon and toolbar options allow you to customize the selections that your users see when using this database:

Ribbon Name: This drop-down list (when populated) lets you select a custom ribbon for this database. Customizing the ribbon is outside of the scope of this book.

Shortcut Menu Bar: Similar to the Ribbon Name drop-down list, you can select custom menu bars for the current database.

Allow Full Menus: This option is the default if you don't specify a custom menu.

Allow Default Shortcut Menus: This option is the default if you don't specify a custom shortcut menu.

Name AutoCorrect Options

The Name AutoCorrect features were plagued with problems in earlier versions of Access, but you could simply disable the features. They're enabled by default in Access 2007. These options assist you when you rename tables or fields so that such objects as queries, forms, and reports recognize the new name.

Track name AutoCorrect info: Access stores the information to correct naming errors. However, Access doesn't repair these errors until you select the Perform name AutoCorrect option.

Perform name AutoCorrect: Checking this option lets Access repair naming errors as they occur. Access will rename tables and fields in objects such as queries, forms, and reports when you change the names of the tables and fields in the table.

Log name AutoCorrect changes: Checking this option lets Access track the changes it makes in a table named AutoCorrect.log.

Filter lookup options for current database

The options in this section control several features such as the size of the value lists that appear in the Filter By Form window, whether or not you can display values for indexed or non-indexed fields, and whether or not the value lists appear in the controls in a form when you use Filter By Form. These options are as follows:

- **Local indexed fields:** Displays a list of values in the Filter By Form window for a local indexed field. *Local* means in a table in Access, not linked in some way.

  When you index a field, Access sorts and finds records faster. An index can be based on a single field or on multiple fields. The primary key field in a table gets indexed automatically, and you can choose other fields to index as well.

- **Local nonindexed fields:** Displays a list of values in the Filter By Form window for a nonindexed field in a local table.

- **ODBC fields:** Displays a list of values in any ODBC-connected table's field.

- **Don't display lists where more than this number of records read:** The default number of records is 1,000. You can change this number if 1,000 is too many or too few records to display.

Datasheet

The following sections describe the ways you can customize datasheets, and Figure 17-7 shows the default selections for each parameter.

Default colors

You can set the default colors for contrast and to make viewing your data easy on the eyes. You can see the gridlines, but they aren't annoying in any way.

Watch Your Step

When using colors and fonts, use font colors that have contrast to the background colors so you can easily read the data. Make background colors subtle and inoffensive to the eye. Use a simple font that's large enough for users to read comfortably at a screen resolution of 1024 x 768.

You can change any of these settings to suit your preferences or special needs:

- **Font color:** This sets the color for the text in the datasheet. The default is black.

- **Background color:** This sets the color for the background color of the datasheet. The default is white.

- **Alternate background color:** This sets the color for the background for every other row of the datasheet. Set it to a color different than the Background color to see the background colors alternate from row to row. The default is light gray.

- **Gridlines color:** This sets the color for the gridlines that appear between rows and columns. The default is light gray.

Gridlines and cell effects

The following options set the appearance of the lines and cells in the datasheet. These settings are

- **Default gridlines showing:** You can choose to display Horizontal and/or Vertical gridlines. The default is both.

- **Default cell effect:** Flat, Raised, or Sunken. Flat is the default. Flat cell effect makes the datasheet look like a spreadsheet. The Raised and Sunken options give the datasheet a 3D look.

- **Default column width:** This sets the width of the columns for tables and query result sets. 1" (one inch) is the default width.

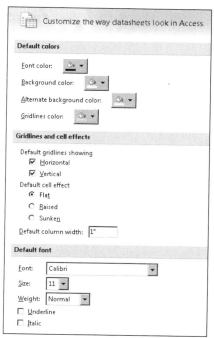

Figure 17-7: You can customize your datasheet's appearance.

Default font

The following options define the default font for datasheets and query result sets. These settings are

- **Font:** Select a common font that's available in a wide range of operating systems (such as Windows 2000, Windows XP, and Windows Vista). The default is Calibri.

  Arial is a common alternative to Calibri.

- **Size:** You must test the appropriate size for you and your users. Usually, most users find a font size from 10 to 12 acceptable. The default for the Calibri font is 11.

- **Weight:** Normal is the default for all fonts. You can select a different weight, but be sure to test it to see how others react to the change. Some fonts don't view well in weights other than Normal or Bold. Be careful when choosing other weights such as Thin, Extra Light, Semi-Bold, Extra-Bold, and Heavy.

- **Underline:** This option underlines data in every cell. The default is no underline.

- **Italic:** This option italicizes data in every cell. The default is no italics.

Object Designers

The Object Designers options affect the defaults when you're creating or modifying tables, queries, forms, and reports. You can also modify error-checking behavior in Object Designers.

Table design

The following options affect the defaults when you're creating or modifying tables:

- **Default field type:** Text is the default field type. Most of your fields (columns) are probably Text, so this makes a good default value.

- **Default text size:** The default size of this field is 255. It's also the maximum size for this field type.

- **Default number field size:** The default is Long Integer, which has the largest range of numbers available. The range is from –2,147,483,648 to 2,147,483,648.

- **AutoIndex on Import/Create:** The default setting is ID;key;code;num. These keywords generate an index on newly created fields that contain the keyword in the field name when you import or create a new table or field.

You can also add your own custom keywords to the list if your keywords aren't in the list.

- **Show Property Update Options buttons:** If you change a field's property in Table Design View, you can choose to update related properties of controls on forms and reports that are bound to that field.

Query design

The following options affect the defaults when you're creating or modifying queries:

- **Show table names:** This option is selected by default and shows the Table row in the query design grid, which makes queries easier to design, especially for queries based on multiple tables.

- **Output all fields:** This option isn't selected by default. If you select it, this option tells the query to select all fields by default. In SQL, the statement is

  ```
  SELECT * FROM Table_Name
  ```

- **Enable AutoJoin:** This option is selected by default, which enables the query builder to join tables automatically (because joined tables generally make queries run faster).

- **Query design font:** The default is Segoe UI. Select something simple and standard, such as Arial.

- **Font size:** The default is 8 for Segoe UI. You must test different sizes to know which works best for the font you choose.

- **SQL Server Compatible Syntax (ANSI 92):** Nothing's selected by default. Select this option when you want to run queries against Microsoft SQL Server databases. You can check to make the syntax compatible for the database you're currently using, or for all new databases you create.

- **This database:** By default, this option isn't selected. Select this option if you want the current database to generate queries that comply with SQL Server syntax.

- **Default for new databases:** By default, this option isn't selected. Select this option if you want all new databases to generate queries that comply with SQL Server syntax.

Forms/Reports

The following options affect the defaults when you're creating or modifying forms or reports:

- **Selection behavior:** Partially enclosed or Fully enclosed are the choices for this behavior. Partially enclosed is the default. This selection means that when you're designing a form or report, you can select any part of a field to include it in the selection. Fully enclosed means that to select a field or control, you must fully enclose the control or field to select it. The selection you choose is a matter of personal preference, but if forms are very complex, you should consider using Fully enclosed to avoid selecting the wrong control.

- **Form template:** The default form template is Normal. You can create a form template, name it, and enter its name in the Form template text box. You can name the new form Normal, but you should give the new form a new name in case you want to revert to the Normal template.

- **Report template:** The default report template is Normal. You can create a report template, name it, and enter its name in the Report template text box. You can name the new report Normal, but you should give the new report a new name in case you want to revert to the Normal template.

- **Always use event procedures:** Selecting this option starts the Visual Basic Editor instead of displaying the Choose Builder dialog box when you click the ellipsis button on a property sheet for any event. By default, this option isn't selected.

Error checking

Have all the check boxes in this section selected so you can use the maximum error checking possible — especially during the development (creation and modification of a database application) phase. Before deploying an application, you can unselect any or all of these options, but by default, they're all selected.

Proofing

You may be somewhat familiar with proofing tools in programs such as Microsoft Word, in which you use a spell-check dictionary, a thesaurus, and AutoCorrect options. This section defines how to change the Access settings for correcting and formatting the contents of your databases.

AutoCorrect options

AutoCorrect is the feature that corrects words as you type. For instance, if you type teh, AutoCorrect changes that word to the for you. You may never realize that you spelled it incorrectly because of AutoCorrect.

Click the AutoCorrect button to see commonly misspelled words (or shortcuts to create symbols such as copyright or trademark), and what the text is replaced with. You can also add your own text if you know of words that you often mistype.

When correcting spelling in Microsoft Office programs

The following options for correcting spelling are self-explanatory, except for the custom dictionary. You can build your own custom dictionary for your specific needs.

For example, if you work in a chemical laboratory, you may need to add terminology that isn't included in a regular dictionary to your custom one.

Click the Custom Dictionaries button to add words to your dictionary. You can create one or more new dictionaries by clicking the New button.

Watch Your Step

If you use a custom dictionary, don't select the *Suggest from main dictionary only* option in the "When correcting spelling in Microsoft Office programs" section. If you choose that option, your custom dictionaries aren't consulted.

Advanced

Most of the options in the Advanced section are a matter of personal or professional preference because only a few of them affect users unless those users assist in design and development. (This book doesn't cover personal preference options in detail.)

Editing

These options are personal-preference selections based on how you like to work in Access.

The Editing options include two exceptions to personal preferences:

- **Datasheet IME control:** IME (Input Method Editor) allows the user to enter and edit Chinese, Japanese, and Korean characters.
- **Use Hijiri Calendar:** This is a lunar calendar commonly used in Islamic cultures.

Display

The Display options affect all users, whether or not they perform any design or development activities:

- **Show this number of recent documents:** This option is the number of documents shown in the right pane after you open Access but before you select a database to open. The default is 9.

- **Status bar:** Hide or show the status bar on the bottom frame of the Access window. The default is checked.

- **Show animations:** Hide or show any animations in the application. The default is checked.

- **Show Smart Tags on datasheets:** Hide or show Smart Tags in Datasheet View. This option affects users only if you allow Datasheet View in the database. The default is checked.

- **Show Smart Tags on forms and reports:** This option affects all users. The default is checked.

Printing

These settings define the print margins for reports. You must adjust them to print on letterhead, in a special format, or with some printers. The numbers in the Left, Right, Top, and Bottom margin text boxes are your defaults.

General

The following options define the settings for displaying errors and feedback while using the application. This section also defines the format for the year as well as the options for the Web. The options are

- **Show add-in user interface errors:** This option is disabled by default. When disabled, this option prevents users from seeing any add-in-related errors in the database.

- **Provide feedback with sound:** Feedback sound is disabled by default. When enabled, Access plays various sounds while the user is working with the database.

- **Use four-digit year formatting:** You can apply this option to this database or all databases. By default, this option isn't selected, leaving the year in two-digit format. This option affects all users.

- **Web options:** If you use links in your application, you can choose the link color, followed (visited) link color, and whether you want to underline links.

Advanced

The following options (the "Advanced of the Advanced," so to speak) define other settings such as modes of opening the database, record locking, and interfacing with other applications. The settings are

- **Open last used database when Access starts:** This feature affects only your copy of Access, and is a personal preference item.

- **Default open mode (Shared or Exclusive):** Shared is the default choice and lets other users open the database while you have it opened. Always set this option to Shared unless you have some compelling reason (such as doing maintenance) for selecting Exclusive mode, which means only you can make changes to the database. This setting affects other users of shared databases.

- **Default record locking (No locking, All records, Edited record):** The default is No locking. You should change this setting in shared databases to Edited record so while you're editing a record in the database, some other user can't begin editing that same record until you've saved your changes.

Information Kiosk

Database locking is a fairly complex topic that requires analysis of your usage habits, including the number of users, the type of data, and so on.

- **Open databases by using record-level locking:** By default, this option is selected. If it's deselected, Access uses page-level locking as the default for the open database. Page level locking may improve performance, but locks more than one record which may prevent other users from editing a record, even if you're not editing that same record.

Adjust the remainder of the Advanced selections (timeout and refresh values) only if you begin to experience latency (slowness) issues with your databases. The default values for these selections are considered optimal for most cases.

Customizing by Using the Quick Access Toolbar

You can usually find the Quick Access Toolbar at the very top-left of the active program's window. (Figure 17-8 shows the Quick Access Toolbar.) If it's not in the top-left, look for it below the Ribbon; you can choose where it appears. You can add commands to this toolbar by choosing the Customize drop-down list at the far right of the toolbar. It's called the Quick Access Toolbar in all of the Microsoft Office 2007 applications, and the name has nothing to do with the program named Access. Quick Access refers to the ability to perform a subset of tasks quickly without the need to search for them.

Figure 17-8: Customizing the default Quick Access Toolbar.

By default, the Quick Access Toolbar is configured with Save, Undo, and Redo selections.

When you first open the Customize option from the left navigation menu in Access Options, you see Popular Commands below *Choose commands from* — and the current (default) selections (Save, Undo, and Redo) listed below *For all documents (default)* underneath Customize Quick Access Toolbar. Figure 17-9 shows the Customize section in Access Options.

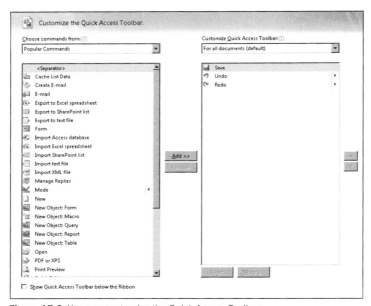

Figure 17-9: You can customize the Quick Access Toolbar.

Any changes that you make to the Quick Access Toolbar alter the toolbar for all Access databases. You can select the current database from the drop-down list under Customize Quick Access Toolbar. Any changes made to the current database (for example, the Issues database) are made to that database only. To add more commands to the Quick Access Toolbar, follow these steps:

1. **Select your current database from the drop-down list below Customize Quick Access Toolbar.**
2. **In the list below Popular Commands, select Open and New, then click Add.**
3. **Click OK.**

Access pauses for a moment while creating the custom Quick Access Toolbar, then displays the new toolbar attached to the default one. Figure 17-10 shows the new Quick Access Toolbar for the Issues database.

Figure 17-10: This customized Quick Access Toolbar now includes the Open and New icons.

You can select commands from about 35 different options below *Choose commands from* to customize your Quick Access Toolbar. To see all the available options (more than 35), choose All Commands from the *Choose commands from* drop-down list.

If, at some point, you decide to remove all of the custom commands, you can click the Reset button. This step resets the Quick Access Toolbar to its original state.

You can remove any selection from a custom Quick Access Toolbar by selecting the item and clicking Remove.

Add-Ins

The Add-ins section assists you in managing your Microsoft Office add-ins.

Trust Center

The following sections offer detailed information about each aspect of the Trust Center and how to use this information to suit your needs.

Online information

Access's online information explains Microsoft's position on privacy and protecting its customers' privacy, maintaining security, and gathering information. Links to Microsoft resources are given if you want more information.

Protecting your privacy

The hyperlinks in this section display information about Microsoft's privacy statements for Access and Office as well as their Customer Experience Improvement Program:

- **Show the Microsoft Office Access privacy statement:** This online information link takes you to Microsoft's privacy and use statement about the Microsoft Office 2007 system. It explains how your information will be used, Microsoft's regard for your privacy, and activation of the product. Click the link to learn how to activate your copy of Access.

- **Microsoft Office Online privacy statement:** This generic page on www.microsoft.com explains your privacy rights, information use, and Microsoft's position on user privacy.

- **Customer Experience Improvement Program:** This online resource from Microsoft explains the CEIP. Microsoft does a lot of research and uses feedback to improve and design its products. This is one of the ways in which Microsoft gathers that information.

Security and more

The hyperlinks in this section display information about protecting your privacy and security from Microsoft Office Online:

- **Microsoft Windows Security Center:** Clicking this link launches the Security Center applet on your computer. The Security Center has information about your personal firewall, antivirus protection, and automatic updates from Microsoft Support.

- **Microsoft Trustworthy Computing:** An online resource from www.microsoft.com that informs you about such topics as new security features in Microsoft products, protecting your privacy, and protecting your assets.

Microsoft Office Access Trust Center

The Microsoft Office Access Trust Center and Trust Center settings should look a little familiar if you created a trusted location and made yourself a trusted publisher in Chapter 15.

Trusted Publishers

This category provides a list of trusted publishers of content and the expiration date for each publisher's certificate. This interface provides methods for you to view and remove trusted publishers.

Trusted Locations

In the Trusted Locations interface, you can specify folders in which you want to keep databases, and those databases' content is trusted for users to open. Using this interface, you can

- **Add new location:** Browse to a new location on your local computer or network folder to set up that location as a trusted location.
- **Remove:** Delete a trusted location.
- **Modify:** Add a description, change the trusted location, or add subfolders to the trusted location.

You can also make network locations trusted or disable all trusted locations, thus requiring all content to be signed and trusted.

Add-ins

This section changes trust settings for third-party add-ins. You can choose to use add-ins only from trusted publishers or to totally disable all add-ins.

Macro Settings

These settings are for macros in an untrusted location. Your settings depend largely on the level of security you need at your site. The options are

- Disable all macros without notification.
- Disable all macros with notification.
- Disable all macros except digitally signed macros.
- Enable all macros.

I have mine set to "Enable all macros" because I'm in a trusted environment and don't plan to use outside databases unless I've checked them carefully — but mine is a unique situation. You should always create the safest environment for your applications.

Message Bar

The message bar, if enabled, resides just above your database objects. Your two options for the message bar are

- Show the message bar in all applications when content has been blocked.
- Never show information about blocked content.

The default is to show the message bar, but you may want to turn this option off before deploying a production database to other users. This way, the users won't be able to easily enable content that may not be trusted.

Privacy Options

The Privacy Options seem to have less to do with privacy and more to do with support. The reason they're in a section about privacy is perhaps because some limited information is exchanged between your computer and Microsoft when accessing and getting updates from Microsoft Office Online.

Check out the section "Protecting your privacy," earlier in this chapter, to see how Microsoft gathers and uses this information.

The options in this section are

- **Search Microsoft Online for Help content when I'm connected to the Internet:** This option provides you with the latest information available from Microsoft and works just like the offline/local version of Help.

- **Update featured links from Microsoft Office Online:** When you first open Access, you see links and information, including templates, that keep you up to date on downloads and new features, patches, and news.

- **Download a file periodically that helps determine system problems:** This part of Microsoft's new maintenance program for their applications is disabled by default.

- **Sign up for the Customer Experience Improvement Program:** I discuss this option in the section "Protecting your privacy," earlier in this chapter. Provide customer feedback to Microsoft on your experiences with their products.

Resources

The Resources section is a convenient list of informational links and utilities to keep your software up-to-date and in good working order. You also get various methods of contacting support. Figure 17-11 shows the list of resources.

Get updates

The Check for Updates button opens Internet Explorer to the Microsoft Update page and checks your computer for needed updates. After the check is complete, you're given the option of an Express or Custom installation of those updates.

The Express installation takes place without intervention unless you must accept a license agreement or indemnification notice.

The Custom installation button allows you to pick and choose the updates you want to install.

Figure 17-11: You can get the help you need through Microsoft's online resources.

Run Microsoft Office Diagnostics

The Diagnose button launches the Microsoft Office Diagnostics Wizard.

The first page of the wizard warns you that the process can take up to 15 minutes to complete. You're prompted to click Continue to proceed.

The next page of the Diagnostics Wizard displays the tests that it will perform on your system. The tests are

- Check for known solutions
- Memory Diagnostic
- Compatibility Diagnostic
- Disk Diagnostic
- Setup Diagnostic

Click Run Diagnostics to continue. After the diagnostic is complete, you receive a summary of any issues that the wizard found and whether it made repairs. A Details link gives an in-depth summary of repairs.

Contact us

The Contact Us button launches a contact link to `http://office.microsoft.com`. You can choose from links for Professional Support, Online Communities, and Feedback.

Activate Microsoft Office

The Activate button launches the activation site for Office 2007. The product requires activation before you can use any downloads, templates, or updates. If Office is already activated, you receive a message saying that the product is already activated.

Go to Microsoft Office Online

The Go Online button launches the Office 2007 Online System page. Here, you can find links to help, downloads, clipart, templates, Office Live, updates, and much more. Visit this site often to keep abreast of the latest information for Access and other Office 2007 products.

About Microsoft Office Access 2007

The About button launches the About Microsoft Access dialog box that displays license information, registration information, and version numbers. If you contact Microsoft Technical Support, you're directed to this page so you can provide them with the Product ID.

AutoCorrect: An Office feature that changes mistyped words to correct ones.

Smart Tags: Links to active content such as maps, sound, and video.

Practice Exam

1. **When you make changes in the Current Database section, your changes:**

A) Affect all users permanently

B) Affect all users temporarily

C) Affect all users in a shared environment

D) Affect the current user only

2. **The quickest way to find technical support contact information is to:**

A) Search `www.microsoft.com`

B) Click the Contact Us button

C) Ask your local computer shop

D) Do an online search for technical support

3. **You can change the Quick Access Toolbar in:**

A) A shared database

B) All databases

C) Both A and B

D) None of the above

4. **True or False (explain why): The Quick Access Toolbar buttons are affected by Microsoft's security settings.**

_____

_____

5. **The "Compact on close" option does what when enabled?**

A) Strips the database of personal information

B) Resets all options back to their original settings

C) Repairs and compacts the database

D) Performs diagnostics on the database

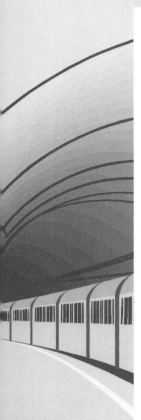

6. Taking part in the Customer Experience Improvement Program:

A) Enhances your privacy

B) Requires that you submit personal information over the Internet

C) Lets you tell Microsoft what you like about Access and Office

D) None of the above

7. Microsoft uses information from surveys and feedback programs for:

A) Verifying that you aren't using pirated software

B) Sending you information about other Microsoft products

C) Product enhancement

D) None of the above

8. What is a trusted location?

A) A folder that you identify as a trusted source for opening files

B) A folder that you use for database storage

C) A network drive mapped with a user name and password

D) An encrypted folder

9. What must you do before you're allowed to download content from Microsoft for Office 2007?

A) Activate the product.

B) Call technical support.

C) Create a trusted location for your databases.

D) None of the above.

10. When should you change the default file format for Access?

A) When you want the files to be smaller

B) When you want to compact and repair a database

C) When you want to share data with Excel

D) When you need to be compatible with older versions of Access

Connecting Access to the Web — Level I

STATIONS ALONG THE WAY

- Assessing your Web development skills
- Creating a Web database
- Installing a Web server
- Installing a programming language
- Starting and stopping Windows services
- Making the ODBC connection

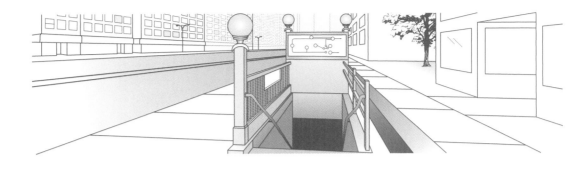

 # Enter the Station

Questions

1. What's a Web database?

2. What are the advantages and disadvantages of using a Web database?

3. How do I implement a Web database?

4. What kinds of preparations must I make before implementing a Web database?

5. Do I need to figure out a programming language?

6. What's a Web server?

7. What's a Windows service?

8. How do I start and stop Windows services?

9. How do I look at a database by using a Web browser?

10. What kind of connection do I need to implement a Web database?

Express Line

If you're familiar with Web databases, then skip ahead to Chapter 19.

This chapter introduces you to the concept of Web databases. This is a preparatory chapter for the exercises in the next. In this chapter, you can prepare a computer to become a Web database host. You can install a Web server and a programming language, and you can find out how to prepare the ODBC connection for the database.

Considering Access as a Web Database

A Web database is a database that you access by using a Web browser (such as Internet Explorer), a programming language, and a Web server. Microsoft Access may seem an unlikely candidate for a Web database, but you can use it that way. Web databases are an integral part of most company intranets, and the skills needed to support them are highly valued. Creating a Web database can solve many problems for you and your users.

Advantages of Web databases

A Web database can

- Provide access to data by using only a Web browser.
- Provide Internet access to data.
- Significantly lower the cost of using a database.
- Make a database available to more users.
- Reduce adoption time of a new data-based application.
- Provide users a familiar Web interface.

Disadvantages of Web databases

Using a Web database has some disadvantages, as well. You must weigh these disadvantages for each individual case:

- Development time increases.
- Skill-level requirements for the development team are higher.
- Maintenance needs aren't decreased.
- The risk of data corruption may be increased.

Getting the Essential Web Database Skills

You need to have some basic skills to create and maintain a Web database. Although you don't necessarily need all of them, you should probably become familiar with as many of them as you can if you plan on creating and maintaining Web databases. The skills needed to create and maintain a Web database are

- **HTML:** Any good HTML editor with a Design mode can alleviate the need for you to figure out HTML tags if you don't already know HTML.

- **A programming language (such as Perl, PHP, ASP, Java, or .NET):** You need to use only one programming language. They're all different but perform tasks in a similar fashion. The language you use is a matter of preference. I prefer PHP because it has a C-language programming syntax but also has elements of shell scripting and HTML. I use PHP in the examples in this book.

- **Installing software on a Windows computer:** You need to be able to install the programming language and Web server tools if they're not already on the computer you're using. You'll also need to make sure you have rights to install software.

- **Building and maintaining databases with Microsoft Access:** This entire book is designed to help you develop this skill.

- **Web-server management:** Chapters 18 and 19 review basic Web server management skills using Internet Information Server (IIS). These skills include installing, configuring, and navigating around in IIS.

Transfer

Appendix A lists books and Web sites that give you ample reference for study in the vast and fascinating area of Web development.

Preparing Your System

In the following sections, you can find out how to prepare your system to become a host for a Web database. You can use either your desktop computer or a server to which you have administrative access. (Administrative access is necessary because you install software that requires that level of access.)

In general, the changes you make to your system during this process don't harm your system when you perform those changes according to the instructions in this chapter. But sometimes things go wrong, and each system is different. The procedures in this chapter should work on any desktop or server system that has Windows NT, Windows 2000, Windows XP, Windows Vista, Windows NT Server, Windows 2000 Server, or Windows 2003 Server.

In addition to Access running on a Windows operating system (desktop or server), this project requires two additional components:

- **PHP:** The programming language
- **Internet Information Server (IIS):** Microsoft's Web server

Transfer

If you already have PHP and IIS installed on your system, you can skip ahead to the section "Selecting an Access database," later in this chapter.

Installing the PHP programming language

PHP (or PHP: Hypertext Preprocessor) is a scripting language that you can use to bring dynamic content to HTML pages. Small and large corporations, alike, use PHP. It's a very popular language that offers

- A simple structure and syntax
- A worldwide community of users
- Open licensing
- Flexibility and scalability
- An extraordinary number of modules to support every major database
- Cross-platform capability

Being very popular, PHP enjoys many community-based Web sites and resources that you can use free of charge. Its open licensing means it's free to download and use, which makes it an extremely viable choice for companies working within tight budgets. *Cross-platform capability* means that programs built with PHP can work on any operating system with few, if any, changes.

Information Kiosk

The full name of PHP is *PHP: Hypertext Preprocessor* — which abbreviates as *PHP*. It's a *recursive acronym* because it includes its own name in the acronym. Recursive acronyms are a very popular naming idiosyncrasy in the Unix/Linux world. Other famous examples of recursive acronyms are PINE (Pine Is Not Elm) and GNU (Gnu's Not Unix).

To install PHP to your workstation or server, you need access to the Internet. Follow these steps to install PHP:

1. **Open Internet Explorer, enter** `www.php.net` **into the address field, and press the Enter key.**

2. **Click the downloads link at the top of the page.**

3. **Under Windows Binaries, select the PHP zip package by clicking the link.**

4. **Select the highlighted link to download PHP from one of the mirror sites.**

5. **When prompted to Open, Save, or Cancel on the File Download dialog box, click Save.**

6. **Save to a location such as** `C:\Temp` **or another location that you can go back to for the file.**

7. **Close Internet Explorer.**

8. **Browse to the file you downloaded, double-click the file to open it, and click Extract.**

9. **When prompted for a location to extract the files, enter** C:\PHP **in the Extract to location and then click Extract.**

10. **Close the zip application.**

    PHP is now installed on your system.

11. **Right-click My Computer and select Properties.**

12. **Click the Advanced tab on the System Properties applet.**

13. **Click the Environment Variables button.**

14. **In the lower pane (System variables), scroll down until you see the variable Path.**

15. **Select Path and click the Edit button.**

    The Variable value field should be highlighted.

16. **Press the right arrow key on your keyboard once and enter the following text exactly as shown:**

    `;C:\PHP`

17. **Click OK three times.**

    The System Properties applet closes.

Setting up the IIS Web server

I use IIS in the examples in this book because IIS is available in every newer version of Windows and is the native Web server software. It's a standard Web server that serves many Web sites worldwide. IIS is free, customizable, robust, and easy to configure and maintain. For a Windows-centered solution, it's the clear choice.

Installation

To install IIS, follow these steps:

1. **Open the Control Panel by clicking Start → Settings → Control Panel.**
2. **Double-click Add or Remove Programs.**
3. **Click Add/Remove Windows Components.**
4. **Scroll down the list until you see Internet Information Server (IIS), select it, and click Next.**

   You may be prompted to place your original Windows installation CD or DVD in the CD/DVD drive so that these components can be installed.

5. **After IIS is installed, close the Add or Remove Programs applet and Control Panel.**

Configuration

After you install IIS, you're ready to configure it to work with PHP for this example. Follow these steps:

1. **Click Start → Programs → Administrative Tools → Internet Information Services.**

   The Internet Information Services applet launches. Your computer name appears in the applet.

2. **Click the plus sign (+) next to your computer name to reveal more objects.**
3. **Right-click the Web Sites folder and click Properties.**
4. **Click the ISAPI Filters button and click Add.**
5. **Enter** php **as Filter name, enter** C:\php\php5isapi.dll **into the Executable field, and click OK.**

   A red arrow appears next to the php filter — you can ignore this arrow for the purposes of these steps.

6. **Click the Home Directory tab and click Configuration.**
7. **Click Add, enter** C:\php\php5isapi.dll **into the Executable field, enter** .php **into the Extension field, and click OK twice.**
8. **Click the Documents tab and then click Add.**
9. **Enter** index.php **into the Default Document Name field and then click OK twice.**

If you want to stop the IIS Admin service by issuing a command from the command line, follow these steps:

1. **Click Start → Run, and then type** cmd **into the Run field. Click OK.**

A command prompt opens.

2. **Enter the following commands exactly as shown:**

```
NET STOP IISADMIN <ENTER>
```

3. **When prompted to answer whether you also want to stop the World Wide Web Publishing service, type** Y **and press Enter.**

A notification appears, saying that the services have been stopped successfully.

Figure 18-1 shows the detailed output from this command.

Figure 18-1: The NET STOP IISADMIN command stops the IIS Admin service.

 Information Kiosk

The World Wide Web Publishing service is another name for Internet Information Service (IIS), the Microsoft Web server. In some versions of Windows, IIS is known as Personal Web Server (PWS).

4. **To start the IIS Admin service, type** NET START IISADMIN **at the command prompt and then press Enter.**

The IISADMIN service starts, but the command's feedback doesn't mention the World Wide Web Publishing service. Figure 18-2 shows the results of starting the IIS Admin service.

5. **To start the World Wide Web Publishing service, type** NET START W3SVC **at the command prompt and then press Enter.**

Figure 18-3 shows the command window after starting the World Wide Web Publishing service.

Figure 18-2: The NET START IISADMIN command starts the IIS Admin service.

Figure 18-3: You can start the World Wide Web Publishing service by using the NET START W3SVC command.

Information Kiosk

You can stop and start the World Wide Web Publishing service (or any service) by using its formal name (in this case, World Wide Web Publishing). You must use double quotes around the name because the name of the services contains spaces. The commands look like this:

```
NET STOP "WORLD WIDE WEB PUBLISHING"

NET START "WORLD WIDE WEB PUBLISHING"
```

6. **Close the command prompt by typing** EXIT **and then pressing Enter.**

Transfer

If you use the command prompt to stop and start the IIS Admin service and the World Wide Web Publishing service, you can skip ahead to the following section.

If you don't like working at the command line, Windows has a graphical interface for working with services. To get to the Services applet, follow these steps:

1. **Right-click My Computer and click Manage.**

   The Computer Management application launches. This Computer Management console is the central management point for your computer. The workstation and server versions look exactly the same.

   The Computer Management console is shown in Figure 18-4.

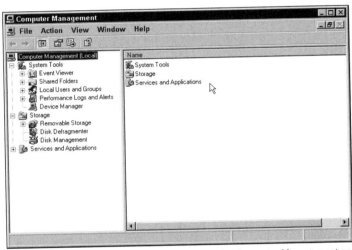

Figure 18-4: You can start and stop Services in the Computer Management console.

2. **Double-click Services and Applications.**

3. **Double-click Services.**

   The Services applet opens, showing the list of all services available for this computer. The list can be long.

4. **Scroll down the list until you see IIS Admin.**

   See Figure 18-5 for a closer look at services — specifically, IIS Admin.

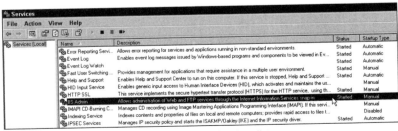

Figure 18-5: Look for the IIS Admin entry in the Services list.

Each service in the Services list has the following attributes:

Name: The formal name of the service.

Description: A full description of the service's purpose.

Status: The current status of the service — Started, stopped (blank), or Paused.

Startup Type: Describes how the service is started. The types are

- **Automatic:** Starts when the computer is booted.

- **Manual:** Starts when you launch an application or by some other manual means.

- **Disabled:** The service is currently disabled and isn't functioning.

Log On As: Normally you log on as the user account that controls this service — in particular, as Local System or Network Service (built-in accounts for running system services). You can use other user accounts to run services if those accounts have sufficient privileges.

In Figure 18-5, you can see that the service controls appear as icons on the tool bar above the service listing. The four controls are

Start service: Starts the highlighted service. It's grayed out for a started service.

Stop service: Stops the highlighted service.

Pause service: Temporarily suspends a service.

Restart service: If available, this control stops then restarts a service with no further intervention.

After you install the programming language (for example, PHP) and set up the Web server (for example, IIS), you're ready to connect to a database. The rest of this chapter shows you how.

Connecting to a Database

To get into an Access database using PHP, you must create a connection to it. You need to select the Access database you want to connect to and create an ODBC connection to the Access database.

Selecting an Access database

You must carefully choose the database that you want to use as your Web database. Consider the kind of data you want to present and the sources of that data.

Your first thought might be to split a database and use the back-end database for your table sources. (Chapter 16 covers splitting a database.) Splitting your database works only if you have physical tables in your database. Splitting a database strips out all forms, reports, macros, and linked tables. Access strips out linked tables from all sources.

One solution is to split the database into a front-end and back-end database. Follow these steps to split the database:

1. **Select the database you want to use.**
2. **Split the database so that only physical tables remain.**
3. **Use the back-end database to link your other data sources.**

The other option is to use the full database with all the other objects intact, just as if you were using them in Access. Deciding to use a full database is a wise choice. Leaving the other objects in the database doesn't reduce the performance of a Web database.

Using a Web-based solution is, in effect, "splitting" your database without the hassles of actually splitting it. When you use Access to split a database, what you get is a database in two pieces — one that contains only tables (the back-end database) and another that contains all other objects that have links to the tables in the back-end database. Web databases, on the other hand, use your existing database as a back-end data source through ODBC (the link); a Web server processes Web pages (forms and reports) and serves them to a client (your Web browser).

A Web database is a more efficient solution than splitting the database in Access. Here's why:

Services are back-end by design.

Web servers, ODBC connections, and database servers such as SQL Server run a very efficient *Agent mode,* which means they run in a listening state waiting for a client to connect.

Access doesn't have to be open for Web service to use the Web database.

Access is a client program that you must have open in order to use Access databases. This is good architecture for single-user applications or ones that are shared with a limited number of other clients.

Splitting services and creating client/server and multi-tiered applications greatly increase the efficiency of those applications because the applications don't have to run in graphical mode.

The fact that Access doesn't have to be open for you to use an Access database is one of the greatest features of a Web database solution. Why is a book about Access saying something like that?

The answer lies in the solution. If you're using Access as it was designed (as a desktop application), then it's a perfect solution. But if you want to use an Access database for a Web database solution, which isn't part of Access's design, then you must change the way you use Access. Don't use Access to work with the Web database. Use Access for design purposes only. (It's a great design tool.)

ONE FARE **TCP/IP is a polite protocol, which makes it another efficiency built in to a Web database solution.**

- In networking terms, a *polite* Web server listens a lot and doesn't talk much. IIS, for example, does nothing except listen for connections to its service. It doesn't broadcast or advertise its own existence — nor does it use some "keep-alive" activity to maintain itself. Polite means, in effect, that these back-end services respect your precious network bandwidth. They don't speak until spoken to. Think about it like this: Your favorite Web site waits for you to type its name into a browser before you can use it. The Web site doesn't reach out to your computer and start your browser for you, nor does it contact you in any way before you connect to it.

- Applications such as Access must maintain a constant open connection to the objects they're connected to. This constant connectivity requirement is one of the reasons why the Upsizing Wizards exist in Access. The two upsizing options provided in Access are two ways that you can circumvent this constant connectivity issue: Split the database into a front end and a back end or upsize to SQL Server to provide those back-end services from a database server.

ONE FARE **Web browsers are light clients.**

Web browsers are the preferred method for connecting to databases in high-volume user environments, such as the Internet. When you connect to a Web site that offers a search field in which you can type keywords, you have no idea what type of database is on the back end. It may be Oracle, SQL Server, MySQL, or even Access. You don't have to install a special application or other piece of software to search for information by using this search field. Nearly every computer is equipped with a Web browser. It's the universal client for all Web applications. The drivers, software, and connectivity are handled by the programming language, Web server, and ODBC (or other) connectivity.

ONE FARE **Client/server architecture is more efficient from standard application architecture.**

A service is efficient also because you don't need a front-end application running to use the service.

Preparing the ODBC connection to the database

ODBC is the method you must use to connect to an Access database when using IIS as the Web server and PHP as the programming language. You must create the ODBC connection as a system data source.

The database that I use in the examples in this section is the Grades database as it exists at the end of Chapter 7. This database contains the Grade_10 table, the Grade 10 Test Scores form, a `Grades.txt` linked table, and so on. It has all the elements a Web database needs: tables, linked tables, forms, reports, and queries. If you don't have this database, you can download the database from this book's Web site.

The rest of this chapter uses IIS Admin for examples. If IIS Admin isn't running on your computer, follow these steps to start it:

1. **Select IIS Admin from the list of Services and click Start Service.**

The IIS Admin service starts. The World Wide Web Publishing service doesn't.

2. **Scroll down to the bottom of the list of Services, select World Wide Web Publishing, and click Start Service.**

The World Wide Web Publishing service starts.

To create the ODBC connection to an Access database, follow these steps:

1. **Click Start ➜ Programs ➜ Administrative Tools ➜ Data Sources (ODBC).**

2. **Click the System DSN tab, then click Add.**

Figure 18-6 shows the System DSN tab in the ODBC Data Source Administrator.

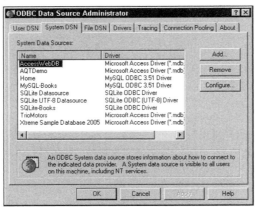

Figure 18-6: You can create a connection to an Access database in the ODBC Data Source Administrator.

3. **Scroll down until you see Microsoft Access Driver (*.mdb, *.accdb), select that driver, and click Finish.**

The ODBC Microsoft Access Setup dialog box opens.

4. Enter a name (for example, AccessWebDB) into the Data Source Name field.

You can see the ODBC Microsoft Access Setup dialog box in Figure 18-7.

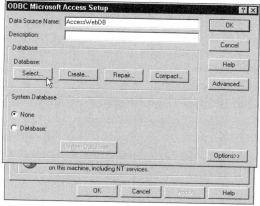

Figure 18-7: Name your data source in ODBC Microsoft Access Setup dialog box.

5. Click Select in the Database section.

6. Browse to the database that you want to use, select that database, and click OK.

I chose the database that I mention in the introduction to this section, named `Database4.accdb`. I made a copy and named it `AccessWebDB.accdb` for this example.

For this example, the data source AccessWebDB is now listed in the ODBC Data Source Administrator, which is shown in Figure 18-8.

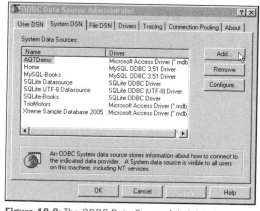

Figure 18-8: The ODBC Data Source Administrator.

7. Click OK to close the ODBC Data Source Administrator.

Your computer now has an ODBC connection to the Access database. You can use this connection to add, edit, and delete data from the Access database through a programming language such as PHP.

Stopping the IIS Admin Service

When you want to stop the IIS Admin service, follow these steps:

1. **Select IIS Admin from the list of Services by clicking it.**

2. **Click the Stop Service button on the toolbar.**

The Stop Other Services dialog box appears, warning you that stopping IIS Admin will also stop the World Wide Web Publishing service.

3. **Click Yes.**

The IIS Admin and World Wide Web Publishing services are stopped. If you want to see the status of the World Wide Web Publishing service to make sure it's stopped, scroll all the way to the bottom of the service list.

Internet Information Server (IIS): The Microsoft Web server. This application allows a computer to serve Web pages to other computers through a network.

IIS Admin: The management service for the Microsoft Web Server (IIS).

Internet Server Application Programming Interface (ISAPI): Through this interface in IIS, programming languages such as PHP can interact with IIS. You use the ISAPI filters when you install IIS.

PHP (PHP: Hypertext Preprocessor): A programming language that works well with Web servers and Web databases. It has an easy C-language type syntax and many flexible components that make it one of the most popular programming languages in the world today.

service: A program that runs in memory but has no direct interface for the user. Programs have been created to configure and work with services, such as Windows's Services applet.

 *continued*

Transmission Control Protocol/Internet Protocol (TCP/IP): This is the language of the Internet. One host speaks to another on the Internet by using this suite of protocols. Services such as database servers, mail servers, and Web servers all communicate through TCP/IP.

Web server: A generic term for the service that supplies Web pages to Web browsers when a browser requests information.

World Wide Web Publishing: The name of the Microsoft Web-server service.

Practice Exam

1. True or False (explain why): A Web browser, such as Internet Explorer, functions as a universal client.

_____

_____

_____

2. When connecting to a Web database over the Internet with Internet Explorer, you need to know:

A) The type of database used on the back end

B) The type of services used on the server

C) The ODBC connection name

D) Nothing about configuration of the services

3. IIS is an excellent choice for a Web server because:

A) It never crashes.

B) It's a native Windows application supplied by Microsoft.

C) It's open-source.

D) It works only for small applications.

4. Selecting a programming language for a Web database application is based on:

A) Personal preference

B) How much the language costs per user

C) How similar it is to the C language

D) Whether it's supplied by Microsoft

5. Converting a regular database to a Web database is essentially the same as:

A) Upsizing to SQL Server

B) Splitting the database

C) Encrypting the database

D) None of the above

6. A service can be stopped and started by:

A) Using the graphical Services interface

B) Rebooting the server computer

C) Using the command prompt

D) All of the above

7. When a database is split, which objects remain in the back-end portion of the database?

A) Forms

B) Reports

C) Linked tables

D) Local tables

8. Which of the following isn't a good reason to convert a database to a Web database?

A) To allow Internet access to data

B) To allow more users to use the database

C) To reduce maintenance needs on the database

D) To decrease costs of operating a database

9. Why is TCP/IP called a polite protocol?

A) It broadcasts randomly to any client.

B) You can start it at the command line.

C) It waits and listens for a client to connect.

D) Its service is set to Manual.

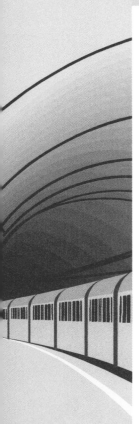

10. **What's the "language of the Internet"?**

   A) Microsoft

   B) PHP

   C) TCP/IP

   D) IIS

Connecting Access to the Web — Level II

STATIONS ALONG THE WAY

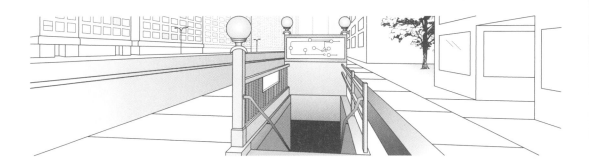

Enter the Station

Questions

1. What is HTML?

2. Do I need a special program for creating and editing HTML files?

3. How do I set up IIS to use PHP?

4. What are tags?

5. How do I create a form?

6. What happens to the data from a form?

Express Line

If you're already thoroughly familiar with HTML and IIIS, then skip ahead to Chapter 20.

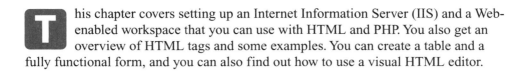

This chapter covers setting up an Internet Information Server (IIS) and a Web-enabled workspace that you can use with HTML and PHP. You also get an overview of HTML tags and some examples. You can create a table and a fully functional form, and you can also find out how to use a visual HTML editor.

Setting Up a Workspace

After you finish the preparative work, which you can read about in Chapter 18, you're ready to begin the second phase of constructing and implementing a Web database. You need a workspace that you can use for your Web application. A *workspace* is a folder that the Web server is aware of. This folder is the location in which you store your Web pages.

In the following sections, you can test folder functionality by creating some very simple HTML (Web) pages and PHP scripts.

Exploring the IIS folder structure

IIS has its own unique layout with which you must become familiar. The following sections introduce you to this layout. After you tour the folders on the file system, you can then look at the same structure from within the Internet Information Services application.

In the section "Creating the workspace folder," later in this chapter, you can set up a workspace for your first Web application. Then, in the section "Web-enabling the workspace" (also later in this chapter), you can enable that workspace so IIS can use it to deliver content to a Web browser.

You can then test the setup by creating HTML and PHP files in the workspace in the section "Testing the workspace," later in this chapter. You can create HTML and PHP files by using the Free HTML editors that are available online for you to download, install, and use in these exercises. Alternatively, if you want to take a no-frills approach, you can use text editors such as Notepad (which comes with the Windows operating system) to create the file. (I tell you about my own favorite editors in the section "Working with Web Pages," later in this chapter.)

You can then find out how to interact with the files both by using a Web browser and at the command line in the section "Testing PHP Functionality."

Analyzing the IIS physical folder structure

When you install IIS, it creates a folder and subfolders on your computer; it uses these as its environment. The default location for the installation is `C:\Inetpub`.

Information Kiosk

Inetpub is a leftover abbreviation for Internet Publications from the mid-90s when IIS was first included with the Windows NT product. This and other aspects of its folder nomenclature are a bit outdated but still fully functional.

Under the Inetpub directory, you find

- **Adminscripts:** Contains scripts to manage IIS by using a Web browser.
- **iissamples:** Example files written in VBScript.
- **mailroot:** Contains the files necessary to support the Microsoft SMTP (mail) service.
- **wwwroot:** The default Web site folder and supporting files.
- **ftproot:** The folder that supports an FTP service. This folder is typically installed by default on a server computer. It's an optional selection.

The wwwroot directory is the default location in which you place your HTML pages, subfolders, graphics, and all other Web site supporting files. This is the default location but not the *preferred* location for these files.

In the section "Creating the workspace folder," later in this chapter, I demonstrate how to create a new workspace and explain in more detail why wwwroot isn't the preferred location for creating workspaces and Web sites. The main focus of the discussions of IIS are centered on wwwroot and other folders created elsewhere.

I don't cover the other folders under C:\Inetpub in this book.

Comparing physical and virtual folder structures

The following locations exist in IIS under the Internet Information Services application. If your installation is on a server, rather than a workstation, you see different sites and folders. The version of IIS you're using also has an effect on the folders that exist. I'm using IIS and IIS Manager version 5.1 on Windows XP Professional. Windows Server 2003 uses IIS version 6.0. To examine the graphical IIS application, follow these steps:

1. Open the IIS Manager application by selecting Start → Programs → Administrative Tools → Internet Information Services Manager.

IIS appears on-screen, as shown in Figure 19-1.

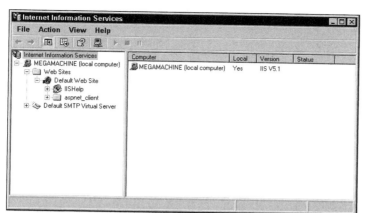

Figure 19-1: Internet Information Services (IIS) manager.

IIS offers you some useful resources:

- **Default Web Site:** `C:\Inetpub\wwwroot`.

- **IISHelp:** `C:\windows\help\iishelp` contains the online help files for IIS.

- **aspnet_client:** `C:\Inetpub\wwwroot\aspnet_client` contains support files for ASP.NET Web pages.

2. **Click Default Web Site to view the locations of folders and associated files.**

The Default Web Site corresponds to the `C:\Inetpub\wwwroot` directory. The IISHelp folder is `C:\windows\help\iishelp`, but the IISHelp directory has an icon that denotes a Web application.

Figure 19-2 shows where to find IIS Help IIS Manager icons.

Figure 19-2: The IISHelp application icon appears under Default Web Site.

A Web application, such as IISHelp, doesn't have to be a folder under `wwwroot`, and in fact, most aren't. Subfolders of an application are designated with a normal folder icon.

Creating the workspace folder

You need to create a workspace folder in which to work and place files that you can use as your Web site for a Web application. The first step in this process is to create a folder; the folder doesn't have to be a subfolder under `wwwroot`.

Because I don't know how your computer is configured, I'm going to make some generic assumptions about Windows computers. To create a new folder, follow these steps:

1. **Open My Computer.**
2. **Double-click the** `C:` **drive.**
3. **Right-click an empty space in the** `C:` **drive window, select New, and then click Folder.**
4. **Enter** Access-web **into the highlighted New Folder name field and press Enter.**

    This location, `C:\Access-web`, is your workspace for the rest of the examples in this book.

You may ask at this point, "What makes this folder different from any other on my computer?" The simple answer is: Nothing — right now, this is just a regular folder, no different from any other.

You simply need a folder that you set aside to contain nothing else but the files and folders created in the upcoming exercises.

Web-enabling the workspace

The preceding section tells you how to create your workspace, but that workspace contains no special functionality beyond that of any other folder. The folder must be Web-enabled to be useful as a Web application folder.

To *Web-enable* this folder, you must make IIS aware of the folder's existence and set some basic attributes for the folder. Follow these steps to get that done:

1. **Open the IIS Manager application by selecting Start ➜ Programs ➜ Administrative Tools ➜ Internet Information Services Manager.**
2. **Select Default Web Site by clicking it.**
3. **Right-click Default Web Site, select New, and then select Virtual Directory.**

    The Virtual Directory Creation Wizard opens.
4. **Click Next.**
5. **In the Alias field, enter** AccessWebDB **and click Next.**
6. **Browse to** `C:\Access-web`, **click OK, and then click Next.**

    The "Read" and "Run scripts" (such as ASP) options are selected by default.
7. **Select "Execute (such as ISAPI applications or CGI)", click Next, and then click Finish.**
8. **Right-click the AccessWebDB application and then select Properties.**

9. On the Virtual Directory tab, click the Configuration button.

10. Click Add.

11. In the Add/Edit Application Extension Mapping text box, enter C:\php\ php5isapi.dll.

12. Enter .php into the Extension field and click OK three times.

Your workspace is now Web-enabled and ready to use with IIS.

Testing the workspace

PHP files are very different from HTML files. HTML files are just text. They're sometimes called HTML documents. HTML doesn't execute in any way; it's merely *parsed* (read) by the browser. PHP files are actually scripts, which means they're executed.

When IIS gets a request for a PHP file from your browser, it parses the PHP file through `php5isapi.dll`, which you set up in IIS in the preceding section. Because the PHP program has internal HTML definitions, it assumes you've already done some basic HTML formatting. (You can see this assumption demonstrated in the browser test later in this section.)

Because HTML is text, the browser can deal with it directly or through the Web server. You can simply double-click an HTML file, and it opens in Internet Explorer. It looks the same as if it had been served by the Web server. It also functions the same as if it had been processed by the Web server.

PHP, on the other hand, is a script that needs a parsing program to be read correctly by the browser. You can't open a PHP file in Internet Explorer by double-clicking it. Even if you configure Internet Explorer to open PHP files directly, those files don't render correctly because they're scripts and must be processed by the PHP parser.

These concepts become clearer as you work through the rest of this chapter.

Testing HTML functionality

You now have a fully functional Web server and Web application container. No need to go into exhaustive detail about how HTML documents are created. In this section, you simply test your site to make sure it really works.

To test the site, you have to create a minimal HTML file that can confirm your site is functional. Follow these steps:

1. Open Notepad by clicking Start → Run, entering Notepad into the Open field, and clicking OK.

Windows Notepad opens.

2. Enter the following text into Notepad exactly as shown:

```
<HTML>
<HEAD>
<TITLE>Test File</TITLE>
<BODY>
Success!
</BODY>
</HTML>
```

3. Click File, click Save, browse to `C:\Access-web`, select All Files in the Save As Type field, and enter test.html as the file name.

4. Click Save.

5. Open Internet Explorer, enter http://localhost/AccessWebDB/test.html into the address field, and then press Enter.

Your browser should display the word `Success!`

The success of this test proves that the Web server recognizes the folder you created — and has it properly registered as a Web folder (virtual directory).

Testing PHP functionality

The test of functionality in this section is the definitive test for the Web folder you create in the preceding sections. Depending on the functionality you're looking for, you should test your PHP files at the command line, as well as in Internet Explorer.

You start this example by creating a simple PHP file. Follow these steps:

1. Open Notepad.

2. Enter the following text, exactly as shown, into Notepad:

```
<?
echo "Success!";
?>
```

3. Click File, click Save, browse to `C:\Access-web`, select All Files in the Save As Type field, and enter `test.php` as the file name.

4. Click Save.

Command line test

When the PHP file is ready to use, you can test your system's PHP functionality from the command line by following these steps:

1. Click Start, click Run, enter cmd into the Open field, and click OK.

The command prompt opens.

2. Type the following text at the command prompt:

```
cd \Access-web <ENTER>
```

3. Type the following text at the command prompt:

```
php test.php <ENTER>
```

If the word `Success!` appears on the screen, you've set up PHP correctly to work at the command line and parse PHP files.

Browser test

To test your PHP file, follow these steps:

1. Open Internet Explorer.

2. Enter http://localhost/AccessWebDB/test.php **into the Address field and then press Enter.**

Your browser should display the word `Success!`

This test proves that the Web server is correctly displaying PHP files to browsers when requested.

Working with Web Pages

A *Web page* is really just another term for an HTML page because you view an HTML page with a Web browser. Web is short for World Wide Web, which you see abbreviated in homepage addresses as www.

To produce Web pages, you need some sort of text editor. A *text editor* is any program that allows you to enter and save text to a file. Notepad is an example of a simple text editor that you can use to create Web pages. In fact, you use Notepad in the preceding section to create a simple Web page.

You can find many free and commercial programs for creating Web pages, generally known as HTML editors. Type "HTML editor" into any search engine and you get a lot of hits.

If you're pressed for time, don't worry — I've done this bit of research for you: Here I use Notepad, as well as another program (called Selida 2) for higher-level editing. You can use any text editor you want, but Selida is free, easy to use, and has a lot of useful tools for creating Web pages.

If you don't already have a favorite HTML editor, download Selida to work through the exercises in this section. To do so, follow these steps:

1. **Open Internet Explorer, enter** http://selida.camelon.nl **into the address field, and press Enter.**
2. **Click Download from the left navigation list.**
3. **Read the indemnification clause and click Yes.**
4. **Select the latest full version of the program for download.**
5. **Click Save when prompted, save the file to a location with which you're familiar, and click Save.**
6. **Locate the file you download in Step 5 and double-click it to install Selida 2 on your computer.**
7. **Follow the prompts for the installation.**
8. **When the installation is complete, close Selida.**

    You use Selida in editing procedures given later in this chapter.

HTML basics

Although HTML is an acronym for HyperText Markup Language, HTML isn't really a formal programming language. It's actually a series of tags that describe the way a document looks and behaves when viewed with a Web browser.

You can find many good books on HTML, as well as HTML tutorials and Web sites dedicated to explaining HTML. I'm not going to give you an in-depth discussion of HTML, but you need a basic understanding of it — how it works, and its limitations — before you can do any effective programming in PHP or any other related language.

Tags

HTML tags are special designations that describe and format text in an HTML file. In HTML code, you surround text that needs formatting with an opening tag and a closing tag. *Tags* are keywords and abbreviations that describe some attribute for the text; they tell the browser how to display the text on-screen.

For example, if you want to make some text bold, you surround that text with the tag for bold, which is <B>. The text would look like this in the HTML file:

```
<B>Hello There.</B>
```

The opening tag for bold text is <B> and the closing tag is </B>. The text in the HTML file doesn't change in the editor. To view the text, you either have to use an

HTML editor with a Preview mode or use Internet Explorer to open the HTML file with which you're working.

An opening tag is the tag attribute enclosed in pointed brackets < >, and the closing tag has the slash in it to designate it as a closing tag </ >.

Watch Your Step

You must enclose text in an opening and a closing tag. If you forget your closing tag, all text after the opening tag carries the attributes of the opening tag. Some HTML editors automatically insert an opening and closing tag for you. In an editor such as Notepad, you must supply all tags yourself.

To fully demonstrate the HTML tags discussed in this section, follow these steps:

1. **Open a new file in Notepad.**
2. **Enter** <B>Hello There</B> **into the file.**
3. **Save the file in the** C:\Access-web **folder as** tags.html.
4. **Open Internet Explorer and enter the address** http://localhost/ AccessWebDB/tags.html **into the address field, and then press Enter.**

   You should see **Hello There** in bold letters in your browser.

Keep Notepad and Internet Explorer open to this page so that, when you make new changes in Notepad, you can see them on-screen in Internet Explorer by refreshing the page.

Structure

The following sections talk about basic structure tags for an HTML document. They aren't explicitly required for all valid HTML documents, but I suggest you get familiar with using them. Most good HTML editors pre-format your HTML document by using these tags.

<HTML></HTML>

The <HTML> tag encloses the entire contents of an HTML document. You've already used this tag if you tested the HTML functionality of your workspace (earlier in this chapter). That test file has all the elements needed for a complete HTML file.

The HTML document looks like this:

```
<HTML>
Content
</HTML>
```

\<HEAD>\</HEAD>

The \<HEAD> tag has special significance for HTML files. It holds the title of the document and scripts for the file. You can't see the contents of the \<HEAD> section in the browser.

The \<HEAD> section is the first section of an HTML document. This section can cover one or many lines in the document. The entire \<HEAD> section resides above any content.

Here's an HTML document that includes the \<HEAD> tag:

```
<HTML>
<HEAD></HEAD>
Content
</HTML>
```

\<TITLE>\</TITLE>

The \<TITLE> tag is an optional part of an HTML document. When you add a \<TITLE> to your document, the title appears in Internet Explorer's title bar. The \<TITLE> resides in the \<HEAD> of an HTML document. In the HTML test you can perform in the section "Testing HTML functionality," earlier in this chapter, you use Test File as the \<TITLE>.

Here's the HTML file with the TITLE section:

```
<HTML>
<HEAD><TITLE>Example Document</TITLE></HEAD>
Content
</HTML>
```

\<BODY>\</BODY>

The \<BODY> tag of an HTML contains all of your content: text, forms, images, links, buttons, and so on. The \<BODY> is the material that you can see in Internet Explorer when you view a Web page.

The exercises in the rest of this chapter focus on the \<BODY>. (You can do some interesting things in the \<HEAD> portion of an HTML document, but that's beyond the scope of this discussion.)

Each of the following sections focuses on a particular set of tags to format text in the \<BODY> of an HTML document.

Here's the HTML file with a complete skeleton structure:

```
<HTML>
<HEAD><TITLE>Example Document</TITLE></HEAD>
<BODY>
```

```
Content
</BODY>
</HTML>
```

Spacing

The following sections explain how to format your text by using spaces, new lines, indentation, and paragraphs. These tags are very powerful tools. With them, you can format HTML documents to look like regular documents.

<P></P> and <P>

The <P></P> tag was originally used to separate paragraphs of information by a full line of white space above and below the enclosed text. You can also use <P> by itself to create a line of white space below its location.

For an example of both versions of this tag — which illustrates the difference between them — follow these steps:

1. Open the `tags.html` **Notepad file created in the "Tags" section (earlier in this chapter).**

2. Enter the following text into the file:

```
<P>This is a paragraph with space above and below</P>
This is a plain text sentence.
<P>
This is an unformatted sentence.
```

3. Refresh your browser by clicking the Refresh button or pressing the F5 key on the keyboard.

The formatted text appears on-screen.

</BR> and

The
</BR> tag is similar to the <P></P> tag in that it creates a link break above and below the enclosed text. A <BR> by itself creates a line break below it. To see this tag in action, follow these steps:

1. Open the `tags.html` **file if it's not already open.**

It's the same one created in the "Working with Web Pages" section, earlier in this chapter.

2. Enter this text into the file:

```
<BR>This is a sentence with line breaks above and       ↵
below.</BR>
This is another unformatted sentence.
<BR>
And another.
```

3. Save `tags.html` **and refresh your browser to see the update.**

The formatted text appears on-screen.

The ` ` tag is very different than most tags because it has no pointed brackets surrounding it. This is the non-breaking space tag. *Non-breaking space* means that this tag adds a space exactly where you place it but doesn't start a new line. It's equivalent to a space between two words.

One idiosyncrasy of HTML is that you can have only one space separating any two words or tags. Sometimes, when this restriction isn't convenient, the non-breaking space comes to your rescue. You can place as many of these tags as you need into a document — one right after the other.

To demonstrate non-breaking spaces, follow these steps:

1. **Open the file** `tags.html` **if it's not already open.**

It's the same one created in the "Working with Web Pages" section, earlier in this chapter.

2. **Enter the following text into the file:**

```
<P>
Two non-breaking spaces:  Two spaces.
<BR>
Five non-breaking spaces:         ↵
 Five spaces.
```

3. **Save the file and refresh your browser.**

The formatted text appears on-screen.

<BLOCKQUOTE></BLOCKQUOTE>

A `<BLOCKQUOTE>` tag originally was meant to make excerpts or quotes stand out from surrounding text. You can use it for other purposes, such as creating space to make a page look less cluttered. You can also stack `<BLOCKQUOTE>` tags to indent text farther and farther.

You need a fairly large block of text to reap the benefits of the `<BLOCKQUOTE>` tag, so for this example, include the preceding paragraph between the `<BLOCKQUOTE>` tags. To demonstrate block quotes, follow these steps:

1. **Open the** `tags.html` **file if it isn't already open.**

It's the same one created in the "Working with Web Pages" section, earlier in this chapter.

2. **Enter the following block of text into the file:**

```
<BLOCKQUOTE>A BLOCKQUOTE originally was meant to
make excerpts or quotes stand out from surrounding
text. It can also be used for other purposes, such as
creating space to make a page look less cluttered.
You can also "stack" BLOCKQUOTE tags to indent text
farther and farther.</BLOCKQUOTE>
```

3. **Save the file and refresh your browser.**

The formatted text appears on-screen.

You don't need to include a <P> or <BR> tag before a block of text separated by <BLOCKQUOTE> tags. That's because the <BLOCKQUOTE> tag makes this separation automatically as part of its format.

Text

I call this section "Text" because, in general, you format small portions of text by using these tags. The exception to this statement is the <PRE> tag. You use the rest of the tags in the following sections for emphasis of some kind — I cover bold text, italicized text, enlarged text, and preformatted text.

<B></B>

The <B> tag formats enclosed text with boldface type. Like any special text tag, you should use it conservatively and only to emphasize something that you want to stand out from surrounding text.

At the very beginning of the "Tags" section (earlier in this chapter), you use the <B> tag. Check the first line of tags.html in that section:

```
<B>Hello There</B>
```

The old form of this tag is <STRONG></STRONG>, but hardly anyone uses that tag anymore. It's deprecated (that is, abandoned as obsolete) in favor of <B></B>.

<I></I>

The <I> tag italicizes enclosed text. To demonstrate italicized text, follow these steps:

1. **Open the tags.html file if it isn't already open.**

It's the same one created in the "Working with Web Pages" section, earlier in this chapter.

2. **Enter the following text into the file:**

```
<I>Hello There</I>
```

3. **Save the file and refresh your browser.**

The formatted text appears on-screen.

The <BLOCKQUOTE> tag from the section "<BLOCKQUOTE></BLOCKQUOTE>," earlier in this chapter, removed the need to put in a leading line break before this line of text.

The old version of this tag is <EM></EM> (emphasis), but it's now considered obsolete, so it's deprecated in favor of <I></I>.

<U></U>

The <U> tag may confuse some readers because traditionally links are underlined. Because of this potential confusion, use this tag sparingly and only when bold or italics can't give the proper emphasis. To demonstrate underlined text, follow these steps:

1. **Open the** `tags.html` **file if it isn't already open.**

It's the same one created in the "Working with Web Pages" section, earlier in this chapter.

2. **Enter the following text into the file:**

```
<BR>
<U>Underlined Text</U>
```

3. **Save the file and refresh your browser.**

The formatted text appears on-screen.

<H1></H1>

You use the <H> tags to format Headings. The <H> tags bold and enlarge the text that they enclose. The <H1> tag makes the text very large and bold. It's the largest of the Heading tags. To demonstrate the <H1> tag, follow these steps:

1. **Open the** `tags.html` **file if it isn't already open.**

It's the same one created in the "Working with Web Pages" section, earlier in this chapter.

2. **Enter the following Level 1 Heading into the file:**

```
<H1>Today's Headlines</H1>
```

3. **Save the file and refresh your browser.**

The formatted text appears on-screen.

You don't need to put in a line break before the <H1> tag line because Headings automatically format white space above and below them.

 Watch Your Step

Headings can be very effective when you use them in moderation on a Web page, but they can have an amateurish effect if you overuse them. Many newcomers to HTML use Headings for everything. Use other types of text formatting when possible to make your few headings really stand out.

<H2></H2>

The Level 2 Heading (as you might expect) is smaller than a Level 1 Heading. As the level number increases, the size of the type decreases. <H1> is the largest, and <H6> is the smallest. To demonstrate a Level 2 Heading, follow these steps:

1. Open the `tags.html` file if it isn't already open.

It's the same one created in the "Working with Web Pages" section, earlier in this chapter.

2. Enter the following Level 2 Heading into the file:

`<H2>Today's Top Story</H2>`

3. Save the file and refresh your browser.

The formatted text appears on-screen.

<H3></H3>

The <H3> tag creates a Level 3 Heading, which is a little larger than regular text and looks different from standard text that appears in boldface. The characters appear to be spread out a bit more horizontally than standard text. To demonstrate a Level 3 Heading, follow these steps:

1. Open the `tags.html` file if it isn't already open.

It's the same one created in the "Working with Web Pages" section, earlier in this chapter.

2. Enter this Level 3 Heading into the file:

`<H3>Yesterday's News</H3>`

3. Save the file and refresh your browser.

The formatted text appears on-screen.

<H4></H4>

The Level 4 Heading is the same size as standard bold text, which makes it a seldom-used heading type. Compare its size and weight to regular bold text. To demonstrate a Level 4 Heading, follow these steps:

1. **Open the `tags.html` file if it isn't already open.**

It's the same one created in the "Working with Web Pages" section, earlier in this chapter.

2. **Enter this Level 4 Heading into the file:**

```
<H4>Special Caption</H4>
```

3. **Save the file and refresh your browser.**

The formatted text appears on-screen.

<H5></H5>

I rarely use — or see — Level 5 (or, for that matter, Level 6) Headings used on contemporary Web pages. These Headings are extra bold and small — which makes them a little difficult to read, even on new, higher-quality computer screens. If you use these Headings, use them sparingly and in very high-contrast designs (such as black text on white background). To demonstrate a Level 5 Heading, follow these steps:

1. **Open the `tags.html` file if it isn't already open.**

It's the same one created in the "Working with Web Pages" section, earlier in this chapter.

2. **Enter the following Level 5 Heading into the file:**

```
<H5>Can You Still Read This?</H5>
```

3. **Save the file and refresh your browser.**

The formatted text appears on-screen.

<H6></H6>

Okay, some Web sites still use Level 6 Headings for copyright notices or indemnification headings, but even these headings are becoming very rare. To demonstrate a Level 6 Heading, follow these steps:

1. **Open the `tags.html` file if it isn't already open.**

It's the same one created in the "Working with Web Pages" section, earlier in this chapter.

2. **Enter this Level 6 Heading into the file:**

```
<H6>Copyright 2007</H6>
```

3. Save the file and refresh your browser.

The formatted text appears on-screen.

<PRE></PRE>

The <PRE> (preformatted text) tag is one of the most useful tags for those of you who like full control of the way text looks on a page. Ordinarily HTML ignores white space unless you format that space by using tags — but the <PRE> tag gives you full creative control. It's especially great for those who do free-form poetry.

The text that you enclose in the <PRE> tag looks exactly how you format it, with spaces, tabs, returns, justifications, and so on. It defaults to an old typewriter font (Courier), but you can find out how to change this attribute in the "Fonts" section (later in this chapter). To demonstrate preformatted text, follow these steps:

1. Open the `tags.html` file if it isn't already open.

It's the same one created in the "Working with Web Pages" section, earlier in this chapter.

2. Enter this text into the file, exactly as you see it here:

```
<PRE>
             This is how                    preformatted     ↵
    text         works!


    Any text
                            Anywhere on the page with ↵
    no HTML                    tags.
    </PRE>
```

3. Save the file and refresh your browser.

The formatted text appears on-screen.

Justification

All text in a browser is left-justified unless you give the text some alternate formatting. With HTML tags, you can center, right justify, or fully justify text. Justification refers to where the text lines up with the rest of the text. Normal *left-justified* text, as you see in this paragraph, is lined up on the left side. All the text is flush with the left margin and jagged on the right. *Centered* text centers the text in the middle of the page. *Right-justified* text is flush with the right margin and can have a jagged left margin. *Fully justified* text is spread out so it's flush with both the right and left margins. Fully justified text looks neat and clean at the edges, but sometimes the spacing of words is a little strange.

In contemporary style, left-justification seems to be the norm. Centered text is reserved for headlines, large titles, or section separations. Fully justified text is still used in some cases. Right-justification as a design technique is handy if you need to line up field labels on a form or report (you'd get a look very similar to design elements of forms and reports in Access).

Most of the time, centering also involves stacking other tags with the centered text for added emphasis.

Information Kiosk

When you stack tags, they must be properly *nested* (enclosed). Work from the inside (the text) outward.

<CENTER></CENTER>

You usually use centering with other emphasis tags, such as a Heading or Bold tag, to give that extra punch to the text. In the example in this section, you stack <H1> with <CENTER>. You must act on your text with the <H1> tag first, and then use centering to create the effect you want. To demonstrate centered text, follow these steps:

1. Open the `tags.html` **file if it isn't already open.**

It's the same one created in the "Working with Web Pages" section, earlier in this chapter.

2. Enter the following text into the file:

```
<CENTER><H1>Big Story</H1></CENTER>
```

3. Save the file and refresh your browser.

The formatted text appears on-screen.

<P ALIGN=RIGHT></P>

You may find part of this tag familiar. Right-justification is actually an enhancement of the <P></P> tag, which I discuss in the section "<P></P> and <P>," earlier in this chapter. Many HTML tags have enhancements that make them very versatile. To demonstrate right-justified text, follow these steps:

1. Open the `tags.html` **file if it isn't already open.**

It's the same one created in the "Working with Web Pages" section, earlier in this chapter.

2. Enter the following text into the file:

```
<P ALIGN=RIGHT>Text that is Right-Justified.</P>
```

3. Save the file and refresh your browser.

4. Enter the following addition for another example of nested tags:

```
<P ALIGN=RIGHT>Text that is Right-Justified.<BR>    ↵
More text.</P>
```

5. Save the file and refresh your browser.

The formatted text appears on-screen.

<P ALIGN=FULL></P>

Full justification is another twist on the same concept as right justification, which I discuss in the preceding section. You need a lot of text to see the effect of full justification. Use this paragraph of text for a convenient example.

To demonstrate justified text, follow these steps:

1. Open the `tags.html` file if it isn't already open.

It's the same one created in the "Working with Web Pages" section, earlier in this chapter.

2. Enter the text into the file:

```
<P ALIGN=FULL> Full justification is another twist    ↵
on the same concept as right-justification. You need   ↵
a very long sentence to see the effect of full         ↵
justification. Use this paragraph of text for a        ↵
convenient example.</P>
```

3. Save the file and refresh your browser.

The formatted text appears on-screen.

Fonts

A *font* is the typeface of a letter. Fonts come in a variety of styles: sans-serif, block, script, and so on. You have a great variety of fonts to choose from. Make your choices carefully — a font that you use to promote a band doesn't work for promoting stocks and bonds.

The same rules that apply for fonts in Access forms and reports apply for fonts on Web pages. They should be

- Clean
- Easy to read
- Without much variety

The three most popular styles are

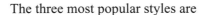 Arial

Times

Courier

Courier is losing its popularity, but many sites still use it because it has a typewriter-like "retro" feel to it. You can find several variations on these three fonts, but Arial and Times are widely used and respected as standards.

<FONT FACE></FONT>

The default font face (typeface) for HTML is Times, and you see the Times font face in `tags.html`. You can change the face for a single letter, word, paragraph, or an entire page by using the <FONT FACE> tag.

I like to use the Arial font because it's clean, seems larger than normal on-screen, and is very readable. To custom format a font, follow these steps:

1. Open the `tags.html` file if it isn't already open.

It's the same one created in the "Working with Web Pages" section, earlier in this chapter.

2. Enter the following text into the file:

```
<FONT FACE="Arial">Hello. Do you see the          ↩
difference?</FONT>
```

3. Save the file and refresh your browser.

Do you see how much larger Arial appears for standard text? In the section "<FONT SIZE></FONT>," later in this chapter, you can find out how to change font size without resorting to a Heading.

<FONT COLOR></FONT>

You can specify the color you use for your font in the <FONT> tag, as well as the font face. Although this section may seem to imply that you have to use a separate or nested tag for the color, you don't. You can stack the attributes in a single tag.

Here's the font-face example from the preceding section:

```
<FONT FACE="Arial">Hello. Do you see the difference?</FONT>
```

You can add a color after the font face, as shown here:

```
<FONT FACE="Arial" COLOR="blue">Hello. Do you see the      ↩
difference?</FONT>
```

These days, you can use the actual color you want (if it's supported), but a few years ago, you had to use hexadecimal code (a special six-character designation) for the color. Web designers all had hex-code charts taped up near their desks for easy reference. That's just a bit of historical trivia — you don't have to worry about hex color codes. To demonstrate adding color to a font face, follow these steps:

1. Open the `tags.html` file if it isn't already open.

It's the same one created in the "Working with Web Pages" section, earlier in this chapter.

2. Enter the following text to specify the font face and color in the file (or change the text you entered in the preceding section):

```
<FONT FACE="Arial" COLOR="blue">Hello. Do you see    ↵
the difference?</FONT>
```

3. Save the file and refresh your browser.

The formatted text appears on-screen.

<FONT SIZE></FONT>

As with color (which you can read about in the preceding section), you can stack font size into a <FONT> tag that already has the other font attributes. The following line of HTML, for example, specifies font face, color, and size:

```
<FONT FACE="Arial" COLOR="blue" SIZE=4>Hello. Do you    ↵
see the difference?</FONT>
```

The SIZE attribute has a range of 1 (smallest) to 7 (largest). To demonstrate specifying font size, follow these steps:

1. Open the `tags.html` file if it isn't already open.

It's the same one created in the "Working with Web Pages" section, earlier in this chapter.

2. Enter the following text in the file (or change the text you entered in the preceding section):

```
<FONT FACE="Arial" COLOR="blue" SIZE=4>Hello. Do    ↵
you see the difference?</FONT>
```

3. Save the file and refresh your browser.

The formatted text appears on-screen.

4. Close Notepad (`tags.html`) but leave Internet Explorer open for use with other examples.

Form elements

Forms are your main method of communication with a Web database when you want to select, insert, update, or delete data. You select data by using forms to generate reports or display records. Data-entry forms are developed to assist users in their everyday tasks of managing data.

Forms make it easy for users to interact with your data. A well-designed form is easy to use, makes good use of screen space, and requires very little creativity from the user.

In the following sections, you can build a fully functional form and script designed to decipher the data and display it in a browser.

<FORM></FORM>

In HTML, the entire page isn't generally dedicated wholly to a form, although it certainly could be. A form is simply an aspect of an HTML page.

To create a form, you must declare the <FORM> tag in your HTML page. A form by itself isn't very useful; you have to include some sort of script that extracts the form data and submits it — either through e-mail to an e-mail address or to a database. Both methods are very common.

I've never seen the <FORM> tag used by itself. It always has certain attributes that define its destination.

Here's a very common example of a form:

```
<FORM METHOD=POST ACTION="submit.php">
```

The METHOD=POST attribute means the form will submitted through a POST — that is, the form's data goes to a script for processing. The ACTION="submit.php" attribute defines the file (script) to which the data from this form is being submitted. You can name the file anything you want. I usually name it something related to the data that's being submitted to it.

You must place all other form elements between the opening <FORM> tag and the closing </FORM> tag. To begin a new form, follow these steps:

1. **Open Notepad and enter the following text:**

```
<HTML>
<HEAD><TITLE>Form One</TITLE></HEAD>
<BODY>
<FORM METHOD=POST ACTION="submit.php">
</FORM>
</BODY>
</HTML>
```

2. **Save this file as** form.html **in your** C:\Access-web **folder.**

Leave Notepad open because you'll be using it again later in this chapter.

Don't bother viewing this form in Internet Explorer because there's nothing to see right now. As soon as you have elements in your form, you can view them.

Form elements have certain attributes that are common to them all — NAME and VALUE:

- **NAME:** Required for all form elements. This attribute becomes the name of the variable that holds your data for that form element. This aspect of forms becomes clear after you complete this form and the script to receive the data.

- **VALUE:** Optional. I use VALUE as a default answer in case the user doesn't give one.

<INPUT>

The <INPUT> tag can contain various versatile and powerful attributes. This one tag can take the form of a check box, a radio button, a hidden field, a text field, a submit button, or a reset button.

You use a different <INPUT> tag for each form element you need. In other words, if you need three text fields, a submit button, and a reset button, then you need five different <INPUT> tags — each identifying the type of input required. The next five subsections look at these variations, one at a time.

Text field

The code in this section shows a common type of Text field used in forms shown with available Text-field attributes. The only required value is NAME. I added FName for first name. VALUE is a default value. SIZE is the screen size of the field in characters (letters). MAXLENGTH is the maximum number of characters that are allowed in this Text field.

 Information Kiosk

A Text field is a field that accommodates small amounts of text, such as a name, city, Zip code, phone number, and so on.

Here's what the HTML looks like that specifies a Text field:

```
<INPUT TYPE="TEXT" NAME="FName" VALUE="" SIZE=0      ↩
MAXLENGTH=0>
```

Check box

The check box is a very popular form element, especially for survey questions. The example shown in this section is a standard check box with attributes. I entered CB1 for NAME. CHECKED is either blank (unchecked) or "checked". To have the check boxed in "checked" state means that the user has to uncheck the box if she doesn't want that option.

Here's what the HTML looks like that specifies a check box:

```
<INPUT TYPE="CHECKBOX" NAME="CB1" VALUE=" "
CHECKED="checked">
```

Radio button

The radio button has the same attributes and options as the check box. Here's an example with a value of RB1 for the NAME:

```
<INPUT TYPE="RADIO" NAME="RB1" VALUE=" " CHECKED="checked">
```

Hidden

The Hidden field is very handy for passing values to a script or database. The field doesn't appear on the page.

Here's what the HTML looks like that specifies a Hidden field:

```
<INPUT TYPE="HIDDEN" NAME="HF1" VALUE="TEST">
```

Password

The Password field is useful if you want to keep entries private because the information typed into it is *masked* (hidden from prying eyes by an on-screen string of neutral characters). You can use the Password field to validate your users before allowing them access to other forms and the database.

Here's what the HTML looks like that specifies a Password field:

```
<INPUT TYPE="PASSWORD" NAME="PASSWD" VALUE=" ">
```

Submit button

The Submit button sends the form data to the receiving script identified in the FORM ACTION declaration. The value that you enter into the VALUE attribute appears on the Submit button. You can enter any value you want here. I chose to use Send for the value of this button.

Here's what the HTML looks like that specifies a Submit button:

```
<INPUT TYPE="SUBMIT" NAME="Submit" VALUE="Send">
```

Reset button

The Reset button is customarily located near the Submit button; it's used to reset the form to its default values. In effect, it wipes out any information you've selected or entered, instead of submitting the information. (It's handy when you change your mind about the data you're entering.) The VALUE attribute is displayed on the button.

Here's what the HTML looks like that specifies a Reset button:

```
<INPUT TYPE="RESET" NAME="Reset" VALUE="Clear">
```

<SELECT></SELECT> and <OPTION></OPTION>

The SELECT tag allows you to set up a drop-down list with as few or as many options (each specified with its own OPTION tag) as you want to use. A SELECT list lets you limit the responses that a user can enter for a particular item.

A typical SELECT list — in this case, with several OPTION tags — looks like this:

```
<SELECT NAME="CHEESE">
<OPTION>Gouda</OPTION>
<OPTION>Havarti</OPTION>
<OPTION>Sharp Cheddar</OPTION>
</SELECT>
```

Building a form

You create the basic skeleton for a form (form.html) earlier in the "<FORM> </FORM>" section of this chapter. If this basic form needs some specialized features, you can add a few form elements to demonstrate how forms operate and how the receiving script processes the information sent to it. To build a form with various elements, follow these steps:

1. Open form.html in Notepad, if it's not already open.

2. Add the following form elements to form.html:

First Name:

```
<INPUT TYPE="TEXT" NAME="FName" VALUE="" SIZE=25      ↵
MAXLENGTH=40>
     
```

Last Name:

```
<INPUT TYPE="TEXT" NAME="LName" VALUE="" SIZE=25      ↵
MAXLENGTH=40>
     
```

Test1:

```
<INPUT TYPE="TEXT" NAME="Test1" VALUE="" SIZE=3       ↵
MAXLENGTH=3>
<P>
<INPUT TYPE="SUBMIT" NAME="Submit" VALUE="Submit">
   
<INPUT TYPE="RESET" NAME="Reset" VALUE="Clear">
```

3. Save the file in Notepad.

4. Open Internet Explorer if it's not already open, type http://localhost/ AccessWebDB/form.html **into the address field, and then press Enter.**

5. Close Notepad but leave Internet Explorer open with `form.html` displayed.

Does the form look the way you thought it would? Take a look at the form elements, labels, and attributes carefully and compare them to what you see on-screen.

Building the script

Each form needs a script to which it can submit its data. The script must be configured to receive and process the data. PHP is perfect for processing form data. The form you create in this section displays data you're submitting on-screen — in Internet Explorer. This is a very common process, to show the user the information that's about to go to a database.

You can find out how to configure this PHP in Chapter 20, which explains PHP scripting, so don't get bogged down in the details right now.

Each of the NAME values in your form, `form.html`, appears on-screen in the browser. To build a script that can receive data from a form, follow these steps:

1. Open a new file in Notepad and enter the following text into that file:

```
<?
echo $FName;
echo "<BR>";
echo $LName;
echo "<BR>";
echo $Test1;
?>
```

2. Save the file as **submit.php**.

3. Open the Internet Explorer page for `form.html` (http://localhost/ AccessWebDB/form.html); then enter your first name, your last name, and a test score.

4. Click Submit.

Do you see what you expected? (I'm still always thrilled at successfully submitting data to another page or to a database.)

<TEXTAREA></TEXTAREA>

The <TEXTAREA> tab creates a configurable field for text. You can enter a considerable amount of text into a Text Area field. In the following code, I configured the Text Area to have 5 rows and 30 columns of characters:

```
<TEXTAREA NAME="NOTES" ROWS=5 COLS=30></TEXTAREA>
```

Tables

Tables are an extremely important and useful part of HTML. Tables can be very simple, or extremely complex and nested. To work with complex tables, you need a good visual editor or a great imagination. In the following sections, I cover only the simplest table configurations so that my demonstrations are clear.

<TABLE></TABLE>

The <TABLE> tag comes with standard attributes for formatting the basic character of the table. Here's an example of a typical opening <TABLE> tag definition:

```
<TABLE CELLPADDING=5 CELLSPACING=5 WIDTH=600 BORDER=0>
```

CELLPADDING and CELLSPACING relate to how individual cells are configured. (Cells make up the spreadsheet-like configuration of a table.) WIDTH is an optional parameter. If it's absent, then the table is dynamic in width and shrinks or expands to fit the data it contains. BORDER refers to the thickness of the border surrounding the table and cells. If you set BORDER to 0 (zero), then the table and cells have no border. You can set BORDER=1 for testing purposes so you can see the table design. After you're satisfied with the design, you can get rid of the border by setting BORDER=0.

<TR></TR>

The <TR> tag defines table rows and usually does little more than hold the <TD> tags that define table columns, which I discuss in the following section.

<TD></TD>

The <TD> tags enclose table data. <TD> tags also define a column in a table.

Building a table

A table is composed of rows and columns, much like a spreadsheet: Table rows and table data create cells. The example in this section provides you with a very simple table that has all standard table attributes defined. To create this table, follow these steps:

1. Open a new file in Notepad.

2. Enter the following text into the file:

```
<TABLE CELLPADDING=5 CELLSPACING=0 WIDTH=600 BORDER=1>
<TR>
<TD>Row1 Column1 </TD>
<TD>Row1 Column2 </TD>
</TR>
<TR>
<TD> Row2 Column1</TD>
```

```
<TD> Row2 Column2</TD>
</TR>
</TABLE>
```

3. **Save the file as** table.html.

4. **Open Internet Explorer, enter** http://localhost/AccessWebDB/table.html **into the Address field, and then press Enter.**

You can now experiment with CELLPADDING and CELLSPACING to see the effects each has on the look of the table.

5. **Change** CELLPADDING **from 5 to 10 in** table.html **and note the difference.**

Continue changing CELLPADDING — and experiment with CELLSPACING — to see how these numbers affect the on-screen look of the table.

6. **Change the** WIDTH **value from 600 to** 400.

You can also remove the WIDTH attribute completely.

Also get a feel for the BORDER width by changing BORDER from 1 to 2, for example.

7. **Close Notepad when you're finished with your experimentation, but leave Internet Explorer open for the exercises in the following section.**

Tables play an important part in Chapter 20 when presenting data for reports. The discussion of static and dynamic content in the section "Using Access Forms and Reports," later in this chapter, is a prerequisite for Chapter 20. Knowing the difference between static and dynamic content, and understanding the changes that you need to make to display each, is very important to your success in implementing Web databases.

Miscellaneous

The tags in the following sections didn't really fit anywhere else in the scheme of this chapter, so I filed this highly useful list of oddballs under "Miscellaneous."

<A HREF></A>

The <A HREF></A> tag is perhaps the most important tag in all of HTML: It's the tag that defines a hyperlink. Without this tag, hypertext really wouldn't be hyper at all; it would just be text. To demonstrate a hyperlink tag, follow these steps:

1. **Open a new file in Notepad and enter the following text:**
```
<A HREF="http://www.kenhess.com">Author's Web Site</A>
```

2. **Save the file as** misc.html **in Notepad.**

3. **Open Internet Explorer, enter** http://localhost/AccessWebDB/misc.html **into the Address field, and then press Enter.**

4. Click the link that appears on your page.

This click not only demonstrates how hyperlinks work, but it also gives you a gratuitous tour of my Web site.

5. Click the Back button on Internet Explorer until you return to the `misc.html` page.

<!–Comments–>

The `<!--Comments-->` tag defines a comment. A *comment* is a description of what's going on in a file, but it doesn't appear when you view the page by using a Web browser. You use comments to document what you're doing so you can troubleshoot later as needed. To demonstrate commenting, follow these steps:

1. Open the file `misc.html` in Notepad if it isn't already open.

2. Enter the following comment into the file:

```
<!--This link is the Author's Web Site.-->
```

3. Save the file and refresh your browser.

The formatted text appears on-screen. The exclamation point tells the browser that this is a comment, so the browser doesn't display it.

You can place comments anywhere in an HTML file. Be generous with them. It doesn't cost anything in performance to put them in, and it can save you a lot of page-maintenance headaches later.

<HR>

The `<HR>` tag defines a Horizontal Rule, which is a practical tool for separating parts of a Web page as part of the overall design. A Horizontal Rule can have a specific WIDTH, a SIZE (thickness), and a COLOR. The default rule appears with SHADE (shading). To turn off shading, use NOSHADE.

If you don't enter a WIDTH parameter, the Horizontal Rule has a dynamic width (browser width), which you may prefer. To demonstrate a Horizontal Rule, follow these steps:

1. Open the file `misc.html` in Notepad if it isn't already open.

2. Enter the following Horizontal Rule into the file:

```
<HR SIZE=1 WIDTH=500 COLOR="navy">
```

3. Save the file and refresh your browser.

The formatted horizontal rule appears on-screen. Experiment with different SIZE, WIDTH, and COLOR parameters to see how they affect the overall look.

Images

Images (pictures) can greatly enhance your Web pages. Although an in-depth discussion of images is a bit beyond the scope of this book, I give it a bit of space here because images are such a prevalent element of Web pages. Like text, images are left-aligned unless you specify an alignment for them. Use the same alignment (justification) for images as you do with text.

Before you place an image in a Web page, consider these factors:

- Decide where you want the image on the page.
- Know the relative path to the image.
- Know the size of the image.
- Decide whether you want a border on the image (usually, you won't; borders can add visual clutter).
- Decide whether you want the image to also be a hyperlink.
- Define your ALT text (if you want ALT text).

Users read Web pages from top to bottom, so you must decide on a position for your image on the page.

The *relative path* means where the image is located in relation to the page that holds it. Most Web designers designate a folder, which they name `images`, to hold all of the images — and they place it in the same folder as the Web pages. (Here the relative path is `images/picture.jpg`.)

You can figure out the size of an image by following these steps:

1. **Right-click the image.**

2. **Select Properties.**

3. **Click the Summary Tab.**

4. **Click the Advanced button to see the width and height of the image.**

The other Advanced selections are a matter of personal preference, but most designers don't place a border on images.

Information Kiosk

ALT text is a label for the image that pops up when you place your mouse cursor over that image. Internet users with text-based browsers can also see this text.

Here's an HTML example that shows standard image insertion into a Web page:

```
<IMG SRC="images/home.jpg" WIDTH=87 HEIGHT=20 BORDER=0  ↩
ALT="Image Text">
```

Figure 19-3 shows an excerpt from my `misc.html` page, displaying the image and ALT text.

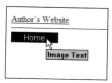

Figure 19-3: On my page, placing the cursor over the Home image makes the ALT text appear.

To make the image a hyperlink, place the hyperlink tag (`<A HREF="website">  Image Tag </A>`) around the image tag, like this:

```
<A HREF="http://www.yourpage.com"><IMG SRC="images/  ↩
home.jpg" WIDTH=87 HEIGHT=20 BORDER=0 ALT="Image Text"></A>
```

This code creates a hyperlink for your image that opens `www.yourpage.com`. Your entire image is now a clickable hyperlink.

Using Access Forms and Reports

You can export Access forms and reports as HTML files. These forms and reports have already been designed to work with the data in tables, so it only makes sense to use tables as a basis for Web forms and reports.

Presenting static information

Exporting Access forms and reports to HTML files is a viable way to create Web pages in which you can present data. Before Access exports the form or report to HTML, Access executes any queries or macros on which the form or report depends.

The big drawback to using this method is that the forms and reports are static; they don't change automatically in response to a change in the data. If data is added, removed, or updated in the database, you must export the forms and reports again.

Forms exported to HTML aren't very useful. You can't use them to enter or search for records. The main reason to export forms to HTML is to use them in the design of dynamic forms.

Reports, on the other hand, are useful when exported to HTML if you want to simply view static report data. You can also use static report data as a starting point when you're designing dynamic reports.

To export a report to HTML from Access, follow these steps:

1. **Open Access and the AccessWebDB database.**

2. **Select a report by clicking it.**

3. **Click the External Data tab.**

4. **Click the More drop-down list in the Export group, and then select HTML Document.**

   The Export Wizard launches.

5. **In the File Name field, enter**

   `C:\Access-web\Grade-Report.html`

6. **Select *Open the destination file after the export is complete* and click OK.**

7. **Click OK on the Output Options dialog box and any other dialog boxes until the Web page opens.**

8. **Click Close on the final Export Wizard dialog box.**

9. **Add a new record to the database and refresh the Report Web page.**

   The new record doesn't appear on the Web page.

10. **Export the report again by following Steps 2 through 8 and refresh your browser to see the new record.**

Presenting dynamic information

To present dynamic information in a Web-based format, you must create a Web application. This chapter and Chapter 20 explain how to create a Web application. You can display your data easily and dynamically through Web pages if you use a scripting language such as PHP.

Creating HTML Pages

Creating HTML pages isn't a particularly difficult process, but you can create those pages in even easier ways than by using Notepad. Notepad works fine for many instances, but you need a better editor for higher level design work.

In the section "Working with Web Pages," earlier in this chapter, you can download Selida, a visual HTML editor. To use Selida to help create an HTML page, follow these steps:

1. **Open Selida.**

Selida places you into Source Edit mode (in the lower screen) with a preview in the upper screen. Your cursor appears in the body of the document, waiting for input.

2. **Type** Hello There **and look at the upper screen.**

This preview shows you exactly what your page will look like when you view it in a browser. Try out some of the examples in earlier sections in this chapter.

3. **After you experiment a bit with a few tags, click the drop-down list in the upper-right corner of the new document and select Taglist, as shown in Figure 19-4.**

Figure 19-4: Selecting the Taglist in Selida 2.

The currently available tags appear in a scrollable list.

4. **Insert a table by clicking Insert on the menu bar and clicking Table.**

The Table Wizard launches.

5. **Click the +/– (plus/minus) buttons to add/subtract rows and columns, creating a table with three columns and three rows. Click Next.**

6. **Select Center for Table Alignment, Middle for Cell Vertical Alignment, and 1 for the Border; then click Next.**

7. **Select the default data for the cells. Select** *Non-breaking space* **and click Finish.**

A tiny 3×3 table appears on the page.

8. **Select Insert → Form to start the Form Designer.**

When creating a form to send data to a script, select Post as the Method and application/x-www-form-urlencoded as the MIME Post Method. Also, specify a script to receive the data in the Actions field. (In this example, I use receive.php). Figure 19-5 shows how to create a form.

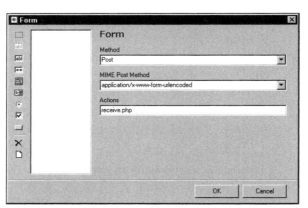

Figure 19-5: Select your form settings in the Form dialog box.

9. **Select a text box from the left menu, give it a Name (for example,** FName**), a Width (size), and a Maximum authorized length, as shown in Figure 19-6.**

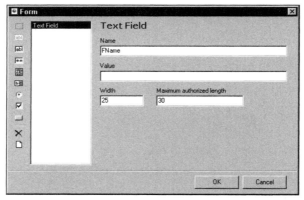

Figure 19-6: Specify a text box's attributes.

10. **Click OK.**

The text box now appears in the preview pane.

With this visual editor — and what you know of HTML from reading this chapter — you can create some basic Web pages. It's good practice to experiment and work with Selida (or some other editor that you feel comfortable with) until creating HTML becomes as natural to you as working with text in Microsoft Word.

font: The typeface of letters and numbers.

HTML (HyperText Markup Language): The set of text tags you use to create pages that users can view in a Web browser.

HTML editor: A program designed to work with HTML tags and files.

script: A file whose attributes make its instructions executable.

tag: A descriptor for formatting text specific to HTML.

workspace: A folder on a computer that's designated for HTML files.

Last Stop

Practice Exam

1. An HTML editor is:

A) Any text editor

B) A text editor specifically for HTML

C) A program that writes your Web page for you

D) A folder on a Web server

2. HTML is really just a set of:

A) Folders

B) Programs

C) Web servers

D) Tags

3. The `<H1>` **tag should be used for:**

A) Fine print

B) Hidden information

C) Titles and headings

D) Standard text

4. The Title of a Web page is located in the:

A) Body

B) Head

C) Foot

D) Folder

5. An example of a font is:

A) Arial

B) Folder

C) IIS

D) Web-enabled

6. True or false (explain why): You need a functional Web server to view HTML files in a Web browser.

_____

_____

_____

7. Where must form data be sent for processing?

A) A Web server

B) A Web browser

C) A folder

D) A script

8. Why is it important to name HTML items that require input or a choice?

A) The names identify the variables.

B) Naming these items improves security.

C) It helps you keep track of the data.

D) The names are all there is to the data.

9. Which tag would you use to insert a space between two paragraphs?

A)
</BR>

B) <FONT></FONT>

C) <P></P>

D) <TR></TR>

10. **Which of the following is correct?**

A)
Hello There</B>

B) <B>Hello There</>

C) <B>Hello There</P>

D) <B>Hello There</B>

Introduction to PHP

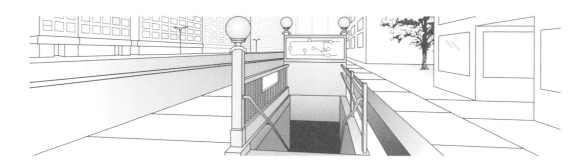

 # Enter the Station

Questions

1. What are variables?

2. How can I incorporate a loop into my program?

3. Is there a correct way to combine HTML and PHP?

4. How do I handle form data?

5. How can I prevent users from entering blank values into my database?

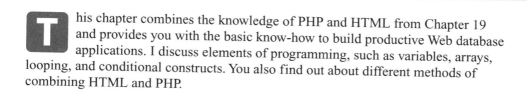

his chapter combines the knowledge of PHP and HTML from Chapter 19 and provides you with the basic know-how to build productive Web database applications. I discuss elements of programming, such as variables, arrays, looping, and conditional constructs. You also find out about different methods of combining HTML and PHP.

Getting the Basics of Programming

This book explains programming from a PHP perspective, which is a traditional top-down, global variable, C-language point of view. PHP is probably the easiest programming language I've ever used. It's generally forgiving, and gives ample and accurate error feedback.

Newer versions of PHP have been designed with most of the *enterprise-level* (very large network) attributes of Java. Some larger companies are actually opting to use PHP rather than Java because of PHP's lower overhead, ease of use, and true cross-platform capability.

When figuring out a new programming language or programming for the first time, work through the examples to give yourself a sense of accomplishment. You should also read other resources on that language to get other perspectives.

To create a PHP file, you must use the PHP tag (`<? ?>`). This tag tells the Web server to execute this information by using the `php5isapi.dll` file that you configure in Chapter 18.

Here's a simple PHP file:

```
<?
echo "Hello There";
?>
```

This PHP file contains the essentials for a successful PHP script: Opening and closing tags, and output (echo). In PHP, rather than a period at the end of each sentence, you use a semicolon (;).

Creating output

Output is the main goal of any programming language. Without some sort of output, you'd have little use for a language. Output can be an action, a message, both, or an error.

Most of the time, output is an action that sends a message to the screen or a Web browser. Creating output with PHP is very easy as shown in Chapter 19. When you send the variables from `form.html` to `submit.php`, you create output. The input is data that you enter on the form, and the output is sent to the Web browser through variables in `submit.php`.

In PHP, output is generated in the form of an echo to the screen or Web browser. Open submit.php (from Chapter 19) in Notepad and view that file's contents. Every bit of information that file sends to the screen is sent by using the echo function.

Here are the submit.php file contents:

```
<?
echo $FName;
echo "<BR>";
echo $LName;
echo "<BR>";
echo $Test1;
?>
```

The echo function provides output for the form data and for HTML formatting. Although you don't see the <BR> tags on the screen (just like in HTML), you do see the effect of the tags. Each line of programming ends with a semicolon.

Variables

Variables are placeholders for information that have no specific value of their own. Variables take on values assigned to them by some external method. When you enter your name and grade into form.html, you're assigning your first name to a variable, your last name to a variable, and a grade to a variable.

Those variables are then sent with their assigned values to submit.php, where their values appear in Internet Explorer. If 30 different people used that form, they'd each see the names and grade that they entered, but the variable itself doesn't change. The value assigned to it changes 30 times.

You can give variables any name you want, but I suggest using something descriptive enough that you can easily recognize it months later when you come back to it.

You can assign variables a starting value by setting the variable equal to the value, like this:

```
$day1 = "Monday";
$month1 = "January";
```

After you assign a value to a variable, you can call this value at any time by using the variable name, like this:

```
echo $day1;
```

You can "stack" variables to make visual sense, like this:

```
echo $day1 $month1;
```

Follow these steps:

1. Create a new PHP file in the `C:\Access-web` **folder with Notepad and enter the following text into that file:**

```
<?
$day1 = "Monday";
$month1 = "January";
echo "$day1 $month1";
?>
```

2. Save the file as `variables.php`.

3. Open Internet Explorer and enter http://localhost/AccessWebDB/ variables.php, **then press Enter.**

Scalar variables

Scalar variables are simple variables that have one value. The value can be a number or a string. A *string* is a collection of letters, symbols, or numbers. In other words, numbers such as a Zip code can be a string if you don't perform mathematical operations on it.

The differences between numbers and strings are fairly obvious after you see them written out:

- This is a scalar numeric variable. It has a single number as its value:

  ```
  $Test1 = 90;
  ```

- This is an example of a scalar string variable. Its value is a single string:

  ```
  $FName = "Bob";
  ```

  A string may also include numbers, like this:

  ```
  $serialno = "XG1141";
  $zip = "76470";
  ```

- A string variable's value is enclosed in quotes (double or single), but numeric variable values aren't.

You may be asking yourself why you'd set a variable to a specific value when you could just use the value itself. You may find using variables representing strings, rather than retyping those strings every time you want to refer to them, a handy technique.

For instance, you can use a date function that's very convenient for inserting dates into databases or displaying dates on a Web page.

Here's the `date` function:

```
$today = date("m-d-y");
echo $today;
```

The variable $today displays the date as month-day-year (for example, 02-15-07). Using a variable in this way allows you to set this variable once and use it forever because, each day, $today changes according to the date function.

Array variables

Most variables are scalar, as described in the preceding section, except those related to extracting data from a database; those variables are array variables. An *array variable* is a variable that holds multiple values. When you select data from a database, you get multiple records that are set to a single variable.

Here's an example:

```
$sql = "SELECT First_Name, Last_Name, Test1 FROM Grade_10";
```

Because this query result set has more than one student listed, $sql has many values. The result set looks like a table of data. You can iterate through these values by using a loop (as shown in the following section).

Consider the following example of an array:

```
$fruit = array("apple", "banana", "grapes");
echo $fruit[1];
```

In response to this command, you see the word banana. Why don't you see apple?

Well, PHP is a computer language, and counting starts at 0. The array looks like:

```
$fruit[0] = "apple";
$fruit[1] = "banana";
$fruit[2] = "grapes";
```

The same thing (sort of) happens when you select data from a database. You extract a sufficiently complex array of data from the database that it needs special functions (PHP programs) to extract the data and present it to the screen.

Loops

A *loop* is a programming technique that takes a list of values and iterates through them one at a time until they're complete. Looping is one of those essential constructs in programming that automates pulling one piece of data at a time for what can be thousands of iterations. Looping can be fun because you don't have to do it by hand. The computer does this looping very rapidly.

During the loop, you can act on members of the list, write messages to the screen, write to a file, echo data to the screen, and so on.

Loops are essential when pulling data from a database. Without them, you'd have to select one row of data at a time rather than all of the rows you want.

Here's an example of a simple while loop:

```
<?
$num = 0;
while ($num < 10) {
echo $num;
echo "<BR>";
$num = $num + 1;
}
?>
```

Can you tell what this loop will produce? I'll walk you through its execution.

Originally, $num = 0. When $num enters the while loop, its value is 0 (which is less than 10), 0 is echoed to the screen, <BR> is echoed to the screen, and 1 is added to $num (which is 0).

$num now equals 1. It doesn't reset to 0 because $num = 0 is outside the loop. $num is caught inside the loop until it's not less than 10. 1 is less than 10, so 1 is echoed to the screen, <BR> is echoed to the screen, and 1 is added to $num (which is 1).

$num is now 2, which is less than 10, so the loop repeats again. The loop repeats until $num = 10, which is not less than 10. At the point where the loop test is false, the loop ends.

Is 10 echoed to the screen? To use a loop in a PHP script, follow these steps:

1. **Open a new file in Notepad and name it** loop.php.
2. **Enter the code from the while loop into the file.**
3. **Save the file.**
4. **Open Internet Explorer and enter** http://localhost/AccessWebDB/loop.php **into the address field, then press Enter.**

   You can now see whether 10 is echoed to the screen.

Extracting rows of data from a database is similar to what happens in this loop. The loop that extracts rows from a database does so, one at a time. You extract the first row, echo its contents that you want displayed, and repeat the loop until you have no more rows to extract. The PHP function fetch_array keeps track of how many rows there are. It would be very difficult and time-consuming to use a manual row count first and then iterate through the rows, until you have no rows of data left.

The fetch_array function does this for you for the current result set. If someone adds records while you're iterating through your array, you see only the records that existed when you executed the SQL statement. Refreshing the page can pick up any new records. If you had to do this manually, you'd always have to get a fresh row count before you could display new records.

Arrays

The type of array you work with when dealing with database data is an associative array. Sometimes, you hear this type of array referred to as a key-value pair. The key in a key-value pair is the variable, and the value is the value of that variable.

When you pull data from a database by using an SQL statement, the resulting array looks something like the following:

```
$sql = "SELECT First_Name, Last_Name, Test1 FROM Grade_10";
$row = array("First_Name" => "Bob", "Last_Name" =>  ↵
"Jones", "Test1" => 90);
```

In the array, First_Name is the variable (key) and Bob is the value of one key-value pair. Last_Name and Jones are another key-value pair, and Test1 and 90 are the last key-value pair in this row.

To extract the values from this array, you'd use these echo statements:

```
echo $row["First_Name"];
echo $row["Last_Name"];
echo $row["Test1"];
```

You can represent these array variables more concisely by making them look like standard variables. That way, you can more easily work with them and combine them to look more natural on the screen. To exchange the more complex array variables for simpler ones, use the following examples:

```
$fname = $row["First_Name"];
$lname = $row["Last_Name"];
$test1 = $row["Test1"];
Now you can display the results:
echo "$fname $lname $test1";
```

To demonstrate extracting data from an array, follow these steps:

1. Open a new file in Notepad and name it array.php.

2. Enter the following text into the file:

```
<?
$row = array("First_Name" => "Bob", "Last_Name" =>  ↵
"Jones", "Test1" => 90);
$fname = $row["First_Name"];
$lname = $row["Last_Name"];
$test1 = $row["Test1"];
echo "$fname $lname $test1";
?>
```

3. Save the file.

4. Open Internet Explorer and enter http://localhost/AccessWebDB/array.php in the address field, then press Enter.

Combined with a while loop, you can extract all of the data from a queried result set.

Conditions

A condition in programming is easy for parents to understand because it involves a behavior and consequences. Usually, a conditional statement takes the form of an if-then or an if-then-else configuration.

Sometimes, you hear conditional statements called *branching* in programming.

If-then statements look like this:

```
if (condition) then (consequences);
```

Consequences aren't always negative consequences. You have multiple possibilities for consequences. An if-then-else statement can demonstrate multiple consequences:

```
if (condition) then (consequences) else (other
consequences);
```

In PHP terms, the if-then and if-then-else syntax is either

```
if (Test1 < 70) echo "Fail";
```

or

```
if (Test1 < 70) {echo "Fail";} else {echo "Pass";}
```

In PHP, the word "then" is implied, so you don't have to write it out. When you have more than one possibility, you must enclose the possibilities in curly brackets { }.

Follow these steps:

1. Open a new file and name it array.php.

2. Enter the following conditional statements into the **array.php** file:

```
echo "<P>";
if ($test1 > 85) echo "Woo Hoo!";
echo "<P>";
if ($test1 < 70) {echo "Fail";} else {echo "Pass";}
```

3. Save the file and refresh your browser.

Files and commands

By using PHP, you can interact with the file system, which means you can open files, edit files, remove files, and so on. You can also run some system commands through PHP, which is both useful and potentially dangerous.

The danger of running commands on your system by using a PHP script is a matter of access. Depending on how security is set up on your system, running some commands can have devastating results. You can do some things to prevent some of the danger.

My favorite example of interacting with the file system is opening a file and reading its contents. If you can read a file, you can probably also edit, copy, move, or remove the file. As a Web developer, I can allow certain users to edit configuration files by using this feature, or I can allow a user to create a file and then open it in Internet Explorer.

To create a PHP file that reads the contents of a file, follow these steps:

1. **In Chapter 3, you can create a file named `Grades.txt`. Copy that file into the `C:\Access-web` directory.**

2. **Create a new file named** read.php **and enter the following text into it:**

```
<?
$grades = file_get_contents("Grades.txt");
echo $grades;
?>
```

3. **Save the file.**

4. **Open Internet Explorer and enter** http://localhost/AccessWebDB/read.php **into the address field, then press Enter.**

   This isn't a very friendly way to view this file. All of the data runs together, which it makes for very poor reading and deciphering.

5. **Make the following change to `read.php`:**

```
echo "<PRE>$grades</PRE>";
```

6. **Save the file and refresh your browser.**

To write content to a file, follow these steps:

1. **Enter the following text into a new Notepad file:**

```
<?
$file1 = "C:\Access-web\chapter20.txt";
$filename = fopen($file1, "w+");
fwrite($filename, "This is a test.");
?>
```

2. **Save the file to `chapter20.php`.**

3. **Open Internet Explorer if it's not already open and enter** http://localhost/AccessWebDB/chapter20.php **in the address field, and then press Enter.**

   A blank Web page appears because there is no output specified — only input.

4. **Open the `C:\Access-web` folder to see the new file you created.**

5. Open the file by double-clicking it.

6. To get instant feedback on the file's contents, enter the following two lines inside the chapter20.php file after the **fwrite** line:

```
$readit = file_get_contents($file1);
echo $readit;
```

7. Save the file and refresh your browser.

Information Kiosk

Creating and writing content to files is easy, but you need to remember to give the user feedback so that he knows the operation was successful.

Everyone always asks, "How can I get a directory listing?" You can get a directory listing in many ways, but the following is my favorite. It's very easy to do and gives you exactly what you need in a nice format.

To create a PHP file to read the directory contents, follow these steps:

1. Open a new file in Notepad and enter the following text:

```
<?
echo "<PRE>";
system("dir");
echo "</PRE>";
?>
```

2. Save the file as **dirlist.php**.

3. Open Internet Explorer if it's not already open and enter http://localhost/ AccessWebDB/dirlist.php **into the address field, then press Enter.**

The preceding example also introduces you to the concept of running system commands through the system function. Using this function, you can run any command that can run in Command Line mode.

Watch Your Step

Don't use the system function to launch Notepad or other graphical Windows components. This function is strictly for launching command line applications. If you try to launch a graphical application by using the system function, you could crash IIS or the Windows host.

The scripts in this section may cause your browser to display the message `Warning:` `system() [function.system]: Unable to fork.` If you receive this message, the following procedure can remedy the problem so that you can run command line utilities by using PHP:

1. **Open Windows Explorer and browse to `C:\Windows\System32` or `C:\Winnt\System32`.**

   Find the `cmd.exe` file.

2. **Right-click `cmd.exe` and select Properties from the list.**

3. **Click the Security Tab.**

   If you don't have a Security tab, skip to the Security Tab instructions in the following list, then return here.

4. **Select the Internet Guest Account (COMPUTERNAME\IUSR_ COMPUTERNAME) and select Read & Execute from the Permissions pane.**

5. **Click OK.**

Now, you can use the examples in this section.

To enable the Security Tab in File/Folder Properties, follow these steps:

1. **Select Start → Settings → Control Panel.**

2. **Open Appearance and Themes, then open Folder Options or Folder Options.**

   How your computer is set up determines which option you see.

3. **Click the View tab.**

4. **Scroll all the way to the bottom of the list and deselect *Use simple file sharing (Recommended)*.**

5. **Click OK.**

You can now see the Security tab in File/Folder Properties. Return to the preceding list of instructions to set permissions on `cmd.exe`.

Database connectivity

Connecting to a database through Web pages and PHP is fun. It's also addictive. After you do it, you'll find a million different applications for it, and all hopes of ever being a normal user of Access will be lost forever. (Okay, maybe it's just me, then.)

In Chapter 18, you create the ODBC (Open Database Connectivity) connection that you use in this section to connect to the database by using a PHP function. To use the ODBC function, follow these steps:

1. **Open a new file in Notepad and enter the following text:**

```
<?
$connect = odbc_connect("AccessWebDB", "", "");
?>
```

The function `odbc_connect()` connects to an ODBC data source. The formal syntax for the function is

```
odbc_connect("ODBC DSN", "username", "password");
```

Because an Access ODBC DSN (Data Source Name) uses a database file without a user name and password, you don't need a user name and password in the function.

2. **Save the file as `connect.php`.**

3. **Open Internet Explorer and enter `http://localhost/AccessWebDB/connect.php` into the address field, then press Enter.**

The Web page is blank because you didn't specify any output.

You need to make an important addition to a function such as `odbc_connect()` to customize any errors. You want to customize errors for your pages so that the default errors are suppressed. Default errors give away too much detail about the structure of your site.

To see the default error message, follow these steps:

1. **Change `AccessWebDB` in the `odbc_connect` function to AccessWebDE.**

2. **Save the file and refresh your browser.**

The error displays the complete path to your PHP script.

Custom error functions take the form of

```
or die("Could not make the connection");
```

You also need to add the @ sign to the beginning of the function because that sign suppresses the default error messages:

```
@odbc_connect()
```

3. **Enter the whole connect string into your file, like this:**

```
$connect = @odbc_connect("AccessWebDE", "", "") or ↵
die("Could not make the connection");
```

4. **Change `AccessWebDE` back to AccessWebDB and save the file.**

Embedded SQL

There's a bit of controversy over whether to use embedded SQL or stored procedures for Web databases. For Microsoft Access, you don't have a choice. Access doesn't have stored procedures available. *Stored procedures* are coded programs that are database objects, such as macros or modules. You can *fire* (launch) these stored procedures externally by using a scripting language such as PHP.

Embedded SQL means that the SQL statements are included in the code *(embedded)* with the rest of the variables, loops, conditions, and other pieces of a script. I prefer embedding the SQL even if stored procedures are available because embedded SQL makes the Web applications easier to debug if errors occur.

You enter SQL statements into a PHP file, just as you enter them into the Query Builder in SQL View. Each SQL statement is set equal to a variable.

Here's an example of an SQL statement in a PHP file:

```
$sql = "SELECT First_Name, Last_Name, Test1 FROM Grade_10";
```

I used `$sql` for the variable in this statement, but the variable name isn't important. I try to keep my variables somewhat consistent for different situations. If I have three SQL statements in a PHP file, I use something like `$sql1`, `$sql2`, and `$sql3` for the variable names.

To create a new file that contains embedded SQL, follow these steps:

1. **Open the file `connect.php` if it's not already open.**

2. **Enter the SQL statement into the file.**

3. **Save `connect.php`.**

   The file still has no output to Internet Explorer because you haven't defined output in the text. The SQL statement must be executed against the database. Right now, it's just sitting there.

4. **Execute the SQL statement by adding the following line of code to `connect.php`:**

   ```
   $results = odbc_exec($connect, $sql);
   ```

   This line executes the SQL statement (`$sql`) through the ODBC connection (`$connect`) by using the `odbc_exec` function. The extracted information from the executed SQL statement is now held in a result set array (`$results`). This array is similar to the array you create in the section "Arrays," earlier in this chapter.

5. **Enter this looping code into `connect.php`:**

   ```
   while ($row = odbc_fetch_array($results)) {
   $fname = $row["First_Name"];
   ```

```
$lname = $row["Last_Name"];
$test1 = $row["Test1"];
}
```

The first line begins the while loop that will extract each row of data according to the SQL statement that's executed. The function `odbc_fetch_array()` extracts rows of information from the result set (`$results`). The rest of the loop sets easy-to-use variable names for the array variables.

6. **Print the information to the screen for each row by entering this text into connect.php:**

```
echo "$fname $lname $test1<BR>";
```

You must place this line inside the loop or you see only the last row of information.

The complete `connect.php` file looks like this:

```
<?
$connect = @odbc_connect("AccessWebDB", "", "") or ↩
die ("Could not make the connection");
$sql = "SELECT First_Name, Last_Name, Test1 FROM ↩
Grade_10";
$results = odbc_exec($connect, $sql);
while ($row = odbc_fetch_array($results)) {
$fname = $row["First_Name"];
$lname = $row["Last_Name"];
$test1 = $row["Test1"];
echo "$fname $lname $test1<BR>";
}
?>
```

The example in this section is the basis for all content involving embedded SQL in PHP. The following section shows you how to create a form to enter data into the Grade_10 table. This integrates HTML, PHP, and SQL.

Creating a data-entry form

To create a data entry form, follow these steps:

1. **Create a new file in Notepad and enter the following text into it:**

```
<HTML>
<HEAD><TITLE>Grade Entry Form</TITLE></HEAD>
<BODY>
<FONT FACE="Arial">
<CENTER><H2>Grade Entry Form</H2></CENTER>
<FORM METHOD="POST" ACTION="postgrades.php">
First Name: <INPUT TYPE="TEXT" NAME="first" SIZE=25>
     
```

```
Last Name: <INPUT TYPE="TEXT" NAME="last" SIZE=25>
     
Test1: <INPUT TYPE="TEXT" NAME="test1" SIZE=4>
<P>
<INPUT TYPE="SUBMIT" NAME="SUBMIT" VALUE="Submit">
     
<INPUT TYPE="RESET" NAME="RESET" VALUE="Clear">
</FORM>
</FONT>
</BODY>
</HTML>
```

2. Save the file as **grade_entry.html.**

Examine grade_entry.html to see that it contains elements from preceding exercises.

3. Open a new file in Notepad and enter the following PHP code into it:

```
<?
$connect = @odbc_connect("AccessWebDB", "", "") or  ↩
die ("Could not make the connection");
$sql = "INSERT INTO Grade_10 (First_Name,            ↩
Last_Name, Test1) VALUES ('$first', '$last',         ↩
'$test1')";
$results = @odbc_exec($connect, $sql) or die         ↩
("Could not write to the database");
echo "You successfully entered: $first $last $test1  ↩
into the database.";
?>
```

4. Save the file as postgrades.php.

5. **Open Internet Explorer if it's not already open and enter** http://localhost/ AccessWebDB/grade_entry.html **in the address field, then press Enter.**

6. **Enter** http://localhost/AccessWebDB/connect.php **in the browser's address field and press Enter.**

You can see that your data really was written to the database.

Form data

Understanding form data can give you a deeper understanding of how data is posted to a script and what the script does with the data after it receives that data.

Consider the grade_entry.html form from the preceding section:

```
<HTML>
<HEAD><TITLE>Grade Entry Form</TITLE></HEAD>
<BODY>
<FONT FACE="Arial">
<CENTER><H2>Grade Entry Form</H2></CENTER>
```

```
<FORM METHOD="POST" ACTION="postgrades.php">
First Name: <INPUT TYPE="TEXT" NAME="first" SIZE=25>
     
Last Name: <INPUT TYPE="TEXT" NAME="last" SIZE=25>
     
Test1: <INPUT TYPE="TEXT" NAME="test1" SIZE=4>
<P>
<INPUT TYPE="SUBMIT" NAME="SUBMIT" VALUE="Submit">
     
<INPUT TYPE="RESET" NAME="RESET" VALUE="Clear">
</FORM>
</FONT>
</BODY>
</HTML>
```

When the Submit button is clicked, the variables, along with their assigned values, are posted to the receiving script (postgrades.php).

How does this data look to the receiving script?

The raw data from a form posting, called the Query String, looks like this for grade_entry.html:

```
first=Bob&last=Jones&test1=85&SUBMIT=Submit
```

On some Web sites, you see Query Strings hard coded into the address of a particular Web page which means that a data entry form is being bypassed. Here's an example of a hard-coded Query String:

```
http://www.somepage.com/form.php?ID=1&Name=Test&Date=010207
```

In the case of this Query String, the variables would look like this:

```
$ID = 1
$Name = Test
$Date = 010207
```

Hard-coded variables make it easy for a Web developer to make choices for the user based on that user's previous choices.

For instance, say you fill out a Web form and enter the response Red for your favorite car color. After you click the Submit button, you're redirected to a page in which you can browse red cars.

If someone else fills out the form and enters White, then she is redirected to a page of white cars.

Using variables that are carried from page to page builds a sort of intelligence into the pages and provides the user with a richer experience. It also prevents the user from repeating responses on other forms.

How does the receiving script extract the variables and values from the data that's posted to it? The entire block of data is posted to the receiving script (for example, `postgrades.php`) in this format. PHP knows to separate the variable/value pairs at the `&`. The variable and value of the Submit button are also appended to this Query String but are of no value.

Integrating PHP and HTML

You have a bit of experience with integrating PHP and HTML already. You can integrate the two languages in these different ways:

- Use HTML for forms and static pages, and use PHP for dynamic pages.
- Use HTML and include embedded PHP snippets.
- Use PHP files that have all HTML embedded as PHP.

You don't get any particular advantages or disadvantages when you use any of these methods. When I first began developing in PHP, I used HTML files for static pages and forms. I never really liked using PHP snippets embedded into HTML, although it's a very popular method of dealing with the HTML/PHP mixture.

In the past two or three years, I've been using the third method in the preceding list, which is pure PHP. For all HTML code, I use echo HTML code, and the PHP code stands alone in the file. I chose this method because, for me, pure PHP is easier to trace when I need to locate errors. The most difficult method is the PHP snippets method. The code is very hard to look at and is somewhat tedious to debug.

The first method in the preceding list uses files that are named with `.html` for HTML files and `.php` for PHP files. This naming system keeps your files very organized and separated for some programmers. Using snippets basically involves a regular HTML file that contains PHP tags and a bit of PHP script. The catch is that you have to name the files with the `.php` extension or the PHP doesn't work. The pure PHP method also requires that all files receive the `.php` extension.

PHP snippets

PHP snippets isn't an official name for this method at all. It's just the name I gave it. This method is very similar to Microsoft's ASP (Active Server Pages) scripting in the way code is handled within an otherwise normal HTML file.

Here's an example of a PHP snippet embedded in an HTML file:

```
<HTML>
<HEAD><TITLE>Test File</TITLE></HEAD>
<BODY>
```

```
<FONT FACE="Arial">
<CENTER><H2>Test File</H2></CENTER>
<?
$today = date("m-d-Y");
echo $today;
?>
</FONT>
</BODY>
</HTML>
```

 Watch Your Step

You must name any file that has PHP code in it with the .php
extension or your web browser simply ignores the PHP code.

You can use as many PHP code snippets as you want in a file. The PHP doesn't all
have to reside within a single set of PHP tags. Here's the preceding file with more
HTML and more PHP:

```
<HTML>
<HEAD><TITLE>Test File</TITLE></HEAD>
<BODY>
<FONT FACE="Arial">
<CENTER><H2>Test File</H2></CENTER>
<?
$today = date("m-d-Y");
echo $today;
?>
<P>
This is the test file for HTML and PHP.
<?
echo "<PRE>";
system("NET ACCOUNTS");
echo "</PRE>";
?>
</FONT>
</BODY>
</HTML>
```

To create an embedded PHP file, follow these steps:

1. **Create a new file in Notepad and enter the Test File code into it.**
2. **Save the file as test1.php.**
3. **Open Internet Explorer if it's not already open and enter** http://localhost/
   AccessWebDB/test1.php **in the address field, then press Enter.**

Information Kiosk

The NET ACCOUNTS command displays information about user account settings on your computer.

If you want to use this method of mixing HTML and PHP, I recommend that you create your entire HTML file first, then add the PHP script snippets. This way, you keep the coding separate from the design.

Use HTML for the general layout, design, and static page content, and include PHP to insert dynamic information (such as dates, file lists, SQL, and loops).

Totally PHP

Most professional PHP programmers use this method of creating files with both HTML and PHP. Plenty of developers use the other methods, too. You often hear this method referred to as *pure PHP,* which means that all content is written from a PHP perspective.

Each file begins with an opening PHP tag (<?) and ends with a closing PHP tag (?>). All HTML is echoed and placed in quotes.

Watch Your Step

When using a pure PHP programming method, you need to use double quotes for echoing HTML output and single quotes for any other quotation marks, or vice versa. For example, you need to format a hyperlink consistently in one of these two ways:

```
echo "<A HREF='http://www.wiley.com'>Wiley
Publishing</A>";
echo '<A HREF="http://www.wiley.com">Wiley
Publishing</A>';
```

You receive error messages if you use only one style of quotation mark for both PHP and HTML.

Here's the Test File example from the preceding section:

```
<HTML>
<HEAD><TITLE>Test File</TITLE></HEAD>
<BODY>
<FONT FACE="Arial">
<CENTER><H2>Test File</H2></CENTER>
<?
$today = date("m-d-Y");
echo $today;
?>
<P>
```

```
This is the test file for HTML and PHP.
<?
echo "<PRE>";
system("NET ACCOUNTS");
echo "</PRE>";
?>
</FONT>
</BODY>
</HTML>
```

The pure PHP file looks like this:

```
<?
echo "<HTML>
<HEAD><TITLE>Test File</TITLE></HEAD>
<BODY>
<FONT FACE='Arial'>
<CENTER><H2>Test File</H2></CENTER>";
$today = date("m-d-Y");
echo $today;
echo "<P>
This is the test file for HTML and PHP.
<PRE>";
system("NET ACCOUNTS");
echo "</PRE>
</FONT>
</BODY>
</HTML>";
?>
```

In the line <FONT FACE='Arial'>, I changed the double quotes to single quotes because I used double quotes for the echo function.

Adding a table to a PHP file so you can display results is a little tricky. For this example, I use the connect.php file that you used in the section "Database Connectivity."

Here's the connect.php file:

```
<?
$connect = @odbc_connect("AccessWebDB", "", "") or die  ↩
("Could not make the connection");
$sql = "SELECT First_Name, Last_Name, Test1 FROM Grade_10";
$results = odbc_exec($connect, $sql);
while ($row = odbc_fetch_array($results)) {
$fname = $row["First_Name"];
$lname = $row["Last_Name"];
$test1 = $row["Test1"];
echo "$fname $lname $test1<BR>";
}
?>
```

A simple table containing data looks like this:

```
<TABLE CELLPADDING=5 CELLSPACING=0 WIDTH=500 BORDER=0>
<TR><TD>Ken</TD><TD>Shay</TD><TD>56</TD></TR>
<TR><TD>Tom</TD><TD>Evans</TD><TD>94</TD></TR>
<TR><TD>Sue</TD><TD>Cleary</TD><TD>100</TD></TR>
</TABLE>
```

Using a table in a situation such as this can be tricky because you need to place the <TABLE> tags outside the loop and all of the rows of data (<TR></TR>) inside the loop.

Here's the solution in a pure PHP file:

```
<?
$connect = @odbc_connect("AccessWebDB", "", "") or die ↵
("Could not make the connection");
$sql = "SELECT First_Name, Last_Name, Test1 FROM Grade_10";
$results = odbc_exec($connect, $sql);
echo "<TABLE CELLPADDING=5 CELLSPACING=0 BORDER=0>";
while ($row = odbc_fetch_array($results)) {
$fname = $row["First_Name"];
$lname = $row["Last_Name"];
$test1 = $row["Test1"];
echo "<TR><TD>$first</TD><TD>$last</TD><TD ALIGN= ↵
'RIGHT'>$test1</TD></TR>";
}
echo "</TABLE>";
?>
```

This code makes a very nice table layout for your data. I used ALIGN='RIGHT' because the test scores are numbers and should be right-justified for clarity.

The table in the preceding code has no column headings to explain the data that it displays. You can remedy this absence by adding another static row of data before the loop begins, like this:

```
<TR><TD>First Name</TD><TD>Last Name</TD><TD>Test 1 ↵
</TD></TR>
```

If you prefer more of a separation for the column heads, you can bold them by adding the <B> tag, like this:

```
<TR><TD><B>First Name</B></TD><TD><B>Last Name</B></TD> ↵
<TD><B>Test 1</B></TD></TR>
```

The entire file now looks like this:

```
<?
$connect = @odbc_connect("AccessWebDB", "", "") or die ↵
("Could not make the connection");
$sql = "SELECT First_Name, Last_Name, Test1 FROM Grade_10";
```

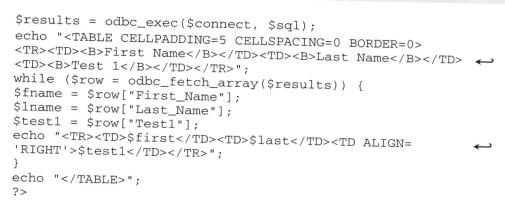

```
$results = odbc_exec($connect, $sql);
echo "<TABLE CELLPADDING=5 CELLSPACING=0 BORDER=0>
<TR><TD><B>First Name</B></TD><TD><B>Last Name</B></TD>
<TD><B>Test 1</B></TD></TR>";
while ($row = odbc_fetch_array($results)) {
$fname = $row["First_Name"];
$lname = $row["Last_Name"];
$test1 = $row["Test1"];
echo "<TR><TD>$first</TD><TD>$last</TD><TD ALIGN=
'RIGHT'>$test1</TD></TR>";
}
echo "</TABLE>";
?>
```

To create a PHP file with a table in it, follow these steps:

1. **Open a new file in Notepad.**

2. **Enter the preceding code for this pure PHP file into the file.**

3. **Save the file as** phptable.php.

4. **Open Internet Explorer and enter** http://localhost/AccessWebDB/
phptable.php **into the address field, then press Enter.**

Error checking

When programming for public consumption, you must take into account that some
users are going to make mistakes. Some users may also purposely make errors to test
your coding skills. For both types of user, you need to include something called error
checking.

Error checking consists of validating text that's entered into forms. It involves catch-
ing variables and values from a form and checking them before an SQL statement
processes them. The most common kind of error checking, especially if users are
entering data into a database, is preventing blank responses.

You can implement error checking for the preceding example simply.

Here's how this error checking works:

- A conditional statement checks one or more variables for empty (NULL)
values.

- If any value is empty, the script is halted.

- If all values contain data, then the script is allowed to continue.

The generalized conditional statement looks like this:

```
if ($variable =="") {echo "There are missing values";}
else {the script continues}
```

In practice, you list all required variables in the `if` clause. The `echo` part of the `then` clause is usually more direct, such as, "There are missing values, please click the back button on your browser to finish filling out the form." The `else` clause allows the script to flow normally down the page — you don't include a continue statement or command. The continue statement here represents the rest of the script.

List each variable for which you require a value in a way that tells the PHP script that if `$variable1`, `$variable2`, or `$variable3` is empty, the script halts. So, if any of the variables are empty, the script halts.

You can list the variables in an *and* fashion, which means if `$variable1`, `$variable2`, and `$variable3` are all empty, the script halts. You probably want to use the first conditional statement, but the second type of conditional exists if you ever have a situation in which one or two variables can be empty, but not all three.

You can have as many variables in your if-then-else statement as you need. You're not limited to three.

Here are some examples of each type of conditional:

```
if ($variable1 == "" || $variable2 == "" || $variable3 ↩
== "") {
echo "You are missing some data, please click back on ↩
your browser and fill-in the form completely."; } else {
the script continues}
```

The `||` (double pipe) symbol means "or" in programming languages. You can find the pipe symbol on your keyboard, paired with the backslash (\).

Here's the same conditional statement, but now it contains the variables that use the *and* syntax:

```
if ($variable1 == "" && $variable2 == "" && $variable3 ↩
== "") {
echo "You are missing some data, please click back on ↩
your browser and fill-in the form completely."; } else {
the script continues}
```

The `&&` (double ampersand) symbols mean "and." The `==` (double equal signs) mean "equivalent to," and you use them to test equality. You use a single `=` (equal sign) for assignment of values.

For instance:

```
$fruit = "banana";
```

Or:

```
$cost = 15;
```

To put a test such as this into practice, use the `postgrades.php` file (from the "Creating a Data Entry Form" section):

```
<?
$connect = @odbc_connect("AccessWebDB", "", "") or die
("Could not make the connection");
$sql = "INSERT INTO Grade_10 (First_Name, Last_Name,
Test1) VALUES ('$first', '$last', '$test1')";
$results = @odbc_exec($connect, $sql) or die ("Could
not write to the database");
echo "You successfully entered: $first $last $test1
into the database.";
?>
```

I prefer to place these types of conditionals very early in the script — before any variables are affected. Here's an example

```
<?
$connect = @odbc_connect("AccessWebDB", "", "") or die
("Could not make the connection");
if($first == "" || $last == "" || $test1 == "") {
echo "You are missing some data, please click back on
your browser and fill-in the form completely."; } else {
$sql = "INSERT INTO Grade_10 (First_Name, Last_Name,
Test1) VALUES ('$first', '$last', '$test1')";
$results = @odbc_exec($connect, $sql) or die ("Could
not write to the database");
echo "You successfully entered: $first $last $test1
into the database.";
}
?>
```

To implement a conditional statement, follow these steps:

1. **Open postgrades.php.**

2. **Enter the conditional statement (shown in bold) into the file like this:**
```
<?
$connect = @odbc_connect("AccessWebDB", "", "") or
die ("Could not make the connection");
if($first == "" || $last == "" || $test1 == "") {
echo "You are missing some data, please click
back on your browser and fill@@hyin the form
completely."; } else {
$sql = "INSERT INTO Grade_10 (First_Name, Last_Name,
Test1) VALUES ('$first', '$last', '$test1')";
$results = @odbc_exec($connect, $sql) or die
("Could not write to the database");
echo "You successfully entered: $first $last
$test1 into the database.";
}
?>
```

Remember to place the ending } before the closing PHP tag or you receive an error.

3. **Save the file.**

4. **Open Internet Explorer and enter** http://localhost/AccessWebDB/grade_entry.html **into the address field, then press Enter.**

5. **Enter the name** Nick **in the First Name field, enter** Barnes **in the Last Name field, leave the Test 1 field blank, and click Submit.**

A message appears, telling you that you're missing data.

6. **Click the back button on Internet Explorer, enter** Nick **for the First Name field,** 71 **for the Test 1 field, and leave the Last Name field blank. Click Submit.**

You receive the same missing-data message.

7. **Enter** Nick **into the First Name field,** Barnes **into the Last Name field, and** 71 **into the Test 1 field, then click Submit.**

This time, you receive a message saying you've successfully entered Nick Barnes 71.

8. **Enter** http://localhost/AccessWebDB/connect.php **into Internet Explorer's address field, then press Enter.**

The data for Nick Barnes appears only once in your database.

9. **Replace the** || **with** && **in the conditional for** `postgrades.php` **and enter new student data with first one, then two, and finally three pieces of data missing.**

10. **Check your results each time by using the** `connect.php` **page to view the data.**

Only when all three values are blank do you receive the missing data message.

A good question to answer at this point is, "How much of the contents of the PHP file has to be enclosed in the conditional statement?"

The answer depends largely on the design of your PHP page. You may have common elements that you want on all pages. In that case, you begin the conditional statement below any required page information but above any form variables.

As for the closing bracket (}), you need to place it below any point that has anything to do with form variables but above any required information on the page.

Required information includes logos, page titles, copyright statements, navigation features, and so on.

array: A set of variables that share the same name but each has a unique identifier.

condition/conditional: A type of programming statement that tests a situation as true or false and makes a decision based on that true or false answer. An if-then or if-then-else statement is a good example of a conditional statement.

construct: A part of a programming language that performs some action and is somewhat self-contained (such as a loop or conditional statement).

embedded: Placing one language within another for added functionality.

file system: The physical location that contains files and folders. The file system, or filesystem, refers to all of the files, commands, folders, and the underlying magnetic organization on the physical drives.

loop: A programming construct that directs the flow of a program to return to a point within the program until all results have been iterated.

snippet: A piece of code.

variable: A named object that holds a value or values for use within a program.

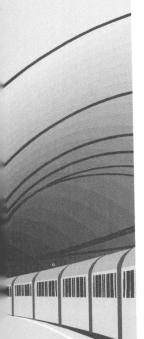

Last Stop

Practice Exam

1. In the following loop, what is $num?

```
$num = 0;
while ($num < 5) {
echo $num;
$num = $num + 1;
}
```

A) A conditional

B) A loop

C) A variable

D) A test

2. In the loop from Question 1, why is $num **set equal to 0?**

A) 0 is an arbitrary starting point.

B) You must set objects like $num equal to 0.

C) In the computer world, counting starts at 0.

D) All of the above.

3. An if-then-else statement is known as a(n):

A) Arbitrary statement

B) Loop

C) Variable

D) Conditional statement

4. An SQL statement placed inside a PHP file is said to be:

A) Embedded

B) A construct

C) Variable

D) Looped

5. Why do you have to use a loop to iterate through a result set extracted from a database?

A) You don't have to — you can use either a conditional statement or a loop.

B) A loop extracts the rows one at a time from an array.

C) Because a loop is embedded.

D) Because you have to use echo.

6. In the following array, which president is `$president[1]`?

```
$president = array("Bush", "Clinton", "Johnson",
"Nixon");
```

A) Bush

B) Clinton

C) Johnson

D) Nixon

7. In the array from Question 6, which president is `$president[4]`?

A) Clinton

B) Johnson

C) Nixon

D) None of the above

8. A scalar variable can have how many values associated with it?

A) None

B) One

C) Two

D) Many

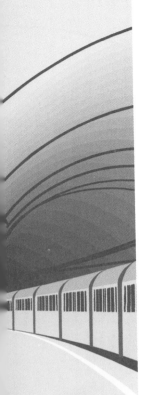

9. In the following Query String sent to a script, identify a variable and the corresponding value:

`Name=John&State=TX&Item=Plate`

A) Name, State

B) John, TX

C) Name, Plate

D) State, TX

10. In the following part of an if-then statement, what do the || represent?

`if ($variable1 == "" || $variable2 == "" || $variable3 == "") {`

A) And

B) But

C) Or

D) None of the above

A

Resources

Internet Resources

Internet resources are very important to professionals who need to interact with other professionals on a particular topic. The worldwide resources available — and the online communities — are numerous and fascinating.

Included in this list of resources are Web sites that I have used for information over the years. I have also added a bit of information about each for you.

Access

office.microsoft.com: This is the "mother ship" for all things related to Microsoft Access. I suggest you visit it often and get involved in some of the online communities that are available for Access users and programmers.

www.4guysfromrolla.com: This site has been around for years and is an excellent resource for those who program using Microsoft technologies such as ASP, ASP.NET, and SQL Server.

www.15seconds.com: This is another interesting and informative site that focuses on Microsoft technologies. I have gleaned much from it over the years.

PHP

www.php.net: The home page for all things PHP. Here you will find all of the PHP resources right from the source. The online manual is invaluable. Besides the online manual, users of the site post practical solutions for the functions so you can see how they work in practice. This is the first Web site I visit when seeking anything PHP–related.

www.phpclasses.org: This is a community-supported site that offers downloadable classes that are pages of PHP code you use for free. There are about 30 categories of classes available, and they include just about everything imaginable. You need to register (free) and can join the mailing list to get updates on all the new classes that are added daily.

www.phpbuilder.com: PHP Builder is the absolute best online community resource for PHP and database information that I have seen. I visit it often — more often when I have a problem — I just can't solve. The users are helpful and very knowledgeable. I have never been disappointed by this community. You have to register to post (free).

www.devshed.com: DevShed has been around a long time and has gathered much respect and resources in all areas of programming. There are lots of annoying ads on the pages, but if you can ignore those, you will find that DevShed is a top-notch resource for tutorials — and assistance on the toughest issues you may encounter.

SQL

www.sqlcourse.com: When I first found this site, I stayed up all night reading and learning from it. There are links to many resources from here — but most valuable of all is the free SQL tutorial. Check out the links to Access and PHP information.

This free resource is one of my favorites and I owe the contributors a great debt of gratitude.

www.sqlcourse2.com: A companion site to www.sqlcourse.com, with more resources, links and tutorials.

www.sswug.org: The SQL Server Worldwide Users Group site. They have a mailing list and a lot of resources. You can register for free but some of the content is for subscribers only.

Answer Key

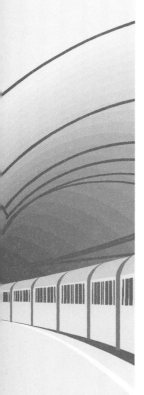

Chapter 1

1. **Which of the following is the best definition of a database?**

D) An object that stores a collection of related data

2. **You have three notebooks filled with information that you want to put into Access. One notebook contains the names and addresses of your friends and family, another contains information related to your home-based business, and the third contains information about your music collection. When using Access to organize and store this data, you would:**

D) Create three databases, one for each of the three general types of information.

3. **Which of the following would be the best name for a database that holds information for the Destructo Demolition company?**

D) Destructo Demolition Company

4. **Which of the following steps is the most important when designing a new database?**

B) Remove redundancies.

5. **When developing a naming convention for your databases, you should:**

A) Use simple, easily decipherable names.

6. **True or false: You can create a new database from within Access. If true, explain how.**

True. Open Access and click Blank Database.

7. **If you delete a database accidentally, you may be able to retrieve it if:**

C) It's still in the Recycle Bin.

8. **What's the true purpose of a database?**

C) To store and retrieve data

9. **True or false: A database should contain data that's related.**

True. That is the definition of a database.

10. Explain why you shouldn't name three new databases Stuff, Miscellaneous, and New.

Specific, descriptive database names are far more useful.

Chapter 2

1. Which of the following would be the best table name for storing information about a postage-stamp collection?

B) `Stamp_Collection`

2. You've accidentally deleted a table from your database. Describe the steps you'll take to recover it.

It can't be recovered.

3. About how many columns should you limit a table to?

C) 15

4. What are the characteristics of a good naming convention?

A) Simple, descriptive, and short

5. True or false: The order in which you create the columns in a table is very important. Explain why or why not.

False. Columns are part of the definition of a table; their order is not.

6. Database tables are very similar to spreadsheets because they're:

D) Made up of columns and rows

7. Describe the process of adding a new column to a table.

Access provides a prompt for a new column automatically. Click into the Add New Field field and enter the name.

8. Which of the following is true of database tables?

C) Tables are dynamic entities.

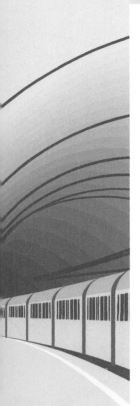

9. **True or false: You can delete only very small tables by using the method shown in this chapter. Explain why or why not.**

False. Any size table may be deleted along with all of the data in it.

10. **Write down the column names and data types that you would use to create the table for the following scenario. Imagine you are asked to develop a table to store information about company employees, using the following information as a guide: Name, address, phone number, salary, city, state, Zip code, number of dependents, and marital status.**

Name (text), Address (text), Phone (text), Salary (currency), City (text), State (text), Zip (text), Dependents (number), and Marital_Status (text).

Chapter 3

1. **Why would you export data from Access?**

A) To share information with others

2. **Which type of file do you create when you need to export data but don't know the application that will use it?**

C) Text

3. **What's the default name for any file that's exported?**

D) The name of the exported table.

4. **To use a SharePoint server, you must know:**

C) The URL of the SharePoint server

5. **What's the greatest advantage of exporting to a text file?**

D) Almost any application can use it.

6. **Importing data into Access is an excellent way to:**

A) Get a lot of data into Access quickly.

7. **You must use caution when importing data into Access that will be appended to an existing table. Why?**

B) The names and number of columns in the external file must match the Access table exactly.

8. **Using a SharePoint Portal Server with Access is a great way to:**

D) Share data

9. **When importing data, Access automatically attempts to assign a primary key to the table. Why?**

B) It is a feature of good design.

10. **What's one major advantage of linking to rather than importing data from external sources?**

A) Linked data is lower maintenance.

Chapter 4

1. **What's the main purpose of a filter?**

D) To get a small number of relevant hits

2. **What's the main purpose of a query?**

D) To show specifically selected data

3. **What do aggregate functions do?**

A) They summarize data.

4. **What's a hit?**

C) A positive result

5. **Why would you want to use a rounding function?**

B) It makes numbers easier to deal with

6. **Why wouldn't you use calculated fields in a table?**

A) It's poor design.

7. **What type of queries have you read about in this chapter?**

A) Aggregate

8. **How can you narrow the number of hits returned from a query?**

B) By using the Simple Query Wizard

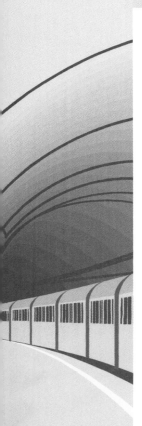

9. Why would you want to summarize your data?

D) Access doesn't allow calculated fields.

10. Which of the following are aggregate functions?

A) Max, Min, StDev

Chapter 5

1. What's the basic query that only reads data?

A) Select

2. If you want to change data in a table, which type of query would you use?

C) Update

3. If you want to add data to a table, which type of query would you use?

B) Append

4. If you want to remove entire records from a table, which type of query would you use?

D) Delete

5. If you want to make a backup of a table, which type of query would you use?

B) Make Table

6. To update or delete data in a table in another database, which type of query would you use?

C) Update

7. List the steps to update information in another database.

Create a Link to the other database table that you want to update and update as you would any other table

8. Which type of query can be performed without enabling content or creating a trusted location?

A) Select

9. **What would be the purpose of using a query to make an exact duplicate of a table?**

   D) It's a simple way to make a backup of a table.

10. **By creating a trusted location, you perform this task:**

    A) Trust all databases in that location.

Chapter 6

1. **Why is it important to customize your forms with colors, fonts, and navigational elements?**

   B) It gives the form a more professional look and feel.

2. **What's the purpose of tab order?**

   A) Tab order assists the user when entering data.

3. **What's the default tab order?**

   B) The order in which the fields were created.

4. **Which of the following is a good design scheme for a form?**

   C) A few colors, normal fonts, and correctly sized data-entry fields.

5. **Why do you need to resize data-entry fields?**

   B) So that data entry is less confusing for users.

6. **To create a Button control, you must be in:**

   C) Design View

7. **To fully test your forms before allowing users to use them, you must be in:**

   A) Form View

8. **What lets you change attributes such as fonts, fields, and background colors for a form?**

   D) Property Sheet

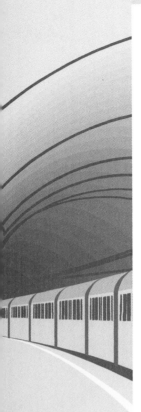

9. Which attribute lets users make sure they're using the correct form for data entry?

B) The title

10. Which two items are sometimes added to give a form a more professional look and feel?

A) A Date and Time feature and a logo.

Chapter 7

1. Which view gives you the most creative freedom and lets you fully edit a report?

C) Design View

2. Which view gives you an exact preview of the way the report will look when a user views the report?

A) Report View

3. Which view gives you an exact preview of the way the report will look when printed?

D) Print Preview

4. When adding a new field to a report that's not table-bound, how do you bind the field to the table?

A) Add an expression to the field that references table fields.

5. Which type of summary function is built into Access?

B) Column-oriented

6. What action do you take if you have too many columns on your report to be viewed on one page in Portrait mode?

B) Change the orientation of the report to Landscape mode.

7. What must you do before you can create a report based on multiple record sources?

C) Create a relationship between the two tables.

8. Reports are great for presenting what type of data?

A) Summary

9. What's the quickest way to create a new report based on a single record source?

B) Use the Report Wizard.

10. What's the purpose of using summary data on a report?

B) It makes the data easier to find and interpret.

Chapter 8

1. Why might you need an offline mode for SharePoint?

D) You may need to work in a place where the SharePoint server isn't available.

2. What's the best reason for making a list or database private?

A) Security.

3. Why would you set up an e-mail alert for a file or list?

A) To track any changes that occur on the file

4. After creating a new event, why should you use SharePoint to edit the event?

C) SharePoint has a more user-friendly, richer interface for editing events.

5. True or false: It's necessary to publish all changes to a database after that database is shared on a SharePoint site.

B) False

6. What happens when you synchronize SharePoint data?

C) All data is updated in both lists and databases.

7. A Table in Access is converted to what kind of object in SharePoint?

D) List

8. True or false (explain why): SharePoint lists are initially read-only.

False. Access databases saved in SharePoint sites open as read-only.

9. True or false (explain why): Someone can steal your data without being able to edit it.

True. Anyone who can read your database can make a local copy.

10. What is one advantage to moving your database(s) to a SharePoint site?

A) Your network administrators are more likely to perform backups on a SharePoint site.

Chapter 9

1. True or false (Explain why): Normalization is a lengthy and unnecessary process.

False. Normalization varies in the amount of time it takes, and makes your database more usable.

2. True or false (Explain why): Databases should be normalized to the highest possible degree.

False. The needed degree of normalization is specific to each database.

3. Generally speaking, which normal form is sufficient for most database implementations?

D) 3NF

4. What's the purpose of enforcing referential integrity?

B) To prevent orphaned records in the database

5. What's a benefit of normalization?

B) Accuracy

6. What component of a table do you need to have before attempting to normalize a database to the First Normal Form (1NF)?

A) A primary key

7. How can you resolve a many-to-many relationship?

C) Create a junction table.

8. True or false (explain why): All relations are tables.

True. But not all tables are relations. A table must have specific characteristics to be a rotation.

9. Which of the following relationship types is the most common?

B) 1:∞

10. Which of the following is not a true normal form?

A) ONF

Chapter 10

1. True or false (explain why): Maintaining data integrity is a good reason to limit a user's possible responses to a read-only list of choices.

True. Prompts and Tool Tips can encourage the user to enter only the desired data type.

2. You should remove scroll bars from text boxes because:

D) Both A and B.

3. Status-bar messages are useful if:

C) You need to supply some bit of extra information to the user.

4. What should you always supply for every field, button, or other control on a form?

D) ControlTip Text

5. Which data type would you use for user feedback on a form?

B) Memo

6. Why would you provide a default entry for a field?

D) It provides a prompt for the user.

7. Tool Tips are also called:

B) ControlTip Text

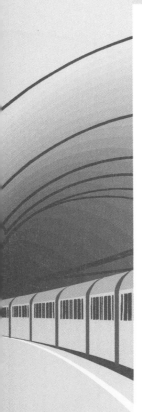

8. Buttons can perform which of the following?

D) All of the above

9. Which property lets you open a form from another form by using a combo box?

C) List Items Edit Form

10. When you open a saved form by using the left navigation pane in Access, which view are you in?

A) Form View

Chapter 11

1. Macros are minimally composed of:

D) Actions and arguments

2. An argument is a:

B) List of parameters

3. The main reason for constructing and maintaining a Switchboard is:

A) User convenience

4. True or false (explain why): A multi-step macro and a macro group are the same thing.

False.

5. Macro groups are created mainly for what reason?

B) To reduce clutter

6. Macros execute in what type of fashion?

D) Top-down

7. True or false: You can launch external programs from within Access by using macros.

True

8. One of the advantages to creating and using macros is:

C) No knowledge of VBA is required.

9. What's the one requirement for using the RunApp macro action?

B) A full path to the program

10. What's the main purpose of using macros in an Access database?

C) Automation

Chapter 12

1. True or false: You can export all objects in a database to another database at once.

False

2. True or false: You can import all objects in a database to another database at once.

True.

3. What must you check before altering a database template that you downloaded from a Web site?

C) Licensing

4. When evaluating a template, you should:

B) Thoroughly test the template.

5. When would you need to export a table instead of importing a table to create a template?

C) When tables need to retain all of their data

6. What should you check when evaluating any template?

A) References from current users

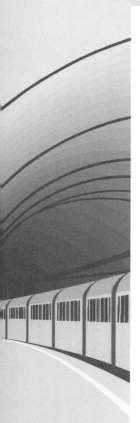

7. **When is it okay to put data into data tables and leave the data in a template that you create?**

   B) When supplying a database as a demonstration database.

8. **Aside from using a template in a business or personal situation, templates also offer value for:**

   D) Teaching

9. **True or false: It's okay to change a template that you download from the Internet, change it, and sell it as your own.**

   False

10. **If you create a template that you want to share freely, what information should you still include in the template?**

    B) Licensing and copyright

Chapter 13

1. **The Data Manipulation Language is responsible for which of the following actions?**

   D) Removing data

2. **Which of the following keywords removes a table from a database?**

   B) DROP

3. **Which SQL keyword is used more than any other?**

   B) SELECT

4. **Which of the following is necessary to isolate a single record in a SELECT query (statement)?**

   C) WHERE

5. **SQL is a language because it has _____ and _____?**

   D) Syntax and semantics

6. **It's possible to completely empty a table with which keyword?**

A) UPDATE

7. **Which of the following keywords would you use to change the spelling of a person's name in a table?**

D) UPDATE

8. **Which keyword would you use to create an index on a column?**

A) ALTER

9. **The SELECT . . . INTO keyword is one way to:**

A) Create a new table with data already in it.

10. **What would you use to remove a column from a table?**

C) ALTER TABLE

Chapter 14

1. **ODBC is an acronym that stands for what?**

B) Open Database Connectivity

2. **To use ODBC to connect to a foreign database, what must you have in place?**

A) ODBC drivers for the foreign database

3. **A DSN connection string usually contains which of the following pieces of information?**

B) Database, table, and driver name

4. **Open Source means:**

C) The program code is available.

5. **When linking tables through ODBC, you're prompted for what before each table is linked?**

B) The primary key

6. Access can make an ODBC connection to SQL Server very easily because:

C) SQL Server support is built into Access and Windows.

7. True or false: You may connect only to databases that have a client/server architecture.

False

8. True or false: A DSN can only be created from within Access.

False

9. When you connect to a foreign database through ODBC, you can work with the tables from those databases the same way you would if they were:

A) Local

10. Using ODBC is advantageous because:

C) It lets you connect to a wide array of foreign databases.

Chapter 15

1. When is it appropriate to trust a publisher's signed content?

D) If you trust the publisher

2. True or false: After you trust it, a publisher or source of content may never be "untrusted."

False

3. Changing a file extension to what makes it vulnerable to editing by a user?

A) .accdb

4. Which file extension designates the file as encrypted and password protected?

A) .accde

5. If you forget the password for an encrypted database, you may:

D) Both A and C

6. True or false: Network drives aren't secure and therefore shouldn't be used as trusted locations.

False

7. When using file, folder, and share permissions to secure a location:

A) Use groups to set access.

8. When selecting a password for a database, you should:

C) Use a non-dictionary word.

9. You can create a certificate to sign a package simply with the:

D) SelfCert tool

10. Access 2007 doesn't support user-level security from older versions of Access. What has taken this security's place?

D) All of the above

Chapter 16

1. True or False: Backing up databases is a necessary activity.

True

2. You need to upsize a database when:

B) You need greater database security.

3. You should use automated maintenance because:

A) It moves the responsibility of the task to a computer.

4. You should analyze performance on databases:

C) Before you deploy them to users

5. When should you perform backups?

D) Daily when no one is using the databases

6. **You can upsize to SQL Server by using:**

   C) ODBC

7. **What two things should you try before upsizing to SQL Server?**

   A) Performance analysis and database splitting

8. **You can save a table as which of the following?**

   D) All of the above

9. **Why would you want to save a table as a PDF file?**

   B) It's a very common file type.

10. **What particular aspect of a table are you looking for when considering splitting that table into two or more tables?**

    D) Redundant data

Chapter 17

1. **When you make changes in the Current Database section, your changes:**

   A) Affect all users permanently

2. **The quickest way to find technical support contact information is to:**

   B) Click the Contact Us button

3. **You can change the Quick Access Toolbar in:**

   C) Both A and B

4. **True or False: The Quick Access Toolbar buttons are affected by Microsoft's security settings.**

   False

5. **The "Compact on close" option does what when enabled?**

   C) Repairs and compacts the database

6. **Taking part in the Customer Experience Improvement Program:**

   B) Requires that you submit personal information

7. **Microsoft uses information from surveys and feedback programs for:**

   C) Product enhancement

8. **What is a trusted location?**

   A) A folder that you identify as a trusted source for opening files

9. **What must you do before you're allowed to download content from Microsoft for Office 2007?**

   A) Activate the product.

10. **When should you change the default file format for Access?**

    D) When you need to be compatible with older versions of Access

Chapter 18

1. **True or False: A Web browser, such as Internet Explorer, functions as a universal client.**

   A) True

2. **When connecting to a Web database over the Internet with Internet Explorer, you need to know:**

   D) Nothing about configuration of the services

3. **IIS is an excellent choice for a Web server because:**

   B) It's a native Windows application supplied by Microsoft.

4. **Selecting a programming language for a Web database application is based on:**

   A) Personal preference

5. **Converting a regular database to a Web database is essentially the same as:**

   B) Splitting the database

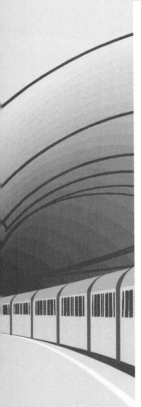

6. A service can be stopped and started by:

D) All of the above

7. When a database is split, which objects remain in the back-end portion of the database?

D) Local tables

8. Which of the following isn't a good reason to convert a database to a Web database?

C) To reduce maintenance needs on the database

9. Why is TCP/IP called a polite protocol?

C) It waits and listens for a client to connect.

10. What's the "language of the Internet"?

C) TCP/IP

Chapter 19

1. An HTML Editor is:

A) Any text editor

2. HTML is really just a set of:

D) Tags

3. The `<H1>` tag should be used for:

C) Titles and headings

4. The Title of a Web page is located in the:

B) Head

5. An example of a font is:

A) Arial

6. **True or false: You need a functional Web server to view HTML files in a Web browser.**

False

7. **Where must form data be sent for processing?**

D) A script

8. **Why is it important to name HTML items that require input or a choice?**

A) The names identify the variables.

9. **Which tag would you use to insert a space between two paragraphs?**

C) <P></P>

10. **Which of the following is correct?**

D) <B>Hello There</B>

Chapter 20

1. **In the following loop, what is $num?**

```
$num = 0;
while ($num < 5) {
echo $num;
$num = $num + 1;
}
```

C) A variable

2. **In the loop from Question 1, why is $num set equal to 0?**

A) 0 is an arbitrary starting point.

3. **An if-then-else statement is known as a(n):**

D) Conditional statement

4. **A SQL statement placed inside a PHP file is said to be:**

A) Embedded

5. Why do you have to use a loop to iterate through a result set extracted from a database?

B) A loop extracts the rows one at a time from an array.

6. In the following array, which president is $president[1]?

`$president = array("Bush", "Clinton", "Johnson", "Nixon");`

B) Clinton

7. In the array from Question 6, which president is $president[4]?

D) None of the above

8. A scalar variable can have how many values associated with it?

B) One

9. In the following Query String sent to a script, identify a variable and the corresponding value:

`Name=John&State=TX&Item=Plate`

D) State, TX

10. In the following part of an if-then statement, what do the || represent?

`if ($variable1 == "" || $variable2 == "" || $variable3 == "") {`

C) Or

Index

Special Characters

A

B

E

Enable design changes for tables in Datasheet View setting, 359
Enable Layout View for this database setting, 359
enabled content, 76–77
Encode As dialog box, 220, 222
encryption, 313–314, 322
English-language databases, 357
Environment Variables button, 384
error checking, 366, 461–464
evaluations, template, 249–253
event lists, 162–166
Event tab, 216, 217, 219, 225, 226
Excel, 35–38, 42–46
Excel button, 216, 217
Excel file, 45, 216, 217, 223
Excel format, 32
Excel SharePoint List, 31
Excel-linked spreadsheet, 46
Exclusive mode, 314, 330, 369
executable content, 76, 315
execute-only database, 320–321
Exit buttons, Switchboard, 214–215
explicit field name, 129
Explorer window, 34
export, defined, 47
Export File Warning, 221
Export group, 255, 432
Export Text Wizard, 45
Export to File text box, 45
Export Wizard, 432
Export_Macros group, 222–224
exported data, 32–33, 44–47
exports, automating, 216
Express installations, 374
expression, defined, 137
Expression aggregate function, 67
Expression Row function, 66
expressions, 133, 136
external data
   linking to, 41–42
   sources, 31–33, 41–44, 47
External Data tab, 31, 34, 36, 38–45, 145, 152, 255, 292, 298, 300, 432

features
   Date and Time feature, 103
   Default record locking feature, 369

editing, 130
Open databases by using record-level locking feature, 369
Open last used database when Access starts feature, 369
security features, 282
Time feature, 103, 106, 120
fetch_array function, 445
Field list, 274
Field List window, 101, 200
Field Options area, 37
Field Properties window, 272
Field Separator, 270
fields
   adding to reports, 134–136
   calculated, 62, 134
   Cascade Delete Related Fields, 177, 178
   Cascade Update Related Fields, 177, 178
   Comments field, 197, 198, 220
   data fields, shrinking, 98
   Data Source Name field, 293, 300, 393
   defined, 26
   Foreign Key field, 178, 271
   ID field, 87, 98, 101, 104, 123, 124, 146, 148, 151, 172, 177, 191, 198, 272, 276, 294
   Status Bar Text field, 203, 205
   Subject_ID field, 191, 198
File Data Source tab, 347
File Download dialog box, 338, 384
file extensions, 320–321
File Format drop-down list, 45
File Name drop-down list, 318
file system, 465
File text box, 45
File Type drop-down list, 331
file-based RDBMS, 299
file-copy database backups, 333–334
file-oriented tools, 335–339
files
   delimited, 45–46
   and PHP, 447–450
   writing content to, 448–449
Filter By Form window, 362
filter lookup options, 362
filters, 53, 54, 58, 68
fire stored procedures, 451
First Normal Form (1NF), 176
First Row function, 66
First_Name text(50) field, 270

Folder Options, 450
Folder Properties dialog box, 308
folder structure, Internet Information Server,
    401–405
folders
  creating, 404
  Databases folder, 311, 312
  Default database folder, 357
  Folder Options, 450
  Folder Properties dialog box, 308
  folder structure, Internet Information Server,
    401–405
  Outlook Folder, External Data tab, 32
  shared, 311–312
  virtual folder structure, Internet Information
    Server, 402–403
  Web application folder, 404
  Web folder, 406
  Web Sites folder, 385
  wwwroot subfolder, 403
<FONT COLOR></FONT> tags, 420–421
<FONT FACE></FONT> tags, 420
Font option, 363
<FONT SIZE></FONT> tags, 421
fonts
  color of, 362, 421
  default datasheet, 364
  size of, 365, 421
  steps to custom format a, 420
  Web page, 419–421
Foreign Key field, 178, 271
foreign keys, 170, 271–272
form, defined, 117
form control, 189
Form Design Tools area, 115, 191
Form dialog box, 434
Form drop-down list, 213
Form Layout Tools tab, 100
Form Name drop-down list, 227
Form template, 366
Form View, 111
Form Wizard, 187, 189, 190, 195
<FORM></FORM> tags, 422–423
Format tab, 100, 101, 136, 216, 218–220, 225
forms
  advanced form construction, 187–189
  compiling data in, 193–196
  creating, 97, 193, 425–426

customized
  basic process for creating, 103–107
  with controls, 101–103
  overview, 99–100
  selecting theme, 100–101
  customizing, 98
  data and PHP, 454–456
  data-entry, 453–454
  editing title, 102
  enhancement of
    buttons, 198
    default entry prompts, 202
    limiting users, 199–200
    opening by context, 198–199
    overview, 197
    scroll bars, 197–198
    status bar, 203
    Tool Tips, 200–202
  Form Wizard, 189–192
  navigation of
    custom navigation controls, 114–116
    Design View, 112–113
    Form View, 111
    Layout View, 111
    overview, 107
    record navigation, 107–108
    record search, 110–111
    tab order, 108–110
  Object Designers options, 365–366
  overview, 95–99
  and Web databases, 431–432
  Web page, 422–426
ftproot directory, 402
fully justified text, 417
functions
  aggregate, 65–68
  summary, 133–136

G

General options, 368
GNU (Gnu's Not Unix), 383
Go Online button, 376
Gradebook button, 215
Gradebook form, 195, 196, 198, 210, 224, 226
Gradebook table, 180, 238

P

S

single records, changing, 83–84
single-entity data, 175
SIZE attribute, 421
Size option, 363
Smart Tags, 368, 376
snippets, 456, 465
Software Development Kit (SDK), 253
Source Edit mode, 433
space tags, HTML, 411–413
spell-checking, 367
spreadsheets, Excel, 36–38
SPS (SharePoint Portal Services)
  lists
    contact, 155–159
    event, 162–164
    linking to, 43
    overview, 33, 154–155
    personal or public task, 160–161
    problem issues, 161
    and table creation, 39
  overview, 141–143
  remote data
    copying databases to Sharepoint, 146–151
    moving information to Sharepoint, 145–146
    overview, 143–144
  working offline, 152–154
SQL (Structured Query Language)
  data types, 264–265
  embedded, 452–454
  Internet resources, 470
  overview, 261–264
  sub-languages
    Data Control Language, 282–283
    Data Definition Language, 268–274
    Data Manipulation Language, 274–282
    overview, 265–267
    syntax definitions, 267–268
SQL command, 264
SQL keyword, 266, 267, 282, 284
SQL query, 262, 266, 269, 278
SQL Query window, 269, 278
SQL Server, 4, 287–296, 303, 328, 329, 346–351, 365, 390, 391, 397, 469, 470
SQL Server Compatible Syntax (ANSI 92) option, 365
SQL Server database
  connecting to, 294
  upsizing to, 348–349

SQL Server Upsizing Wizard, 290
SQL Server Worldwide Users Group (SSWUG), 470
SQL statement, 264, 267–274, 278, 445, 446, 452, 453, 461, 467
SQL View, 262, 269, 270, 273, 274, 277–279, 452
SQLite, 292, 299–300, 301
square brackets ([ ]), 81, 267
SSWUG (SQL Server Worldwide Users Group), 470
stand-alone macros, 210, 218–220, 228
Start service control, 389
start-up options, 240
Startup Type attribute, 389
statements
  conditional statements, 463–464
  CREATE INDEX statement, 271
  CREATE statement, 270, 275
  CREATE TABLE statement, 269–270, 275
  CREATE VIEW statement, 270
  DELETE statement, 281
  DROP INDEX statement, 273
  DROP TABLE statement, 273
  echo statements, 445
  if-then-else statement, 462
  Microsoft Office Access privacy statement, 372
  Microsoft Office Online privacy statement, 372
  privacy statements, Microsoft, 372
  query statement, 62
  SELECT statement, 277–279
  Show the Microsoft Office Access privacy statement link, 372
  SQL statement, 264, 267–274, 278, 445, 446, 452, 453, 461, 467
  UPDATE statement, 280, 281
static content, 428
static data, 459
static forms and reports, 431–432
statistical analysis, 66
Status attribute, 389
status bar, 203
Status bar option, 368
Status Bar Text field, 203, 205
status bars, 203
Status-bar messages, 204
StDev Row function, 66
Stop service control, 389

stored procedures, 451
strings, 443
structure tags, HTML, 409–411
Structured Query Language (SQL)
  data types, 264–265
  embedded, 452–454
  Internet resources, 470
  overview, 261–264
  sub-languages
      Data Control Language, 282–283
      Data Definition Language, 268–274
      Data Manipulation Language, 274–282
      overview, 265–267
      syntax definitions, 267–268
Student combo box, 199
student forms, 190
Student Information Form, 190, 199, 212,
  221, 222
Students table, 172, 177, 180, 182, 190, 193,
  195, 197
Subject combo box, 194
Subject list, 191, 194
Subject_ID field, 191, 198
Subjects table, 172, 173, 177, 181, 182, 194, 195,
  200, 216
submit.php file, 442
subsets, data, 90–91
Suggest from main dictionary only option, 367
Sum Row function, 66
summary data, 62
summary functions, 65–68, 130, 133–136
Switchboard form, 211, 213, 215, 225
Switchboard Items table, 211
Switchboard list, 211
Switchboard Manager button, 211
Switchboard Manager Wizard, 211, 212
Switchboard tables, 254
Switchboards, 211–215, 228
synchronize, defined, 164
Synchronize button, 154
Synchronize option, SharePoint Lists, 33
syntax, defined, 283
syntax definitions, 267–268
Syntax element, 263
System DSN tab, 297, 392
system function, 449
System Properties applet, 384
System Tools, 331

T

Tab Index property, 109, 110, 113
tab order, 108–110
Tab Order screen, 112, 113
Table Analyzer Wizard, 343, 344
Table Design View, 365
Table drop-down list, 75, 80
Table relationships, 168, 181, 189
Table tab, 22, 58
<TABLE></TABLE> tags, 427
tables
  adding columns to, 180–181, 274
  adding data to, 25–26
  alterations to, 22–23
  Analyze Table Wizard, 343–345
  copying without copying data, 255
  creating, 19–22
  creating relationships between, 128–129
  deleting, 23–25, 273
  exporting data, 44–47
  external data sources, 31–33
  gathering data, 31
  importing data
      Access, 33–35
      Excel, 35–38
      overview, 33
      Sharepoint Lists, 39
      text files, 39–41
  linking to external data, 41–44
  linking while connecting to SQL Server,
    294–295
  locking, 73
  Make Table queries, 89–91
  names, 169, 291
  Object Designers options, 364–365
  overview, 15–18
  relationships
      database normalization, 174–177
      designing databases, 179–184
      overview, 128–129, 167–169
      referential integrity, 177–178
      Relational Data Model, 169–172
      types of, 172–174
  saving as queries, 338
  SQLite, 300–304
  updating data across, 84–86
  Web page, 427–428

Text Box, 45, 134–137, 188, 197, 199, 366, 405, 434
Text button, 222
Text data types, 265
text editor, 407
text files, 32, 39–46, 49, 220–222
Text Import Wizard, 46
Text Qualifier, 45
text tags, HTML, 413–417
<TEXTAREA></TEXTAREA> tabs, 426
Text-linked table, 46
themes, defined, 117
Third Normal Form (3NF), 175, 176–177, 230
This database option, 365
Time button, 103
Time dialog box, 103
Time feature, 103, 106, 120
Times font style, 420
TITLE section, 410
Title tab, 113
<TITLE></TITLE> tags, 410
Tool Tips, 200–202
toolbar options, 361
toolbars
 Custom Quick Access Toolbar, 371
 Customize Quick Access Toolbar, 370, 371
 Default Quick Access Toolbar, 370
 New Quick Access Toolbar, 371
 Quick Access toolbar, 355, 369–371, 377
top-down fashion, 209
totally PHP, 458–461
<TR></TR> tags, 427
Track name AutoCorrect info option, 361
Transactions table, 249
TRANSFORM keyword, 282
Transmission Control Protocol/Internet Protocol (TCP/IP), 395
transparent data, 143
Trust all from publisher option, 319
Trust Center, 371–374
Trust Center Settings button, 316, 320
trusted computing, 315–316
trusted connection, 347
trusted location, 78, 322
Trusted Location dialog box, 316, 317
trusted locations, 78–80
trusted publisher, 322
Two_Tables tab, 130

U

<U></U> tags, 414
Underline option, 363
underlined text, 414
unique identifier, 176
Update button, 81, 85
Update featured links from Microsoft Office Online option, 374
UPDATE keyword, 280–281
Update queries
 across tables, 84–86
 changing single records, 83–84
 overview, 81–83
UPDATE statement, 280, 281
updates, Microsoft, 374–375
upsizing tools
 Database Splitter, 345–347
 overview, 345
 SQL Server, 347–351
Upsizing Wizard, 290, 348, 349
usability, template, 252–253
Use Access special keys setting, 359
Use four-digit year formatting option, 368
Use Hijiri Calendar option, 367
Use Windows-themed controls on forms setting, 359
user name, 291
User name setting, 357
user-level security, 283, 307–312
users, form, 199–200

V

Value Access, 276
VALUE attribute, 423, 424
Values list, 274, 275
Var Row function, 66
variables, 442–444, 461, 462, 465
VBA (Visual Basic for Applications), 209,228, 238
VBScript, 402
View drop-down list, 219
View tab, 450
views, 270
Virtual Directory tab, 405

X

XML File, External Data tab, 32
XML File format, 32
XPS (XML Paper Specification) format, 32
XPS dialog box, 339
XPS Document Viewer, 32

Y

Yes/No data types, 265

Z

Zero Normal Form (0NF), 176

Elevate your education.

The L Line puts learning on the express line. Each book gives you a crash course in the skills you need to master concepts and technologies that will advance your career or enhance your options. Discover how quickly you can reach your destination on The Express Line to Learning.

What you'll find on *The L Line*

- Pre-reading questions to help you identify your level of knowledge
- Real-world case studies and applications
- Complete tutorial coverage with plenty of illustrations and examples
- Easy-to-follow directions
- Practice exams that let you evaluate your progress
- Terminology overviews to clarify technical jargon
- Additional online resources

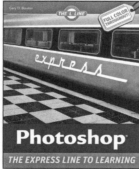

WILEY
Now you know.

Give more at the Office.

Master the skills you need to make yourself indispensable in the business world.

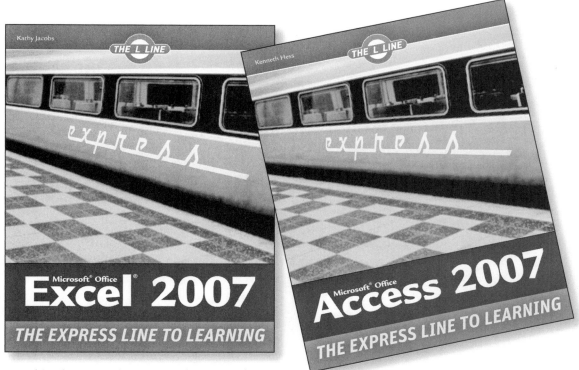

Excel is the second most-used Microsoft Office application. Conquer the newest version of the world's most popular spreadsheet program with *The L Line*, focusing on common practices and skill sets that professionals need.

ISBN-10: 0-470-10788-X
ISBN-13: 978-0-470-10788-1

Proficiency in Access 2007, the Microsoft Office database application, is increasingly in demand. Gain the skills you need with *The L Line*, including plenty of practical examples that prepare you for the real world.

ISBN-10: 0-470-10790-1
ISBN-13: 978-0-470-10790-4

The more you know, the farther you'll go.

Jump aboard *The L Line*, the direct route to sharper skills and better opportunities.

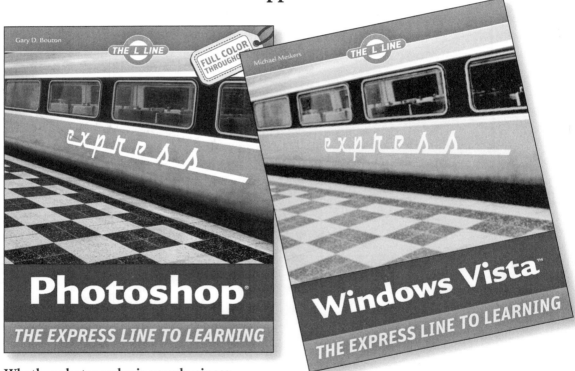

Whether photography is your business or your passion, Photoshop expertise is essential. Master the number one image-editing software, including painting and drawing, using layers, retouching, correcting color, creating Web graphics, and more.

ISBN-10: 0-470-09746-9
ISBN-13: 978-0-470-09746-5

Become an expert with Windows Vista, the first major Windows upgrade since XP. Here's what you need to become proficient with Vista's new features, including everything from the task-based interface to the Sidebar feature and the enhanced file system.

ISBN-10: 0-470-04693-7
ISBN-13: 978-0-470-04693-7

WILEY
Now you know.